Thucydides on Politics

Thucydides famously declared his work to be 'a possession for all time', and so it has proved to be, as each age and generation has seen new things to admire in it and take from it. In the last hundred years, Thucydides has been interpreted and invoked in support of many different positions in politics, political theory and international relations. Geoffrey Hawthorn offers a new and highly original reading, one that sees him as neither simply an ancestor nor a colleague but as an unsurpassed guide to a deeper realism about politics. In this account, Thucydides emerges as sensitive to the non-rational and the limits of human agency; sceptical about political speech; resistant to easy generalisations or theoretical reductions; and opposed to any practical, moral or constitutional closure in politics.

The book will be of interest to students of politics and classics.

GEOFFREY HAWTHORN is Professor Emeritus of international politics, University of Cambridge.

Thucydides on Politics

Back to the Present

Geoffrey Hawthorn

CAMBRIDGE
UNIVERSITY PRESS

CAMBRIDGE
UNIVERSITY PRESS

University Printing House, Cambridge CB2 8BS, United Kingdom

Published in the United States of America by Cambridge University Press, New York

Cambridge University Press is part of the University of Cambridge.

It furthers the University's mission by disseminating knowledge in the pursuit of education, learning and research at the highest international levels of excellence.

www.cambridge.org
Information on this title: www.cambridge.org/9781107612006

First published 2014

A catalogue record for this publication is available from the British Library

ISBN 978-1-107-03916-2 Hardback
ISBN 978-1-107-61200-6 Paperback

For Nell and in memory of Bernard Williams

Contents

Preface and acknowledgements

Thucydides' account of 'the war of the Peloponnesians and the Athenians, how they waged it against each other' between 431 and 411 BC, has never been easy to read. At the end of the first century BC, in the earliest comments on the text that survive, Dionysius of Halicarnassus said that those who could master its Greek 'are easily counted'. Lorenzo Valla, presenting his translation into Latin to the Pope in 1452, explained that the eight books into which it had come to be divided, 'these eight towns, just so that you know this, my Imperator, for perhaps you know not what sort of towns you ordered me to take, are situated in the loftiest regions, in craggy mountains, and defy missiles, battering rams, ladders, trenches and the mines of sappers'. Thucydides knew, and made no apology. 'The absence of the element of fable in my work may make it seem less easy on the ear, but it will have served its purpose well enough if it is judged useful by those who want to have a clear view of what happened in the past and what – the human condition being what it is – can be expected to happen again some time in the future in similar or much the same ways. It is composed to be a possession for all time and not just a performance-piece for the moment.'

Yet it stops suddenly, in mid-sentence, seven years before the war had ended (though there are insertions that Thucydides could only have made, if it was he who made them, when it had). And its style apart, the text is unusual. No one had written as he did, and no one was to do so in the same way again. It is more than a chronicle, recalls epic, has elements of tragedy and is intended to be of use; but Thucydides' few conclusions do not convince and he does not say what its use might be. It falls across all our genres and is diminished when assigned to any.

Its subject though is clear. It is politics: men (all men) seeking power over others, using it to pursue ends that are sometimes clear, sometimes not, never being sure what the outcomes will be. We habitually write politics as history, science or theory, and many have been tempted to read Thucydides in one or other of these ways. But this is not how he writes. He presents politics as they were practised, neither writing beyond what his subjects could see or drawing readers into conspiracies of hindsight. He has no conceptual ambition, favours no one kind of explanation, harbours no *telos*, evinces no one opinion, and is neither a cynic nor a moralist. In his grasp of the non-rational and the limits of human agency, his ability to see all sides and his disinclination to arrive at any conclusions, he is not so much an ancestor of the present-day study of politics and international relations (let alone the study of present-day politics and international relations) as an ancient who offers a critical purchase on the ancestries we have. He allows one to see that politics is rarely admirable but always unavoidable, owes less to reason than we might suppose and allows no practical, moral or constitutional closure.

Unlike Thucydides himself and many of those who have written about him since the First World War, I fall at Polybius' insistence (and Clarendon's after him) that one should not write about high politics or war without having known them, and I am not a classicist. This aside, it may seem idle to offer yet another book on a text on which there are so many, impertinent to offer conclusions on a text one of whose more remarkable qualities is to offer almost none of its own. But I read it in ways that others do not, and have been unable to resist writing for those who might like to think again about it as well as for those who do not know it. To do justice to all that has been said would require a different and much longer book; the 'reception' of Thucydides, as of much else from the time, has become an academic speciality in itself. I can at best allude to other readings, which I do towards the end of Chapter 1, the start of Chapters 9 and 15, and in notes throughout. I end with thoughts on its interest now.

The story is crucial; one's understanding expands in the course of it, and I raise questions of an interpretive kind as they seem to me to arise. In no case is the moment I choose the only one at which they do so. Questions of power, interest, strategy, opportunity and decision, not to mention those of necessity and contingency, present themselves throughout; emotion, reason and judgement are always in play; the mismatch between word and deed pervades the text; and at no point can it be said that character does not matter. But the narrative would have been diverted if I had considered each whenever it arises and drained if I had considered them all at once.

For those unfamiliar with the text, I provide a synopsis at the end; some might like to look at this first. And because the story can be bewildering without a ready frame in which to set it, I start with a few maps and a short list of relevant happenings in and around Greece at the time. Everything else that a non-classicist might need in order to decide for him- or herself – a sensitive and accessible translation of the text, notes on its more problematic or contentious parts, full synopses, a glossary of terms, a list of characters and many detailed maps, together with an excellent introduction, a range of ancient opinions and a full index of names and topics – are provided in Jeremy Mynott's authoritative edition for *Cambridge Texts in the History of Political Thought*, which I use throughout. In my notes, *TWPA* refers to Mynott, *HCT* to the commentary by Arthur Gomme, Antony Andrewes and Kenneth Dover and *CT* to that by Simon Hornblower; I say more on the commentaries in a note on reading at the end. I describe Thucydides' account as 'the text', reserving 'book' for one or other of the eight into which the text has been divided, and cite the passages I quote or refer to by book, chapter and section (as in 1.1.1). I leave my references to other texts, ancient and early modern, to be pursued in standard editions. The 'Hellenes', as they had come to think of themselves, did not refer to their political entities in the singular; I follow convention in using 'Sparta' and 'Spartans' etc. interchangeably to refer to the political community at issue, which will sometimes be large ('Athens'), sometimes small ('Plataea') and frequently in question ('Thrace'). I despair of consistency in rendering Greek names and only hope that my decisions do not offend. All dates are BC except where obviously not.

My acknowledgements are many. To the undergraduates reading Politics at Cambridge in the 2000s who found themselves taking a course on Thucydides, not all of whom will have known that it was their enthusiasms, curiosities and sheer intelligence that prompted me to think about writing and to whom I apologise for having been less clear at the time than I may be now; to the colleagues who tolerated my eccentricity and presented me with a copy of the Holkham bust of the man (he has since sat staring at me), in particular to Glen Rangwala, who shared the teaching, to Helen Thompson, whose collusion in the conceit that Thucydides was among us made academic hard times less so, and to Joy Labern, who made them human; to the often spellbinding qualities of the classical scholarship on Thucydides; to the memory of Frank Walbank, whose question on an early sketch ('where's the argument?') haunted me throughout; to Neville Morley for inviting me to join his project on the reception of Thucydides; to Richard Fisher, Elizabeth Friend-Smith, Maartje Scheltens, Chloe Dawson, Gillian Dadd, Christina Sarigiannidou and their colleagues at the Cambridge University Press and the Press's three acute and constructive readers; to Gloria Carnevali, Paul Cartledge, Stefan Collini, Mark Fisher, Kinch Hoekstra, Polly Low, Derin McLeod, Gillian Moore, Paul Seabright, Helen Thompson and John Thompson for being so ready to take time to read a draft, point to obscurities, correct mistakes and suggest improvements; and to Ronald

Vance and Douglas Hyland for the cover image. My greatest debt is to Jeremy Mynott, who was preparing his edition as I was writing and without whose constant encouragement, generosity and advice – linguistic, literary, analytical and editorial – I really could not have done what I have; I thank the Press for permission to quote from his translation and use maps from his edition. My longer debts are to Bernard Williams, who has given my unformed intuitions what shape they have, and to Gloria, who has done so much for one man in her life by living so gaily and so long with this other.

Cambridge

Chronology 545–323 BC

This situates the events that Thucydides considers. I summarise what he does in a synopsis of his text at pp. 241–6.

545–510	'Tyranny' in Athens
c.513	Persia invades Europe
507	Political reform in Athens: beginnings of democracy
506	Spartan invasion of Athens collapses
c.505	Sparta forms Peloponnesian 'league'
490	First Persian invasion of Greece: Greeks defeat Persians at Marathon
481	Greek request for support against Persia from Syracuse
480–479	Second Persian invasion of Greece: Persians defeat Greeks at Thermopylae; Greeks defeat Persians at Salamis, Plataea and Mycale
478	Athens forms Delian 'league', which becomes dominion or 'empire'
c.466	Death of Pausanias (Spartan); flight of Themistocles (Athenian)
466–461	Civil war in Syracuse; democracy proclaimed 463
465–456	Helot revolt at Sparta
465–460	Thucydides born
460–446	'First Peloponnesian war': conflicts between Sparta and allies and Athens and allies; ends with 'thirty-year peace'
460–429	'Age of Pericles' at Athens
459–454(?)	Athenian expeditions to Cyprus and Egypt
454	Treasury of Delian league transferred to Athens
451	Thirty-year peace between Sparta and Argos
449(?)	'Peace of Callias' between Athens and Persia
448(?)	Accession of Perdiccas II (Macedonia)
444–433	Foundation of Thurii; Athenian treaties with Leontini and Rhegion

441–439	Revolt of Samos (from Athens) and surrender
c.437	Athenian expedition to Black Sea
437–436	Foundation of Amphipolis
435	Dispute between Corinth and Corcyra over Epidamnos
433	Athenian alliance with Corcyra; battle of Sybota
433–432	Renewal of Athens' treaties with Leontini and Rhegion
432–430	Revolt of Potidaea and surrender
432	Meetings at Sparta
431	Theban attack on Plataea
	Peloponnesian invasion of Attica
	Athenians sail round Peloponnese
430	Plague at Athens
	Peloponnesian invasion of Attica
	Athenian expedition to Peloponnese
	Phormio (Athenian) despatched to Naupactos
429–427	Siege of Plataea
429	Phormio defeats Cnemos (Spartan)
428	Peloponnesian invasion of Attica
	Revolt of Mytilene, to 427
427	Peloponnesian invasion of Attica
	Internal war at Corcyra
	Athenian expedition to Sicily, to 424
	Plague again at Athens
426	Demosthenes (Athenian) in western Greece
	Nicias (Athenian) attempts to take Melos
425	Peloponnesian invasion of Attica
	Athenian capture of Spartans at Pylos; Athenians refuse Spartan offer of peace; Athens reassesses tribute from dominion
424	Athenians unsuccessfully intervene in Megara; fail in Boeotia
	Brasidas (Spartan) captures Acanthos, Amphipolis and Torone
	Thucydides goes into exile
	Conference of Siceliot states at Gela
423(?)	Athens renews peace with Persia
	Truce (to 422) between Athens and Sparta
422	Cleon (Athenian) retakes Torone; he and Brasidas die at Amphipolis
	Athenian envoys in Sicily and Italy

421	'Peace of Nicias' and fifty-year alliance between Athens and Sparta
	Destruction of Scione
420–419	Intense politicking between Peloponnesian states, Boeotia and Athens
418	Sparta defeats Argives and Athenians at battle of Mantinea
	Fifty-year alliance between Sparta and Argos
417	End of oligarchy in Argos, renewed alliance between Argos and Athens
c.416	Tissaphernes becomes Persian satrap at Sardis
	Athens takes Melos
415–413	Athenians in Sicily
415	Alcibiades (Athenian) flees to Sparta
414	Athenians land in Laconia
413	Spartans occupy Deceleia; renew war
	Perdiccas II dies
412–411	Revolts of Athenian subject states
	Treaties between Sparta and Persia
411	Coup in Athens: rule of 400 and then '5,000'
	End of Thucydides' text
	Athenian naval victories in the Hellespont
410	Athenian naval victory over Sparta and Persian land force at Cyzicus (Black Sea); Athens rejects Spartan offer of peace
	Democracy restored at Athens
409	Hannibal (Carthaginian) destroys Selinus and Himera in Sicily
408	Athenians retake Byzantium
407	Alcibiades returns to Athens
406	Athenians defeated at Notium; Alcibiades withdraws; Athenian victory at Arginusae
	Hannibal takes Acragas (Sicily)
405	Athenians conclusively defeated at Aegospotamoi (Hellespont)
	Dionysius succeeds at Syracuse; makes peace with Carthage
405–404	Siege of Athens
404(?)	Death of Thucydides
404–403	Peace between Sparta and Athens; 'Thirty tyrants' rule Athens until democracy restored under Sparta's aegis
404–371	Spartan hegemony in Greece

Maps

Based on maps previously published in Jeremy Mynott, *Thucydides: The War of the Peloponnesians and the Athenians*, Cambridge University Press, 2013. © Cambridge University Press 2013, reproduced with permission.

Maps

Map 1. Greece and the Aegean

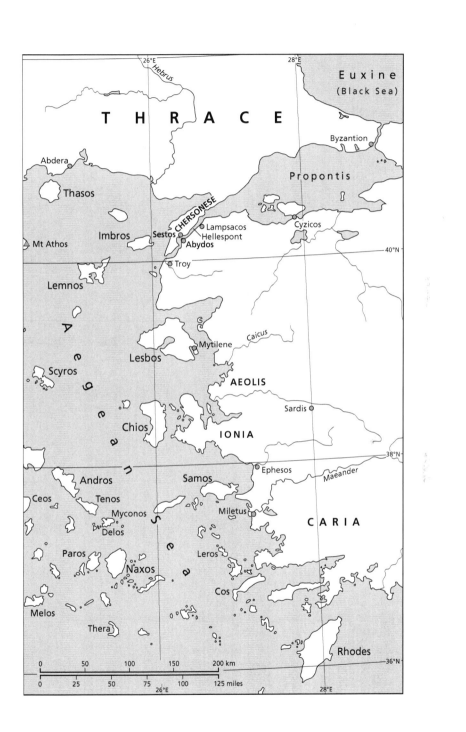

Euxine
(Black Sea)

THRACE

Hebrus

26°E   28°E

Abdera

Byzantion

Propontis

Thasos

CHERSONESE

Imbros   Sestos   Lampsacos   Cyzicos
Mt Athos   Abydos   Hellespont

40°N

Troy

Lemnos

Caicus

Mytilene

Aegean

Lesbos

Scyros   AEOLIS

Sardis

Chios   IONIA

38°N

Ephesos

Andros   Samos   Maeander

Ceos   Tenos

Myconos   Miletus   CARIA

Delos

Paros   Leros

Naxos

Cos

Melos

Thera

Rhodes

36°N

| 0 | 50 | 100 | 150 | 200 km |

| 0 | 25 | 50 | 75 | 100 | 125 miles |

26°E   28°E

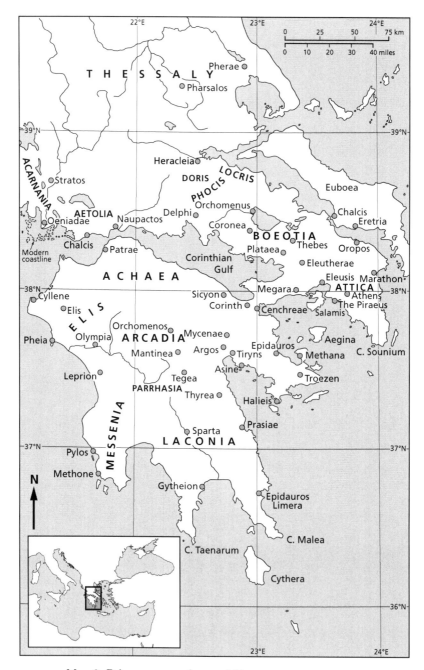

Map 2. Peloponnese and central Greece

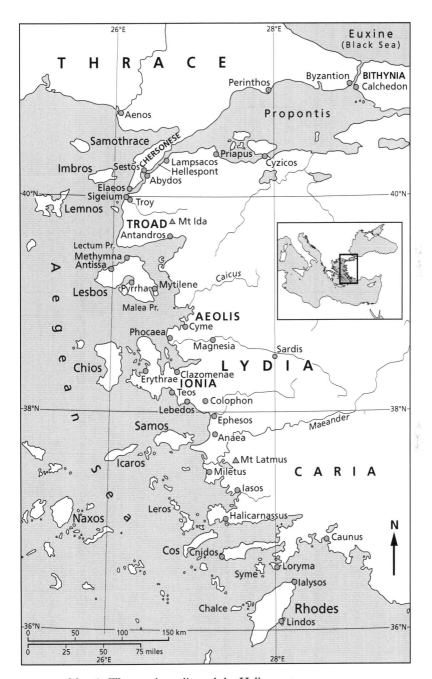

Map 3. Western Anatolia and the Hellespont

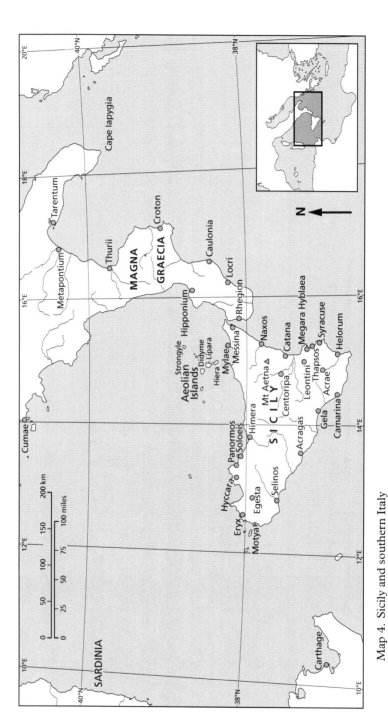

Map 4. Sicily and southern Italy

1   The text

Thomas Macaulay often read while he walked. 'Walked out over West-
minster Bridge', he wrote in his journal for 24 November 1848, 'and back
by the Hungerford Bridge. Read the first book of Thucydides – excellent.
I never liked him so much'; 26 November, 'after breakfast – read Thucydides during some time. Finished the third book'; 1 December, 'began
the sixth book of Thucydides – very good'; 2 December, 'walked home
and began the seventh book'; 3 December, 'finished the seventh book';
4 December, 'staid at home all day – a miserable rainy day – making
corrections for the 2nd edition [of the *History of England*]. Then read
the eighth book of Thucydides – not every word – but particularly the
account of the Athenian revolutions.' 'On the whole', Macaulay reflected
later that afternoon, 'Thucydides is the first of historians. What is good
in him is better than anything that can be found elsewhere. But his dry
parts are dreadfully dry; and his arrangement is bad.'
   Few can have read so much difficult Greek prose so quickly; the text
in a modern English translation can run to nearly 600 pages. Few certainly will have read any of it while walking through the stink and noise of
London in the 1840s or, as Macaulay also had, while taking a shave.[1] But
many have read the first seven of the eight books into which the text has
been divided with comparable enthusiasm. They too are drawn into the
story of men in what Thucydides called 'the war of the Peloponnesians
and Athenians', 'dealing sensibly, foolishly, sometimes catastrophically,
sometimes nobly' as Bernard Williams put it 'with a world that is only
partly intelligible to human agency'.[2] But many have shared Macaulay's
dismay in reading on. They too have found the narrative in book 8, up to
what he calls the 'Athenian revolutions' of 411, to be 'dull and spiritless'
and lacking in drama, an aimless sequence in which he seems 'to grope his
way like a man without a clue'; 'a series of not even well-connected out-
lines'; running on 'flat and monotonous, offering no outstanding feature

---

[1] Macaulay 2008: II 5–11. Being shaved, Sullivan 2009: 140.
[2] Williams 1993: 164.

as a starting point for analysis'; 'a bald record of quarrels, back-stabbing and inconclusive struggles' which after the account of the 'revolution' in Athens (more exactly a coup) 'breaks off in mid-stream' and offers no end; a sequence that is simply stuffed with too many facts. One Marcellinus, writing probably in the seventh century AD, thought that Thucydides must have been ill when he drafted it, in a state in which 'the intellect' is in 'little sympathy' with the body, 'more unstrung'. In an otherwise fine lecture in 1981 on epic and tragedy in Thucydides, Colin Macleod declared that 'it is clear, indeed, that the whole history, or what remains of it, finds its culmination' not in book 8 but at the end of book 7.[3]

Yet book 8 is as absorbing as any in the text, as central to the qualities of Thucydides' political understanding as it is to the story he has to tell. It is true that there is no set piece of the kind that he presents in the earlier books and nothing to attract those concerned with what politics might ideally be. By its eighteenth year, few of those involved in what was by now an urgent war had the will or the time to make any but the most instrumental of arguments about the rules of rule. But although it has none of the drama of the debates on large questions, only those who are deaf to politics could see in it no more than quarrels, back-stabbing and inconclusive struggle. The shifting alliances, antagonisms and suspicions between those who were notionally on the same side as well as not; their assumptions, fantasies, ostensible interests, declared intentions and apparent motives; their mutual appreciations, enmities, confusions, loyalties and deceptions; the combinations and collisions of reflection, risk, caution, courage, cowardice, cunning and stupidity; not to mention the distribution of good luck and bad in what Thucydides calls the 'unaccountable contingencies of human life' (8.24.5), are the stuff of success and failure in politics and war. And he writes of them with his best dispassionate passion. His story of the political contests between the mid 430s and 416 in the first five books has shown that where fear, anger and frustration combine in allies and antagonists few of whom have a steady conception of what they can do to allay these feelings and where none can achieve a decisive advantage, each will need to respond in one opportunistic move after another; the consequence of which is to prolong a state of affairs from which all, not without ambivalence, are hoping to escape. His resumption of the story in book 8, after the Athenian campaign in Sicily in 415–413, shows the difference that having more

---

[3] Also Ch. 14 below. Reactions to book 8, Cornford 1907: 244, Schwartz from 1919 quoted by Pouncey 1980: 175 n. 16, de Romilly 1963: 53, Crane 1996: 256, Thucydides 1972b: xv cited by Rood 1998: 251; also Ch. 14 below. Marcellinus in Mynott *TWPA*: 601–6. Book 8 as drafts to be revised, Andrewes *HCT* V: 1–4, also Ch. 2 n. 1 below, and Ch. 15 below. Connor 1984b: 213f. Macleod 1983e: 141.

practicable strategies for winning (or not losing) was to make. As I explain in Chapter 14, the conflict had become more determined, the desperation greater and the politicking more intense. Even though Thucydides writes it in a different way, it continues what David Lewis described as his 'most remarkable achievement': the capacity 'to transmute even military' – and one can add political – 'narrative into a commentary on the human condition'; what in *The Gay Science* Nietzsche said was the wider Greek disposition to be superficial out of profundity.[4]

But this is a reaction to Thucydides now. One cannot presume that it is how he hoped or expected to be read. He announces that 'Thucydides of Athens wrote the war of the Peloponnesians and the Athenians, how they waged it against each other', starting to do so at its outset 'in the expectation that this would be a great war and more worthy of account than any previous one. He based this judgement on the grounds that both sides came into the war at the height of their powers and in a full state of military readiness; and he also saw that the rest of the Greek world had either taken sides right at the start or was now planning to do so' (1.1.1).[5] This is not as obvious as it seems and may not be true. His narrative goes on to explain that the war's outset, as outsets do, predated its onset, but he would have been prescient indeed if he foresaw a 'great war' at the faltering start. This however is incidental.

More interesting is that whenever Thucydides did start to write or to think about doing so, his purpose was almost the opposite of that of his most prominent predecessor. Herodotus had in the middle of the fifth century written his *historie* of the war in 499–478 between the Greeks and Persians (and perhaps given readings from it in the 430s at Athens and other places) in order that 'human events of the past do not become erased by time and that the great and wondrous achievements displayed by the Greeks and the barbarians, and especially their reasons for fighting each other, do not go unrecognised'.[6] At the end of the first century BC,

---

[4] Lewis 1992c: xiv, Nietzsche 2001: 8–9: 'Oh, those Greeks! They knew how to *live*: what is needed for that is to stop bravely at the surface, the fold, the skin; to worship appearance, to believe in shapes, tones, words – in the whole Olympus of appearance!' On Nietzsche and Th., Ch. 11 below.

[5] This first sentence is in effect Th.'s title page, and for this reason, though not for this reason alone, Mynott *TWPA* translates it literally. The key word is *sunegrapse*, 'wrote', and 'the war' its direct object; 'he wrote the war' which he thinks *axiologotatos*, especially worthy of *logos* (a discussion, description or reasoned account). Also Ch. 2 below.

[6] *Historie* is the word in the Ionic dialect in which Herodotus chose to write, perhaps following Homer and the Ionian scientific writers; he was originally from Halicarnassus (modern Bodrum), where the dialect was Doric. In Attic, in which Th. writes and which modern dictionaries of ancient Greek take as standard, the word, not used by Th., was *historia*. Th.'s wish to distinguish himself from Herodotus, Lang 2011. Th.'s relation to Herodotus is an exception to the great German historian Felix Jacoby's observation that

Dionysius of Halicarnassus declared that 'the superiority of Herodotus' judgement to that of Thucydides in his choice of subject matter is directly related to the superiority of the story of the wonderful deeds of the Greeks and barbarians to that of the pitiable and terrible sufferings of the Greeks'; this last, in Thucydides, 'was quite inappropriate for one who was a Greek and an Athenian'.[7] There is much of political interest in Herodotus. But Thucydides' considerations were quite different from his and from those of Dionysius, by which time what we think of as 'classical Athens' was an already glorified past. He set out to write what happened with an eye, as he says, on the 'usefulness' of a truthful account. Unlike Herodotus, he lived through the events he describes 'when I was of an age to appreciate what was going on and could apply my mind to an exact understanding of things'. And since 'it so turned out', he explains, 'that I was banished from my own country for twenty years, [I] had the time to study matters more closely; and as consequence of my exile I had access to activities on both sides', to those of the Peloponnesians as well as the Athenians, and perhaps also, though he does not say, to those of the Macedonians and Thracians though not probably to the Persians (5.26.5).

His identification as Thucydides son of Olorus suggests a relation to two political Athenians: Cimon, a grandee whose father-in-law was an Olorus and a Thracian king, and through his mother to a Thucydides son of Melesias, both of whom were opponents of Pericles, the 'first man' in Athens at the start of the war.[8] The writer Thucydides son of Olorus appears to have been elected as one of the city's ten generals, *strategoi*, in the spring of 424, in the war's seventh year, and in the following winter was relieved of his command after he had he failed to prevent a Spartan force taking the city of Amphipolis (4.104–7) and been forced or chose to go into into exile. (We do not know why he had stayed at his station on Thasos when for the previous two months the Spartan Brasidas had been capturing Athenian cities less than 40 miles to the west. But another Athenian general was stationed at Amphipolis itself and Thasos would have been a suitable place for a second. In any event it was midwinter and even Brasidas' own men would probably not have expected him to march them through a day and night of storm and snow to capture the city.) If Thucydides could not have been elected general before the qualifying

---

in Greek historiography 'polemic usually names its object, borrowings are anonymous', quoted by Hornblower 2006: 310.

[7] Quoted by Mynott *TWPA*: 594–5.

[8] Rusten 1989: 2 gives two possible family trees. The opposition of Thucydides son of Milesias is unclear, Andrewes 1978. We know nothing about the Thucydides of Pharsalus whom 'our' Th. mentions as the representative at the Piraeus of the *golpistas* in Athens in 411, 8.91.7.

age of thirty, he can have been born no later than the mid 450s and in the absence of any other evidence can be presumed to have died, as Marcellinus says, in his early fifties, soon after the end of the war in 404 to which he refers in his so-called 'second preface' in book 5 and another late insertion (2.65.12). Marcellinus mentions a memorial that was raised to him in Attica, but he is not known to have returned to Athens; it was said that he had been murdered on his way back there.[9] Thucydides himself explains that he owned the right of working gold mines in Thrace, possibly at Scapte Hyle on the mainland opposite Thasos, by virtue, Marcellinus suggests, of having married a woman who owned mines at that place, and he was thought by Brasidas to have had influence with the leading men in the area. This would explain why his first posting had been in the north and how, when having been relieved of his command and gone into exile, he was able to travel through Greece and have the leisure, Marcellinus says, relaying a no doubt fanciful story, in which to sit beneath a plane tree at Scapte Hyle and write what he had learnt.[10]

The writing was central. His work was 'composed to be a possession for all time', not another competitive performance-piece for the moment (1.22.4). We receive it in the collation and still contested editing of two families of medieval manuscripts and a papyrus fragment from the third century BC. There is no reason not to believe that the text became stable quite early; few now expect to discover anything that will surprise us. The original will have been written on papyrus, in capital letters without spaces between the words and sentences or any other kind of punctuation; and the fact that it was written (or dictated to be written) would have meant that Thucydides could have made deletions, additions and other revisions, which he plainly did. Its Greek reminded Henry Wade-Gery of 'English prose before Dryden and Addison . . . a language largely moulded by poets: its precision is a poet's precision, a union of passion and candour', and we might with Kenneth Dover believe that he thought of what he dictated more as sounds than as marks on a roll. There would have been no division into books, chapters and sections, and there are few grounds for believing that these later separations reveal much about his own conception of the text.[11] It seems clear that the original stopped

---

[9] A suggestion that Th. lived longer and started writing later, Fornara 1993. The rumour of murder, Pausanias, 1.23.9.

[10] The mines were originally Thracian; Athens may have taken ownership of them after 460, Bissa 2009: 35–6, who adds that unlike undemocratic states, Athens tended to devolve such matters to private contractors. Nicias' father had had a share in the silver mines in Attica. Marcellinus in Mynott *TWPA*: 601–8.

[11] Wade-Gery 2012, from 1949. Sounds rather than marks, Dover in *HCT* IV, 408. But it is said that each book would have more or less filled a standard papyrus roll, and

where ours does, suddenly, in the middle of an event and a sentence in the late summer of 411, and that nothing of the end of book 8 or the rest of the work (apart perhaps from notes and drafts and possible false starts) has been lost. Three writers appear to have taken up the story and it has been said that Xenophon, who did so directly, may have had a hand in editing what Thucydides had written. Yet although one of these three, the author of the so-called *Hellenica Oxyrhynchia*, is thought from the fragments that have surfaced to be good, none was to imitate him.[12]

It is less clear whom Thucydides was writing for. Literacy was extending in the later fifth century and so were schools; he himself mentions an establishment for boys in a remote small town in Boeotia in 413 (7.29.5). But though a short manuscript might be had for little more than the daily wage (at least in Athens) of a manual worker, longer ones would have been expensive. Pupils may have had to memorise them, and poorer teachers may have had to do so too. Thucydides may have more often been encountered in the social settings of readings aloud. And it is possible that parts at least of the text may have been circulating before the end of the war. James Morrison wonders whether he might have hoped that it would be discussed, although as with any defeated people one can only guess at how many Athenians after the end of the war would have been able with equanimity to dwell on an account of events which they knew only too well had ended their overseas empire and brought 'sufferings unprecedented in any comparable period of time' (1.23.1).[13]

---

that the length of works may have been determined by how much a roll could contain, Maehler 2012. On revision, Allison 1997: 240 n. 6. On the relation between the books and Th.'s conception, Andrewes *HCT* V: 379. On the changes in the ways in which he distinguished events, Dewald 2005; Ch. 14 below. What we now have as the sections of chapters are said to have been separated in the seventeenth century.

[12] Xenophon carries on from Th. 8.109: 'After this, not many days later...' (*Hellenica* 1.1.1). Marcellinus mentions and dismisses the story that book 8 was put together by Th.'s daughter, a story so unlikely for the time, Hornblower remarks, that it might be true, Hornblower 1994: 136. Th.'s immediate reception, with reservations about 'imitiation', Hornblower 1995.

[13] Morrison 2006: 172–4, following suggestions in Thomas 1992: 104. Hammond 1973: 59, presuming that Th. expected to return to Athens after the end of the war, suggested that in the atmosphere of the 'quisling junta regime' in the city then, he may have been nervous about setting out any extended reflection on the war. On one recent definition of empire, 'a hierarchial system of rule acquired and maintained by military coercion through which a core territory dominates peripheral territories, serves as an intermediary for their main interactions, and channels resources from and between the peripheries' (Mann 2012: 17), Athens' *arche* was one, although juridically the Athenians did at first distinguish between states that were subject and those that were independent, Gomme *HCT* I: 36–43. On Athens' 'empire' itself, de Ste Croix 1954 and other essays in Low 2008. But as Mann says, his definition allows all kinds and mixtures of military, political, economic and 'ideological' domination. It also fails to capture the arguable intention of some Athenians to create what might be described as a 'greater Athenian

Athens' defeat was to turn many citizens away from its immediate past to reinvocations of the glories of the Persian war. Anyway, Athenians can seem to have shown little interest in what their historians told them; only military men may have been curious.[14]

Historia, inquiry, had on one interpretation been thought of by the Greeks as judgement on the judgements of others; thus perhaps Herodotus. On another interpretation, new in the later fifth century and evident in medical writing of the time, it may have begun to be thought of as inquiries in the pursuit of truth; thus almost certainly Thucydides, although he does not use the word, perhaps because Herodotus had.[15] 'From the evidence I have presented', he says, 'one would not go wrong in supposing that events were very much as I have set them out; and no one should prefer rather to believe the songs of the poets, who exaggerate things for artistic purposes, or the writings of the chroniclers, which are composed more to make good listening than to represent the truth, being impossible to check and having most of them won a place over time in the imaginary realm of fable. My findings, however, you can regard as derived from the clearest evidence available for material of this antiquity' (1.21.1).[16] So also on the near-present. 'As to the actual events of the war . . . I resolved not to rely in my writing on what I learned from chance sources or even on my own impressions, but both in the cases where I was present myself' – in Athens in the later 430s and early 420s – 'and in those where I depended on others I investigated every detail with the utmost concern for accuracy. This was a laborious process of research,

---

state', Morris 2009. One thinks also of the ambiguities in this respect of China and Russia after 1935. I prefer to think more loosely of 'dominion', to be specified as and when.

[14] The interest of contemporary historians, Thomas 1989: 201–3, Hornblower 1995, who at 61 mentions their increasing attention to the Persian war. On military men, Hunt 2006.

[15] Darbo-Peschanski 2007. The meanings of inquiry were naturally more complex and variable than this might suggest, Lloyd 2002: 15–20. On Th. and medical writing, Ch. 15 below.

[16] Mynott *TWPA* notes that this is just one sentence in the Greek, difficult enough in construction to have led to a range of different translations. Cameron 2003: 42, he adds, gives a super-literal version which shows what a tough read Th. has always been: 'From the stated evidences, nevertheless, someone would not go wrong by considering what I have recounted to be very much of that kind [i.e. reliable]; not, rather, believing as the poets have sung with decorated exaggeration concerning these matters or as the chroniclers, in a manner more attractive to hear than true, have composed things that are incapable of being disproved and things that have – many of them in time – won their way into the fabulous in a way that cannot be believed; but (one would not go wrong) considering [what I have recounted] to have been researched from the clearest evidences, given that the matters are sufficiently ancient.' Flory 1990 reads 'the imaginary realm of fable' in Th. to refer to tales of the 'chauvinistic' kind that Dionysius praised Herodotus for writing.

because eyewitnesses at the various events reported the same things differently, depending on which side they favoured and on their powers of
memory' (1.22.2–3), though as Peter Hunt observes, Thucydides never
says that witnesses were hard to find.[17]

Truthfulness about the present however was not the limit of his ambition. The text, he says, 'will have served its purpose well enough if it
is judged useful by those who want to have a clear view of what happened in the past and what – the human condition being what it is –
can be expected to happen again some time in the future in similar
or much the same ways' (1.22.4). Josiah Ober takes this to mark the
invention of a political science. But that says nothing about Thucydides, and, as I explain in a moment and again in Chapters 8 and
15, what he may have meant would be foreign to the 'sciences' of politics in the modern Anglo-American sense. As I argue at the end of
this book, it also obscures the ways in which he was critical of politics
itself.[18]

One aspect that he would expect to recur 'some time in the future'
would be the tension between *logoi*, words, reasonings – how politicians
describe events, justify their attempts to direct them and attempt to persuade others – and events themselves, *erga*, things done. Thucydides
was writing at a time when written narratives were new and there was
enthusiasm still for the art of oral persuasion. In the new 'democracies'
in Greece (the term dates from the first part of the fifth century) men
could not succeed if they did not speak well, and in the later fifth century
fashionable 'sophists' as they came to be called, travelling teachers of
philosophy and rhetoric, were explaining how to do that. Indeed *rhetor
kai strategos*, or just *rhetor*, was coming to connote 'politician', and in
the fourth century many of those whom we might now think of as intellectuals were to blame 'demagoguery' for the deceptions, divisions and
self-destructions of the war. Thucydides only once lapses into suggesting
anything so simple.[19] For him, there are the truths of events, the truths
(as well as the deceptions and outright falsehoods) of speech and the
truths that are revealed in the often distant relation between the two, and

---

[17] Hunt 2006.
[18] Canfora translates, when similar things are in 'the process of occurring', Nicolai 2009:
390. Moles 1999 is an intricate and illuminating analysis of 'a possession for all time'.
A political science, Ober 2006.
[19] Wallace 2007 persuasively suggests that the sense of sophist purveyed by Plato and
accepted until recently by many (Grote and Popper were exceptions) is excessively
pejorative; but that critical thinking, of which Th. was a part, was more common in
Athens in the later fifth century.

to draw attention to these differences was itself a political act in a society in which, like many since, competing rhetorics could distort and falsify.[20]

There was nevertheless a difficulty. 'As to what was said in speeches by the various parties either before they went to war or during the conflict itself, it was difficult for me to recall the precise details in the case of those I heard myself, just as it was for those who reported back to me on cases elsewhere. What I have set down is how I think each of them would have expressed what was most appropriate in the particular circumstances, while staying as close as possible to the overall intention (*gnome*) of what was actually said' (1.22.1). The tension in this last sentence has been much discussed, but though Thucydides can be complex and condensed and often both at once, he is rarely obscure. On this, which plainly matters to him, he may be being quite clear. He heard only a few of the speeches himself and would rarely have had a transcript of any;[21] he tried hard to recover the point of what was said in those he did not hear; where he could not, then – like a dramatist but working with what we know or (on the whole) believe to be real characters – he wrote what particular speakers would have wanted to say as the speakers they were at the moment in question; and although each of the speeches that he presents was given by a particular man (or set of men) at a particular moment, and although he does often do something to capture their voice, he wrote most of them up in a style that is evidently his own. In many cases, the 'overall intention' in what was said will have been just that. In introducing the Syracusan Hermocrates' warning to a gathering of Siceliots (Greek Sicilians) at Gela in the summer of 424 about the dangers of presenting the Athenians with a divided island, a speech that he would not himself have heard, Thucydides writes that Hermocrates 'spoke words *such as these*' (4.58.1, my emphasis). In others, he may have been able to be more exact. In introducing the address that Pericles made in the winter of 431–430 on the occasion of the funeral of the first Athenians to be killed in the war, he writes that when the moment came Pericles 'stepped forward from the tomb and mounted the platform that had been set up so that he could be heard by as many as possible in the throng, and spoke as follows' (2.34.8), which gives the impression that he was there and would have written down something close to what Pericles 'actually said'.

---

[20] Lloyd 2012, also Ch. 15 below. Parry 1972 and 1981 (the first an extension of the second and perhaps an indication of *The Mind of Thucydides* which Parry did not live to write) reify the contrast into Th.'s tragic vision of a civilisation of intelligence brought down by war. An excellent discussion, Greenwood 2006: 57–82.

[21] Thomas 2003 suggests that speeches were beginning to be written down, although it is less likely that political speeches will have been; Th. does not mention transcriptions.

What he does not explain is how he selected the speeches he did from the many that would have been given in the years that he covers; or why, when there was a debate, as in Athens in 430 over whether to pursue the war after the second Spartan invasion of Attica and an epidemic in the city, he sometimes selected those from one side only. (In this instance, some have suspected that he did not want to give voice to one of the new arriviste politicians, Cleon, as he again may not have wished to do when Cleon scorned a Spartan proposal for peace in 425 (4.21.3).)[22] But where he does present only one side, he usually conveys a sense of the other; he often makes it clear where he is picking out part of what someone had said; and when someone seems to have been responding to or otherwise reflecting what someone else had said at a different time or in a different place, there can be a plausible explanation. A reader might be surprised that an Athenian commander addressed his crews before engaging Spartan ships in terms that almost exactly mirrored those in which Spartan commanders a mile across the water were addressing theirs (2.87, 2.89), but Thucydides makes it clear that the problems facing the one were the reciprocal of those facing the other and would have been plain to both.[23] This is also one of the instances at which he writes as though several men spoke in unison. It is most charitable to suppose that he will not always have known just who did address the audience at hand, or that he ran what he took to have been similar speeches together.

Uncertainties remain. But one can say that Thucydides used the speeches he selected to convey what he took to be the political and military judgements and practical reasonings of men who were living the war, attempting to understand it, hoping to direct actions in it and trying to persuade others of why they were doing what they were. They are the repositories of reason, good and bad, in the text. As such, they serve to reveal the distances between what was thought and said and what transpired. They serve also in the first three books and the beginning of the sixth to move the story along, conveying a drama that is unavoidably absent from accounts of politics in which persuasion is more difficult to see. They may be varying mixtures of report and reconstruction and in this respect as well as their selection contain a measure of Thucydides' own sense of what mattered. But few suspect that in Coleridge's nice

---

[22] Plutarch, *Pericles*, 33, quoting the contemporary comic dramatist Hermippos, suggests that Cleon was already active against Pericles. On the 'new politicians' in Athens, Connor 1992, Rhodes 2000.

[23] The speeches in question at 2.86.6–89; I discuss them briefly in Ch. 6 below, where see n. 10.

phrase his imagination completely 'disimprisons the soul of fact' about what was said. We have either to take each as his approximation of what men said or ignore them altogether, for there is no other record. And if we ignore them, we cease to read what he wrote.[24]

One Philistos of Syracuse, a fourth-century writer now glimpsed only in the work of others, may have been the one historian who modelled himself on Thucydides. Later ancient commentators, writing in different kinds of political circumstance, tended to read the text as a sourcebook for rhetoric or, despite the distance that Thucydides insisted on, as a chronicler or memorialiser.[25] It was only when he began to be read in the later fifteenth and sixteenth centuries that he was taken to have something to say to the politics of the day. Kinch Hoekstra recovers a crescendo of interest in what he could be taken to suggest about the grounds on which states should and should not go to war.[26] It was Thomas Hobbes in the mid 1620s, making the first direct translation from Greek into English, who made one of the most powerful cases for the quality of the text itself. One feels oneself to be present, Hobbes said; the 'pithiness', 'strength', 'purity' and 'propriety' of Thucydides' style casts 'the reader into the same passions that they were in beholders'; the reader may accordingly 'from the narrations draw out lessons to himself, and of himself be able to trace the drafts and counsels of the actors to their seat'; in this way does Thucydides 'secretly instruct the reader, and more effectually than can possibly be done by precept'. The text, Hobbes emphasised, combines *truth* and *elocution*'; 'in *truth* consisteth the soul, and in *elocution* the body of history. The latter without the former, is but a picture of history', a mere image of reality; 'and the former without the latter, unapt to instruct'. In his own work, Hobbes had hoped that 'elocution' would not be necessary; that the truths revealed by 'civil science' and philosophy would be self-evident to reasonable men. It was only later that he came to see that just as deception could exacerbate division and self-destruction, so right speech was required to give right reason force and show what was needed for civil peace. But by then he had left this text behind, retaining

---

[24] One commentator at least believes that Th. simply invented the speeches, Yunis 1996: 61–6. If so, he occasionally invented a lie which he was then able to expose, 4.85.7, 4.108.5. On the almost complete absence of speeches in book 8: Ch. 14 below. On what can be discerned about the settings, Westlake 1973.

[25] Herodotus was older than Th. and it is almost universally assumed that in so far as there is any effect of the one on the other it is of Herodotus on Th. A contrary view, Irwin 2007. On later writers' inabilities to understand 'the special mix of practical political and rhetorical examples' in Th., Nicolai 2009: 384–9, cf. Hornblower 1995. More widely, essays in Fromentin, Gotteland and Payen 2010.

[26] Hoekstra 2012, 'crescendo' at 31.

only the motives of fear, honour and interest (what in *Leviathan* he calls safety, reputation and gain) that Thucydides puts into the mouths of Athenians (1.75.3, 1.76.2) and imputes to the Spartans.[27]

To Hobbes and his predecessors in Venice, the Low Countries and Spain, Thucydides was a connoisseur of the political arts; a source of maxims and examples from a rediscovered past. In France, Italy, what became southern Germany and a little later in Scotland and England, he was to be taken up by those who were beginning to have an interest in pasts themselves. 'All preceding narratives', said David Hume, 'are so intermixed with fable, that philosophers ought to abandon them, in a great measure, to the establishment of poets and orators'; 'the first page of Thucydides is, in my opinion, the commencement of real history'.[28] 'History' is not to us a misplaced description of what Thucydides is doing, even if it is not the only thing, and even if he was working through his ideas about how to write it as he did so. Whatever else it may and may not be, his is a narrative in which things that existed are explained by others that have done so, an account in which the questions that can be asked of the past, one might say, are questions of a kind that can be asked of the present. They are also questions that can be asked of characters and events in fiction, as long as we are aware that these are bounded by the fiction. If one's sole interest is in Thucydides as a writer, one can read him in the way one reads a history play or an historical novel. As it is, suggests Williams, he was the first writer we know of in the West to describe real pasts standing in a determinate relation to each other and the real present.[29]

Leopold von Ranke, who wrote a now lost dissertation on Thucydides in the late 1810s or early 1820s, was among those who went on to make the case for what is now seen as the start of professional history writing. This was not an end in itself. Ranke's own vaunted method may have been empirical, his early interest classical, and Thucydides may have been an early model, but his own time was Romantic. The history that he championed in the 'national awakening' in Germany after 1813 promised to recover a past as an identity for the present.

---

[27] Thucydides 1989: 575–8, xxii. Hobbes appears to have finished his translation two or three years before it was registered in 1628 and published in 1629. Skinner 2002a: 62 remarks that his introduction is itself a model of forensic oratory; more comprehensively on Hobbes' rhetoric, also Skinner 1996: 244–9, and on the substance of motive, Hoekstra 2007.

[28] Hume, 'Of the Populousness of Ancient Nations' II.11.98. Hume later relaxed the measure and rather spoiled the point: 'the Peloponnesian war is a proper subject for history, the siege of Athens [in 404] for an epic poem, and the death of Alcibiades [in the same year] for a tragedy', *An Enquiry Concerning Human Understanding*, III, 14.

[29] Williams 2002: 149–71.

Wilhelm Roscher, who attended Ranke's seminar in Berlin in 1839–40, may have captured Thucydides' wider appeal. In his sensitivity to motive and the wider movement of things, said Roscher, his aversion to metaphysics, and his ability to bring everything together with style and effect, he was more than a mere historical handworker. Macaulay agreed: he 'surpassed all his rivals in the art of historical narration, in the art of producing an effect after the imagination, by skilful selection and disposition'.[30]

Macaulay himself regretted only that Thucydides did not draw the lessons of what he recorded. Hobbes had not hesitated to do so and at comparable moments of collective anxiety, readers since have been similarly unrestrained. But where Macaulay may have thought there were several lessons to be drawn, most readers, usually to confirm their existing opinion, have extracted just one. Hobbes took Thucydides to be suggesting that the moderate tyranny in Athens between 546 and 527 and what was 'democratical in name' but 'in practice monarchical' under Pericles in the 430s were the kinds of regime under which men could best live peaceably together.[31] Revolutionaries in the late eighteenth century were more drawn to what they saw as Sparta's egalitarian republicanism, and those of a liberal inclination who turned away from them rejected what Benjamin Constant regarded as the false liberty of all the ancients (a conception that Hobbes had also disdained) in favour of a liberty for 'moderns' in large commerical societies that had been unknown in the ancient world. In what was to become the United States, in which battles between ancients and moderns were less evident and classical texts less often invoked, republicanisms in the Spartan and Athenian manner were rejected in favour of a state in which the powers of the people and the state would be contained. It was those pressing for reform in England in the first half of the nineteenth century who saw some promise in what Thucydides describes for fifth-century Athens.

Thucydides has more recently been invoked on almost all sides. The most unusual reading in the United States in the twentieth century, perhaps the most unusual reading of any kind anywhere, was that of Leo

---

[30] On Roscher, Morley 2012, who notes that he may not have been widely read at the time; on Th. and early nineteenth-century German historiography, Süssman 2012. Macaulay 1889: 138.

[31] Thucydides 1989: 572–3. Hobbes' references are to 2.65.9, where Th. remarks that under Pericles Athens was coming to be ruled by the first man, and 6.54.5, where he says (in Hobbes' translation) that in ruling Athens in the third quarter of the sixth century Peisistratus held 'virtue and wisdom in great account for a long time, and taking of the Athenians but a twentieth part of their revenues, adorned the city, managed their wars, and administered their religion worthily'. On the Peisistradids, see Ch. 12.

Strauss in the late 1950s and early 1960s. In writing of cities at war, Strauss said, Thucydides is seeking to impress what he never describes, the virtue that is 'first for us', 'inherent in the city as such', 'natural', 'pre-philosophic', pre-political and peaceful, 'subject and subservient to the divine'. More liberal Americans have in different ways pressed the lasting value of what Pericles said of Athens in the 430s: that 'a spirit of freedom governs our conduct' under rules of rule in which 'we are all personally involved either in actual political decisions or in deliberation about them' (2.37.2–3, 2.40.2).[32] In foreign affairs, what sixteenth- and seventeenth-century readers in Europe had taken Thucydides to insist on was recast in the idiom of a 'realist' science of international relations. There is a lasting and overriding truth, it was claimed, in what he has Athenians say to leaders at Melos; 'judgements about justice are relevant only between those with an equal power to enforce it and that the possibilities are defined by what the strong do and the weak accept' (5.89). 'Neo-conservative' adventurers after the United States' 'Cold War', drawing on native liberal internationalists as well as realists, took heart from what they read to be Athens' commitment to implanting democracy overseas, its suspicion of multilateral alliances and its dislike of Persian 'multi-culturalism'. After the attacks on New York and Washington in 2001, some were to recall the resentment at Athens' dominion and if they were disinclined to react with force, invoked Thucydides to warn of rash ventures abroad. Those more directly concerned with military matters have meanwhile welcomed his text as the first treatise on strategy in the West.[33]

Classical scholars, as one would expect, have paid more attention to the text and to what it reveals about its own time. Between the 1840s and the 1970s philologists and historians tried to discern when, how and in what order Thucydides wrote what he did in order to discover what he might have been intending. But the answers could only be found within the text itself, and as it became clear that this revealed almost nothing on which all

---

[32] On eighteenth- and nineteenth-century revolutionaries and liberals, Urbinati 2012; against 'ancient liberty', Constant 1988. On nineteenth-century England, Potter 2012. Strauss 1964: 139–241, esp. 174, 240–1, on the interpretation of whom I am helped by Pippin 2003; also, following Strauss, Orwin 1994. Another modern conservative reading, Samons 2004, contested by Hansen 2006a. Among liberal commentators, Farrar 1988: 126–91, arguing that Th. was sympathetic to democracy, and Ober 1998: 52–191 and 1996 (a critical review of Farrar), arguing that he was not. Reflecting on the wider appeal of Athens, Dunn 2006: 23–70.

[33] Ancient and modern 'realisms' in the study of international relations, Low: 2007: 7–32 and important reflections on Th. in his time at 222–48. (There is also much of relevance on Athens in the analysis of fourth-century speeches in Hunt 2010.) Early modern instances, Hoekstra 2012. Modern 'realisms' in the note on reading at the end of this book. Th. as strategist, Platias and Koliopoulos 2010.

could agree, the questions died and there seemed no reason not to go back to taking the work as a whole. Some who did so, drawing on epigraphic evidence, attended to its accuracy, some emphasised the importance it gives to reason and some dwelt on the unreasoned tragedies of politics and war. Others again read it as literature, examining its structure and style and restoring it to its cultural context. To a few, reacting against the West's wars abroad since the 1960s, recoiling at Thucydides' preoccupation with war and high politics, impelled to unmask grand narrative and to privilege the response of the reader over the intentions of the author (a move difficult to resist with an author whose intentions have been so difficult to discern), it has become 'no longer a startling thought that what Thucydides gives us is the Peloponnesian war as defined by the ideology of a particular class of aristocratic and wealthy Athenian males'.[34]

But nobody's 'ideology' is all of a piece. Thucydides, straining to 'decontextualise' himself from Athens and being adrift from the city for the larger part of his writing life, reveals little.[35] He is inclined to moderation, *sophrosune*, in politics. But this goes deeper than a fixed preference for one kind of rule over another. The categories of 'oligarchy', 'democracy' and 'tyranny' run across principled conviction, constitutional form and the practicalities of government and were as coarse to him as they are to anyone who thinks for a moment about them now; he can be sceptical of attitudes to them all.[36] He also qualifies the generalities on which any putative ideology must rest. In suggesting that people are always disposed to 'indulge in uncritical hope for what they want but use their sovereign powers of reason to reject what they would prefer to avoid' (4.108.4), he takes pains to show that at two important moments, when one of their kings warned the Spartans in 432 against going unprepared to war and when an Athenian commander in the winter of 412–411 criticised the urgings of another to ally the city with Persia, each was speaking reasonably against what he ultimately wished for (1.82.1, 8.48.4). Thucydides suggests that in some respects Peisistratos' tyranny in Athens in the sixth century stood in flattering contrast to the democracy there in the 420s and 410s (6.54.5); yet although he sees the part that demagogic competition in Athens had played in the city's defeats (2.65.4, 6.15.3–4, also

---

[34] Th.'s composition, magisterial essays by Andrewes and Dover *HCT* V: 361–437 and a criticism of their assumptions, Connor 1984a. Reading Th. as history and literature, Dover 2009. Th. writing history, Pelling 2000, Greenwood 2006.

[35] Th.'s ideology, Dewald 2005: 13, also Hunter 1973 (discussed in Dover 2009) and, among others, Badian 1993. 'Decontexualising' himself, Moles 1999; 'adrift from locality', Davidson 2005. On ideology, also Ch. 5 below.

[36] Wisely on *sophrosune*, Andrewes *HCT* V: 159–60. As 'an oligarchic code word', Hornblower 1994: 192; Humble 2002 notes that Athenian oligarchs were inclined to attribute *sophrosune* to rule in Sparta. Also Ch. 4 n. 3 below.

4.28.3, 6.63.2, 7.24.3), he remarks on the pragmatic good sense of the *demos* when it had to pull itself together after Sicily (8.1.4) and does so again after the coup against the democracy in 411. His observation on the tendency of war to incite wider violence does not square with his accounts of the restraint urged by Athenians in 427 and again in 421 and 415 (3.82.2, 3.46–7, 5.16.1, 6.10). And as in collective actions, so also in his portrayal of individuals, who are invariably complex, often contradictory and in their thoughts and actions governed more by circumstance than any ideology or theory would easily allow.

When therefore Thucydides says that what happened in the course of this war 'can be expected to happen again or some time in the future' and in 'much the same ways', one might be wrong to take him to have been saying that he had discovered enduring connections of cause and effect. He may instead have meant that events would continue to move in unexpected ways and that those involved in them would continue to be as wise, foolish, surprised, delighted, frightened and cast down as those in his own story; that the more enduring happenings as well as the 'unaccountable contingencies of human life' are at once too numerous, too varied and too contradictory to be subsumed in any but the blandest of inclusive characterisations and general explanations. Twenty-one years of fear, hope, fury, frustration and suffering – twenty-seven by the time that he came to make his final revisions – may have seemed to him to signify nothing beyond themselves. If there is a lesson to be learnt, this might be it.

But Thucydides does not openly state it. Lessons turn on generalities and generalities on retrospection, and apart from two small exceptions that I suggest we do well to disregard, he does not offer that. He writes the past as the present it was for those who were living it and attempting to deal with an unknown future. He is in this respect more like a dramatist without a chorus or a modern novelist than an historian or social scientist pressing a thesis. But even those who write fictions can be inclined to answer a question they have posed or meet an expectation they have raised and thus bring matters to one or another kind of resolution. He does not. Even if he had managed to write the last six years of the war, it would not have been out of character for him to finish simply by saying that it had ended and with it, the writing that Thucydides of Athens had set out to do; knowing that as Gregory of Tours was to say about the Frankish monarchies a thousand years later, things would just keep on happening, some good, some bad.[37]

---

[37] Gregory's remark comes at the start of the prologue to his *Histories*, Heinzelmann 2002: 101–4. Heinzelmann argues that he deflected the 'charge of glorifying only famous men

This might seem to suggest that Thucydides does little more than elaborate the obvious about politics and military action. Men try for what they wish for when they think they can, sometimes succeeding and often failing. It is for the reader to give whatever 'meanings' he or she may wish to give – causal, dispositional, associational or consequential – to his account of their doing so. The significance in what he writes is the significance one chooses to give to it.[38] Yet he would not have continued to be read by those with an interest in politics and war if he did not convey an acute sense of the ways in which the obvious can manifest itself, not least in the fact that people engaged in politics and war often do not have a full sense of what they are doing and why. One can see why Hobbes should have regarded him as 'the most politic historiographer that ever writ'. Not only does he take readers back to the 'drifts and counsels of the actors to their seat', leaving the futures of their present open, and refrain from digressing 'to read a lecture, moral or political, upon his text'. In going 'no further than the acts themselves evidently guide him', Hobbes said, he also enters men's hearts.[39]

This is not now an idiom of ours and earlier commentators, innocent of the sobrieties of recent historiography and political science, might have agreed that its disappearance is our loss. The disposition in the Greek fifth century and before not to separate motive, intention and action has been thought to mark what anthropologists used to call a primitive mentality. But to insist on these separations can lead those who favour reason to privilege the explanatory value of reasoned intention over unreflected motive and to underrate the significance of action. It is impulses and commitments of a pre-reflective kind, what one of Thucydides' protagonists called 'invisible forces' (3.45.5), forces for which we still have no agreed and satisfactory names, formed in feeling and shaped by culture and experience, that determine what people care about and direct their intentions, and these commitments and what people derive from them are most reliably – one might say most truly – expressed in what they do. This is not of course to say that in politics, thought and talk are incidental. *Logoi*, the accounts people give, their analysis, reflection, calculation and debate, are important *erga*, 'things done', political acts to be seen as such in the light of others. It is Thucydides' grasp of this simple truth

in the pagan tradition' by insisting that he had to describe the bad in order the more effectively to demonstrate the goodness of good Christians. With the exception of the ways in which he writes Pericles and (more arguably) Nicias, Th. stands apart from any evaluative purpose of this kind, Christian (of course) or pre-Christian.

[38] A useful catalogue of kinds of 'meaning(fulness)', with no particular reference to history or politics, Nozick 1981: 575.

[39] Hobbes, Thucydides 1989: xxii.

(which Nietzsche, though he did not extend it to politics, so admired), his ability to convey it and, as I suggest at the end of this book, the view he thereby secretes of politics itself that make his writing, in form and content almost out of time, immediate still in our own.[40]

---

[40] The distinctiveness of ancient philosophies of action, Williams 1993. Nietzsche on Th., 2005: 225–6 ('What I owe the ancients', *Twilight of the Idols or How to Philosophise without a Hammer*, 2) and more indirectly, 1997: 60 (book 2, 103). On pre-reflective commitments in Nietzsche, Pippin 2010 and Chs. 4, 11 and 15 among others here.

2   Writing power: Athens in Greece 478–435

'Thucydides of Athens wrote the war' (1.1.1). Many translators have said that he wrote *the* history of the war. Others could say that he wrote *a* history, one of the many that could have been written. But both, the question of history aside, would understate him. The verb he uses, *sun-graphein*, with which he also often signs off his account of a year, was unusual and in a world in which prose was still rare, ambiguous. Literally 'to depict together' and by extension 'to bring together in writing', it can allow us to read him both to say that he wrote up the information he had and constructed the war to make it the one we should know. He may mean both.

Events, *erga*, things done (1.22.2), were as they were; if they happened they happened and had to be recovered. There is no reason to doubt that Thucydides investigated the reports he received 'with the utmost concern for accuracy' and was in reporting as truthful as he could manage. Likewise with the speeches, even if he had more often than not to resort to imagining what the speaker in question would 'most appropriately' have said in the circumstances in which he found himself. And in writing all this down he sought the authority that writing gave.[1] The most extreme contrast would have been with the vagaries of oral exchange in the conditions of internal war, where 'simplicity' of spirit – as Hobbes translates it, 'sincerity' – 'was laughed to scorn and vanished' (3.83.1). 'Men assumed the right to reverse the usual values in the application of words to actions' (3.82.4), and nothing said could be trusted. The comparison would have been with the aspiration of the Athenian general Nicias. Wanting to be sure he could convey the predicament he found himself in in Sicily in 414 and fearing that a messenger's oral account 'would fail to report the true facts, whether through lack of ability in speaking or failure of memory or a wish to indulge mass opinion', Nicias sent a letter so that those in Athens 'should deliberate with a view to the

---

[1] Moles 1999. On authority in ancient historiography more generally, Marincola 1997.

truth of the matter' (7.8.2). To the thinking part of a society in which writing and reading were still rare, Thucydides saw himself offering a text based on critical appraisals of oral accounts by others and his own witness of 'the actions of the things done'. This was inquiry as it should be, 'true and not concealed', as Lowell Edmunds puts it, 'because written; true and not distorted for gratification, because written; true and exclusive, not popularised, because written'.[2]

Thucydides is certainly confident. 'No-one in future ever need enquire how it came about that so great a war arose among the Greeks' (1.23.5). He tackles the question of how it did in book 1, the only one of the eight in which he presses a consistent thesis. It is a complicated construction of seven parts. In the first (1.2–19), which in the older sense of a discourse on antiquity has come to be called 'the archaeology', he describes the rise of Greek power from 'earlier times'. He wants to show what this power consisted in and 'that earlier events were not on the same scale' as the conflict he is writing about, 'either as regards their wars or in other respects' (1.1.3). In the second part, he pauses to explain his methods of inquiry (1.20–2). In the third (1.23–88), he tells how two sets of events on the Greek periphery in the later 430s gave Sparta and its allies cause to engage with Athens. In the fourth, the so-called *pentecontaetia* or 'fifty years', he elaborates on the growth of Athens' power between the retreat of the Persians in 479 and the start of 'the present war' in 431 (1.89–1.118.2, at 118.2). In the fifth (1.119–25), he returns to his narrative to describe reactions to the events on the periphery at a meeting of the Peloponnesian states. Having in the sixth (1.126–38) digressed on the character and fate of leading men after the Persian war in order to give a sense of how Athens and Sparta began to be suspicious of the other, he returns in the seventh (1.139–46) to describe Athens' response to the deliberations of the Peloponnesian league and the Spartan embassies that followed. By the end of book 1, he expects the answer that he gives to his question towards the start and twice repeats to be evident. 'I consider the truest cause [of the war], though the one least openly stated, to be this:

---

[2] Edmunds 2009: 109. This way of putting his project, in itself persuasive, does not warrant Edmunds' two further conclusions: that accepting 'the textual project' as Th. defines it 'depends on the reader's sharing the ideological orientation' of Th. the aristocrat, and that 'Th. the historian thus becomes less important than Th. the writer' (112–13); likewise Loraux 1986b, Allison 1997: 226, in contrast Dover 2009; also Ch. 5 below. Th. continues without comment to explain that when the messengers sent by Nicias arrived in Athens, they gave an oral report of what they had been told (perhaps by Nicias himself) in Sicily, that only then was his letter read to the assembly and that the citizens voted to reject his appraisal and request (7.10.1, 7.16.1), Ch. 13 below. On 'sincerity' in truthfulness, Williams 2002: 84–122. On the more straightforward significance of writing in making an agreement, 5.35.3.

the Athenians were becoming powerful and inspired fear in the Spartans and so forced them into war'; 'They could bear it no longer' (1.23.6, 1.118.2, also 1.88).

The verb translated by Walter Blanco, Martin Hammond and Jeremy Mynott as 'forced', *anankazein*, has its root in the notion of something that tightly binds. Hobbes translates the Spartans being 'necessitated' to war, Henry Dale as being 'compelled'. In a more modern idiom, Richard Crawley and Rex Warner say that war was 'inevitable'.[3] No one can suppose that Thucydides believed in necessities of what we would call a supernatural kind; the gods may have played a part for others but they play none for him. Nor did he imagine anything that could sensibly be described as laws of history.[4] He had the commoner sense of men seeing no practicable choice and perhaps a sense also of a 'necessary identity', an identity such that someone who has it feels bound to act in ways that maintain their identity in the eyes of others; as fifth-century Greeks would often have put it and as the Spartans saw it by the late 430s, to maintain their honour and not suffer shame.[5]

I return to this possibility at the end of Chapter 4 and a further aspect of it in Chapter 10, and pursue the question of necessities more generally in Chapter 9. But one might still be wary of Thucydides' claim that the Spartans were forced into war. Christopher Pelling argues that 'his narrative principle' here is 'to suppress points which have no consequence' for the story as he wants to tell it and to deflect any interest we may have in alternative explanations and 'in the history that did not happen'. To be wary of his claim is not to suppose that it is untrue, although Thucydides does put it very generally. In asking about what did not happen, one merely wants to be sure about what he says did.[6] It helps in this to take what he writes in a more conventionally chronological order.

---

[3] Blanco in Thucydides 1998, Hammond in Thucydides 2009, Mynott *TWPA*, Hobbes in 1629 in Thucydides 1989, Dale in Thucydides 1907, Crawley in 1874 in Thucydides 1996, Warner in 1954 in Thucydides 1972a. The use of 'inevitability' in the sense intended by Crawley and Warner dates from the 1850s. Also Ostwald 1988.

[4] Laws of history, de Romilly 1963. Her more general reflections, Ch. 15 below.

[5] Not only ancient Greeks; Campbell 1964 on an archaic modern community in the northwest; and even in modernity, not only Greeks. It is a further question about ancients and moderns, individual and collective, whether they have one necessary identity or several, and other identities, as we call them, which are not necessary. The question of legal identities is separate and conceptually simpler. I take the idea of a 'necessary identity' from Williams 1993: 122–3, 126–9, though deploy it a little differently.

[6] Cf. Pelling's claim (Pelling 2000: 81) that Th. writes against our interest in things which did not happen with Stahl's suggestion (Stahl 2003: e.g. 92–3) that he emphasises the importance of 'hinges'. On this I favour Stahl, though sometimes differ on what the 'hinge' events were and how to read these, Chs. 9 and 13 below. Thoughts on the more general question, Hawthorn 1991.

This said, we have no need to ask what might have been happening by the fifth century if the remote past had not been as Thucydides says it was. Things would have turned out far too differently. From the few sources Thucydides has and is prepared to rely on and what he believes to be permissible reasoning backwards from the present, he offers a materialist account of Greece from what he calls the 'early times'. His conception is now conventional and will have been so to anyone since the Scottish eighteenth century. But it was original for its time, and although in 'culturalist' times some might express a distaste for its concentration on power, and though archaeologists and historians have refined it, its central point holds. It also operates at a level of explanation that Thucydides was not again to approach.

The first Greek settlements, he suggests, were scarcely settled at all; successive migrations and the conflicts to which they gave rise caused one poorly defended group after another to move on. It was some time before walls were built around collections of dwellings, and some time again before pirates and other private booty-chasers could be subdued by clans and communities who had acquired the resources to impose a monopoly on raids and organise the defence of their territories. Even when settlements did begin to settle, he says, there was no war on land that changed the distribution of power. Those that were fought were particular disputes between neighbouring communities. The Greeks, as Greeks, did not mount distant expeditions 'for they had not yet come together as subjects of the great powers, nor did they of their own accord make expeditions in common as equal partners' (1.15.3). (An exception he does not mention was a fight over the importantly fertile land on the island of Euboea off eastern Attica, which in about 700 BC had prompted other states to take sides [1.15.3].)[7] The Minoans (our term, not Thucydides') had come to parts of the mainland from the island of Crete and a later Mycenaean expedition to Troy was of no material consequence. But these early moments reveal what he takes to be critical. Minoan power and that of the expedition to Troy was the same as that in Persian expeditions (in Phoenician ships) to islands settled by Greeks off the Ionian coast after revolts there in the early fifth century and then to the Greek mainland; the same as the power in the Athenians' eventually successful repudiation of these expeditions which after 478 enabled them to create the league that became their dominion (*arche*) or 'empire': it lay in navies. 'Those who actively developed [these] strengthened their positions greatly in terms of revenue and dominion over others' (1.15.1).

---

[7] A war which acquired something of a mythic standing in later centuries, Boardman 1982: 760–3. It is said to have been the last 'pre-hoplite' conflict.

Thucydides wants to show that by the later 430s the growth of the Athenians' naval power 'was finally clear for all to see and their actions were beginning to impinge directly on the Spartan alliance' (1.118.2). Not all have agreed that this was so. Once the Persians had been defeated in 480–479 the Athenians reoccupied Athens and the Spartans went home. Sparta had led the Greek alliance and its forces on land, but Athens' new navy, financed by silver from mines at Laureion, 50 miles or so south-east of the city, had been just as important. Its architect, Themistocles, who afterwards became one of the first men in the city, saw how naval power could give Athens parity and after the war was over, decided to extend the advantage by rebuilding Athens' walls and strengthening its port at the Piraeus. The Spartans were suspicious; they wanted any new Persian attack to be defended from the south and no line of defence to be drawn between the Peloponnese and the rest of mainland Greece. But they also wanted to be rid of the Persian threat, to this end combined with the Athenians to remove Persians from Cyprus and the small but strategically placed city of Byzantion on the Bosporos, and after clumsily failing to assert themselves in Ionia and the northern Aegean accepted that the Athenians were competent to take command there. Arguing that it was essential to collaborate against the possibility of another attack by Persia, the Athenians formed a league to include these places.

'The Athenians exercised their leadership over allies who were autonomous and participated in deliberations in joint assemblies' on the sacred island of Delos (1.97.1). A navy being essential to their project, the Athenians 'assessed which cities should be required to contribute money for the war against Persia and which ships – the ostensible purpose being to avenge their sufferings by avenging the King's land' (1.96.1). The result was that Athens was able to extend a dominion over *poleis* which, Thucydides does not quite say, the *poleis* themselves were financing. Not all were content to do so. Naxos, the first to rebel, was 'enslaved', Athens laid siege to what had been the considerable sea power of Thasos, near sources of gold and silver in Thrace, and settled the city of Nine Ways on the nearby mainland, where there was wood for masts and oars.[8] Thucydides also does not mention that in 454 the treasury and site of deliberation about tribute and related matters were transferred from the authority of the joint assembly at Delos to Athens, but he makes the point clear: notionally equal allies had rapidly become subjects of an Athenian dominion.

---

[8] Gomme *HCT* I: 622.

The alliance that Athens and Sparta had made to counter Persia was not formally revoked, although Thucydides does mention that the Spartans had secretly promised the Thasians that they would invade Attica to divert the Athenian siege of that island, and that notwithstanding the small number of ships they could call on, he believes that they would have kept their word, had they not been 'prevented by the occurrence of the earthquake' (1.101.2). This took place in 464, and unsettled them. Helots, 'the captured', unfree tenants in Messenia in the Peloponnesian south-west on whom the Spartans depended for a good part of their livelihood, together with two towns there, rebelled. When some of these people barricaded themselves on Mount Ithome, the Spartans asked the Athenians and others to help lay a siege. Themistocles, whose hostility to Sparta might have led him to resist the request, was no longer in the city. (He had been ostracised from Athens in about 470, gone to help anti-Spartan elements in the Peloponnese and when Sparta accused him of having been corrupted by Persia fled east, learnt Persian and become a provincial governor for the King. Thucydides praises his strategic abilities and says nothing about his alleged offences [1.138.3].) Cimon, who had been active in creating the Athenian league, had been hostile to Themistocles, was favourably disposed to the Spartans and persuaded the Athenians to help put down the rebellion. But when his force arrived in 462, the Spartans changed their mind. Perhaps aware (Thucydides does not say) that Cimon's allies were by then losing authority in Athens, they became afraid that the Athenians might be persuaded to side with the Messenians. They accordingly asked the Athenian force to leave and it did, much offended. It was then, suggests Thucydides, that 'an open difference first emerged' between the two powers (1.102.3).

Athens ended the alliance, and despite Cimon's previous successes, most recently in defeating a Persian force in southern Anatolia and subduing Thasos, he was ostracised and went into exile for ten years. It was to be about ten years also (like much in this period, the exact dating is disputed) before the Spartans were able to succeed with the siege at Mount Ithome; when they did, they allowed those rebels who so wished to leave for Naupactos, a city that the Athenians had recently captured on the northern coast of the gulf of Corinth. Meanwhile, Megara, on the isthmus between the mainland and the Peloponnese, was angered by a boundary dispute with Corinth, came over to Athens and caused the Corinthians also to form 'a vehement hatred of the Athenians' (1.103.4). What has come to be described as 'the first Peloponnesian war' had begun.[9]

---

[9] 'The first Peloponnesian war' was not defined as such until the 1950s in Oxford, Lewis 1992b: 111–20. (Rusten 2009: 8 n. 21 tells a nice story from Lewis: candidates in an

In 459 the Athenians defeated a Peloponnesian fleet near Aegina, an island south of the Piraeus which even though it had fought with the Greeks at Salamis in 480 had previously been sympathetic to the Persians. The Athenians occupied the island and, in a moment of cruelty of the kind that Thucydides often mentions to convey unnecessary horror, mobilised their reserves to resist a Corinthian army that was trying to recapture Megara (1.106). In 457 the Athenians moved against a force from Sparta itself that had advanced to recover 'daughter cities' on the mainland north of the isthmus, near Phocis. In part because the Athenians commanded its routes home, in part, Thucydides explains, because Sparta was tempted to see what might come of reports that some in Athens were keen to end the democracy there, the force delayed its return. But the conspiracy in Athens came to nothing and the Spartans defeated Athenians who came out to attack them. This allowed them to go home, but sixty-two days later (Thucydides is suddenly exact) the Athenians won a battle with Phocians and some adjacent Boeotians.

These were the high points of Athenian power on land. Thucydides adds a few more details, including a tussle between Sparta and Athens over the entity that controlled the pan-Hellenic shrine at Delphi, which Athens won. He also recounts the disastrous end for the Athenians in 450 to a long campaign against the Persians in Egypt, in the course of which, he says, Persians had tried and failed to bribe the Spartans into invading Attica (1.109–10). But he does not mention a peace that most believe was concluded with Persia in 449 after an Athenian victory off the coast of Cyprus (in which Cimon died); this would have removed the case for regarding Athens' dominion as a defence against a renewed Persian attack on Greece and for that reason, historians speculate, the authorities may have kept it quiet.[10] Sparta and Athens themselves then agreed a five-year truce. Thucydides says little also about how the Athenians began to retreat on the mainland of Greece. They lost a battle at Coroneia in Boeotia and released their hold there in order to recover prisoners, suffered a brief revolt on Euboea and found themselves unable to prevent

examination at the university in 1959 were surprised to be invited to write about an event of which they had not yet been told.) Gomme, writing in advance of the notion, gives a full list of the known omissions in *HCT* I: 365–9, what he regards as the more 'inexplicable' of these at 369. Against the point of doing so, Price 2001: 357 n. 50. De Romilly's remark (1985: 104), that 'it is impossible to over-emphasise how much Thucydides leaves out of his account' more generally, was rather optimistic about what we know of what he does not write about, and taken literally, could be said of almost any subsequent historian of anywhere.

[10]   The peace of 449 was said to have been agreed by a brother-in-law of Cimon's; some suspect that Cimon himself had attempted one earlier. Even if none was agreed, hostilities with Persia ceased after Cimon's victory in Cyprus in 451. The debate about this, Lewis 1992d: 121–7.

Megara returning to the Spartan side. In 446, they did face a Spartan invasion of Attica itself. This stopped short of Athens, perhaps because the Spartan commanders had been bribed, perhaps because terms were discussed, perhaps for both these reasons. In the following winter, the two powers agreed a full treaty of peace between their leagues to last for thirty years. The Athenians, one of their leaders was later to admit, had needed it (4.21.3). They relinquished the ports they had held in the Megarid and neutral Achaea but it was decided that each side should otherwise keep what it had, that no state should switch from one league to another, as the Megarians had been doing, and that neither side was to attack the other if the side that was attacked was willing to accept arbitration. Sparta was to retain its allies in the Peloponnese and Boeotia and also Megara, all of which were to be self-governing, so long as they did not move to what by this time was coming to be called 'democracy'.[11] Athens was to retain its dominion over states in Greek Ionia and the Aegean. Nothing appears to have been said about those that remained neutral.[12] The first Peloponnesian war was over.

Thucydides remarks at the end of the 'archaeology' that by the start of the second Peloponnesian war in 431, the military resources that Athens alone could command were greater than those that the two powers had been able together to deploy against the Persians in 480–479. The city's revenues had increased and the navies it could use, including those of Chios and Lesbos, which had continued to provide ships and crews rather than money, had grown. (Samos, the third island that had provided ships, had become involved in a war in 440 with another subject state, Miletus, across the water in Ionia, defied Athens' attempt to stop it, been subdued, had its ships confiscated and was thereafter required to provide tribute in money instead, with costs for the trouble it had caused. Thucydides later remarks that the Samians boasted that they had come close to depriving Athens of its command of the sea [8.76.4].) In the 430s the Spartans and their allies had the larger land force, and their army, which they could supplement with lightly armed troops and infantry from its local populations, was the only one in Greece that was what we might describe as 'professional', or full-time. But although the Spartans could

[11] Raaflaub provides a clear account of arguments about the history of 'democracy' in Athens to the 450s in Raaflaub, Ober and Wallce 2007: 1–27. Also Eder 1997, which puts Raaflaub (among others) into perspective. Raaflaub emphasises the importance of Athens' empire to the democracy in contrast to Ober 1996, who emphasises ideology.

[12] Th. gives lists of the allies on each side at the start of the ('second') war at 2.9.2–4. Gomme *HCT* II: 12 sharply remarks that this is 'a meagre and beggarly description . . . with no details of forces, and above all no comparison of the strength of both sides'; also that Th. does not here mention allies of either side in the west, or the Thessalians in northern Greece, who provided cavalry for the Athenians.

call on the Corinthian navy, the Peloponnesians still had too few ships. In the years following the peace in 446–445, the Athenians had pointedly demonstrated their reach across the sea by refounding a colony at Thurii in the instep of Italy, perhaps calling it pan-Hellenic and if so, thereby staking a claim to leadership in Greece;[13] they also consolidated their hold on Nine Ways in Thrace, which they renamed Amphipolis, and paraded ships along the Black Sea coasts, from the north shore of which wheat was exported to Attica. Thucydides does not mention these expeditions. But in the speeches he is to give each side immediately before the start of the war, all remarked on Athens' maritime power.

The facts might therefore seem at first to support the case he is making: Athens' wealth was greater, its navy was supreme, and its potential power had grown. There was no ultimate necessity in this. If the Persians had not threatened Greece, Athens might not have developed a powerful navy at all. Once it had, however, and once others had acceded to the dominion it acquired at sea after the Persian defeat, what followed would have been all but impossible for other Greek powers to resist. Nonetheless, Athens appears to have observed the terms of the peace in 446–445 and not used its power against any state in the Peloponnesian league. The second element in Thucydides' thesis therefore is not yet clear. The Spartans would not appear to have had anything, as he puts it, that they could no longer bear; anything materially to fear.

[13] Andrewes 1978: 6–8 is sceptical.

3   Explaining the war: stated reasons 435–432

Thucydides remarks that Sparta's fear, which he believes to be the 'truest cause' of the war, was 'the one least openly stated' at the time (1.23.6). This is not to say that he reports no one having mentioned it. Corcyraeans spoke of it to Athenians and Corinthians addressing Spartans did their best to fan it. But no Spartan openly acknowledged it. This is scarcely surprising. A state that values the perception of its power will rarely admit to fear of another. If fear is the motive or 'true cause' of hostility it will usually be attributed to a fault elsewhere: to an enemy's greed or real or apparent aggression, or to an ally's failure. Even if the terms in which Thucydides distinguishes between what motivates but is not spoken and what is spoken but may not motivate are unstable, he is clear about the difference.[1] At this moment however he does not identify either as clearly as he might have done. He leaves it to the reader to see how in the years before the start of open hostilities between Sparta and Athens, it was to be exaggerated arguments advanced by an ally of Sparta's in response to events which need not in themselves have been decisive that for a different and deeper reason caused Sparta to move to war, and that for reasons of its own, the leadership in Athens let it do so.

Thucydides gives three arguments on the Peloponnesian side for alleging that Athens was not observing the spirit of the peace of 446–445. He seems not to have taken the first of the three, the restrictions that the Athenians had at some point placed on Megarians' trading, as seriously as the Spartans and some in Athens did (1.67.4, 1.126.3, 1.140.3,

---

[1] There is a large literature on Th.'s use of *aitia* and *prophasis*, commonly rendered as 'true cause' or 'real reason' and 'reason given' or 'pretext'. He was writing at a time when usage was fluid, but most agree on what he meant; see further Mynott *TWPA*: 1.23n; Andrewes *HCT* V, 415–23; and, on reasons 'least openly stated', Richardson 1990. As my argument in this chapter suggests, Hornblower's rendering of 'profound and superficial causes' is not quite right, and this aside, I think he may exaggerate in suggesting that even when properly understood this 'is arguably Th.'s greatest single contribution to history writing', *CT* I: 65.

1.144.2). (It is unfortunately not clear what these restrictions were or when and why they had been imposed. The avowed reason was religious; the Athenians had accused the Megarians of violating sacred land. But Megara was important for control of the isthmus, the Athenians had lost control of it in 446–445 and that grated.) Nor does Thucydides elaborate on the second argument, the claim by leaders on the island of Aegina that Athens had denied them the autonomy promised in 'the treaty' (perhaps the thirty-year peace, perhaps another), a grievance that was to make the Aeginetans 'foremost among the delegates in urging war' in advance of a meeting of Sparta's allies in the autumn of 432 (1.67.2). The arguments that he does consider and at length arose between Corinthians and Corcyraeans over events in the city of Epidamnos in 435 and between Corinthians and Athenians over the city of Potidaea in 432 itself.

Epidamnos (on the site of modern Durrës in Albania) was said to have been colonised or founded 'in accordance with ancient practice' by a Corinthian and subsequently colonised by people from Corinth itself and the island of Corcyra (modern Corfu). 'As time went on', Thucydides writes, 'the Epidamnians became very powerful with a large population; but after internal conflicts lasting many years, it is said, they were decimated as a consequence of a war with the neighbouring barbarians [Illyrians] and were deprived of much of their power'. In 435, 'the common people there expelled the leading men, who then joined the barbarians in attacking the inhabitants of the city and harried them both by land and sea' (1.24.2–5). The 'common people' in Epidamnos regarded Corcyra rather than Corinth as their 'mother-city' and asked the Corcyraeans to reconcile the warring parties. The Corcyraeans refused and the Epidamnians, having first asked the oracle at Delphi whether they should do so, turned to the Corinthians, who were only too pleased to help; 'both as a matter of right', Thucydides explains, 'since they regarded the colony to be at least as much theirs as the Corcyraeans', and in hatred for the Corcyraeans who though also colonists of theirs were 'failing to show them respect'; the Corcyraeans 'did not present the traditional gifts of honour at their common festivals, nor did they bestow the first portion of the sacrifices on a Corinthian as the other colonists did. Instead, the Corcyraeans looked down on them: for in terms of financial power the Corcyraeans were at that time the equals of the richest of the Greeks' – outside Athens, Thucydides may have meant – 'and in terms of military resource they were even stronger, sometimes boasting of their great superiority at sea' (1.25.4). Their fleet of 120 warships (three-deck triremes) exceeded the Corinthians' own, and was at the time second only to the

Athenians' 300 or so.[2] One is left to imagine why the Corcyraeans did not respond to the appeal from Epidamnos; Thucydides offers no hint. They certainly valued their prosperity and independence from the rest of Greece and its troubles. The Corinthians, Thucydides makes clear, were driven by pride or honour (*time*). They resented the Corcyraeans' lack of ancestral respect, were not pleased to be thought less prosperous – all the more so no doubt for being widely acknowledged by others to be pre-eminent in trade across the isthmus and between the seas – and were offended at being thought to be militarily inferior on land as well as at sea. (The weakness of their army will have been shamefully evident when in a move on Megara in 459 it was stopped by a force of mere reservists from Athens.)

The Corinthians' first act in the new dispute was to send fresh colonists to Epidamnos. The Corcyraeans retaliated by besieging the city. The Corinthians set about recruiting allies to provide a naval escort for more colonists in case the Corcyraeans were to impede them. This prompted the Corcyraeans, taking envoys from Sparta and Sicyon, a city near Corinth that was also in the Peloponnesian league, to go to Corinth to make themselves clear. Thucydides summarises their case. 'If the Corinthians had any counter-claims they would be willing to submit to arbitration in the Peloponnese by any states both of them agreed upon; and whichever party it was adjudged the colony belonged to should prevail. They were also willing to submit the matter to the oracle at Delphi. Making war, however, the Corcyaeans advised against. Otherwise, they said, they in turn would be compelled, if the Corinthians forced them into it, to make new friends not of their choosing and different in kind from their current ones, in order to get help' (1.28.2–3). The Corinthians agreed to consider arbitration but, in the usual stand-off in situations of this kind, each side required the other to withdraw first and neither would. The Corinthians declared war on the Corcyraeans, who declared war in return. The Corcyraeans then won a battle at sea and proceeded to besiege Epidamnos itself. The Corinthians did not accept that this resolved the issue and through 434 and the first part of 433 built more ships and sought crews for them from elsewhere. The Corcyraeans meanwhile decided to seek help from Athens. 'When the Corinthians learned of this they too went to Athens to put their case, to prevent the addition of the Athenian fleet to the Corcyraean becoming an obstacle to their settling the war as they would wish' (1.31.1–3).

---

[2]   120, it should be said, is a suspiciously common number throughout the text. But there is no good reason for suspecting the relative magnitudes here.

It is the first exchange of arguments that Thucydides writes; the open-ing act in a text in which, in the politics of war, the claims of the past and of purported principle clash with the demands of the moment and usu-ally lose. The Corcyraeans opened with a polite flourish to their Athenian audience. They agreed that they had been wrong in not having joined with Athens in the peace of 446–445; their failure had been 'more a matter of judgement than character', not something for which they could still be blamed; but they argued that in making an alliance now, they could promise immediate advantage and lasting friendship. The Athenians, if they were to accept their offer, would be able to draw on a navy larger than any except their own and be admired and feared (the Corcyraeans said honoured) in the eyes of others; few great powers, they said, are able to receive as much as Athens could now give. The Athenians should not hesitate to make an alliance with the colonists of others if like us, the Corcyraeans said, those colonists have not been treated as equals and been refused arbitration. And the Athenians should not think that they would be breaking the terms of the thirty-year peace if they were now to accept the Corcyraeans; any state that was not party to the treaty had been free to join whichever side it pleased. It would be outrageous if in the war that no one can deny is coming – 'the Spartans are ready to go to war through fear of you' – the enemies of Athens could recruit mercenar-ies from Athenian territory while the Athenians reject our request. 'We will hold you far more at fault if you are not so persuaded.' The fear you excite, the Corcyraens concluded, 'if backed by strength, will be frighten-ing enough . . . whereas being confident but weak – as a result of rejecting us – will do less to intimidate an enemy who is strong'. Their resources and location on the route to Italy, they reminded the Athenians, would at once reduce the weakness (1.32–1.36.3).

It had been a long speech, and the Corinthians' response was even longer. The Corcyraeans, they said, may indeed regret not being party to an alliance with Athens. But their independence was deliberate and has served them well; they have prospered and been able to act at will. That should have made them more generous to others, not less. To us, the Corinthians said, they have been hostile. They do not respect us as their founder, and although they were initially willing to take their aggression to arbitration they are now in the stronger position and do not. (Thucydides does not think it necessary to remind the reader that the Corinthians were overlooking the fact that the Corcyraeans were already strong and had not attacked when they first offered to go to arbitration.) It is one thing to ally with a previously neutral state, the Corinthians went on, quite another to do so with a state bound historically to the other side which is now rejecting that side. In fact Athenians should see that Athens is bound to us. We provided ships for its battle with Aegina before the Persian war and just a few years ago, in 440, voted against Peloponnesian help for Samos when that island had revolted. (This is the only evidence of a meeting of the Peloponnesian league between 446 and 432. The Corinthians' parallel here was loose: Samos belonged to the Athenian league; for the Peloponnesian league to have taken its side would have been to break the terms of the thirty-year peace.) Helping another in need is the basis for a lasting friendship, the Corinthians went on, and the Corcyreans are now asking you to subvert our own. If now, Athenians, you were to agree to this, you would be preferring 'an uncertain possibility' to what is the 'definite fact' of Corinthian hostility 'very much in the present'. You must realise that the Corinthians are your equals, the Corcyreans are not, and 'it is a surer source of strength to avoid wronging one's equals than to make risky gains in the flush of excitement about some immediate prospect' (1.37–43).

The Corinthians were on unsound ground, and will probably have known that they were. If, as they claimed, mutual need was the basis for a lasting friendship, the Corcyraeans now had a better claim on Athens than the Corinthians, who in simple power, ships and their useful location, were not now equal to the Corcyraeans. This apart, for Corinthians now to offer the 'lasting friendship' of but one member of the Peloponnesian league was dubious; a Corinthian alliance with Athens would break the terms of the thirty-year peace, while an Athenian alliance with Corcyra need not. Corinth could at best try to persuade the other members of the league not to be hostile to Athens, and it would not have been obvious to the Athenians that it would succeed. The Corinthians' best argument would seem to have been that 'the right thing for you to do, surely, is to stand aside from both parties or, failing that, to take the opposite course of joining us' against the Corcyraeans (1.40.4); if the Athenians wanted to maintain the peace, this was not a dispute they should enter.[3]

The Athenians debated the question at assemblies on two successive days. Some historians suggest that this was usual when there was a question of war and peace or of issuing a decree; others claim that it reflects political differences; there may also have been some indecision. None of these possibilities excludes the others, and Thucydides does not explain. On the first day a majority of Athenians inclined to the Corinthian case, on the second to the Corcyraean. Appreciating that if they were to agree a full military alliance with the Corcyraeans against the Corinthians they might indeed be seen to be breaching the terms of the peace, they

---

[3] The debate has standardly been described as an argument between justice and expediency, e.g. by Price 2001: 82–9; a subtle discussion of the difficulties the Corinthinans had in making their case, Rood 2006b.

settled on a formally more defensive bilateral arrangement 'to protect each other's territory against attacks, whether on Corcyra or Athens or the allies of either' (1.44.1). Yet as Thucydides presents it, their argument was in part the same as the Corcyraeans'. Perhaps reporting truly, perhaps imputing his 'true reason' for the conflict that was to come, though it is not his practice to anticipate events in this way, he says that whatever the Spartans may have had in mind, the Athenians also, on evidence he does not present, 'thought that there would in any case be a war with the Peloponnesians and they did not want Corcyra, with a fleet of the size they had, to fall into Corinthian hands; they wanted rather to bring the two of them into collision and wear each other out as much as possible, so that the Corinthians and other naval powers would be much weakened, should the need arise and they had to go to war with them' (1.44.2–3).

Their decision therefore was interesting. It was plainly inconsistent with wanting each side to wear itself out and maintaining the wider peace. And it is difficult to see how the Athenians thought they could defend Corcyra against Corinthian attack without being seen to attack Corinth itself; they could only have hoped that a defensive alliance would prevent them being accused of doing so. If on the other hand they knew that they would be seen to attack but were afraid that if they failed to intervene, a reinforced attack by Corinth on Corcyra would leave no Corcyraean navy for them to make use of in the future, then their decision was not what it seemed to be; they would have been resigning themselves, indeed all but committing themselves, to breaking the peace. If they were, they may have been thinking ahead: of making a move to Italy and Sicily, or of sea battles that they might have to fight with the Corinthians anyway, for which they would benefit from Corcyraean support in ships and supplies, although given the Corcyraeans' past history and recent behaviour, it is not obvious that they would have had good reason to rely on the island's support. The Athenians might also have been hoping, perhaps even calculating, that they could win a war with the Peloponnesians in the Adriatic, on land in Greece and in the Aegean and overcome opposition in Italy and Sicily also. Inscriptions do reveal alliances with Halcyae in western Sicily in the 450s or 440s and perhaps Egesta in the 450s (an inscription from 418 may record the renewal of an agreement); according to Plutarch, some in Athens had been advocating a renewed attack also on Egypt and moving against Carthage in north Africa and Etruria (Tyrrhenia) in central Italy; and in 433–432, Athens was to renew its treaties with Rhegion on the Italian side of the strait between Italy and Sicily and Leontini, a few miles north-west of Syracuse.

Thucydides does not enlighten us. He simply reports the Athenians' more limited avowals, muddled or duplicitous though they can seem to have been. But he does say that they did not want to break the peace now, which one can believe, and that in order to avoid doing so, they did order the ten ships they despatched 'not to engage the Corinthians in battle unless they attacked Corcyra or were about to land there or on some other part of their territory, in which case they were to use every means to prevent them' (1.45.3). On the first day of engagements, the Corinthians had the advantage. On the second, when there was still no immediate threat to Corcyraean territory but the battle was becoming 'a rout' (men fighting from the decks of jostling ships 'in a very clumsy and old-fashioned way' (1.49.1)) 'and the Corinthians were pushing on, there came a point where every man got involved in the action and distinctions were no longer made, and the situation finally made it unavoidable that they came into direct conflict, Corinthians against Athenians' (1.49.7). In the fading light of evening, twenty more Athenian ships appeared and the Corinthians, suspecting that the eventual number might be larger, retreated. 'Never before', Thucydides observes in the kind of flourish he often makes, 'had quite so many ships been involved in a sea battle in which Greek fought against Greek' (1.50.2). On the third day, the thirty Athenian ships and what remained of the Corcyraeans' sailed to face what remained of the Corinthian fleet in the harbour into which it had fled. Events had unsurprisingly taken the Athenians further than they appear to have wanted to go.

The Corinthians however were afraid that the Athenians would see them as having broken the terms of the peace and prevent them sailing home, and accordingly reversed the charge. '"You are in the wrong, Athenians, to begin a war and break a treaty. We are here settling a score with our enemies and you are standing in our way and taking up arms against us. If your intention is to prevent us sailing to Corcyra or anywhere else we may wish and if you mean to break the treaty, then start by seizing us here and now and treat us as enemies." So they spoke, and all the Corcyraean forces in earshot immediately shouted that they should be seized and killed.' The Athenians realised that it would be wise to pull back. '"We are not starting a war, men of the Peloponnese, nor are we breaking the treaty, but we have come to help these Corcyraeans here, who are our allies. So if you wish to sail elsewhere we do not stand in your way, but if you are going to sail against Corcyra or against any place of theirs then we will do all we can to stop you"' (1.53.2–4). Both sides, in short, wondered whether they might not have broken the terms of the peace, both hoped that they had not and the Corinthians, Thucydides allows us to conclude, had been given a convenient grievance.

The city of Potidaea in Chalcidice provided the other cause Thucydides expands on to explain why the Peloponnesians believed, or chose to believe, that the thirty-year peace had been broken. By 437, the

Athenians had secured their settlement at what they now called Amphipolis (4.102.2). This was not far from the eastern boundary of Macedonia. Athenian relations with Alexander, the previous ruler of that kingdom, had been good, but on Alexander's death in 452 his sons had started fighting for control.[4] Perdiccas must have appeared to be winning, for in 433 the Athenians made a treaty with him. But two of his brothers were making 'common cause against him' (1.57.2), one in eastern Macedonia, the other in the south-west, and within months of their agreement with Perdiccas, the Athenians had switched their allegiance. They may have calculated that backing the brother in the east could strengthen the security of Amphipolis and backing the other could offer protection for its subject states in Chalcidice; Thucydides does not explain. Amphipolis was certainly valuable for timber and command of the nearby gold and silver mines, the Chalcidicean states for providing a not insignificant proportion (perhaps one-thirteenth) of Athens' monetary tribute; and both were strategically placed to meet threats to Athens' dominion from further east and the south. Alarmed by Athens' switch, Perdiccas started to talk to Sparta about engineering a war with Athens and to Corinth about bringing about a revolt at Potidaea; he also approached neighbouring states 'about joining in the revolt, thinking that if he had these adjoining places on his side as allies it would be easier to manage the war' (1.57.5). It was clever of him to involve Corinth. Though Potidaea paid tribute to Athens, it had been settled by Corinthians who had, in an arrangement which remains obscure, continued to appoint magistrates in Potidaea. Perdiccas' move made the Athenians worry for Potidaea; they feared that other allies 'in the area of Thrace' – in what the Athenians regarded as their dominion in 'Thraceward' region – might also revolt and accordingly ordered the Potidaeans to 'dismantle their wall on the Pallene [southern] side of the city, hand over hostages, expel their magistrates and refuse in future to accept those the Corinthians sent out each year' (1.56.2).

The Athenians took these precautions, says Thucydides, 'immediately after the sea battle at Corcyra' (1.57.1). That was in the early autumn of 433. In the winter, Potidaea sent envoys to the Athenians to see if it could persuade them to maintain the status quo and with Corinthians sent envoys also to Sparta to secure support from there. The Athenians did not concede but what Thucydides calls 'the authorities' at Sparta assured the Potidaeans that if the Athenians were to move against the city they would themselves invade Attica (1.58.1). If the Corinthians had been right in saying that members of the Peloponnesian league had been inclined to help Samos against Athens in 440, and if these included

---

[4] Th. offers a brief history of Alexander's achievement at 2.99.3–6.

Sparta, as they must have done, this would not have been the first occasion on which the Spartans had contemplated breaking the thirty-year peace. But the Corinthians may not have been telling the truth about 440 (they appear not to have recalled their opposition in the league when speaking at Sparta itself) and in any event, that was the league; by the conventions that are thought to have governed that association, any such decision would have to have been agreed by an assembly in Sparta itself. There is no reason however to think that Thucydides was wrong in what he now reports; the Spartans' promise to the Potidaeans was a promise to act against the terms of the peace. Yet they would not seem to have had grounds to act on Potidaea. In ordering the Potidaeans to take down their walls and expel their magistrates, the Athenians had certainly annoyed Corinth, and Corinth was allied to Sparta. But whatever the oddity of having magistrates from Corinth, Potidaea was allied to Athens, the Athenians were in the right by the terms of the thirty-year peace in defending it and the Corinthians in the wrong in acting to subvert them. In any event, the question of attacking the Athenians would formally be for the Peloponnesian league to decide on, and as far as we know, neither Sparta nor Corinth had yet approached the other members.

In the spring of 432 the Potidaeans shrewdly paid their tribute to Athens. But at about the same time (the exact sequence is difficult to reconstruct), an expedition of thirty ships and 1,000 hoplites had set off from Athens to help Perdiccas' two brothers. The Potidaeans, suspecting that this force might be directed against them also, and responding to Perdiccas' attempts to move some of the cities in Chalcidice to a defensively more secure site, made a swift alliance with these cities and thus in effect with Perdiccas, and pre-emptively revolted against Athens. The commander of the Athenian expedition did not hear of this until he arrived in the area, and realising that he could not simultaneously help Perdiccas' brothers and deal with Potidaea, chose to ignore the revolt. The Corinthians however now thought that the danger for them was getting 'close to home' (1.60.1), and despatched a force of their own which arrived in Chalcidice forty days later. Knowing that their first expedition had been unable to act at Potideaea, the Athenians sent a second. To make things easier for themselves, they also came to a new, temporary understanding with Perdiccas, who would thereby have been relieved of the immediate pressure on him, took the Athenian forces out of Macedonia and concentrated on Chalcidice. Perdiccas then switched back to the Corinthians. (It is nicely said that Perdiccas would leave one side without ever really joining another. He did so nine times in the course of the war and his agility served him well. He survived as king until his notably peaceful death in 413 and was succeeded by a comparably successful son (2.100.2).)[5] The battles over Potidaea began in the summer of 432 and were over by the late autumn, when a further Athenian contingent (under Phormio, to be one of the most praised Athenian naval commanders in the war) completed a siege of the city and the defeated Corinthians went home.

The avowed grievances on each side in the late 430s were therefore clear. The Corinthians claimed to have been humiliated by the Corcyraeans and that the Athenians had breached the thirty-year peace by attacking them. On Potidaea, each was seen to have breached the peace by attacking the other. But war had not yet broken out and no party to the peace had withdrawn from it. 'The Corinthians had acted [over Potidaea] as a private matter', and 'the truce still held' (1.66). There is no reason to believe that in writing 'truce' rather than 'treaty' Thucydides is suggesting the thirty-year peace was no more than a suspension of aggression of the sort that both sides had had with Argos on the eastern Peloponnese. But he is in one sense correct to say that in Potidaea the Corinthians had acted 'privately'. As in their action against Corcyra, they had not been authorised by the Peloponnesian league (although it should be said that nothing in what is known of the thirty-year peace stipulates that a state had to be so authorised). He is not however correct if he means that the Corinthians' action over Potidaea was not sanctioned by their government; it had relied on volunteers from Corinth and on mercenaries from elsewhere, but was led by an experienced Corinthian general, and there is no suggestion that this man was acting in a personal capacity. The Corinthians themselves certainly claimed no such thing at a Spartan assembly a few weeks later.

But although the grievances may have been clear and the feelings strong, the arguments were weak. Only Athens' claim to authority over Potidaea could stand inspection, and that was not unambiguous; Potidaea was paying tribute to Athens and in the thirty-year peace had formally been on the Athenian side, but there were Corinthians there and its magistrates were appointed by Corinth. What seems most insistently to have been driving the anger of the Corinthians was the repeated indifference in both Corcyra and Athens to their standing and honour as a serious power. They appear also to have been irritated by having so openly to depend on Sparta. The Corcyreans in turn were irritated by what we might now describe as Corinth's interference in their internal affairs.

---

[5] Perdiccas' agility, Mynott *TWPA*: 1.56.2n; also Ch. 6 below. His son, Archelos, reputedly killed three others with claims to the kingship, one a boy of seven whom he threw into a well to drown, Plato, *Gorgias*, 471c; Hammond and Griffith 1979: 135–6. In the comic dramatist Hermippos' largely lost *The Porters* from 420, 'lies from Perdiccas' were listed among Athens' imports. But see Ch. 10 n. 8 below.

The Athenians' defensive alliance with Corcyra and the Spartans' offer to invade Attica if the Athenians moved against Potidaea could be taken to show that both of the larger powers saw that war between them was not unimaginable. Thucydides says that the Athenians were expecting it and if the Corinthians had been telling the truth, the Spartans, relieved at last from 'wars of their own at home' against helots (1.118.2) and thinking that they had little to fear at that time from Athens, might have sensed some sort of opportunity for themselves in Samos' attempt to escape from Athenian dominion just five years after the peace. But it is moot whether anything Thucydides writes to this point gives either of the larger powers a convincing reason or even a clear motive for moving to a wider war with each other, certainly for doing so at this moment.[6]

[6] A contrary view by the usually precise and reflective Konstan 2001: 381 n. 22, who thinks it self-evident that if one power 'is restless to get out from under the domination of the other . . . there is a permanent motive for attack, residing precisely in the fear that the other party may grow too strong'. It is not clear that Spartans were or felt themselves to be 'dominated' by Athens. And, in this instance, 'permanent' muddies the water.

4 Explaining the war: true reasons 432

The Corinthians did not rest. In the late summer or early autumn of 432 they called members of the Peloponnesian league to a meeting in Sparta to denounce Athens 'for breaking the treaty and wronging the Peloponnesians' (1.67.1). The Spartans, keen no doubt to assert their authority over any such gathering, quickly convened an assembly and invited the allies who believed themselves to have been wronged by Athens to attend and explain their grievances. Thucydides does not suggest that any Spartan spoke. Among those who did, he mentions 'especially' Megarians voicing their resentment at being excluded from ports in Athens' dominion and markets in the city itself. The Corinthians allowed the Megarians and others to 'work the Spartans up' and shrewdly spoke last (1.67.5). When they had, an Athenian delegation which 'happened to be already present in Sparta on other business . . . thought it advisable to come before the Spartans . . . to point out just how powerful their city was' and explain the Athenian position (1.72.1). The Spartans then dismissed all the visitors, talked to each other in a closed assembly, came to a view, invited their allies back to hear it and announced that there would be a full and formal meeting of the league at which the members could decide what action, if any, to take. It is clear from what Thucydides writes that it was the cumulative effect of what they heard on these occasions and the response of the Athenians, not any other kind of 'thing done', that gave the Spartans what was to them a 'true reason' to act. And it was the speed of the subsequent exchanges that caused them to do so when they did.

Thucydides' account of what was said in the open session of the assembly at Sparta has raised doubts. One can understand why he should give the Corinthians' speech at length; they were taking the initiative and their grievances were the most immediate. Yet to an audience which might not have known as much as the Corinthians would have wanted it to know about what had transpired over Corcyra in the autumn of 433 and what was happening now at Potidaea, they are unlikely to have confined themselves, as Thucydides writes them having done, to generalities about the political characters of Athens and Sparta. It is also striking that there should not merely happen to be Athenians in Sparta 'on other state business' (1.73.1) – this would not have been unusual in inter-state relations at the time (5.22.1–3, 5.46.5, 5.50.5) – but that these men should have been able at short notice to speak so abstractly and with no little elegance and force (though like 'the Corinthians', surely not together) on what they regarded as the nature and point of Athens' dominion.

The Corinthians, claiming to be brief, discoursed at length on the Spartans' long-standing disinclination to act even when threatened by the kind of danger that they insisted the Athenians now presented.[1] 'You go on hesitating', they said to their hosts; 'you forget that peace lasts longest for those who use their resources in the cause of justice but demonstrate a clear spirit of resistance when they are mistreated. Instead, your idea of fair dealing is in not offending others and so not being harmed yourself by the need for self-defence' (1.71.1). You have an old-fashioned attitude, they continued, and bind yourselves in an old-fashioned constitution. The issue is not of right but of power; the Athenians know this and are as usual seizing every opportunity to exercise theirs. But even when it's in your interest, you fail to do the same; 'the real agent is not the one who does the enslaving but the one who could stop it and just looks on, even though he claims the distinction of being the liberator of Greece' (1.69.1).[2] (This in spite of the fact that the Corinthians had claimed at Athens that it was they who had voted against action to 'liberate' Samos eight years before.) 'Let none of you suppose', they explained, 'that all this is said more from hostility than by way of criticism. Criticism is between friends and is addressed to failings; accusations are for enemies committing crimes' (1.69.6). But we should be clear, they continued; it is time to stop dithering. Go now and help the Potidaeans and your other allies just as you promised to do, and invade Attica with all speed 'lest you betray your friends and kinsmen to their worst enemies and drive the rest of us to seek out some other alliance in despair' (1.71.4).

In the speech the Spartans invited them then to give, the Athenians were self-righteous and not a little patronising, and were heard to be so, but they advised caution. They did not want to dwell on the past, they said, and did. They reminded their audience that it was they (they exaggerated) who had taken the initiative against the Persians, they who had evacuated their city, they whose ships had been decisive in ending that war, and it was their allies who had asked for protection when the

---

[1] There appears to be no reason to think that the Corinthians' anxiety and anger had anything to do with their internal politics, which were those of a stable and, internally at least, fairly moderate aristocracy (oligarchy) pursued through a council (including perhaps eight generals) that guided an assembly (Salmon 1984: 240–69, also Th. 5.30.5).

[2] A view expressed again by Hermocrates to Siceliots in 424, 4.61.5 and Ch. 8 below.

Spartans had lost interest. It was they, they conveyed, without quite saying so, who had become pre-eminent among the Greeks and deserved to be. They were not to be blamed for the fact that after the 470s most of those in the league they had created came to hate them 'and some had already rebelled and been suppressed, and you were no longer as friendly as before but had become suspicious and at odds with us'; nor were they to be blamed for the fact that it now no longer seemed safe to let their new dominion go 'since any rebels would have been going over to you' (1.75.4). In creating the dominion they had been driven by fear – of the Persians, one presumes, and perhaps also of Sparta, though Thucydides has no Athenian admit to this until much later in the war (6.82.3) and they would naturally not admit it here – by considerations of honour and interest also, and that they had no doubt that the Spartans would have valued the power they now had. 'It has always been established practice for the weaker to be ruled by the stronger.' No people enjoys being ruled by another, but those who rule 'deserve special credit if in following human nature and ruling over others they still behave with more sense of justice than their power would allow them to do'; though of course, the Athenians quickly conceded, no one ever lets justice stand in their way 'when presented with an opportunity to gain something by force', just as appeals to justice, like yours against us now, will always disguise an interest. You should also remember, they added, that you proved yourselves rather inept in attempting to govern others (1.76.2–3, 1.77.6).

'Take your time then in your deliberations', they urged against the Corinthians' insistence on haste, 'since these are matters of real moment; and do not be so swayed by the opinions and objections of others that you add to your own burdens. Think in advance about how unpredictable war can be before you find yourselves involved in one. The longer a war lasts the more likely it is to turn on matters of chance, which we are all equally unable to control and whose outcome is a matter of risk and uncertainty. Men go to war and launch into action as their first rather than what should be their last resort, and only when they come to grief do they turn to discussion. We are not yet in the grip of any such error ourselves and neither apparently are you, so we urge you, while both sides still have the option of listening to good advice, not to break the treaty or transgress your oaths but let our differences be settled by arbitration according to our agreement' in the thirty-year peace (1.78.1–4). Otherwise it will indeed be war.

Commentators differ on how likely it is that Athenians of this kind should have been in Sparta at all, how likely it is that if they were they would have spoken at this assembly, and how likely it is that if they did speak they would have spoken like this; some have even thought that Thucydides will have invented the speech later. Yet all accept that in the closed assembly that followed, he writes Spartans responding in part to what both the Athenians as well as the Corinthians before them had said. In the first flurry of talk here, 'the views of the majority tended to the same conclusion, that the Athenians were already guilty of wrongdoing and that war must follow without delay' (1.79.2.). The reader sees that it was not only in the democracies that excited citizens could quickly bring each other to extreme conclusions. But then 'Archidamos their king, a man with a reputation for intelligence and moderation, came forward' (1.79.2).[3] Archidamos had succeeded in his line to the dual kingship at Sparta in the early 460s, and like the Athenians, though with rather different intent, he thought it important to take a long view. The young, he said, talk only about chance. The more experienced talk of resources and planning. The Spartans were the more effective on land, but much of the territory under Athens' control was only accessible by sea. Sparta had neither the ships nor the funds in a treasury or from private contributions with which to build or buy them and pay for crews, and it had no naval expertise.[4] Nor did it have as many horses or men. It needed time to gather its strengths and acquire more allies, Greek and foreign. If the Athenians should hear our representations, said Archidamos, 'so much the better. But if not, after two or three years have passed we shall be better equipped to take them on, if that's what we decide to do' (1.82.2). If however 'we are goaded by the complaints of our allies into laying waste the Athenians' land before we are fully ready, then we must be careful we do not just create a situation fraught with more disgrace and difficulty for the Peloponnese' (1.82.5). He was not proposing that the Spartans turn a blind eye. 'Certainly not' (1.82.1). But don't be ashamed, he urged the Spartans, of 'that "slowness" and "hesitation" for which they criticise us'. See it as the self-discipline that gives us our self-respect, just as our sense of shame gives us courage.[5] It would be wrong for us to be shamed into

---

[3] Mynott notes that *sunetos* and *sophron*, intelligence and moderation, are interesting terms of praise. On *sunetos* (also 'sagacious', 'quick to understand') see also 3.37.3. Other individuals called *sunetos* are Theseus, Themistocles, Brasidas and Phrynichos, while Pericles is included among those with a reputation at least for *sunesis* at 2.34.6 and claims it for himself at 1.140.1. On *sophron* and its noun *sophrosune*, see 1.32.4n, 1.37.2, 1.68.1n, 1.84.1n, 1.86.2n, 1.8.24.4–5, Mynott *TWPA*, and the glossary there. Archidamos is the only person Th. directly calls *sophron*, though Pericles is said to have ruled *metrios* ('with moderation', 2.65.6), which is in the same general semantic area.

[4] It is not clear that the Spartans had a public treasury at all, Kallet-Marx 1993: 82 n. 35.

[5] Literally, Mynott notes at the relevant point in the text in *TWPA*, '"self-respect (*aidos*) takes the greatest part in self-discipline (*sophrosune*), as courage (*eupsuchia*) does in shame (*aischune*)." *Aidos* and *aischune* are closely related concepts, but I have used two different

complying with the wishes of others. 'The one to come out on top will be the one trained in the hardest school of necessity' (1.84.1–4). So do not vote now, he concluded; 'send envoys to Athens to discuss Potidaea; and send envoys to discuss the wrongs our allies claim to have suffered, especially now that the Athenians are ready to submit to arbitration – since it is not lawful to initiate attacks in such a case, as if against a proven wrongdoer. But at the same time prepare for war' (1.85.2).

One can imagine that Archidamos might just have won the day in suggesting that the Spartans should take strength from the Corinthians' 'criticisms' and the arrogance of the Athenians; why else would he have said they could? But it suited the ephor presiding over the assembly, one Sthenelaidas, to insist that 'the damage is not a matter of words' and then to show that it was exactly that by playing on Archidamos' moderating 'prudence': true prudence, he said, lay in acting as decisively as possible, and if Sparta did not have the resources, its allies did. 'Vote for war then', Sthenelaidas said, 'as the reputation of your city of Sparta demands, and do not let the Athenians grow any stronger. Let us not abandon our allies, but with the gods on our side' – the oracle at Delphi had been heard to tell the Spartans that they should persist – 'let us advance on the wrongdoers' (1.86). Unable to decide which set of shouts was the louder, Sthenelaidas asked those present to rise and divide; it was clear, says Thucydides, that 'a great majority' (1.87.3) accepted that the peace had been broken and that the Spartans were free to go to war.

These meetings would not have taken place without the urgings of Sparta's allies. Yet Thucydides repeats his claim. The division at Sparta went the way it did 'not so much because [the Spartans] were persuaded by the speeches of their allies as because they feared a further growth in the power of the Athenians, seeing that most of Greece was already subject to them' (1.88). The Spartans may not have been persuaded; the Corinthians' case had been almost devoid of content. But they had plainly been incited, and were to be so again when their allies came to address the league. The Corinthians had been afraid that they might lose their connection with Potidaea before the Peloponnesians took any action and had been going round in advance of this meeting 'privately' urging a vote for war. When it was convened, they chose again to speak last. He who holds back for reasons of protection, they said again, can find himself without anything to protect, though the allies would agree that he 'who

---

terms in English here since Th. does so in the Greek. Commentators are divided as to whether in the Greek "takes the greatest part" means "is largely constituted by" or "is the largest element in". I have translated so as to stress the causal relationships, which seem to be the main point.'

overreaches himself in the flush of military success has failed to realise how treacherous is the confidence that carries him along' (1.120.4). But war, they insisted, was now unavoidable and circumstances favoured it. It was essential to plan and members of the league must work together, each contributing what they could. They should also ask for loans from Delphi and Olympia (an unlikely possibility, one imagines) and support from 'the barbarian'.[6] 'The tyrant state established in Greece is a threat to all alike', they said, '– with some already under their control, and others in their sights – let us attack it and bring it to terms' (1.124.3); otherwise we invite slavery and shame our fathers. The members present voted for war and dispersed to make themselves ready (1.127.1). No one, however, had suggested how, when they were, the war might be fought. And if the Spartans themselves did fear 'a further growth in the power of the Athenians, seeing that most of Greece was already subject to them' none said so. Courage, Archidamos had said, came from a sense of shame; but the Spartans now were being shamed by their allies.

Some nonetheless were nervous and, with the authority or example or even perhaps the prompting of Archidamos or one or two of the more cautious ephors, sent envoys to Athens in order to give the Spartans '*themselves*', Thucydides says, 'the best possible justifications for going to war should the Athenians pay no attention to them' (1.126.1, my emphasis). The envoys were not notably diplomatic.[7] Their first move was to remind the Athenians of a curse on the maternal line of Pericles, the foremost man in Athens who 'opposed the Spartans in every possible way and allowed no concessions but kept urging the Athenians on to war' (1.127.3), in the hope that this might cause men there to shame him out of power. The hope was unreal, and the Athenians did not hesitate to remind the Spartans in turn of two curses on them, one by the god at Delphi for defiling a sanctuary in their city to trap and eventually murder the king who had commanded the Greeks at Plataea in 479 and been suspected of siding with Persians, the other for killing helots who had sought refuge in another sacred place. Notwithstanding the humiliation of the first envoys, a second team went to tell the Athenians 'to withdraw from Potidaea and give Aegina back its freedom'; but 'most of all, and

---

[6] By which the Corinthians presumably meant the Persians and also perhaps the Macedonians. Hornblower *CT* II: 391–3, discussing the distinctions between 'Macedonians' and 'barbarians', concentrates on the ethnic (including linguistic) rather than the political, which in this context matters more to the Corinthians and thus to Th. himself. Also Ch. 6 n. 2 below.

[7] On this incident, Hornblower *CT* I: 202, 206. To the criticism that Th. ignores religious sensibilities (e.g. recently Dolgert 2012), one may say that he sees that what can broadly be described as religious talk as one of the currencies of political exchange.

in the clearest possible terms, they kept advising that there would be no war if the Athenians revoked the Megarian decree' (1.139.2). They were heard but not heeded,[8] and a last team of three went to say that '"the Spartans want there to be peace, and there would be if you give the Greeks back their independence"'. This was wholly fanciful, and Pericles saw that it was the moment at which to ask for an assembly in Athens, consider the whole question, as Thucydides puts it, and give the Athenian answer once and for all. Many spoke at this, some to argue that Athens should go to war, others that the decree against Megara, which as the Corinthians (1.42.2) and now the Spartans had said was standing in the way of peace, should be rescinded.

It was unfortunate for the Athenians who favoured a continuing peace that Pericles, says Thucydides, not himself alluding to any such misfortune, was 'supremely capable both at speaking and in action' (1.139.4). Pericles had been elected *strategos*, one of the ten generals in the city, in each of the previous fourteen years. This was the most powerful office in a city which in spite of the agreement with Sparta in 446–445 considered itself still to be on a war footing. Those who held it consulted the council (*boule*), 500 men selected by lot from the ten 'tribes' into which the city had been divided for political purposes after 507, and their recommendations were subject to the approval of the assembly of all citizens, to which they spoke directly. Pericles had had an advantage. His mother had been a niece of Cleisthenes, the aristocrat who in 508–507 had led the political reform of the city after the tyranny, and his father, who had himself benefited from his wife's connections, had commanded the Athenian naval force in a victory in 479 against the Persians in Ionia. But Pericles' pre-eminence had become his own. He was said to have been more withdrawn than some, but was confident and clever. He had previously outsmarted Cimon and Thucydides son of Milesias, rivals who had been more peaceably disposed to Sparta. He had used public subscriptions and his oratorical ability ('persuasion sat on his lips' said the dramatist Eupolis) to command the Athenians and, when he thought it deserved, had not hesitated to use punitive violence to sustain the city's dominion.[9]

Moderns can still refer to Athens in the third quarter of the fifth century

---

[8] Plutarch tells a good story. When Pericles explained to the Spartan envoy Polyalces that there was a law forbidding the repeal of the decree against Megara, Polyalces suggested turning the face of the tablet on which it was inscribed to the wall: 'there's no law against that', *Pericles*, 30.

[9] Pericles' parents, Herodotus 6.131. He ordered the rebels at Samos in 440 to be nailed to planks, hung outside for a week and finally clubbed to death, Plutarch, *Pericles*, 28. Plutarch, unwilling to think ill of Pericles, regards the story as a Samian calumny. Stadter 1973: 258–9 suggests that such punishment was a 'standard procedure' for treason etc., the final clubbing perhaps an act of mercy.

as 'Periclean', and no one whose record has survived is more responsible for this than Thucydides himself; reflecting a remarkable absence
of debate in the city at this time or else editing heavily, he presents the
words of no other identifiable individual in the city until after Pericles'
death in 428 or thereabouts.[10]

In the first speech of his that Thucydides writes, given in late 432,
Pericles had insisted that the Athenians should not concede anything to
the Spartans. They plot against Athens, he said, and prefer war to words.
(If he had been told of what Archidamos and Sthenelaidas had said, he
plainly found it convenient to ignore the one in favour of the other.) Their
envoys may appear to want to discuss terms, he went on, but they come
merely to dictate them; in any event, for Athens to accede on Megara
or anything else would only lead to further demands. He explained that
Sparta was not willing to go to arbitration. 'If people are pressing their
demands on their neighbours and equals without due process of law,
no matter to what degree, it amounts to enslavement just the same'
(1.141.1). He had remarked at the start of his speech that 'we know that
the course of events can go awry as senselessly as the plans of men,[11]
which is why we usually blame luck for things that take an unexpected
turn' (1.140.1) and he was to say at the end that 'I fear our own mistakes
more than I fear the plans of the enemy' (1.144.1). But war, he said,
could not be avoided, and providing that in conducting it the Athenians
did not try to extend their dominion, they had every reason to believe
they would win.

He explained, as Archidamos had, that the Spartans had no capital
or regular source of surplus income, and added that the Peloponnesian
league was not an executive council like Athens' *boule* but a collection
of states more prone to follow their separate interests than to act in a
common cause. As Archidamos had also done, he pointed out that a
Peloponnesian force could defeat the Athenians on land, but Athenians
should think of Athens as an island, and that since they have so many
territories, they can safely sacrifice one for others; this would be a war at
sea for which the Peloponnesians are not prepared and would not fight
well. 'So let us send these envoys back with this response; we will grant
the Megarians access to our markets and harbours if the Spartans for
their part stop expelling us and our allies as aliens (there is nothing in

---

[10] Zumbrunnen 2008 chooses the first and expounds on the dangers of silence in this
democracy and our own. Pericles' death, 2.65.6.

[11] Mynott notes that *amathos* is an arresting choice of word. The core meaning is 'without
learning' or 'stupidly' but it is applied here somewhat metaphorically to events, which
in English too we can talk of as being 'senseless'. Things resist our ability to account for
them (*para logon*) and 'take an unexpected turn'.

the treaty to prevent either of these moves)'; that's to say, the Athenians would stop interfering with the Megarians' trade if the Spartans were to stop interfering with their own. 'We will let the cities [in Athens' present dominion] have their independence, if they were independent when we made the treaty', a provision that would have suited Athens well, since most of its subject states had lost their independence before 446. And 'as soon as the Spartans grant the cities in their own alliance the right to be independent in a way that suits their own individual wishes rather than the Spartans' interests', he concluded, a provision that it would have been difficult to agree on, let alone to implement, 'we are willing to accept arbitration as set out in the treaty, and will not begin a war, but will defend ourselves against those who do' (1.144.2, also 1.19.1). The Athenians voted as he asked, agreeing to the need for arbitration and 'to deal with the complaints on a fair and equal basis' (1.145).[12]

Thucydides remarks later that the Spartans were to acknowledge that they had been the first to transgress in refusing at this moment to submit to arbitration (7.18.2). In 'law', if one may use the word, Pericles was right. But there is nothing in what survives of the terms of the peace of 446–445 to indicate how such arbitration should be conducted and by whom. The example of the Corcyraeans' offer to the Corinthians in 435 (though outside the terms of that treaty) suggests that it was for the contending parties together to agree. If a third party was required now, it is unclear who could have arbitrated between blocs that together encompassed most of Greece; the more significant neutrals, like Argos and Achaea, might lean to one side rather than the other, and in the circumstances of 432 it is not obvious that the Athenians or Spartans would have respected those that did not. As it was, a majority of Athenian citizens appear to have been pleased to face war. Materially, psychologically, militarily, legally and in their command over their allies, if not always, as events were to show but they were not now to know, in the coherence and decisiveness of their internal politics, they believed they had the edge.

One might nevertheless ask, though Thucydides does not, why Athens and Sparta could not have been content with the existing balance of power; the term may not have been in the vocabulary of either, but the condition seems too obvious for neither to have had the notion. A balance had held since 445. Sparta may have thought of breaking it to support the attempted rebellion at Samos in 440 and again in 432 when the Athenians

---

[12] Th. adds that the Spartans 'never again' came to Athens on an official mission. They did not come again before the start of hostilities, but were to return to seek a truce in 425, Ch. 8 below. The principle of 'self-determination' was of course to be deployed with comparable flexibility after 1919 and 1945.

moved pre-emptively against Potidaea; but if it did, its thoughts came to nothing. Athens had stretched the terms of the treaty in its defensive alliance with Corcyra, but in that alliance and at Potidaea it had at least observed the formalities; there had been fighting over Corcyra, but the outcome was a return to the status quo; Corcyra had not been attacked, and it was a part of the Corinthian fleet, not Corinth itself, that had suffered, which naturally annoyed the Corinthians but could have been overlooked if there had been a will to peace. It also seemed likely that Potidaea, although it might lose its political ties with Corinth, would stay with Athens. Alexander's contending sons in Macedonia were concerned only with their own affairs; they were willing to take advantage of whoever might help them against the other, but they had no ambitions elsewhere and Macedonia was not party to the treaty. The Corinthians and the Spartans had suggested seeking support from Persia, but there was no sign at this moment that that empire still had an active interest in Greece.

The Spartans may nevertheless have wondered whether their influence and perhaps their power in the Peloponnesian league could further diminish. Corinth, financially and militarily the most powerful of their allies, had already threatened 'in despair to seek out some other alliance' if Sparta was unwilling to act against Athens. It is not obvious what this could have been. Argos was conveniently placed to contain Athens and recover Aegina, and if the Corinthians were allied to it, they would have easier access to the Aegean, might be able to bring over states in the northern Peloponnese that were not at ease with Sparta and could also perhaps more effectively protect Megara from Athens. But Argos showed no sign now of wishing to sacrifice its independence and neutrality, which had not been compromised by the truce it had with Sparta, and the two states do not appear to have approached each other. Achaea, along the northern coast of the Peloponnese to the west of Corinth, was of less consequence; even if it had been willing to abandon its own neutrality, it would not have added greatly to Corinth's strengths. An alternative alliance, in short, was not now to be feared, and was not to be talked about for another ten years.

The question of power however within the league did remain. Pericles had exaggerated when he said that this was no more than a collection of states each of which cared more for its own interest than any common cause. Its members did at least agree on wanting to protect themselves against the ambitions of Athens; and although Sparta had only one vote, Pericles (for his purpose, one imagines, deliberately) underrated its power and influence within it. But even if Corinth or any other member would be unlikely to leave the league for another, the Spartans themselves would have realised that their influence within it could weaken further if they persistently failed to act on a matter that an important member saw as vital to its own interest or standing. This apart, the Spartans would need to be able to call on Corinth's navy for their campaigns abroad, and looking forward from this point rather than backwards from the end of the war, they may still have been worried about their political control at home; it had taken them a number of years to break the Messenians' siege at Ithome after the earthquake in 464. Thucydides insists that they were less persuaded by their allies than by their fear of Athens. But as the arguments in the league had made clear, they had reasons to fear their allies also.

Nonetheless, the de facto balance of power that had been formalised in 446–445 seems not to have been seriously disturbed. That Thucydides gives no sign of seeing things in this way might after all be because no one else did so. One might now see the outcome of the thirty-year peace in this way, but it may not have been the intention on either side in agreeing it. That was for security, a period of relief in which each could recoup to press the other at some future time. And in the widest sense of the term now, the Spartans' security was slipping. Corinth had criticised them for refusing to meet their commitment to 'liberate' the Greek states, and it may have been speaking for other members of the Peloponnesian league in so doing. The Athenians who addressed the Spartan assembly in 432 had in effect been saying that Sparta had ceased to be the pre-eminent power. In suggesting that their courage derived from a sense of shame, Archidamos had inadvertently given them grounds for declaring the peace to be at an end. The Spartans had not had any control over events at Corcyra and Potidaea or Corinth's part in these, and once the Peloponnesian league had confirmed the vote, just when Phormio's force was sealing the Athenians' siege of Potidaea, Archidamos and those who shared his reservations would have found it politically difficult to secure a delay. The second of the three teams of envoys that Sparta sent to Athens may still have been looking for a way of avoiding conflict; from what Thucydides says of two of the men who were sent on the last of them, it is possible that at least one might have been inclined to play for time (2.12.1–3, 5.13.1–2). But Pericles restated his resistance while they were still at Athens and presented them with terms they would have known their ephors would not accept.

One might imagine a world in which Spartans had decided that to be Sparta in 432 could not be what it had been to be Sparta in 479 or even 446 and that they should concede their pre-eminence. But that would not have been a world in which they were still Spartans. Their pre-eminence in the eyes of other states in Greece had become a 'necessary identity'. If they were to concede, they would no longer be seen by anyone, including themselves, to be the people that they had thought they were and had devoted so much, indeed everything, to remaining. Unless decisively defeated, and perhaps even when they have been, it is not realistic to expect politicians, ancient or modern, readily to abandon their deepest commitments and beliefs, even if it would in the ordinary sense of the word be realistic of them (and often better for all) to do so, and the Spartans were not ready to abandon theirs. One might still ask whether the self-perceptions on each side now warranted war. Thucydides does not, presumably because he thought it obvious that they did. It was the insistence of Sparta's allies, the resistance in Athens, the Spartans' sense of themselves and their internal politics which gave no one body or person the power that Pericles had created for himself in Athens, rather than any further action of any other kind on either side, which led them to act.

Thebes' opportunistic attack therefore on an ally of Athens on the border with Boeotia towards the end of the winter of 432–431, between the formal end of peace and the start of the next fighting season, without apparently consulting Sparta or the league, may have made no material difference. It is almost certain that Archidamos would anyway have led a Peloponnesian army into Attica in the following summer. Though Thucydides does not say, perhaps because he thought that this also was obvious, only Athens was in a position now to stop the conflict extending. What he does make clear is that it could do so only if Pericles thought it should.

5   Judgements 431–430

'Thucydides the censor', said Nicole Loraux, 'stamps his judgement with the seal of objectivity . . . in the austere guise of an impartial observer'; he writes *sub specie aeternitatis*. This cannot be right. The guise that she describes is one of our own. It was Shelley who imagined an 'eye with which the universe beholds itself and knows itself divine'; Henry Sidgwick, excising the divine, who adopted the image; John Rawls, following Sidgwick, who reached for a view of the human condition that any rationally impartial person anywhere could be expected to take at any time this side of eternity. One can choose to imagine that Thucydides was attracted to one or another of the conceptions from which contemporaries might have conjured a distance between any particular observer and his world; to conceptions in Xenophanes or Heraclitus for instance of an omniscient god (though Thucydides gives every sign of being impatient with theologies and divination); or in Empedocles of an endless oscillation between agents of combination and separation; or in Democritos of agent-less atoms colliding, rebounding, linking and delinking; but there is no sign that he was so attracted, and imputing any such conception to him, though not difficult to do, is idle.

A modern critic might nevertheless insist that Thucydides deceived himself in believing that he could obtain a true view of events as they were. No one, the critic will say, can avoid casting human affairs in terms furnished by their culture, fashioned by their character and guided by what matters to them. Thucydides makes no secret of his inclination to political moderation and good government and his distaste for gratuitous suffering (6.54.5–6, 6.81.3–4, 7.29–30, 8.24.4, 8.97.2). He also excites admiration, loathing, compassion and pity and sometimes all at once. But like the tragedians (and unlike the authors of Old Comedy) he does not dictate any. He cares less about his own ethical stance than about the fact that politics and war can destroy the possibility of ethical life itself (2.53.3–4 below, also 3.83.1–2). If 'ideology' connotes a clear and coherent set of beliefs about how human affairs should more generally be, he does not reveal one. His sense of the differences between characters and within them, of the contrary forces of circumstance and of the difficulties in seeing what may happen, is too sure to allow it. He may be fastidious and, as Loraux said, austere, and these are dispositions that one might associate with his class. But he is not just writing the prejudices of that class.[1] If the judgments on the war which he set down at its end and inserted into book 2 are poor – if they are judgements of his and not those of an ancient editor – then as I suggest at the end of this chapter, the explanation lies elsewhere.

The episode which Thucydides says 'marks the beginning of the war between the Athenians and the Peloponnesians and the allies on each side, the point from which they only dealt with each other through heralds and were continuously at war once they had started' (2.1), is a conspicuous instance of the dispassion with which he can so readily excite the passions of a reader; all the more so since it played no part in causing the war and was incidental to its outcomes. It is the story to which he returns in books 2 and 3 of the small and in itself insignificant city of Plataea, and it begins with Thebes. Early in the spring of 431, he writes, 'the Thebans foresaw that there would be a war [between Athens and Sparta] and wanted to take the initiative and seize Plataea . . . while the peace still held and war had not yet openly been declared' (2.2.3). Thebes was one of eleven states in a Boeotian federation that had been allied to Sparta since 447 and had been subduing smaller states in the area; Plataea was some 8 miles to the south of Thebes, on the border with Attica and allied to Athens. Thebans had attempted to seize it in 519 and been stopped by Athens; in 490, Plataea had been the only Greek community to send men to join the Athenians against the Persians at Marathon; in 480, the commanding faction in Thebes had let the Persians use their city as a

---

[1] Quotation from Loraux 2009: 278; also Edmunds 2009: ch. 2 n. 2. Shelley's couplet, 'I am the eye with which the Universe / Beholds itself and knows itself divine', gave Sidgwick words for the point of view he aspired to, Sidgwick 1962: 382, 420; Schultz 2004: 28; Rawls 1971: 587. Loraux was not alone among (post-)moderns in appearing to assume that we have to choose between the impartial observer and the moralist or ideologist, and that since the first is impossible, the second is forced upon us; from which it can follow that the unmasker either aspires to the point of view of the universe or is a moralist herself, and privileged. Stahl 2003: 146 appropriates Th. to 'the position of the impartial observer to which he personally and justifiably lays claim', fortunately qualifying himself in his next sentence and a note (156 n. 72) by explaining that although Th. is not (consistently) partial to any of the parties in the war he is far from impartial to the human condition, especially its suffering. Rood 2006a on Th.'s 'objectivity and authority' (which does not refer to Loraux) is subtle and sensible. On 3.83.1–2 and the destruction of ethical life itself, Ch. 7 below. On our ideas of 'ideology', descriptive, prescriptive and pejorative, Geuss 1981: 4–44. Westlake's inventory of Th.'s 'explicit judgements on ability and character' (Westlake 1968: 5–19) shows most to be reports of the judgements of others. Exceptions are his remarks on Nicias (7.86.5), also Ch. 13 below, and the hapless Hyperbolos (8.73.3).

base for attacks on other Greeks (one reason perhaps for the Spartans' anxiety about Themistocles after 478; they did not want walls that Persians could use to be built north of the Peloponnese (1.90.2)); and in 479, Plataea had been the site of the last Greek battle with the Persians on land.

A Theban force entered Plataea on the moonless night of a sacred day in what we would call March 431 (3.56.2, 3.65.1), let in by a fifth column that wanted to make the place over.[2] Thucydides does not say whether the Thebans and their supporters in Plataea had reason to believe that Athens would not intervene, despite the Spartans having declared that the peace was at an end; if they had no reason to think they would not – they could not have known that Pericles would refuse to engage on land – it was a risky move. In the event, they were clumsy. Instead of following the conspirators' advice to capture Plataea's leading men, they tried at once for a wider acceptance. Most Plataeans were hostile, but thinking that the Theban force was larger than it was, decided to accede. Quickly realising that it was rather small, they spent the rest of the night blocking the streets with carts and knocking through the walls of adjoining houses to co-ordinate their resistance, and 'with a tremendous commotion' attacked the waking invaders just before first light;[3] 'the women and domestic slaves were shouting and screaming at them from the houses and pelting them with stones and tiles, and on top of all this it poured with rain' (2.4.2). The Thebans put up a fight but soon lost their nerve in the rain, mud, noise and dark. Many were cornered and killed, a few reached the walls, most of them jumping to their death, and the rest, 180 of 300, were taken prisoner. The river that ran between Thebes and Plataea had turned into a torrent and reinforcements were delayed. When these did arrive, they let it be known that they would kill all Plataeans living outside the city if the prisoners inside were not released. The Plataeans replied that if they did, the men would be executed. Undertakings were made by each side and the Theban reinforcements departed. The Plataeans had meanwhile kept Athens informed. Thucydides reports that the Athenians at once arrested all the Boeotians present in Attica (a striking indication, if true, of their administrative reach)[4] and when they heard that prisoners

---

[2] A useful anachronism. In 1936, General Mola announced that he had four columns ready to attack Madrid from outside and a fifth within to assist them. As in Spain at this time, so repeatedly across Greece in this war, Ch. 7 below.

[3] Just as people resisting government troops were reported to have done in Aleppo in 2012.

[4] This can suggest that Athens was an exception to the general truth that pre-modern states knew little about those in their territory, Scott 1998: 2. Paul Cartledge explains to me that these may have been Boeotian metics who were required to have an Athenian sponsor and register to be taxed.

had been taken, asked the Plataeans to wait to discuss their fate; the prisoners included a Theban commander, and would have been useful hostages. But it was too late; the Plataeans had executed them all. The Athenians brought in provisions, stationed a garrison, and evacuated the women, children and least able-bodied men. They made no comment that we know of, and nor does Thucydides. He leaves us hearing the commotion and feeling the dread and panic as though we ourselves had been there.

The fact that he describes this incident at the start of book 2 and returns to it there and in book 3 has led some commentators to see it marking one or another motif in his account of what followed: an instance of the ramifications of what can be seen as one long internal war between Greeks; the first of many moments when intelligence was defeated and the unpredictable, in this instance resistance and rain, was decisive; the first moment of unnecessary suffering in this war; the inception of what came in our time to be called a 'total war', without form, style or honour, in which past promises and existing alliances counted for nothing and anyone was attacked as the circumstance of the moment demanded. There is sense in each of these readings, especially the last. But Thucydides does nothing overtly to encourage any and is content later to remark that the Spartans themselves admitted the significance that the Plataean episode had had for them; the attack by an ally of theirs on an ally of Athens, together with their refusal to go to arbitration the year before, had made them the 'transgressors' (7.18.2). But Sparta and Athens had signalled 'the occasion for war' (1.146) at their assemblies in the previous autumn, and the Spartans' later judgement was perhaps occasioned by the fact that in the winter of 414–413, when they voiced it, they were in the ascendant and no longer haunted by the past. Each side did start in earnest to prepare for war after the attack on Plataea, but each would have done so anyway then: the start of spring in 431 was the start of the first fighting season after the declared end of peace.

Optimistically aspiring to create a Peloponnesian fleet of 500 ships against the 300 or so that the Athenians could command, the Spartans ordered more from Italy and Sicily and asked their allies in the league for funds, one presumes to pay for these. 'The Athenians for their part reviewed their existing alliance and sent ambassadors to the places surrounding the Peloponnese – Corcyra, Cephallonia, Acarnania and Zacynthos – seeing that if these could be counted on to be friendly they would be taking the war to the Peloponnese by a process of encirclement' (2.7.3). The Spartans' own first move was on land; as they had thought of doing in the 460s if Athens had laid siege to Thasos, as they had done in 446, as the Corinthians had now been urging them to do, and as

Archidamos had reluctantly said that they might have to do again, they decided to march on Attica. The Athenians expected to retaliate from the sea. All, says Thucydides, were excited. Men across Greece who were too young to have known war were enthusiastic, oracles were consulted, omens were found and an earthquake on Delos was thought to mean something. Everyone felt involved. Most hopes were for Sparta, 'such was the animus most people felt towards the Athenians, some of them wishing to be freed from their rule and others fearing to fall under it' (2.8.4). Archidamos was in command of the Peloponnesian armies and, when these had assembled at the isthmus, he explained that he expected the Athenians to come out to defend their land and the city itself. But he still hoped that terms might be reached, and sent a Spartiate to see if the Athenians might be more inclined to negotiate now that the threat was real. They refused to listen. 'Today', said the envoy when he returned with his escort to the border, 'will be the beginning of great misfortunes for the Greeks' (2.12.3),[5] and Thucydides has no need to say anything more. The war had begun.

Thucydides lists the parties on each side (2.9). Neither he nor any other surviving source offers a plausible estimate of the forces that Archidamos could command; there is only Plutarch's claim that he took 60,000 Peloponnesians into Attica in this first incursion, which is almost certainly an exaggeration.[6] Pericles himself understood the rhetoric of numbers and publicly explained the resources available to the Athenians. Of money, 600 talents, he explained, came into the city every year, largely as tribute. Of the 9,700 that had been stored as coinage, 6,000 remained. The expedition to Potidaea may have accounted for some of the expended 3,700 (by 429, when the siege was lifted, it had cost 2,000 talents (2.70.2)), and some of the rest would have been devoted to public building. A further 500 were coming in from other sources. Of men, there were 13,000 hoplite infantry drawn largely from farmers and the middling classes and a further 16,000 drawn from across the population for the city's walls and its garrisons, together with 1,200 cavalry men and 1,600 foot archers. Four hundred of the wealthiest citizens were slated to serve as trierarchs to fit out a trireme, find a crew and act formally as its commander; the city would itself provide the hulls. What the Athenian navy might be up against is suggested by the ninety ships from Corinth and sixty from other Peloponnesian allies that had sailed to meet the Corcyraeans in 433, and

---

[5] As others have noted, this man (or Th. in writing him) was perhaps recalling his *Odyssey*, 8.81, 'For them the beginning of woe was rolling down upon the Trojans and Danaans [Greeks] through the will of great Zeus'; as does Herodotus in describing the moment at which Athenians sailed against the Persians in Ionia, 5.97.

[6] *Pericles*, 33. Th. has difficulty estimating Spartan numbers; cf. Mantinea in 418 (5.68.2).

the one hundred of its own that Sparta was able to put to sea in 430 (1.46.1, 2.66.1). In short, Athens had more ships and men to man them, but the finances, Pericles failed to say, were not reassuring. The city had money for war for just a few more years.[7]

To deny advantage to the Spartans, Pericles persuaded the Athenians who lived outside the walls to move into the city. It was difficult, says Thucydides, to cope with them all coming in together; they spread onto sacred land, into the spaces between the walls down to the Piraeus and even in the port itself, settling as best they could. Archidamos took his armies first to the Athenian garrison town of Oenoe in the far north-west of Attica. His troops grumbled at his doing this, doing it slowly and lingering when he arrived. He was trying still to give the Athenians time to reconsider.[8] Failing again to persuade them to do so and being unpractised in laying sieges, failing even to take the garrison at Oenoe, he set off south (in what was now mid June, nearly three months since the events at Plataea) and camped at Acharnae, 7 miles north of Athens itself. His tactic, says Thucydides, was simple. He hoped either to draw the Athenians into a land battle or to set them against each other. He had some success in both; cavalry did ride out when the Peloponnesian forces came close to the city,[9] the Acharnaians were angry at Athens' lack of support for them and the Athenians themselves were dividing. 'The whole city was in ferment and feelings against Pericles were running high' (2.21.3) for refusing fully to engage. Exercising an authority that students of procedure in Athens have questioned but perhaps securing

---

[7] A talent was 6,000 drachmas, a drachma six obols. One drachma was roughly the daily wage for an Athenian labourer, though conservative sources suggest that three obols could keep a modest family going for a day. A warship (trireme) cost one talent to build and another to keep afloat and active for a month. The cost to Athens of having 200 of its 300 triremes active for the eight sailing months of March to October would thus be 1,600 talents, more than twice what Pericles gives as the annual tribute; even without public spending on the army or anything else, though not allowing for private contributions, this would mean that the city's capital would be exhausted in about five years of war at sea if 1,000 talents (see below) was to be set aside for the defence of Athens itself and not spent. Yet historians believe Pericles' figures for money and men were broadly accurate. His 'other income' beyond the 600 talents of tribute may have included that from the silver mines in Attica and private contributions. A possible substitution later of a tax on the movement of goods, Ch. 13 below.

[8] Archidamos' troops were cross that in not moving more quickly he lost the opportunity to catch the Athenians outside the city. It is the first of nineteen explicit counterfactuals that Flory 1988 finds in the text; many more are implied and convey Th.'s sensitivity to contingency. Also Chs. 13 and 14 below.

[9] Athens appears to have increased its cavalry from 300 to 1,000 or so at some point between 445 and 438. Thessalian horsemen had proved to be unreliable (1.100.7) and those considering the city's defence from attack on land had evidently decided that such a force could be useful. The increase required public subsidies for animals and fodder, Spence 2010.

the support of others, Pericles refused to allow a debate on his decision, and instead sent one hundred ships, 1,000 hoplites and 400 archers to harass the Spartans and their allies around the coasts of the Peloponnese, despatched a further thirty ships to Euboea to make sure that Athens' subjects there would not take advantage of the Spartan incursion and 'expelled the Aeginetans from Aegina – men, women and children – alleging that they were largely responsible for bringing the war upon them; besides, since Aegina lay close to the Peloponnese it seemed safer to occupy it with replacement settlers of their own' (2.27.1). He also persuaded the Athenians to set aside 1,000 talents to pay for the defence of the city against future attack and to keep their one hundred best ships aside each year for the same purpose. Having failed in its central purpose and caused some damage in the countryside, Archidamos' army departed.

Pericles' judgement – Thucydides gives us no option but to think of it as such, and there is no other evidence – was that there was nothing to be gained and much to be lost in engaging with the Peloponnesians in Attica and that the Athenian navy should be able to deal with any attack from the sea. The expedition he had despatched around the Peloponnese secured Cephallonia, restored a city the Corinthians had taken from a local ruler in Acarnania in the south-western part of the mainland, and expelled a tyrant from another city in the area which it brought under Athens' dominion (though the Corinthians were to help the man take it back a few months later). The purpose appears to have been to demonstrate Athens' command of the sea. The Athenians also made an alliance with Sitalces, the king of Thrace, who persuaded them to restore a Macedonian city and thereby brought Perdiccas to support the Athenian commander Phormio, who was still at Potidaea. And in the autumn of 431, what Thucydides describes as 'the greatest Athenian force ever assembled together' (2.31.2), 10,000 Athenians supplemented by 3,000 resident immigrants and a further number of lightly armed troops, invaded Megara under the command of Pericles himself and wasted land there. The size of this first expedition to Megara (the Athenians were to repeat it twice a year for several years, if not with so many men) and its limited effect were odd; it also perhaps was intended to be no more than a show of power, this time on land. But with the exception of the capture of Cephallonia, none of these ventures was contrary to Pericles' insistence that Athens should not extend its dominion in time of war.[10]

---

[10] Cornford 1907: 249 detected a touch of 'madness' in Pericles over Megara. Thera (modern Santorini) appears to have been added to Athens' dominion sometime between 431 and 426, just possibly therefore before Pericles' death, Lewis 1992a: 409 n. 110.

Nonetheless, at places which mattered to Sparta around the Peloponnese and the Adriatic, in Thrace, Macedonia and Chalcidice, and against Aegina and Megara, the Athenians were aggressively defending what they defined as their important perimeters. In a remark that he plainly inserted later, Thucydides says that they attempted these things when 'the city was at peak strength' (2.31.2) – in what was just the first of what were to be twenty-seven years of fighting. The Spartans and other Greeks had imagined that the Athenians would be able to hold out against the incursions into Attica for only one year, perhaps two, certainly no more than three (4.85.2, 5.14.3, 7.28.3). Pericles' plan was precarious, and he had admitted that the Athenians could fail through their own mistakes.

In these first two years of the war, Thucydides continues to write about Athens through Pericles. In the winter of 431–430, the few cavalrymen who had died in skirmishes with the Peloponnesians in the summer were given a public funeral. In what some historians believe may have been a fairly recent practice in Athens, when the coffins had been covered with earth, 'a man chosen by the city for his wise judgement and public standing [would deliver] over them a suitable speech of praise' (2.34.6). As Macleod remarked, 'funeral speeches, by their very nature, try to draw their audience's gaze away from certain facts',[11] and Pericles, who gave this one, certainly had to do so. The tomb was in what Thucydides describes as 'the most beautiful suburb' of Pericles' now much beautified city (2.34.5). But he would have been addressing a crowd that may have included people from the countryside who had had to abandon almost everything except their families, as well as residents some of whom would have been angry at his refusal to engage the Peloponnesians. He could not meet the discontents of the first, had to face down the second, and saw that he had to divert all to a higher purpose. But Thucydides does not disclose his motive or speculate. He offers an account of what Pericles said and leaves his readers to make what they will of the context and what Pericles made of the occasion.

When the Peloponnesian armies had been assembling at the isthmus, Pericles had sought to convince the citizens of Athens' material strengths. He chose now to emphasise what these strengths allowed. The honourable death of the cavalrymen had to go without saying.[12] What did not, he believed, were the present ease and lasting glory of what they died

---

[11] Macleod 1983e: 149, also Loraux 1986a, Yoshitake 2010, and Socrates in Plato's *Menexenus*.

[12] Yoshitake contests Loraux's suggestion that such orations alluded to the intentions of those whom they commemorated rather than their (alleged) contributions. He also points out that this funeral oration is unusual among the few that survive from the

for. The ancestors had given Athens a dominion that brought wealth and a 'cast of mind' conducive to 'greatness' (2.36.4). The city, he declared, had a politics, 'democracy is the name we give to it', in which merit is rewarded, poverty is no bar to participation and we 'manage our affairs in the interests of the many not the few' (2.37.1). 'We alone regard the person who fails to participate in public affairs not just as harmless but as positively useless; and we are all personally involved either in actual political decisions or in deliberation about them' (2.40.2). In our private lives, he went on, we are free and tolerant; in public, fear makes us observe the law. In our relations with other states, our courage is natural; unlike the Spartans, we do not have to force ourselves and act under stress. In his one claim to a more particular moral quality, interesting not least for the fact that the Athenians who had been present on 'state business' in Sparta in 432 had openly disavowed it, Pericles insisted that 'we make our friends not by receiving favours, but by conferring them' and 'have the courage to be benefactors not from a calculation of advantage but in the confidence of our freedom', a claim that he at once contradicted in remarking that putting people in one's debt has the satisfying consequence of weakening them (2.40.4–5). Indeed 'the city as a whole', he said, 'is an education for Greece' (2.41.1); what Athenians do exceeds their already impressive reputation and anything he could say about it. They should therefore hold their nerve. 'Look not just to arguments about advantage, since anyone could recite at length all the benefits of resisting the enemy, which you know perfectly well yourselves; rather, feast your eyes every day upon the actual power of the city, become her lovers' (2.43.1).[13] He said that the men being remembered at this funeral had given their lives to its cause, and turned finally to their parents: 'you know that you grew up in a world of chance and change' (2.44.1): the death of your sons shows that they did so too, but this is a world of true fortune in which Athenians can die for something truly glorious.

Pericles' oration is the only idealisation that survives of Athens' domestic politics at the time and, outside tragedy, it is one of only three theorisations that do; it was only after 404 that Athenians began seriously

classical period in saying nothing about what these contributions were. This is understandable; Pericles would have had to praise the dead for engaging the Peloponnesians, which was not what he wanted the Athenians to do.

[13] Ludwig 2002: 330 suggests that where the image of erotic love was invoked at all in Greek politics, it referred to feelings that subjects should have for tyrannies. Pericles was therefore taking a risk (although he was later to describe Athens' dominion in this way, 2.63.2). His meaning may well be captured in Ludwig's shrewd observation that '*eros* is at once perfectly free and perfectly committed', 332.

to reflect on what they had nearly lost, and then often argued against it. Because Pericles portrays these politics as many since the advent of modern democracy have wished to see them, his idealisation has also long been the most noted speech in the text. But like all instances of its genre, it played selectively with the truth. As Jonas Grethlein observes, Pericles offered exactly the kind of one-sided 'performance-piece' for the moment, dedicated 'more to make good listening than to represent the truth' (1.21.1, 1.22.4), that Thucydides himself so disdains.[14]

Pericles had to give Athenians reasons to persist which being his, would be reasons to persist with him. Everyone in Athens expected the Peloponnesians to return to Attica in the summer of 430; Sparta had no other tactic. But no one foresaw that a few days after they did so, a 'plague' would arrive in Athens. Pericles had said that his words could not do justice to Athens' glories. Thucydides says that his own cannot do justice to the miseries of this epidemic. The affliction attacked almost everything on the body and within it from the head downwards, and did so in horrible ways; even if they did not die, people often lost their fingers, toes and eyes and men lost their genitals. Yet for all Thucydides' detail – he suffered it himself, he says – there has been no agreement on what it was.[15] Nor is there any contemporary record of how many

---

[14] Grethlein 2010: 220–5. Foster 2010: 210 quotes a recent German scholar on the oration: 'It is like an advertisement for a union of our time, or the description of the essential features of a modern state of the western type'; 2.37.1 did indeed appear (ambiguously attributed to Th. rather than Pericles) as the motto at the head of the short-lived European Constitution in 2004. The second theorisation of the fifth-century democracy is also in Th., a crisp argument to the conclusion that democracy best meets the various needs and interests in a fifth-century city-state, 6.35–40, Ch. 12 below. The third is the entertainingly ironic characterisation of the unknown Old Oligarch, as he is called (it was previously attributed to Xenophon), which may date from the 420s (and may just be a casual piece concocted from other sources). This is that democracy is not rule for the good but is good for Athens. It allows the mob to serve the city's purposes and to profit, and since change requires rebellion by a disenfranchised multitude – the author must have been innocent of 411 – it is here to stay; it is at once 'explicable, despicable and invincible', Ober 1998: 14–27 at 25, text Gagarin and Woodruff 1995: 133–44. Democritos, a contemporary of Th.'s, echoes Pericles' emphasis on the importance of political participation, DK 253 in Gagarin and Woodruff 1995: 159; Democritos was a conventional political thinker and although he was one of few we know of who favoured the democracy, his was perhaps a conventional view; also Ch. 11 n. 2. Loraux 1986a, e.g. 328–37, unsurprisingly suggested that funeral orations were a medium through which Athenians presented their idealisations. On a wider conception of a 'theory' of democracy in the fifth century, Farrar 1988: 15–43, 265–78; on reflections after 404, Shear 2011: 313–22.

[15] Clinical reflection has suggested 'a gastroenteropathy mediated by the central nervous system'; epidemiological analysis has indicated 'either a reservoir disease (zoonotic or vector-borne)', such as typhus, bubonic plague or an arbivoral disease, 'or one of the few respiratory diseases that are associated with an unusual means of persistence', such as smallpox. An examination of DNA in dental pulp from a hasty mass burial in

died in its three visitations between 430 and 427; indeed no other surviving text mentions it. When Thucydides notes its return in 427, he says that a third of the city's hoplites were lost (3.87.2). That was a not uncommon proportion in later epidemics of one kind or another in late ancient and medieval European populations; if in its first outbreak alone in 430 Attica had about 350,000 people and those in the countryside were as seriously affected as those in the city, more than 100,000 may have died.

It shattered Pericles' picture. 'No-one', writes Thucydides in a matter-of-fact way, 'was eager to add to their own hardships for supposedly fine objectives, since they were uncertain whether they would die before achieving them. Whatever gave immediate pleasure or in any way facilitated it became the standard of what was good and useful. Neither fear of the gods nor law of man was any restraint' (2.53.3–4). Yet Athens did manage to mount two expeditions that summer. Pericles himself took 4,000 Athenian hoplites and 300 cavalry with one hundred ships together with an additional fifty from Chios and Lesbos to Epidauros on the north-eastern coast of the Peloponnese and to damage settlements and the countryside south to Laconia. It was as large a force as the one that Athenians were to send to Sicily in 415 (6.31.2). The size is not easy to explain, and Thucydides does not do so. Pericles was unlikely to have been able to hold Epidauros against Spartan resistance on land. Perhaps he simply wanted to get as many soldiers and sailors out of the city as he could afford to; perhaps as a fourth-century historian, Ephoros, is reported to have suggested about this and other things Pericles was doing at the time, he was putting on a show to distract discontent in Athens; perhaps he wanted to bring Argos onto Athens' side in the war; perhaps, as some have imagined, he needed numbers to capture the representation of the Greeks' healing god Asclepios from the sanctuary dedicated to the god in Epidauros.[16] A little later two other generals took

---

Athens that is dated to about 430 (a burial in which children appear to have been more carefully interred than adults) has so far proved indeterminate. General summary in Scott and Duncan 2001: 2–5; questionable evidence of typhoid in excavated remains, Papagrigorakis, Yapijakis and Baziotopoulu-Valavani 2006; comments by others and the authors' reply to these referred to in the bibliography under these names. Th. is believed to be the first person anywhere (in writing) to have suggested ideas of contagion and acquired immunity. On the populations, Hansen 2006b, Golden 2000.

[16] If so, he failed. The cult of the god-like Asclepios was nevertheless spreading, and his snake (a symbol still of medicine) was eventually brought from Epidauros to the Piraeus in 420–19 and thence to the Acropolis in Athens, Hornblower CT III: 140. Ephoros, whose work is lost, may have echoed Aristophanes' criticisms of Pericles in Peace, 605–18 (robustly rejected by de Ste Croix 1972: 236–7) and been a source for Plutarch's Pericles, 19, in which this opinion is expressed. Also on this expedition, Hornblower CT I: 328–9.

the same force north to attack Chalcideans in Thrace and try to take
Potidaea, which was still under siege; but the plague was affecting the
Athenian soldiers, and they passed it on. More than a quarter of the
Athenian hoplites in the force were lost to it and the force accomplished
nothing.

Archidamos' army had departed before even the first of these expeditions had returned. He had inflicted more damage in his second incursion
into Attica than in the first, but Pericles had again refused to engage.
Meanwhile, those who had come in from the Attic countryside were
suffering from their losses and the condition in which they found themselves, and now there was plague. People were in despair, and it was
understandable that they should turn on Pericles. Aware of this and the
fact that a faction had succeeded in sending envoys to Sparta, Thucydides writes that Pericles realised that he had 'to give them fresh heart
and draw the sting of their anger and so restore them to a calmer and
more confident frame of mind' (2.59.3).[17] But this is not how the speech
in which he did so – the speech that Thucydides writes – reads. Pericles seems to have decided that he had now to frighten the citizens into
accepting his opinion of what Athens should continue to do, and in so
doing, one can hear him frightening himself.[18]

He began quietly enough. 'The state can bear the misfortunes of individuals but each one of them is incapable of bearing hers.' All should
therefore act for the common good. 'In your distress at your domestic
misfortunes you are sacrificing our common security, and you are not
only blaming me for advocating war but also blaming yourselves for supporting the decision' (2.60.4). But it is not me, Pericles said, who is to
blame. 'I think I am as good as any man at knowing what has to be

---

[17] Paul Cartledge points out to me that these men must have been able to persuade the
council (*boule*) and assembly, which indicates Pericles' less than total control. It has
become unfashionable (not least among American classicists committed to democracy)
to talk of 'faction' and 'party' in classical Greek states but, as James Madison observed
in *Federalist 10*, these are 'sown in the nature of man', Hamilton, Madison and Jay 2003:
41 (also Alexander Hamilton's criticism of Pericles' rule in *Federalist 6*: 20). I use one
or other word merely to describe a group coming together for a more or less immediate
political purpose; not to suggest an organised and deliberately agonistic body seeking
support for power of the kind that emerged from 'faction' to 'party' (terms that should
in themselves be neither pejorative or approving) in English politics at the beginning
of the eighteenth century and subsequently elsewhere. Factions are of central concern
to Th. (e.g. Ch. 7 below) even if he only once refers to them thus, at Megara in 424
(4.71.1).

[18] Pericles might have appreciated Dean Acheson's observation that 80 per cent of the job
of having a foreign policy for a democracy was managing the domestic ability to have a
foreign policy at all, quoted in Sarotte 2009: 120.

done and communicating it. I also love my city and am above corruption' (2.60.5). He also reminded his audience that the city's strengths were supreme; when luck is not at issue they made it impossible to believe that it can lose in war. (He did not now refer to the possibility of Athenian mistakes.) 'The Peloponnesians have damaged properties outside the city, but you should think of your land and houses just as the show-gardens and ornaments of your wealth' (2.63.3). What matters, he said – perhaps deliberately forgetting that he had previously warned that to extend the city's dominion in time of war would not be wise – is your unassailable command of the sea 'not only the parts you already occupy but anywhere further you might wish to go' (2.62.2).

His tone then sharpened. The truth, he told his audience, is that you are hated. Your present dominion is 'like a tyranny, which it seems wrong to take but perilous to let go'. To give in to fear 'and try to make a manly virtue of non-involvement' is foolish (2.63.2). 'Men who can suggest this would soon destroy their city if they persuaded others to share this view – as they would destroy any other city they set up under their own control elsewhere.' He rose to his theme. 'If you pursue the privileges of prestige you must also shoulder its burdens' (2.63.1). 'Athens has the greatest name in the world because she never yielded to misfortunes but ... lavished her lives and labours *upon war*. She has acquired the greatest power that has ever existed, whose memory will live on for ever, and even if we do now have to accept some eventual loss (everything being subject to natural decline) posterity will always recall that we were the Greeks to rule over most fellow Greeks,[19] that in the greatest of all wars' – the war with the Persians – 'we held out against them, whether in combination or separately, and that we inhabited a city which was the richest in every resource and the greatest' (2.64.3, my emphasis). To be hated for ruling others, he said, does not matter. What does is the larger purpose. In one syntactical ball, as Macleod brilliantly said, Pericles then tore through the gates of oblivion to eternity: 'the brilliance of present deeds shines on to be remembered in everlasting glory' (2.64.5–6).[20] Meanwhile, there was a war to be won. So saying, Pericles undermined his resistance to

[19] Literally, 'we Greeks ruled over most Greeks', which could mean 'we ruled over more Greeks than any other Greek state ever did' or 'we ruled over most of the Greek world, being ourselves Greeks'. Mynott here preserves the ambiguity.

[20] Macleod 1983e: 153. Pericles' reported remark as he was dying, 'no living Athenian ever put on mourning because of me' (Plutarch, *Pericles*, 38), remains enigmatic. Foster 2010 argues that Th. consistently distances himself from Pericles' imperial enthusiasms. Cf. Vogt 2009.

engaging in one, and Thucydides, silently exposing the contradiction, allows one to hear his fear.

When this speech has been discussed at all, it has been common to contrast it with Pericles' funeral oration: the one, on Athens' domestic politics, unruffled and assured; the other, on its overseas dominion, belligerent, anxious and at the end almost hysterical. But each closes with an emphasis on the glory of Athens, each is concerned to impress on Athenians that they owe this and all else they have to their rule over fellow Greeks, and Pericles makes it clear in both that it is he in the present generation who has been guiding them to it. His had become the dominant voice among the descendants of those who had helped to overthrow the tyranny at the end of the previous century; gone on to arrange political competition in such a way that no one family or faction and its clients would again be able to dominate the others; created a navy to resist the Persians and use that navy to establish a profitable overseas dominion; and realised that to maintain their ascendancy they had to share a proportion of the profits with the people. He had conferred the symbolic power of citizenship on free native-born men, thereby including them in the imperial project and guarding his political base, arranged at no great cost to pay them to take time off work to participate in government and serve on juries (although not to pay them to attend assemblies), and in these ways given them the power in the assembly to vote on motions put to them. They had the last word, if not, as it has nicely been said, in their own words. And 'democracy' was the name the arrangement had acquired.[21] (Unlike most since, Athenians had not had to fight for it. Its conditions had ironically been created in part by Spartan help in removing the tyranny.) But the two recent Spartan invasions and the plague had strained the citizens' commitment to what Pericles was now doing, and he was fighting for his political life. The confessedly pro-Sicilian historian Diodorus goes so far as to suggest that he had long since come 'to the conclusion that it would be to his own advantage to embroil the state in a great war' in order to avoid persecution (12.39.3). The citizens, discontented with what they had experienced so far, were offered an offence (which we do not know) on which to fine him and remove him from office; but Thucydides gives no further detail, they could see

---

[21] In 451 Pericles had been instrumental in narrowing citizenship in a city of increasing ethnic plurality to men born of an Athenian mother as well as father; on Athens' social composition, Cohen 2000. It wasn't until after the war, in the 390s, that citizens were paid to attend assemblies. Before that time, only those with the time and resources would find it easy often to attend, especially if they lived at some distance from the city.

no better alternative, the envoys to Sparta were recalled and he was to be re-elected *strategos*.

The Periclean moment in Athens suggests an interesting twist on the commonly cited dilemma of plenty and power with which Herodotus, speaking through a Persian, ended his *historie* and which others were in one way or another to repeat into the early nineteenth century. (De Tocqueville, reflecting on the early United States, said that no regime can at once provide 'poetry, renown and glory' and 'usefully turn the intellectual and moral activity of man to the necessities of material life and employ it in producing well-being'.) Thucydides has nothing to say on this. Through Pericles himself and in the debate about what to do about Mytilene, which I discuss in Chapter 7, he raises the different question, which understandably excites moderns, of the conjunction of liberty at home and empire abroad.[22] In his own voice, if it is his voice and not that of an editor, he is exercised about the different question again of Athens' democracy at home and its effectiveness beyond. Pericles, he says, had the skill, judgement and personal distinction needed to direct and where necessary distract the citizens and control them. 'What was in name a democracy was in practice government by the foremost man' (2.65.8–9). He is right in saying that no one leader after Pericles managed to dominate the city for so long. He also says that they were lesser men. Driven by 'private ambition and personal greed', they lacked their predecessor's 'evident integrity' and were overly susceptible to 'the whims of the people' for whose support they fought (2.65.7–12).[23]

This however is an incomplete assessment of Pericles and wrong about most of the others, as Thucydides' own account will show. A deeper cause of change in the following twenty-five years, the uncertainty and anxiety of war itself, was already evident in Pericles' last speech and in the Athenians' immediate reaction to it. It would have required an exceptional ability to command a majority in the city and direct it steadily through the war. On Athens' overseas policy, Thucydides recalls that Pericles had told the citizens that if they held back, 'looked after their

---

[22] Herodotus, 9.122. de Tocqueville 2000: 234–5, from 1835. On liberty and empire, Raaflaub 1994. Foster 2010 is a close argument (inspired, she acknowledges, by Stahl 2003 – see Ch. 9 below) for reading the whole of Th. 1–2.65 as an argument against Pericles' ambitions for 'empire'. On early modern readings of Th. on liberty and empire, Hoekstra 2012: 31–5.

[23] One may not need to say that the merits of 'the foremost man' (or woman) commend themselves still in even the most apparently democratic of settings: in recalling his notable speech on the occasion of bombings in London in 2005, the elected mayor of that city compared himself with 'Pericles, mayor of Athens', Livingstone 2011: 533.

navy, did not try to extend their empire during the war and did not expose the city to risk... they would prevail'. Thucydides says that they 'did just the opposite of this in every way' (2.65.7). Yet in what he goes on to write, in the first ten years of the war, he shows they did not.

Later, after a peace with Sparta had failed, they did decide on what proved to be the disastrous attempt to subjugate Sicily, and did so in the course of a grandstanding competition before the assembly of the kind that Thucydides so disliked. But again from his own account, he is wrong to say that the expedition failed not so much because the Athenians misjudged their enemy as because they proceeded to embroil Alcibiades, one of the generals they appointed to lead it, in a dispute in Athens itself (2.65.11). In any event, he himself implies that Sicily was a separate war (6.1.1). And his narrative in books 6 and 7 makes it clear that it was indeed a mistake even to have thought of fighting it. To have recalled Alcibiades from Sicily may have weakened the Athenians, though Alcibiades' tactics for the expedition were arguably less sensible than those proposed by another of the three generals sent to command it; and the Athenians could not be held wholly responsible for his subsequent defection to Sparta.

In the last of these late reflections, Thucydides nonetheless suggests that after recovering from the catastrophe that overtook them in Sicily, the Athenians ensured their defeat in the wider war by infighting. He did not himself realise his intention (5.26.1) of writing the moment of defeat, and his explanation that of why it happened in 6.15.3–4, a passage that is as unsatisfactory as 2.65 and for much the same kind of reason, turns entirely on the citizens' later rejection of Alcibiades for his personal extravagance and 'craving' for tyranny. But other historians did provide an account, and one can infer from these that Athens' defeat was not predetermined either by the short-lived coup against the democracy in the city in 411 or by any other internal dispute. The city's politics were certainly turbulent and often self-destructive, but even with the support that a son of the Persian king was eventually to offer Sparta and the emergence at last of an able Spartan naval commander, the defeat was an avoidable disaster. And as I mention in Chapter 14, it occurred just when Athens, it can be argued, could have won.

The most charitable explanation for these judgements on Pericles, on what politics in Athens was to become, on the Athenians' strategy in the first ten years of war, on the reasons for their failure in Sicily and on why they eventually lost the war, is that Thucydides made them in haste in the lasting shock of that defeat; that he was preoccupied by the memory of the debacle at Syracuse in 413 and of the brief interruption of government in Athens in 411; and that he had overlooked what he had written about events between Pericles' last speech in 430, the end of the Sicilian campaign and the recovery from the coup that followed. He also may not have known all the circumstances of military defeat in 405. As historical judgements, they do not do him justice and one can regret that he set them down.[24]

[24] Comparable considerations by Hornblower *CT* I: 340–9, Dover *HCT* V: 423–7 and Andrewes 1992: 496–8. Helen Thompson, in conversation, offers the ingenious thought that Th. might for a moment have been escaping from authoritative narrator to deceptive speaker in order to highlight the truthfulness of his subsequent narrative. Also 6.15, Ch. 12 below; and 6.15 again and 2.65, Ch. 13 below.

6   Absent strategies 430–428

Thucydides allows one to think that Sparta and Athens found themselves at war in spite of themselves. Or more exactly, that each found itself no longer at peace. A majority at Sparta had been hustled into deciding that the treaty of 446–445 had been broken. Some wanted still to delay, but most had been incited to believe that they had been humiliated enough. Some in Athens wanted to come to an understanding, but Pericles had prevailed. He believed that war was unavoidable if the city was to retain its dominion and prosperity and thereby assure its future glory, but that this was not the moment to fight it. Megara could be harassed, there could be raids along the Peloponnesian coast, and Potidaea had to be brought back, but nothing else was immediately feasible. The Peloponnesians should accordingly be allowed to fail, and in Attica they did. They invaded for a second time in 430, returned in 428 and 427, were deterred by an earthquake in 426 and in 425 stayed for just fifteen days before leaving to deal with a threat in the Peloponnese itself. Thucydides does not say as much but his narrative makes it clear: the Spartans could not see how otherwise to take the war to the Athenians and the Athenians could not see how to take the war to the Spartans at all.

Strategika, generalship, was already in the fifth century being seen to involve more than leading men into battle. In Athens, the board of generals appears to have been responsible for deploying the city's forces. In Sparta, the five annually elected ephors recommended action to the assembly there. (The Spartan *gerousia*, a council of elders, was said by a later historian to have been active on the question of whether to go to war with Athens in the 470s, but Thucydides never mentions it, perhaps because he could not discover anything about it (5.68.2), and there seems to be no other sign of its having played any part in the direction of military affairs in the present war.) The connection between political decision and military direction in Athens could not have been much closer; generals led decisions about what to do and commanded the doing of it. In Sparta, as far as one can judge, the decisions were more separate; one or other of the kings and its other commanders had more power in the field than at home. But even in Sparta there was not that sharp separation of politicians and generals that Clausewitz was to deplore in the early nineteenth century. Nor, to most of those engaged in it, was the war of the Peloponnesians and the Athenians, as Clausewitz said of conflicts in general in the ancient world, local and limited.[1] Local passions were certainly as intense as they were in the Greek and so-called Balkan wars in the nineteenth and twentieth centuries. But as in these, smaller entities were drawn into larger ambitions. One can see why when Thucydides looked back he judged it 'the greatest ever upheaval among the Greeks, which affected a good part of the barbarian world too – even, you could say, most of mankind' (1.1.2).[2] And that was not merely his pride in the importance of what he was writing; it is possible that the conflict was coming to be seen in this way even before it began. But although it had been some time arriving, none of those involved knew quite how to pursue it. In neither the nineteenth- nor twentieth-century senses of 'strategy' – of battles dedicated to winning a war or of war fought for a political purpose beyond it – did either side have one. Some have nevertheless believed that Athenians and Spartans must have had one; wars cannot otherwise be fought. Thucydides' silence on the matter thus led Wade-Gery to regard him as 'a first-rate regimental officer, ashore or afloat, who saw war more as a matter of style', had an indifferent understanding of 'the problems of high command' and could not always grasp matters of strategy, even in the more limited sense of the art of campaigning. I suspect that in Greece in 430–428 and indeed until 413 there was little strategy to grasp and that Thucydides lets us see that this was so. He was an intelligent man, and it is not unknown for younger officers to see more clearly than their seniors.[3]

Sparta wanted to retain the reputation that it had recovered in the peace of 446–445. As Archidamos had intimated in his speech to the Spartans in 432, it might hope in time to be able to extend its league, increase its revenues, acquire a strong navy and reduce Athens to impotence. But that remained a hope, and would take time. 'Unless we beat them at sea or cut off the revenues from which they support their navy we will suffer

---

[1] Von Clausewitz 1984: 605–10, 587.

[2] Mynott notes 'here not just "foreigners", since Th. presumably has particularly in mind the non-Greek-speaking peoples affected by the war (like the Thracians). The distinction between Greek and barbarian and the sense of identity that came from this was a matter both of language and culture and was largely formed in the fifth century in the aftermath of the Persian Wars. See Hall 1989'; it was also sharpened by the war itself. But also Ch. 4 n. 6 above.

[3] Wade-Gery 2012; Wade-Gery had been an officer (gaining an MC) in the First World War. Davies 1993, Brunt 1993a, Cawkwell 2011 and Morris 2009, among others, have read strategies into Th.'s account, and Platias and Kolipoulos 2010 read strategic language into Th. to argue that he is Europe's first (known) theorist of the art.

the greater damage. And in that situation it will no longer be possible to conclude an honourable peace, especially if we are thought to be the main instigators of the dispute. On no account, therefore, must we let ourselves be carried away by the hope that the war can be brought to a speedy end if we devastate their land' (1.81.4–6), and there is no indication that those who voted him down had thought hard about what they might be committing themselves to. They might indeed achieve what they had in 446; that the Athenians, when faced again with a march on their city, would either be defeated or come to terms and that Sparta would be able to restore its honour and security. It is not unusual to fight a war as though it were the one before. But the Spartans would have been wise to recall the one before that, as Pericles was indirectly to do (and as the Spartans may have heard that he had) in suggesting that the Athenians should think of themselves as islanders; they had left their city ahead of Xerxes' Persian army in 480–479 and defended themselves from the sea. In the light of what the Spartans had heard Archidamos explain in the winter of 432–431 and what by the summer of 430 they would have realised about how Athens intended to respond, invading Attica would be a poorly considered means to an uncertain end. They may have felt compelled by their allies and their damaged sense of themselves to make some kind of move. But as Archidamos himself had said, it was not clear that the only one open to them could be decisive.

Most commentators have read Pericles and his supporters in Athens to have been thinking more carefully. The city's financial strength lay in tribute and the monetary reserves that this allowed, its advantage in trade, and a navy that was sustained by each to protect both. If these were not defended – the countryside of Attica and in the extreme even the city itself were dispensible – the city's efforts since the 470s would be for nothing. Pericles and his fellow generals may not have been thinking as hard as they might have done about details; about protecting themselves against an attack on their harbour at the Piraeus, for instance, as an attempt in the winter of 429–428 was to show, or about the advantage they might gain by moving quickly to capture an island base off the southern Peloponnese. But the usual observation, that Athens' first priority was defence, is not wrong. Pericles had said as much. He wanted the Spartans themselves to see that they could not prevail. In the battle language of the nineteenth century one could say that against their wish to annihilate he hoped simply to exhaust.[4] The question is what if anything he and those who thought like him envisaged beyond maintaining the status quo.

---

[4] Platias and Koliopoulos 2010: 65. Strategy understood as the use of battle for war was a nineteenth-century conception, understood as the use of war for policy a conception (notwithstanding von Clausewitz in the 1820s, 1984: 605) of the years after 1918.

Pericles had certainly not revealed any grander plan in what he had said in 431–430; he was content merely to emphasise Athens' unassailable command of the sea. Yet as I mentioned in Chapter 3, the city had made alliances in the 450s or 440s with the non-Greek city of Halcyae in western Sicily (and possibly then, possibly later, with Egesta). Plutarch, how reliably we do not know, says that some Athenians had in the 440s been advocating a renewed attack against the Persians in Egypt and moves also against Carthage on the North African coast and Tyrrhenia (Etruria) in central Italy. In 433–432 Athens did reaffirm its treaties with Rhegion on the Italian side of the strait of Messina and Leontini in Sicily, a city a few miles north-west of Syracuse, and one assumes that Pericles and his supporters will have approved of this. If they did, they may already have been thinking of extending what the Corinthians were describing as their 'tyrant state' over Greeks beyond 'Hellas' as well as within it (1.124.3). Ian Morris has argued that this is exactly what they had in mind after the end of the Persian war, when they realised what power they could exercise in the Aegean. If we think of 'imperialism' being exercised over people regarded as foreign and state power being exercised over one's own, a sometimes rather arbitrary distinction, Athens' dominion (*arche*), Morris suggests, was by the 430s more like a 'greater Athenian state' with varying degrees of political, economic, administrative and cultural control over its parts than an empire, though one should note that it did not extend citizenship to those born in its overseas territories. And if Athenian ideas of commanding Egypt, Carthage or Tyrrhenia were serious, the city may also have been vaguely minded to create a multi-ethnic empire of the kind achieved by Persia and now being attempted by the ruling family in Odrysian Thrace. But once the war with the Peloponnesians had begun, any such ideas had to be set aside; as Pericles had said in warning Athenians not to think of extending their control while trying to maintain what they already had, they could not do so until Sparta and Corinth had been subdued (1.144.1). And he had no strategy for that.

Thus in 431 did each power find itself in a war that it could not see how to take to the other. Each could only harness the resources it had and try to acquire more, take what opportunities might present themselves to disadvantage the other, and otherwise try to maintain its position. Hans-Peter Stahl is not quite right therefore when he says that what Thucydides writes about succeeding events shows how plans can be thwarted by human error and the unexpected.[5] What Thucydides does reveal is that when there are no plans and opportunism is the only option, improvisation, haste, hesitation and accident can make success less

---

[5] Stahl 2003: 75–101, also Ch. 9 below.

certain still. There is no necessity in this; things can turn out other-wise. But in this war, each power was to find itself in much the same position in relation to the other at the end of its first, so-called 'Archi-damian' phase in 421 as it had been at the start. In Greece itself indeed, things did not greatly change until 413–412. The Peloponnesians had by then established a fort in Attica (7.19.1–2, 7.27.2–5), and by 412–411, the Athenians were assumed to have been weakened by their losses on an expedition to Sicily and Persian satraps, 'defenders of power' in Persia's empire in Anatolia, were showing an interest again in involving Persia in the Aegean (6.1.1, 8.5.4–5, 8.6.1).

It is true that Thucydides does not say that there was little strategic thinking between 431 and the spring of 413. But nor does he say the opposite. He does not think in these terms. Or at least, he does not use them in his writing.[6] The several set pieces that appear in books 3, 4 and 5 – the Mytileneans' rebellion against Athens' dominion, the Plataeans' attempt to survive, the civil war in Corcyra, the shock of Spartan soldiers surrendering in the southern Peloponnese, an Athenian defeat in Boeotia, a Spartan victory at Amphipolis and Athens' eventual domination of the Cycladean island of Melos – all make the point. Thucydides writes each with drama and effect and plainly thought that each was significant beyond itself. But their significance lies more in what each reveals about the circumstance and experience of war in general and its attendant political complications than about any plan. Where these moves were reasoned at all, and not every one was, none shows Athens or Sparta matching practicable means to more than immediately urgent ends, and none affected the long course of the war or its outcome. Of the conflicts that Thucydides describes in detail up to the short-lived peace of 421 and on to 413, including the Athenian expedition to Sicily – a different war, as he says, 'on almost the same scale as that against the Peloponnesians' (6.1.1, also 6.36.4) – it can seem that only the move in 418 that a faction in Athens made to raise Argos and other allies to engage the Peloponnesians in the Peloponnese itself was directed to changing the shape of the conflict. But even then he does not emphasise the fact.

Sparta's first move beyond Attica in the summer of 430 was to take 1,000 hoplites on one hundred ships to try to bring the island of Zacyn-thos over from the Athenians, who in the previous summer had sent an expedition there and to Corcyra, Cephallonia and Acarnania to assure

---

[6] Lewis 1992a: 409 n. 109, always a careful historian, remarked that what Th. regards as the Athenians' choice of theatre in 425 'could be held to anticipate some of the features of the plan for 424' and that Th. may not mention the connection because 'he was probably already close enough to the highest strategic thinking for his silence to be taken seriously'. The question is whether there was any such thinking to be silent about.

their freedom of manoeuvre in the western sea (2.7.3). The Spartan intention was to frustrate this, although one can wonder whether they thought that success in just one of these places would have had the desired effect. Nonetheless, their fleet was the largest they were able to deploy again until 412, and it would seem to have been sufficient for the task at hand. But the Zacyntheans refused to come to terms. The Spartans' second move was a more spectacular failure. It was to gather funds, and although that might conceivably be seen as a preliminary to strategic thinking, it was similarly ill thought through. Five state envoys – three from Sparta itself; a man from Corinth who had been active against the Athenians at Potidaea; and one from Tegea, a city in the Peloponnese allied to Sparta – together with another from Argos travelling 'in a private capacity' were despatched to go across the Hellespont to seek money and military support from Persia. They travelled through Thrace to persuade its king, Sitalces, to break his alliance with Athens and use what they hoped would be his good offices to convey them across the water. But there were two Athenians at Sitalces' court, present no doubt to keep an eye on the Thracian's alliance with their city, and they asked his son, who had been given Athenian citizenship, to arrest the envoys and send them to Athens. This he did, and the Athenians 'put them all to death that very day, though they were given no trial and had things they wanted to say, and threw them into a pit' (2.67.4). The Athenians said that they were defending their own interests as the Spartans had done when they caught Athenian and allied traders sailing round the Peloponnese in merchant ships. Thucydides suspects that they had a particular dislike of the Corinthian among them, who had been in action at Potidaea. One might more generally observe that then as now, the courtesies granted to those who fought were not always extended to those who had not, especially if these had been engaged in 'intelligence' or what could be regarded as subversion. It is anyway difficult to see how the envoys could have succeeded. Even if the Persian king had been willing to consider support for the Peloponnesians, he would almost certainly have asked in return for control over the Greek cities in Anatolia; the Spartans seem not to have anticipated this, and having presented Sparta to the overseas Greeks as their liberator, could not now have agreed to it as easily as they were to decide they had to in the more pressing circumstances of 412–411. Sparta's one slight satisfaction in the fighting season of 430 would have come from an attack by locals on Amphilochian Argos on the western mainland, a city that was part of a standing alliance between Athens and the adjacent Acarnanians. But that failed also (2.68).

The more deliberate Athenian attempts at this time to raise money and deal with possible revolts in Chalcidice also achieved less than was hoped.

In the winter of 430–429 the Athenians sent an expedition to collect tribute from Greek settlements in south-western Anatolia (whether regular tribute or an exceptional exaction is not clear). Its leader and some of his force were killed, and it seems that no money was gathered. But some of Athens' unanticipated expenses were relieved when in the same winter the rebellious Potidaeans succumbed to more than two years of siege. Their grain was exhausted and in their hunger, Thucydides drily writes, 'some had even tasted each other' (2.70.1). To the annoyance of those in Athens who thought Potidaea deserved a harsh punishment, the generals receiving the Potidaeans' surrender agreed that both the Potideans and their mercenaries could leave, taking money enough for the journey and 'one garment apiece (two in the case of the women)' (2.70.3). Athens sent colonists to the now deserted city, and in the following summer decided to press for advantage in the area.

Despite some irritation with the lenience the generals had exercised at Potidaea, Athens put one of these men and perhaps the other two also in charge of a new force of one hundred cavalry and 2,000 hoplites. The object was to use a fifth column inside Spartolos, a city a few miles north of Potidaea, to bring it over. The interest, one presumes, was in tribute and finding somewhere safely to station a garrison. And it appeared to be a simple task. Both Thrace and Perdiccas' Macedonia were allies and there was no wider danger in the area. But Perdiccas failed to help the Athenians, and they were defeated. Their force was twice driven back both by cavalry and by peltasts, fighters common in the poorer 'Thraceward' regions who ran with javelins and a crescent-shaped wicker shield that gave them their name; too agile for the heavily armed infantry, these troops killed 430 Athenians and all three generals. The rest of the army took refuge in Potidaea and from there returned to Athens (2.79). In the past in centres of Greek settlement, confrontations of orderly infantries had come slowly to replace more improvised contests between lightly armed troops; it was now becoming clear that a hoplite infantry of non-professionals on short-term service was inadequate to the demands of quick strikes and surprise operations on unknown and often rough terrain. If the centre was to succeed against the periphery it was going to have to use the periphery's means.[7]

The Athenians will however have been relieved that the Peloponnesians, afraid perhaps of the plague, had decided not to invade Attica in 429. This together with the surrender of Potidaea will have encouraged them to attack Spartalos. Archidamos instead took Peloponnesians to Plataea. We do not know whose idea this was. Thucydides suggests that

---

[7] Wheeler and Strauss 2007: esp. 215.

Archidamos or others in Sparta wanted to make sure of the support of Thebes and the wider Boeotian federation (3.68.4), but one can wonder why they thought it necessary to do so. Perhaps Sparta made the move because it thought it was a costless way in an otherwise tactically empty summer in which to impress those in Sparta itself and Boeotia and other allied cities who might have begun to grumble about the repeated failure in Attica. Plataea was small and weak, and Archidamos or the ephors or whoever took the decision may have suspected that if the Athenians were unwilling to come out to defend their own city they would be unlikely to do so for an unimportant ally now. In itself, Plataea was unimportant. Its fate could have no consequence for the wider war. But attacking it now was an act of war, and as I have mentioned, the Spartans were to regret the support they gave now to Thebes. Even so, Thucydides had no need to describe events there at length. His reason for devoting three separate narratives to the siege of Plataea and its eventual obliteration, one in book 2 and two in book 3, must therefore be to impress the corollaries of war. And indeed, of the events we know about he could not have found a more vivid demonstration of unreason, betrayal and suffering; nor a more vivid demonstration also of frustration in a power that did not know how to press its larger war.

Archidamos started by wasting the land around Plataea, but stopped when envoys came out to talk to him. Thucydides gives their speech. They reminded Archidamos that after the battle at Plataea against the Persians in 479, the Greek commander, a Spartan, had made the conventional sacrifices, in that case to Zeus as god of freedom, 'and summoning together all the allies, granted the Plataeans the right to hold and occupy their land and city as an independent people [*autonomoi*]; no one was to take up arms against them without just cause or enslave them; and if they did so the allies present would do everything in their power to defend them. This', the Plataeans pointed out, 'was the reward your fathers gave us for the courage and commitment we showed at that time of danger. But you are doing just the reverse – you have come here in company with the Thebans, our worst enemies, intending to make us slaves' (2.71.2–3). Archidamos replied that this was a different war in which Sparta saw things differently, and that the Plataeans should do so too. Greece was now being liberated from other Greeks. 'Best of all would be for you to take your part in that liberation and stay true to the oaths yourselves; but failing that, do as we have already proposed: keep quiet and look after your own affairs, do not side with either party, treat both as friends and neither as enemies' (2.72.1). The Plataeans said that this would be impossible. Their wives and children were in Athens, the Athenians themselves might come and destroy the city's neutrality, and if they didn't, the Thebans would. Archidamos tried another tack. 'You hand over the city and your houses to us Spartans and indicate the boundaries of the land and the numbers of your trees and anything else that can be quantified exactly. Then take yourselves off wherever you like for the duration of the war. When it is finished we will give you back whatever we took over. Until then we will hold your property in trust on your behalf, working the land and paying whatever rent would prove sufficient for you' (2.72.3). It was a self-evidently suspicious offer. The Plataeans said that they would have to consult the Athenians, and Archidamos allowed them to. The Athenians said that they would not abandon them, urged them to stay where they were and hold to their existing alliance, and the Plataeans accepted. Archidamos addressed the justice of his cause to the gods and decided to take the city.

The episode shows how difficult it was for even the dominant land force in Greece to take an all but wholly unequipped opponent before the advent of artillery, and Thucydides relishes the detail. Archidamos began by raising a ramp of wood and earth against the city wall. The Plataeans started to undermine this from the inside and when they were thwarted, turned to tunnelling it out and to building a new wall behind the existing one. Archidamos then brought up siege engines, but the Plataeans found a way of dropping logs on the engines' rams. He seemed to have had no choice but to build a wall of his own and starve those inside it. He nonetheless thought that he might first try to fire the place. The wind was in his favour and the conflagration was fierce, but then it rained and the fires went out. Realising that he had now run out of options, Archidamos sent part of his army home and ordered the rest to construct a new wall round the town and dig a protective ditch beyond it. Inside, eighty Athenians and 510 Plataeans (400 men and 110 women to cook for them) would have to hold out as best they could. Thucydides continues the story in book 3.

Plataea was an opportunity presented to the Spartans by the Thebans. In the same summer, 429, they seized another presented to them by allies in the west of Greece. Thucydides may not have been as engaged with the fate of the Greeks who had settled there, let alone with the local 'barbarians', as he was with the Plataeans or the Greeks who lived on the borders of Macedonia and Thrace; the west was far from his own experience.[8] But his military interests were again aroused, and the venture reveals much about the lack of strategic thinking, the problems of

---

[8] Hornblower 1994: 196 describes Th.'s introduction to this episode (2.80–81.2) as 'a solid slab of clear and unaffected writing to remind us that [his] emotions are not always engaged very intensely'. This however is just his introduction.

distance between the cities and their commanders in the field, and above all, the dangers of relying on allies whose natural first interest was their own. In so far as the Spartans had had any idea of what to do other than try to bring the Athenians to a settlement or defeat them in Attica, it had been to impede their navy along the western coasts. The local Ambraciots and Chaonians now made a fresh suggestion. If the Spartans were to join them with infantry and ships, it would be easy to occupy Acarnania itself, the islands of Zacynthos and Cephallenia, and also Naupactos, an Athenian naval base that was threateningly situated on the northern coast of the Corinthian gulf. The Spartans were tempted. The Athenians could be seriously disadvantaged and a large part of the west would come over to their side. The Spartan Cnemos, who had led the expedition to Zacynthos the year before, still had his fleet and hoplites across the gulf, and was given command. Corinth, together with neighbouring Sicyon, agreed to provide more ships; it welcomed the opportunity to renew the connections it had with the Ambraciots, and it may also have hoped further to secure its passage through the gulf to the Adriatic.

The Ambraciots and Chaonians had explained that taking Acarnania would require ships to take the coast as well as men for the campaign on land. But Cnemos had 1,000 hoplites of his own and 2–3,000 more men from the Acarnanians' 'barbarian' enemies, together with a promise from Perdiccas (notwithstanding the Macedonian's present alliance with Athens) of a further 1,000, and without waiting for ships decided to cross the gulf directly and march on in. His object was the town of Stratos; if he could take that, he believed, the rest of Arcanania might fall. He assembled three divisions. As these advanced, however, they lost sight of each other, and neither Cnemos' own, made up of Spartans and local Greeks, nor the other noticed that in defiance of what had been agreed between them, the third, a crowd of proud Chaonians, had decided to rush ahead to take Stratos and claim the victory. The Stratians saw the Chaonians coming, ambushed them as they arrived, and when they panicked and fled, the second division fled also, and the Stratians then managed to pin down Cnemos' own. Perdiccas' force had not arrived and Cnemos had to move out of Acarnanian reach to a far south-western point (2.80.1–2, 2.81.3–2.82). It was another failure.

The Athenians had been similarly tempted. At the start of Cnemos' campaign against them, the Acarnanians had asked the Athenian admiral Phormio at Naupactos to bring his twenty ships in support. Phormio sent his regrets, explaining that he could not leave Naupactos undefended against the Corinthian fleet that would soon be sailing past to support Cnemos. This did soon appear, forty-seven ships against Phormio's twenty. It kept to the southern coast of the gulf, and Phormio tracked it from the other side. But for the troops on board to reach Cnemos in Acarnania (for whom they would in fact have been too late, for Cnemos was at this moment failing at Stratos) they had to cross to the north, and Phormio was able to engage them in the open sea. The Corinthian and Spartan commanders decided that it would be sensible to adopt the practised tactic of forming a circle, prows facing out, with a space inside for small vessels and a few fast triremes which could defend any gap in the circle and if necessary, attack the attackers. Phormio's response, which the Athenian navy had often used but which might not have been familiar to the unpractised Spartans or even (though this seems unlikely) to the Corinthians, was to sail his own ships round the enemy's circle to tighten it, relying on what he knew would be a breeze that came down the gulf each morning to unsettle the water and make it difficult for the captains to manoeuvre in tight formation. 'Prepositioning in trireme fighting was everything', Victor Hanson observes, and here it worked.[9] Thucydides the war reporter is at his best in describing how the encircled ships 'collided one with another and were fended off with poles; crews shouted warnings and abuse at each other and were quite unable to hear the word of command or their officers; and finally, in their inexperience men failed to lift their oars clear of the water in the swell and so rendered the ships unresponsive to their helmsmen. That was the critical moment for Phormio to give the signal and the Athenians fell on them' (2.84.3). They sank one of the commanders' ships and destroyed others at will as they came at them, with the result that in their confusion the rest fled. Phormio was a skilled tactician. In Sparta, it was assumed that there had been 'some lack of spirit' on their side, and three senior men were sent to advise Cnemos on a second engagement (2.85.2).

Phormio guessed that this would be coming, and asked Athens for more ships. A further twenty were despatched, but despite Phormio's evident need and what one might think would have been his standing in the city, their commander was ordered first to go to support a quite separate venture in Crete, which had hitherto been outside the war. It was, in the circumstances, a strange decision, and after doing what they were asked to do in Crete, the ships were delayed by bad weather and arrived only when the second engagement was over. Phormio therefore had only his original twenty against what were now seventy-seven. Both sets of crews were frightened; the Peloponnesians because of the previous rout, the Athenians because they were outnumbered. The commanders addressed their men in speeches that are remarkable only for the fact that Thucydides takes the liberty of writing them to respond to each other

---

[9] Hanson 2005: 242.

across a mile of water. The Spartans agreed that in what had been Sparta's first sea battle, their inexperience had defeated them. But they reminded the crews of the Spartan spirit and the fact that they now had numbers. Phormio reminded his men of their experience, stressed the importance of discipline, not least in keeping their voices down so that they could hear the navarchs' orders, and explained his tactics for what lay ahead. He would have preferred, he said, to engage the enemy in clear water as before, but the numbers would tell against that; he would therefore keep to the shore hoping, he all but openly confessed, for the best, then rose to a pardonable exaggeration. 'This is a momentous contest for you', he told the crews; 'either you shatter the hopes the Peloponnesians have in their fleet or you bring closer to home the Athenian nightmare' – the nightmare that Pericles had in public at least not appeared to contemplate – 'of losing control of the sea' (2.86.6–2.89).

In the event, Phormio was saved by the quick thinking of one of his officers. He knew that he had to get back to protect Naupactos, and the two fleets tracked each other from each side of the gulf until the Peloponnesians turned across to attack. Phormio immediately lost nine ships (one can wonder whether his reputation was wholly deserved) and the remaining eleven raced to Naupactos, where the first few to arrive turned round and lined up to defend themselves from their pursuers. The last one to arrive was in danger of being lost to the leading Peloponnesian, but its captain, seeing a merchant ship anchored ahead, had the presence of mind to swerve around this and sink his pursuer. Thinking that victory was already theirs and being in poor order, in some cases having actually stopped rowing, the Peloponnesians who were following took fright and sped off to the southern coast. The Spartan general on the ship that had been rammed killed himself – Thucydides names him, Timocrates, 'strength in honour', he was washed up later at Naupactos – and the rest of the fleet made its way back to Corinth under cover of darkness (2.90–2).[10]

Once there, it was tempted by Megarians. Megara had forty ships at Nisaea, on the eastern side of the isthmus, a little more than 20 miles by sea from Athens' undefended port at the Piraeus and the Megarians,

[10] De Romilly 2012: 80–7 saw this episode as a model of rational reconstruction in Th. The two speeches present alternative possibilities, roughly numbers against skill or experience; each makes predictions and, even allowing for the intrusion of chance, one is proved right, the other wrong. The Peloponnesians need not have panicked at the end, though Phormio had predicted that they would. But he might not have won if the opportunity offered by the anchored vessel had not been taken. That itself of course was evidence of skill. But it was a more close-run thing than de Romilly, insistent on Th.'s rational reconstruction of reasoning in fact, allows. And the success was anyway tactical, not strategic.

who had boats but no crews, persuaded the Spartans to attack. The Peloponnesian commanders could not resist, and Thucydides cannot resist the detail. Indeed in what for him is a rare hint of things to come, he makes a point of again mentioning Brasidas, one of the three advisers who had previously been sent to Cnemos from Sparta and the first man there to have been publicly commended in the war for having beaten off Athenians at Methone in the south-western Peloponnese (2.25.3). The Peloponnesians were to sail in the Megarian ships from Nisaea at night, and the crews walked the 3 miles or so across the isthmus to board them there, each carrying his oar, the loop of leather that secured his oar to the ship and the cushion he needed to stop him sliding on his seat.

It was not an entirely foolish venture. The force was small, but the Athenians would probably have noticed the preparation of anything more elaborate, and a surprise attack might just have succeeded. Ships in the Piraeus and the port itself could have been damaged, and although Thucydides does not say so, the Spartans may even have hoped (against hope, he might have added) that the Athenians might offer the concession that invasions on land were failing to secure. But almost as soon as the crews had set off from Nisaea 'they had become frightened of the dangers involved' ('a wind', Thucydides adds, 'is supposed to have held them up as well') and sailed instead to the eastern point of Salamis, an island opposite the Piraeus, where the Athenians, the Megarians might have thought to tell them, had a station to warn of just such a raid from Nisaea. The station was taken off guard, the Peloponnesians took its three ships, and then in a tactically idle but habitual diversion, proceeded to start to waste the territory (2.93.4). This gave the Athenian station time to send a signal by fire to the Piraeus; Athenians there, whose immediate thought was that the port was already under attack, were able to organise a response; and the Peloponnesians, worried now about their vessels, which had been poorly maintained and were taking water, returned to Nisaea. Athens subsequently placed a permanent guard in the Piraeus and henceforth made sure to close it when there was no traffic.

Much later in the war, Thucydides does not here say, a Peloponnesian squadron was to have another chance to take the port. That was at a moment when Athens had few ships there and would have had to bring some back to defend themselves, thus suffering a delay and weakening themselves elsewhere. 'Not only in this but in many other things', Hobbes translates Thucydides to write on this later occasion, the Spartans 'were the most commodious enemies to the Athenians to war withal. For being of most different humours, the one swift, the other slow; the one adventurous, the other timorous; the Spartans gave them great advantage, especially when their greatness was by sea' (8.96.5). As I later explain, in this later instance the Spartan fleet had an easier and more satisfyingly damaging objective at Euboea.

The ventures so far on each side in 430–429 may have been ill-considered. But the Spartans and Athenians continued in the absence of other possibilities to seek what advantage they could from third parties. In the north, the Athenians had managed to save Potidaea but had been defeated elsewhere in Chalcidice and decided to use Thracian discontents with Macedonia to recover. The Thracean kingdom stretched from the Danube down the western coast of the Black Sea and along the northern coast of the sea of Marmara and the Aegean to the river Strymon at the eastern border of Macedonia, northwards from the Aegean into the mountains of what is now southern Bulgaria. It could only in the loosest sense be described as a state. But the Persians had relinquished their power over its southern parts at the beginning of the century and the Odrysians (from Odrysa, the modern Edirne in European Turkey) had begun to try to unify it. Sitalces' father had started the task, and Sitalces was continuing it. It was not easy. The area included a number of mutually antagonistic peoples of whom Herodotus had observed that 'if they were ruled by a single person or had a common purpose . . . would be invincible and would be by far the most powerful nation in the world'. That, Herodotus added, 'was impossible' (5.3.1).[11] In the event, he was right; what was in effect the imperial kingdom of Odrysian Thrace was to reach its height under Sitalces' son and then divide. But Sitalces now was determined. One can suppose that he actually had a strategy, and Athens may unusually have had one also: it would have suited Sitalces' external security to have an alliance with Athens' power in the Aegean and suited Athens to be as sure as it could be of its summer grain route from the northern coasts of the Black Sea. It would also have suited each to have the support of the other in the event of difficulty with Macedonia. At the beginning of the winter of 429–428, Sitalces agreed with the Athenians to make a move against Perdiccas there.

Both had previously believed that they had understandings with Perdiccas: Athens a formal alliance, Thrace a promise. But Perdiccas had not proved constant. He had recently failed to help the Athenians in Chalcidice and had committed himself, it turned out idly, to help the Spartans take Acarnania. To Sitalces, he had given an undertaking which no source explains but which Thucydides says required Sitalces to reconcile him with Athens and withdraw support for his brother Philip in

---

[11] At the end of a chapter of his own on the Odrysians and other peoples in Thrace, Th. uses the same phrase to describe the Scythians on the steppes to the north of the Black Sea (3.97.6).

Macedonia itself; Perdiccas had not obliged Sitalces either. Sitalces himself had meanwhile promised to help Athens in Chalcidice. It may indeed have been Athens' defeat there in the previous summer that prompted his willingness to move, for he took with him the Athenian envoys who had been visiting him and the Athenian general Hagnon, says Thucydides, 'as leader'. He also had with him Philip's son Amyntas, with whom he now intended, Philip having died, to replace Perdiccas. He set off from his own area in Thrace and moved inland across the Rhodope mountains to gather men and come down into Macedonia from the north. 'Many of the independent Thracians joined the army unbidden in the hope of plunder, so that the total number is reported to have been not less than 150,000. The greater part of these were infantry and about a third cavalry. The Odysians themselves supplied the most of the cavalry... Of the infantry, the fiercest fighting force were the independent tribes of swordsmen who came down from Rhodope, while the rest of the mixed mob that followed behind was frightening mostly because of its number' (2.98.3–4). (Thucydides could share the Greeks' disdain for what they regarded as less civilised peoples.)

The Macedonians had no way of resisting this. But Sitalces stopped short of Chalcidice and adjacent Bottiaea, expecting the Athenians to meet him there. They did not come; even if there was a common strategy in the move, there seems to have been no reassuring communication between Hagnon and Athens; Thucydides says that the Athenians had not been convinced that Sitalces would come himself. Sitalces gave up waiting and moved down to the peninsulas to let his men pillage; Greeks as far south as Thermopylae and some of Athens' enemies elsewhere, it is said, began to fear that he might reach them. But Sitalces had now been in Macedonia for a month and winter was pressing (one might ask why someone from a region where winter invariably bit hard would have set off when he did) and the ever agile Perdiccas, unable to resist by force of arms, lit upon the idea of getting him to desist by offering his sister's hand to Sitalces' nephew Seuthes, who was second to Sitalces in power. Seuthes was attracted by the proposition, persuaded his uncle to withdraw, and the promise was one that Perdiccas kept (2.99–101). (Thucydides says no more about the two Thracians until briefly mentioning Sitalces' death in a dispute in Thrace itself in the winter of 424–423 and Seuthes succeeding him (4.101.50).) In not turning up, the Athenians had achieved exactly the opposite of what they intended.

The only other event that Thucydides reports in the winter of 429–428 was a brief and on its own terms successful expedition by Phormio to Acarnania. Cnemos' force of Peloponnesians and local 'barbarians' had failed there in the summer, but the Athenians evidently wanted to be sure that their alliance was as secure as they could make it. Phormio took a modest contingent of 400 Athenian hoplites and a further 400 Messenians (descendants of those whom the Athenians had settled in Naupactos) to expel 'men regarded as unreliable' from Stratos and other places; he had to leave an area of resistance in the west, it being impracticable to campaign in the marshes there in winter. In the spring, he sailed back to Athens with the Peloponnesian ships that he had captured after the battles in the gulf and the Peloponnesians (other than slaves) whom he had taken prisoner for the purpose of exchange in Athens. 'So this winter ended and with it the third year of the war Thucydides wrote' (2.102–3). A few weeks later, in the early summer of 428, Archidamos once again led a Peloponnesian force into Attica. As before, Thucydides writes, Athenian cavalry prevented the invaders' lightly armed troops from approaching too close to the city (3.1.2). But he records nothing more, and the force may have returned within twenty-five or thirty days. The invasion had failed again.

By the start of the fourth year of the war therefore, the early summer of 428, neither side was any further forward. Neither had a strategy for the wider conflict because neither could see what that could be. If either was thinking ahead, Thucydides does not say so, and if one presumes that he would have been interested if either was, it is not unreasonable to infer that they were not. Each was unable effectively to take the war to the other and in frustration was looking to its allies – allies who had a shrewd sense of the two larger powers' susceptibilities but who themselves lacked capacity, were understandably pursuing interests of their own and could not always be relied upon.

7   Speech and other events 428–427

Thucydides' set pieces on events in the fourth and fifth years of the war turn on the reaction of one or other of the two warring powers to their allies. A rebellion in the city of Mytilene on Lesbos was indicative of those states who sought to take advantage of the wider conflict to recover their autonomy; a debate in Athens about how to deal with this resistance reveals more clearly than anything else in Thucydides how the Athenians now saw themselves in relation to their dominion. A descent into internal war in Corcyra indicated how the wider war was inciting factions within the lesser Greek cities to gain advantage over each other. And Sparta's decision to destroy Plataea is in good part explained by its wish to please Thebes. Each reveals how fear, frustration and rage in the two large powers were offering opportunities to lesser states that brought suffering on these states themselves. Each also exposes the growing distance between what was said and done. Thucydides writes speech to show what men were thinking and how they wished to persuade others to think and act. He makes it clear that on Plataea and Mytilene, speech had as little impact on what was done as it did in most of the rest of his story. He makes it clear also that the war of words as well as actions in Corcyra, to be repeated, he says, in other internal wars, was one in which those speaking were not actually *thinking* at all.

If anyone in the fifth century had said that attempts at truthfulness are the first casualty of war – and had meant what we do when we speak of truthfulness rather than, as contemporaries might have done, 'things not forgotten' – it might have been Thucydides. The idea of truthfulness itself of course, however it may have been expressed, would not have been new. It will have been obvious that no one could co-operate with anyone else without relying on it and equally obvious that those who were existentially threatened by others would be driven to say whatever they believed they had to to survive. Truthfulness depends on a shared purpose, and in exchanges in which one party must die or be 'enslaved' there can plainly be none.[1] Physical survival is the limiting case. The survival of identities, beliefs and interests will often have been at issue also, and where they were, there will have been politics, war and pervasive deceit. In the debate at Athens concerning what to do about the rebels at Mytilene, one of the two men whose speeches Thucydides gives went so far as to say that those who spoke in the agonistic exchanges in the assembly in Athens itself had 'to lie to be credible' (3.43.3). And fear, anger and hope can cause men to divide within themselves and slide into self-deception.

Following a stand-off with the Athenians at Mytilene – Athens feared that it might not have had sufficient force to take the city and had been late in responding to rebellion – the Spartans, says Thucydides, 'told' those speaking for the rebels to make their case to those who had gathered at the games in Olympia in the summer of 428. To an audience that will have included Athenians, the Mytilenaeans explained that they had wanted to leave the Athenian league before the war but that Sparta had shown no interest, that they were now trying again, and that the Athenians were blockading them (3.2–6, 3.8). Their speech was elaborately phrased, is written indeed in a recognisably Thucydidean style (3.9–14). But the speakers (Thucydides again makes them plural) knew that they had to impress their good faith and there is no reason to doubt that Thucydides caught what he described in book 1 as the 'overall intention' in what they said.

The Mytilenaeans explained that they wanted to break an alliance that had been founded on mutual fear. When two sides fear each other equally, they said, there is a sound basis for trust. (Thucydides writes them to have said that this is 'the only basis', which was odd when they were seeking the support of an audience that would have needed some other reason to trust them now (3.11.2).) In their relations with Athens, the Mytilenaeans said, trust had gone. Sparta's withdrawal from Ionia and the Aegean after 479 had made it sensible to form a league with the Athenians against any new move from Persia, but this had become oppressive to the smaller states and threatened now to oppress those like Mytilene that were larger and less dependent, though the speakers did not say how it had. What they did say was that they were now seeking an alliance of a different kind, 'well-founded' on good faith (3.10.1). They were withdrawing from the ranks of the oppressed in order not to be colluding with Athens to harm others and rebelling from Athens in order not to be harmed themselves.

---

[1] On truthfulness, its distinction from truth, its importance in survival and what it depends on, Williams 2002. The Plataeans' betrayal, Ch. 5 above.

(They naturally did not remind their audience that it was Mytilenaeans, with Chians, who had helped Athens suppress the revolt on Samos in 440 (1.116.1), which the Spartans may have thought of supporting. Nor did they mention that Chios, which stood in a similar relation to Athens, was expressing no discontent now.) They said that their predicament was acute, that their need for support was urgent, and that it was in the Peloponnesians' interest to offer it: Sparta would recover its reputation for liberating the Greeks, other states under Athens' dominion would be encouraged to break away, and because Athenian ships would be occupied with the Peloponnesians in the northern Aegean, the Spartans would at last be able to conquer Attica and thereby acquire power over the Athenian navy (3.13.1–7). The war would be over.[2]

The case was as fanciful as those that other secondary powers had made. The Spartans nevertheless agreed to what they were asking. This is not to say that they had been persuaded. It is not impossible to imagine that they had already decided to act and had instructed the Mytilenaeans to speak to the wide audience at Olympia in order to advertise Sparta's willingness to liberate the Greeks. They now declared that they would take the Mytilenaeans into their alliance and going beyond the issue of Mytilene itself, instructed their existing allies to send the usual quota of troops to the isthmus (two-thirds of the number each could raise) and prepare for a new invasion of Attica; they also considered an attack on Athens from the sea and asked for ships. The allies however refused to send any men; it was late in the summer and their troops, unlike the Spartans' own, were part-time and required to harvest fruit at home. The confidence of the Spartans themselves nevertheless made it clear to the Athenians that they were regarded as weak, and the Athenians at once responded by raiding the isthmus and preparing a naval expedition of their own to the Peloponnese. This, says Thucydides, suggested to the Spartans that what the Mytilenaeans had said about the Athenians was not true (it can also suggest that the Spartans' intelligence was poor) and that they ought to call off their announced expedition to Attica. Athens meanwhile, seeing that a Mytilenaean attack on the still loyal city of Methynma on Lesbos had come to nothing, sent 1,000 hoplites to cut Mytilene itself off by land as well as sea. Worried about the expense, they raised 200 talents from a special tax and sent a small force to raise contributions in Anatolia, the leaders of which, as had happened two years before, were murdered. The Spartans were by the end of the following winter able to send forty ships.

---

[2] An excellent analysis of what Konstan 2001: 319 n. 22 briskly dismisses as the Mytileneans' 'waffling' in Macleod 1983c: 88–92, and Hornblower *CT* I: 391–2.

Thucydides records nothing more on Mytilene until the start of the spring of 427, by which time the Spartans had managed to insert a man there. Having learnt from him that Spartan help was on its way, the rebels decided not to come to terms with the Athenians. The man acting for the under-aged son of the exiled king from the other royal line in Sparta (Archidamos may have been ill), leading the revived invasion of Attica, waited to hear that the Spartan ships had arrived at Lesbos, which his troops could more quickly reach from Attica. But the commander of these ships, Alcidas, had no appetite for an encounter and loitered. Mytilene meanwhile was running out of food, and Salaithos, the man whom the Spartans had inserted, decided to issue arms to 'the people' there so that they could attack the Athenians in the city themselves. It was a bad mistake. The people at once asked for a fair distribution of the remaining food and declared that they would come to terms with the Athenians if this was not forthcoming. The leaders of the rebellion accepted defeat, the Athenian commander Paches brought his troops into Mytilene, assured the rebels who had taken refuge at an altar that they would be safe, and asked Athens for instructions (3.28). Alcidas, zig-zagging across the sea to the south, reached the Anatolian coast a full week later; he had heard that the rebellion at Mytilene had failed and wanted to confirm that it had. An Elean travelling with him suggested that he might nonetheless make a useful attack on Mytilene at night (3.30). (Elis, whose territory included Olympia, was a member of the Peloponnesian league.) Alcidas was not persuaded, and also resisted a suggestion from Greek Ionians that he raise a revolt in cities there to divert the Athenians and deny them resources. He wanted to get back to the Peloponnese.

Calling in at Ephesos, he started to slaughter prisoners he had taken along the way, prompting some Samians there to point out 'that this was a poor way to be liberating Greece – massacring men who had never raised a hand against him and were not his enemies, and were allies of the Athenians only under duress; if he didn't stop he would convert few of his enemies into friends but would make many more friends into enemies' (3.32.2). Alcidas took the point, released the captives he had, and continued on his flight. Athens' two state triremes happened to be in the area and spotted his ships; not themselves being in a position to take these, they alerted Paches, who used his own to chase Alcidas beyond a point from which he would be unlikely to return. (Thucydides remarks that Paches was relieved not to have caught the Spartan squadron; that would have brought the trouble of custody.) Paches, having himself stopped to put down a dispute in another city on the Ionian coast with duplicity and no little cruelty, despatched Salaithos and leaders of the rebellion at Mytilene to Athens. The Athenians executed Salaithos, whose desperate last card had been to promise that he could persuade the Spartans to lift the siege at Plataea, 'debated what to do about the other men and in their anger decided to kill not only the ones there in Athens but also the whole adult male population of Mytilene, and to enslave the women and children. They particularly condemned the revolt', Thucydides explains, 'because the Mytilenaeans had so staged it despite not being subjects like the others' (which the Mytilenaeans had feared) 'and what made the Athenians really furious was the fact that Peloponnesian ships had dared to venture into Ionia to support them; that, in their view, made it look as though the revolt was not just the result of a sudden decision. They therefore sent a trireme to convey the news of this decision to Paches, with orders to kill off the Mytilenaeans without delay' (3.29–35, 3.36.2–3).

It had been a catalogue of misjudgements. The Spartans were willing to act for the Mytilenaeans but misjudged the Athenians; the Mytilenaeans misjudged the Methymnians on Lesbos, whom they could not get to submit; the Spartans misjudged Alcidas; Alcidas misjudged the reaction to executing the men he had taken prisoner on his voyage; and Salaithos misjudged the mood of ordinary Mytilenaeans. Thucydides reveals that fear, anger and wishful thinking had clouded the minds of almost all. Only Paches and 'the people' in Mytilene had seen things clearly. But even if anyone had remembered how the Athenians had reacted to a revolt on Samos twelve years before, they may not have expected Athens to order the execution of every last man and the sale of all the women and children into slavery; even some Athenians thought that they had been too hasty in voting for 'the savage and extreme decision to destroy an entire city rather than just those directly responsible' for the revolt (3.36.4). We do not know what moved them, but from what was said the next day, one suspects it was remorse. Mytilenaean envoys in Athens and a number of citizens persuaded the authorities to call a second assembly to reconsider the decision. Thucydides writes the speeches that were given at this by Cleon, whom he describes as the most forceful leader in the city at the time and the most influential, and an otherwise unknown Diodotos. In the first debate, Cleon had spoken in favour of the decision, Diodotos against it. In the second, both elaborated on their positions, each now prefacing what he said with sharp and illuminating remarks on the power of speech itself. As June Allison has said, this was an exquisite opportunity for Thucydides. He had characters who were themselves deliberating on the politics of deliberation.[3]

Cleon may have been crude, and commentators have taken Thucydides to be recoiling against him. But Thucydides makes few men simple and

[3] Allison 1997: 83.

shows Cleon also to have been able. Choosing to overlook the fact that the citizens had changed their own minds between the first assembly and the second, Cleon argued that they should 'not be so carried away by cleverness and contests of wit' to make them act against their own judgement, and proceeded himself to carry them back. Witty himself, he told them that 'you have got used to being spectators of words and listening to deeds. You judge the feasibility of future projects from the performances of good speakers, and the facts of past events from the speeches of clever critics, preferring to believe in what you hear rather than in the deeds you can actually witness. You are champions at being deceived by novelties in argument and in your reluctance to go along with received opinions, slaves as you are to fashions for the extraordinary and sceptics of the familiar. The greatest ambition of each of you is himself to be an orator, or failing that to participate in competition with those who make these speeches by trying to appear quick on the uptake and being the first to applaud a sharp remark. You are as eager to anticipate what will be said as you are slow to foresee its consequences. Indeed you are seeking, one could say, some world other than the one we actually live in and you pay too little heed to the here and now' (3.37.5, 3.38.4–7). The delights of oratory cancel common sense, Cleon was saying, and Thucydides would have agreed. Cleon was now using the art of the one to re-implant the other.

Diodotos took Cleon on words at his word. 'I have no fault to find with those who propose to reopen the debate about Mytilene, and I do not support those who object to reconsidering matters of real importance several times over. On the contrary', continued Diodotos, with whom on this Thucydides would also have agreed, 'the two things I consider most prejudicial to good counsel are haste and high emotion: the latter usually goes with folly, the former with crude and shallow judgement. As for words and speeches', he continues, 'anyone who argues seriously that they should not guide our actions is either stupid or has some personal interest at stake: stupid, if he thinks there is any other way to explore the future in all its uncertainty; self-interested, if he wants to argue some discreditable case but concludes that though he cannot speak well enough to carry a bad cause he can slander well enough to intimidate both the opposing speakers and the audience' (3.42.1–2). But it's true, conceded Diodotos in response to what Cleon was suggesting, that all speakers are thought to be in some way self-interested. 'It has therefore come about that good advice honestly given has become as suspect as bad, and the result is that just as the person who wants to urge some dire proposal resorts to deceit to win over the people, so the person with better policies must lie to be credible. This is therefore the only city so clever that it is impossible to do good here openly and without deceit' (3.43.2–3). It was clever of Diodotos to disarm his audience so. And in case anyone should at once suspect what he was himself about to propose, he emphasised that he was taking a long view of the likely consequences of the decision at issue.

In fact the assembly had already had a long view from Cleon, who in substance, if not tone, echoed Pericles. 'I myself haven't changed my mind at all, and I wonder at those who now want to reopen the ... debate' (3.38.1, cf. 2.61.2). 'The empire you hold is a tyranny, and one imposed on unwilling subjects who for their part plot against you. They accept your rule not because of any sacrifices you may make to please them but because of the superiority that derives from your own strength rather than from their goodwill' (3.37.2, cf. 2.63.2). Neither compassion nor fairness therefore, let alone – he continued in fine oratorical form – your love of fine speeches should affect you. The situation is clear. If what the Mytilenaeans are doing is right, you are wrong. But Athens needs its dominion. If you allow one state to secede, others will think that they can do so too, and you will find yourself in a general war with your allies. To believe otherwise, he said, is to 'give the empire up and go round doing good in safety' (3.40.4). 'Let them now be punished, therefore, in the way the crime deserves, and do not let the blame fall on the ruling few while you absolve the people. They all joined in attacking you, though if they had taken our side they could now be back in possession of their city. They judged, however, that siding with the rulers presented the safer option and so joined in the revolt with them' (3.39.6). It is justice as retribution, not fairness, that's at issue and is in our interests.

Cleon and Diodotos were markedly less hypocritical than the Athenian speakers had been about Athenian power at Sparta in the autumn of 432, right though those men had been to say that subjects who had been treated well would be more angry than if they had not been (1.77.1–5). The Mytilenaeans themselves had agreed with this and so did Cleon; they 'ought never to have been privileged by us over the other states from the start, and they would not then have got so much above themselves' (3.39.5). Diodotos agreed that neither compassion nor fairness was at issue. But nor were retribution or deterrence. 'We are not engaged in a legal dispute with them about rights and wrongs', and you, citizens, should set anger and pity aside (3.44.4). This is a strictly political debate about how best the Mytilenaeans can serve our interests, and destroying them does not. You should understand, Diodotos went on, that they had erred. 'In every case it is desire and hope that do the greatest damage: desire leading and hope following; the one conceiving the project, the other suggesting that good fortune will smooth the way; and so these invisible forces count for more than the threats we can actually see' (3.44.5). It is not words that obscure, he said, but the impulse behind them. Beyond these 'invisible forces', Diodotos continued, 'fortune too plays an equal part in the motivation. She can present herself unexpectedly and so tempt individuals (and cities too) to take risks even beyond their means when the stakes are highest – freedom versus the rule of others – and when the individual as one of a crowd is deceived into overestimating his own powers. In a word, it is a fact of human nature – and it is very naive of anyone to believe otherwise – that when people are really committed in their hearts to doing something, they cannot be deterred by force of law or any other threat' (3.45.6). The destruction of one ally would not therefore deter the rest. It would be more sensible to allow Mytilene to 'come to terms while it still has the capacity to refund our expenses and resume its contributions for the future' (3.46.2). Anyway, said Diodotos, Cleon was wrong to include 'the common people' in the conspiracy at Mytilene;[4] they had been forced into acting as they have (which may have been true) and were everywhere loyal to Athens (which was probably unknowable). 'What you should do, even if they were guilty, is pretend that they were not, to prevent the only faction still loyal to us from becoming hostile.' Truth, transparency and political good sense, he was saying again, do not always coincide. It is in our interest to put interest before justice by appearing to be just. 'Put on trial at your leisure the Mytilenaeans whom Paches identified as the guilty ones and sent over [to Athens], and let the rest live their lives' (3.47.2, 4; 3.48.1).

Democracy, Cleon had declared at the start of his speech, is incapable of ruling subjects (3.37.1). Subjects are not citizens, and it is inappropriate to discuss terms of agreement with them. Diodotos agreed, and was more consistent than Cleon and those who had defended Athens' dominion at Sparta in 432 in openly dismissing the substance of justice. Pericles also had avoided it. What mattered was maintaining Athens' dominion. The difference between Cleon and Diodotos was merely that one was afraid of what might follow if Athens did not use extreme force, the other of what might follow if it did. In the event, the vote at the second assembly went narrowly in favour of Diodotos, but Thucydides is careful not to say that it did so for Diodotos' reasons. He enjoys describing how the second decision was conveyed to Mytilene with unusual speed, the men eating a mess of barley, oil and wine on the move and taking it in turns to sleep, the ship, meeting no headwind, arriving just in time to stop

---

[4] The usual belief, Konstan 2001: 289 n. 58.

Paches implementing the first.[5] 'So close did Mytilene come to disaster' (3.49.3). As it was, the Athenians put the Mytilenaeans in Athens to death and had Mytilene's walls pulled down. They confiscated its ships, imposed a monetary tribute, put its settlements under Athenian control and divided the land outside Methymna into 3,000 plots: 300 for the gods, whose concerns would be attended to by Athenians, the rest for colonists from Athens to rent to their previous owners. These measures left Chios as the last autonomous state in what no one now regarded as an Athenian league.

But even if it was a change of mood rather than force of argument (together with the dawdling of the first ship and the lack of wind against the second) that had prevented the execution of all the men at Mytilene and the enslavement of the women and children there, the occasion of a second debate had at least allowed a change to prevail. At Plataea, as the Plataeans concede at the start of their last encounter, their death was already decided, and their speech and those of the Spartans and attendant Thebans, in which all, in face of the fact, dissemble, was grimly idle. Thucydides has already explained in compelling detail how in the winter of 428–427, with careful preparation on a night of wind and rain and no moon, 212 individuals (120 Plataeans, the rest Athenians) had managed to get over the walls that Archidamos had built and reach Athens. The Athenians had not themselves been willing to relieve the siege, but were pleased to receive the Plataeans who had escaped and confer a form of citizenship on them (3.20–4). By the end of the summer of 427, the 200 Plataeans and twenty-five Athenians who remained in the city could hold out no longer and surrendered to the Spartans.[6]

The Spartan commander (whom Thucydides does not name) said that he would punish 'the guilty' and see that no harm came to the rest. He fed those who were starving, waited for no fewer than five judges to arrive from Sparta, and when they had, asked the Plataeans a single question:

---

[5] It is an important indication of Th.'s tone, Mynott notes, that the adjective *allokoton* for the first mission means 'strange, unusual, uncouth, against the grain, unwelcome', less morally disapproving than those chosen by some other modern translators. This apart, one wonders how Paches would have been able actually to carry out a massacre on the scale demanded by the first assembly; Mytilene in 427 was not a French village harbouring members of the resistance in 1944, and the Athenians did not have automatic weapons. Polly Low tells me that the sources are almost universally silent on how mass killings were accomplished in the fifth century.

[6] Th. liked numbers when he could get them. Those here however do not exactly square with those he gives in book 2. But his account of the escape (in which the Plataeans again took advantage of a dark night and heavy rain) is as detailed and vivid as his description of the imposition of the siege. Both are fine examples of a different kind of set piece in the text. The history and nature of Plataean citizenship at Athens is unclear: 3.55.3 and Hornblower *CT* I: 449–50.

had they done anything in the present conflict to benefit Sparta and its allies (3.52)?[7] Two Plataeans (one called Lacon, which suggests a past connection with Sparta) replied. They had no illusions. They said at the start that they were aware that the trial was a matter of life and death, doubted whether the judges were impartial, knew that the Spartans were acting to please a third party, and feared that the outcome had been decided. 'What we say in response to that "short question" of yours, as to whether we have rendered any benefit to the Spartans and their allies in this war, is that if you put the question to us as your enemies then you were not wronged just because you received no positive benefits from us; but if you are thinking of us as friends you yourselves are the ones more at fault for taking the war to us' (3.54.2). The Spartans' question was about advantage. The Plataeans took the issue to be one of justice. In framing the occasion as a trial, the Spartans had invited that. The Plataeans knew that this was a show, put on by the Spartans for themselves and the Thebans, and the Spartans will have known they knew. Nonetheless, justice was the Plataeans' only suit, and they could not but press it. They knew that it would not succeed and all but confessed the fact towards the end of a speech which they knew they had stretched to a pitiable length; 'we must bring this speech to an end, however difficult that is for men in our situation, since it brings ever closer the moment of mortal danger' (3.59.3).[8]

It was the Spartans, said the Plataeans, who had suggested that they should ally with the Athenians at the end of the Persian war. And unlike the Thebans, they had gone on to fight with the Spartans, Athenians and other Greeks against the Persians. They had sent men to help Sparta against the revolt of Messenian helots. And they had kept their alliance with the Athenians as a defence against the Thebans. 'We have been rejected by everyone – we Plataeans who gave everything and more for Greece – and we are now deserted and unprotected. Not one of our former allies is here to help us, and you Spartans, our only hope, are frail friends, we fear' (3.57.4). Balance our previous merit, they argued, against our present offence, if it is one, and think also of yourselves. 'This course would not befit your reputation . . . neither the offence against the common tradition of the Greeks and against your ancestors, nor the destruction of us, your benefactors' – in Plataea, where one of your generals promised us lasting honour and your war dead are buried in a

---

[7] Herodotus 1.67 describes five *agathoergoi* ('benefactors') who each year passed out of the ranks of knights and were occupied in missions for Sparta.

[8] Th., 'like the tragedians, here and often uses rhetorical skills in order that they should be seen to fail; that not only heightens the pathos but also draws our attention to the reasons why they fail', Macleod 1983g: 113.

place we preserve as sacred – 'to satisfy the private enmity of others when you yourselves have not been wronged. Instead, you should spare us and let your hearts be moved to regard us with compassion and restraint; fix your minds not only on the terrible fate we shall suffer, but also on the manner of men we are who would suffer it, and the vagaries of misfortune which may at any time afflict even the innocent' (3.59.1).

The Spartans had no question for the Thebans who were also present, and the Thebans had not intended to speak. Nor would they have asked to, they explained to the Spartans, 'if these men had actually answered your question briefly instead of turning on us with their accusations, mounting a long defence of themselves on matters irrelevant to the issue in hand and against charges that were never made, and also praising themselves for things no-one had ever criticised' (3.61.1); if, that is, they had talked of advantage, in which pity has no place, rather than justice. But the Thebans were anxious lest the Spartans should start to waver, and briskly defended themselves. Their charge against the Plataeans' alliance with Athens was that Plataea had not been content with protection but willingly supported Athens' aggression against Aegina and Boeotia itself. The Thebans' own past friendship with the Persians counted for nothing now; it had been engineered by an unlawful government and imposed without consent. Against the accusation of aggression against Plataea itself, they reminded the Spartans that they had themselves been invited into Plataea by those of its own citizens who cared for its future and had subsequently been betrayed over an agreement to return Theban prisoners if the Thebans would stop attacking Plataeans outside the walls, neither of which the Plataeans had deigned to mention in their present speech. 'Pity', the Thebans said to the Spartans, 'is due more to those who do not deserve their suffering, but when men suffer just deserts, as these do, there is by contrast cause for celebration. As for their present desolation, that is of their own making. The better allies they rejected of their own free will. They broke the law, without provocation on our part, moved more by hatred than by justice in their decision, and they have not paid back a compensating penalty.'

'Do not let us be pushed aside by their words', the Thebans concluded to the Spartans. 'Show by example to the Greeks that you set before them a contest not of words but of deeds, and that in the case of good deeds a short answer suffices, but in the case of misdeeds speeches tricked out with words are just a concealment. But if leaders will only do what you are now doing – summarising the essential question for everyone and then passing judgement – there will be less seeking after fine words to justify foul deeds' (3.67.4, 3.67.6–7). The Spartans repeated that the Plataeans had refused neutrality and since none among them was able to say that he had done anything to help Sparta in the war, the Spartans led them and the Athenians who were present with them off to be executed, took the women into slavery, and after allowing some displaced Megarians to live there for a while, razed what there was, built a hostel for visitors to a sanctuary on the site, and rented the rest of the land to the Thebans.[9] 'In practically every respect', writes Thucydides, 'this Spartan antipathy to the Plataeans arose from their wish to please the Thebans, since the Spartans thought they might be useful to them at this point in the war' (3.68.4). And actions, as the Thebans said they should, had trumped words.

Nonetheless, the arguments over Plataea and Mytilene were replete with moral claims grounded on selective views of the past, including the claim that the past supported no claim. Convention required such arguments and, where they could, speakers made them. (Commentators suggest that Thucydides must commonly have shortened what speakers said in the course of reconstructing it. That is not the impression here.) Honesty in debate, Diodotos had argued, was honourable, even if it could defeat prudent action for the good of the city; it is unjust to make us suffer, the Plataeans had replied to the Thebans, for what we regarded as an act of sacred duty; pleas for compassion, the Thebans said, had no purchase on knowingly bad acts; loyalty to one side, they added, was disloyalty to another. Where speakers could not invoke any moral quality in what they had done, they pleaded necessity. Cleon justified Athens' dominion in this way and Diodotos the common people's support for the rebels in Mytilene; the Thebans likewise excused their service to the Persians; the Plataeans, when not claiming loyalty, explained what they were bound to do as allies of Athens. Facts meanwhile were suborned to the purpose at hand or simply ignored. In what was said at Plataea indeed it is not easy to see that there was a serious attempt on any side to be truthful about all that had transpired; the only certain sincerities were in the Spartans' terse certainty, the Thebans' vindictiveness and the Plataeans' desperation.[10] This was war; ambitions were urgent, nerves were on edge and there was anger everywhere. Even in the rhythms of the Greek fighting seasons, time could press and what mattered was the desired outcome, not truthfulness. One can be struck less by the fact that

---

[9] The intention was plainly to erase Plataea. One may see the common (if laborious) practice of ravaging an enemy's land to be a milder act of hostility. Lendon 2010: 293–4, inclined to attribute all he can to the search for honour and an opportunity to shame, sees it as a means of humiliation, especially where, unlike here, a direct attack has not been practical. Also *hubris*, Ch. 11.

[10] Price 2001: 125 differs: not so much manipulations as representations of states of mind; 'lies are deliberate, but not so every untruth'.

speech was idle than by the fact that men in these circumstances gave time to it at all.

The Plataeans knew that their trial was a sham and its verdict certain, and that nothing they could say to the Spartan judges would alter that. Yet they were driven to a more emotional and affecting rhetoric and deeper moral outrage than any other speakers in the disputes at this point in the war, more indeed than any in Thucydides' story. And they knew what they were doing. The Thebans knew too. Even the Spartan judges, the Thebans had feared, 'might be moved . . . to relent in some way' (3.60). The dispute over Plataea, they said at the end of their speech, was 'not of words but of deeds'; 'in the case of good deeds a short answer suffices, but in the case of misdeeds speeches tricked out with words are just a concealment'. They would have agreed with Cleon when he derided the Athenians for having become 'used to being spectators of words and listening to deeds' which they would do better to 'actually witness'. But they knew that in dismissing words, they were adding force to what they said: words of dismissal were deeds that had a force of their own.

The extreme instance of this, extreme in what it says about the fortunes of truthfulness and speech itself in politics and war, and not without its own ironies, were conflicts, *staseis*, internal wars within the cities themselves.[11] As the wider war went on, writes Thucydides, 'practically the whole Greek world was in turmoil as everywhere there were rival efforts by the leaders of the populace to bring in the Athenians and by the oligarchs to bring in the Spartans. In time of peace they would have had neither pretext nor inclination to ask for help; but when these states were at war any faction seeking radical change' – *neoterizein*, doing something new – 'readily found allies who could be brought in both to help damage their opponents and to bolster their own position' (3.82.1). The leaders of the oligarchic revolt in Samos may well have tried to do this in 441–440, the popular factions did so in Corcyra after 435 and in Spartolos in 429, the Theban and anti-Theban factions had done so in Plataea and so had the oligarchs at Mytilene. In the Ionian city of Notium in 430 and again in 427, when Paches had intervened, there were attempts to call in the Persians and then the Athenians. But Thucydides sees Corcyra in 427 to have been the first instance in the war of truly 'violent passion' in internal strife, and some of the *staseis* that followed as 'a fact of political life' in Greece to have been even worse. He explains the genesis and nature of the one to convey the character of them all (3.85.1, 3.82.3).

---

[11] Loraux 1991: 49 noted that the word was pejorative: 'each city preferred to place its own divisions under the all-encompassing heading of *diaphora*, whereas the civil wars of its neighbours were categorised as *stasis*'.

It is not clear when the Corinthians had returned the 250 'leading men' from Corcyra they had taken prisoner in 433; some historians think it may have been as early as 430, others that it was later. Thucydides has already said that the Corinthians had intended to bring these men over to their side in order to recover Corinthian influence on the island. What is certain is that by the summer of 427 they were back, working to persuade any Corcyrean who would listen that the city should abandon its alliance with Athens. They accused 'the leader of the people' of enslaving the island and he countered by alleging that they had cut props for their vines from a sacred place. Out of patience, or seeing an excuse, they stormed the council chamber and killed him and sixty others.[12] As Thucydides puts it, they then forced Corcyreans to agree that no outsiders should be allowed in the city unless they came in just one ship and in peace, and warned Athens not to interfere. They may have known that the first ship to call would be from Corinth, carrying mercenaries and envoys from Sparta to help them suppress the popular cause. This the visitors attempted to do, but they were routed two days later and quietly departed. On the day after that an Athenian general arrived with twelve ships and 500 Messenian hoplites from Naupactos and received what he believed were assurances of peace from both sides. The popular party asked if he might leave five of his ships with them and take their opponents back to Athens in five of their own. The opponents refused to go, and the popular party sacked their houses and chased them to a temple on an offshore island.

Four or five days after this, fifty-five Spartan ships arrived to the south of Corcyra under the command of Alcidas, who was now back from the Aegean, with Brasidas again as advisor. (Alcidas was still an admiral. Thucydides elsewhere remarks on the Spartans' respect for rank (5.66.3–4); as in the case of Cnemos, they could doggedly reappoint the doubtfully competent.) In a subsequent battle at sea, the twelve Athenian ships and the Corcyraeans themselves were outnumbered, the Corcyraeans only being saved from destruction by the Athenian commander protecting their retreat. Alcidas took his ships to a harbour on the mainland to the south, but the people in Corcyra feared that he might return, and decided to seek a settlement. Brasidas suggested that it would be to

---

[12] 3.84, which has not been agreed to be by Th. (but see Mynott's note), suggests that 'the people' were the poorer citizens. It is not easy to settle on simple descriptions of the antagonists. Since in the chapters that are agreed to be his Th. also talks of those opposed to the ambitions of Corinth and Sparta as 'the people', I refer to the 'the popular party' in the broadest sense of that term. This is not to say all 'the people' were poor, pro-democratic and pro-Athenian, and conversely. Then as now, of course, though not to Th. himself, 'the people' (*demos*) would have been a natural term of populist enthusiasm and of abuse by their enemies.

Alcidas' advantage to refuse this and attack again, but hearing that sixty more ships were on their way from Athens, Alcidas did neither and went home. The popular party had also heard of the sixty ships, and confident once more of external support, executed some of the opponents who had refused to sail to Athens and offered a trial to the rest in the temple on the island. When these people realised what was coming to them, they 'set about putting an end to each other's lives right there in the temple precincts; and some hanged themselves from trees, while others took their own lives any way they could'. For seven days the man in charge of the sixty Athenian ships, the newly appointed general Eurymedon, looked on as the city proceeded to tear itself apart, and then sailed away (3.70–81, 3.85.1).

Thucydides' account of the fury in the fighting between Corcyraeans is famous. 'Death came in every shape and form, and everything that is liable to happen in such a situation did take place – and worse besides' (3.81.5). But his explanation is incomplete, and, I will suggest, perhaps deliberately so.[13] 'Stasis', he writes, 'always does and always will happen while human nature remains what it is.' Its circumstance now was the wider war and 'war is a violent master; it robs us of the means of providing easily for our daily life and needs, and it usually generates passions to match our circumstances' (3.82.2–3).[14] The political passions in Greece at this time were couched in the rhetoric of principled allegiance and opposition to what the two large powers were taken to embody. The combatants bandied 'specious slogans professing the cause either of "political equality for the masses" or "aristocracy – the government of moderation"; they pretended in their speeches to be competing for the public good, but in fact in their struggle to dominate each other by any available means they brazenly committed all manner of atrocities and perpetrated even worse acts of revenge, with no regard for the constraints of justice and the public interest; each recognised only the limitations set by their immediate appetites, and each stood ready to indulge to the full the animosities of the moment, either by passing unjust votes of condemnation or seizing control with brute force' (3.82.8).

Jonathan Price suggests that Thucydides is unusual in concentrating on *stasis* as 'a state of mind' and on 'the actions and speech patterns arising from it', together with the conditions in which the combatants found

---

[13] Price 2001: 12 remarks that 'the language [of 3.82–3] is perhaps the most difficult in the entire work. Native Greek speakers in antiquity had trouble with it, and modern interpretations vary to an absurd degree.'

[14] Cf. Aristotle, *Politics*: 1334a 25–7: 'war compels men to be just and temperate, whereas the enjoyment of good fortune and the leisure which comes with peace tend to make them insolent'.

themselves, rather than as other Greek writers did on where they had previously stood in relation to each other.[15] Thucydides was certainly struck by the 'states of mind' in Corcyrea and how they affected speech. 'The usual values in the application of words to actions' were inverted. 'Reckless audacity' – daring without *logismos* – 'came to be thought of as comradely courage, while far-sighted hesitation became well-disguised cowardice; moderation was a front for unmanliness; and to understand everything was to accomplish nothing. Wild aggression was a mark of manhood, while careful planning for one's future security was a glib excuse for evasion. The trouble-maker was always to be trusted, the one who opposed him was to be suspected. The man who devised a successful plot was intelligent, the one who detected it still cleverer; but the man who thought ahead to try and find some different option was a threat to party loyalty and must have been intimidated by his opponents' (3.82.3).[16] 'Those who found a good-sounding explanation' for what Thucydides calls their 'dreadful deeds' would enjoy 'the better reputation'. The oppositions were as fierce within parties as between them and one can believe that lingering resentments from past migrations, successive layers and displacements of settlement and other differences and disputes had been excited also.[17]

This analysis is Thucydides' undoubted strength. His arguable weakness is in not explaining the importance of where Corcyreans had previously stood in relation to each other. The fears, angers and opportunities of the wider war might explain how men (and women behind them) were prompted to turn against each other, how this exposed longer-standing differences of other kinds and how it incited some that had not previously existed. But difference and competition do not in themselves explain the fury. This, one can argue, arose in the disruption of everyday relations. In the settlements in which there was *stasis* the combatants would have lived and worked alongside each other, would often indeed have been more or less close kin and participated in rituals and other acts of solidarity, and would have had a thick sense of each other. However much they may have been aroused by the warring of the external powers and

---

[15] Price 2001: 30–9 at 30.

[16] On 'party loyalty' Mynott notes that *hetaireai* were party associations or clubs with both a political and a social function, sometimes called *synomosiai* or 'sworn associations'. See also 8.54, Hornblower *CT* I: 484 and Aristophanes, *Knights* 475–7. At 3.82.6 Mynott uses 'associations' to translate *synodoi*, which he believes does not here mean much more than 'gatherings'.

[17] Th. is also not concerned with the trifles that precipitated the strife in Corcyra (cf. Aristotle, *Politics*: 1304a 5 on Mytilene). But in order to counter what he regards as a persistent political myth he does explain the personal angers that led to the end of the tyranny of Peisistratus and his sons in Athens in 514 (6.53.3–59), Ch. 12 below.

however speciously and abstractly they may have come to describe themselves, they were not just *polemioi*, impersonal foes in the name of one or another purportedly principled allegiance or affiliation, but had become *echthroi*, enemies of an intensely personal kind. Their extremes of rage would have arisen in the inversion of relations which had sustained their deeply felt sense of who they were – of their 'identities', as we might say – and their senses of 'self'.[18]

Thucydides does not disguise his horror, and his critics have pounced. They claim that his attention to inversions of language and connection rest on a conviction of true value which he hides (though not from these critics) in his guise of impartial observer; that in writing (as Mynott carefully translates him to do) that the 'simplicity of spirit, which is such an important part of true nobility, was laughed to scorn and vanished' (3.83.1), he betrays a regret for the certainties of an old hierarchical order.[19] But as I suggested in Chapter 5, no one at this time is likely to have aspired to be impartial. And one does not need to be an aristocrat to be appalled by extreme disruption and the suffering that can ensue; Thucydides himself remarks that people of all classes were prone to destructive dispute except those 'in the middle' who 'either because they would not take sides or because their very survival was resented' fell prey to both parties (3.82.8). Hobbes may not always have translated Thucydides in a way that was true to the text, but he may exactly capture his sense in having him say that it was 'sincerity (whereof there is much in a generous nature)' that 'was laughed down'. Sincerity is an impulse to truthfulness and is tested less by where people are more enduringly placed or place themselves socially, by class or ethnos, than by the more immediate circumstances in which they find themselves, especially if these are extreme and disruptive and threaten what Williams called 'the normal expectations of trustful exchange' and life itself.[20]

What Thucydides says about civil strife is convincing. But if in one respect he does not quite bring out the explanation he is pointing to, in another he may more deliberately refrain. Civil strife inverts values and subverts the semantics of peace. What has been bad or unacceptable in the one becomes good and acceptable in the other, and there are

---

[18] 'What did I lose? My dignity! And believe me, someone will pay for that!' a refugee from the Kosovan war remarked in the spring of 1999, Abrahams, Stover and Peress *c.*2001: 16. Kosovars and Serbs had lived in reasonable peace in the former Yugoslavia before 1991. Even the most self-aware and otherwise sensitive of combatants in wars *between* states, by contrast, confess that they give little thought to the person they're killing.

[19] Ch. 5 above nn.1 and 2. Also Hornblower *HCT* I: 487, who has no doubt that Th.'s observation 'is a clear, absolute and [my emphasis] *conservative* authorial rejection of the "relativistic" moral teaching of certain of the sophists' (elaborated in 1994: 186–90).

[20] Williams 2002: 119.

corresponding semantic transfers. And since what does become acceptable in conflict of this kind arises from fear, rage and hatred and serves to exacerbate all three, it is not surprising that the transfers serve to license violence and foment it. From the perspective of peace it is perverse indeed; if the sincerities of peace and their disposition to political truthfulness produce truths, the distortions of pathological action produce evident falsehoods. Yet the combatants in internal strife and revolution can believe what they say, and in the sincerities of comradeship bring word and deed into a new alignment. A world turned upside down can have its internal coherence; the truth of peace may be a casualty of war, but internal war may produce truths of its own. In practice of course, as Thucydides says of *staseis* and as we know from subsequent revolutions and other extremes of ideology and party-speak – and a long string of satires – these cannot be sustained. Such talk will be semantically riven, turn against itself and become unliveable.[21] Some words can be deeds that destroy those who speak them.

Thucydides' account of *stasis* in book 3 is the most overtly theoretical in his text. (His generalities on the responses to the 'plague' (2.53), when people were driven to abandon their conventions, or on hope at moments of desperation, are of a more straightforwardly empirical sort.) But he does not follow the mischievous sophists of his time. They could show how worlds could indeed be turned upside down and made coherent. His grip on enduring truths of the human condition remains bleakly sure.

---

[21] Thus Hobbes, for whom the two principal features of civil war are individuals appropriating the right to judge 'good and evil' and the absence of a sovereign power, Hobbes 1991: 223, 225. Connor 1984b: 99 sees both in Th.'s account of what he calls 'moral anarchy'. Th.'s account of the inversion of values is the only discussion in Greek of *paradiastole*, redescription, which occupied Hobbes, Skinner 2002b: 90 and *passim*. Such discussions dropped away after the early modern period. In George Orwell's *Animal Farm* the mask has famously become the face, hypocrisy vanishes and true terror has come to stay. The declarations of the Ministry of Truth in his *Nineteen eighty-four* – 'war is peace', 'freedom is slavery', 'ignorance is strength' – have succeeded; nicely discussed by Runciman 2008: 184–8. Jokes, which Th. does not consider, are at their most intense (and often their best) under oppression; one doubts whether they are as good, or even common, in civil war.

8   Meaning and opportunity 426–424

Thucydides claims that he saw at the start that the war would be 'more worthy of account than any previous one . . . on the grounds that both sides came into the war at the height of their powers and in a full state of military readiness' and that 'the rest of the Greek world had already taken sides . . . or was now planning to do so'. In the same opening section but in what must have been a late insertion, he writes that it was 'certainly the greatest ever upheaval among the Greeks, and one which affected a significant part of the barbarian world too – even, you could say, most of mankind' (1.1.1–2). But beyond these remarks on its scale and effect, together with two incomplete and arguably misleading views on why Athens was defeated, the first of which I mentioned at the end of Chapter 5, the second of which I come to in Chapter 12, and his apparently considered view that it was one long war (5.26.2–4, but cf. 7.28.3 and Chapter 14), he ascribes no one meaning – dispositional, associational or consequential – to it, and draws no lesson.[1]

His exile did give him time 'to study matters more closely', but he makes no mention of considering them more broadly (5.26.5); even if he had written ten books rather than eight, as Hunter Rawlings imagines him thinking of doing, the end of the tenth might well have been as inconclusive as the end of the fifth.[2] His inclination always was to take readers back to what Hobbes called 'the drifts and counsels of actors to their seat', to shape his account by what the actors themselves thought they were doing, in so far as they thought about it at all, rather than by what he and the readers knew had happened later. He does in this respect write rather like a modern novelist or in the parts of the text that contain speeches, a dramatist without a commenting chorus. But as I said in Chapter 1, authors of fictions usually convey the sense of an

---

[1] Rutherford 1994 is a concise account of the kinds of lesson that Th. just *might*, without saying so, be thought to have had in mind.
[2] Rawlings 1981, reviewed by Westlake 1982. I come to a different reading of the end of the fifth in Ch. 11 below.

ending, which he does not. Writing against a culture that had long been infused with the anticipation of meaningful outcomes – though a culture that Francis Dunn suggests was in this respect changing – he offers what Henry James, writing about someone else, described as a 'frank provisional empiricism that is more telling than any premature philosophy'.[3]

This is nowhere more telling than in his accounts of the temptations into which the central contenders were drawn in the sixth and seventh years of the war. Each was reduced to responding to opportunities that were for the most part presented by third parties. Or so, reading Thucydides, it can seem. He says nothing about strategies or even about how those in each decided what more immediate moves to make and not. One can suppose that in Athens it will have been the board of generals and the council that did so, that in Sparta the ephors will have been important, and that in Athens and even to some extent in Sparta the assemblies would have had a say. But commanders in the field had considerable discretion, and on both sides and throughout in these years there were continual differences of opinion and changes of mind.[4] A reader intent on finding considered plans risks dscovering what did not exist. Agents – it is often difficult to be more specific – were often acting simply for the sake of it, acting to spoil another side rather than to achieve anything considered for their own. It is not difficult to see why Athens as well as Sparta should act in areas to the north of the Corinthian gulf and in Attica; why Sparta as well as Athens should do so in Chalcidice and southern Thrace; and why Athens should cause what disturbance it could around the Peloponnese. Nor is it difficult to see why each power should pay attention to Persia; both were always in need of funds. The puzzle is Athens' venture to Sicily.

As I mentioned in Chapter 3, the Athenians had made alliances with the non-Greek cities of Egesta and Halcyae in the middle of the century (and were perhaps to renew their alliance with Egesta in 418) and in 433–432 had reaffirmed their treaties with the Siceliot cities of Leontini in the east and Rhegion on the Italian side of the strait of Messina. What John Davies describes as the 'Dorian super-state' that had ruled over the south and east of Sicily from Syracuse since 480 had collapsed in

---

[3] On what have respectively been described as foreshadowing, backshadowing (conspiring with readers to offer judgements in retrospect) and sideshadowing (writing the past as the present it was for those living in it), Morson 1994, also Bernstein 1994; Morson on sideshadowing referred to in Grethlein 2010: 249. The same point in Dunn 2007: 115–50, in the context of a wider account; also Ch. 15 below. Connor 1984b: 17 is one who likens Th. to a modern novelist, which in other respects is apposite. Henry James on Sainte-Beuve quoted by Holder 1964: 494.

[4] Though as 8.15.1 suggests, the Athenian assembly appears to have been given the opportunity to vote on tactics when matters were more urgent.

the 460s. ('Dorian' rather than 'Ionian' in that its inhabitants descended from the supposedly ancient Greek-speaking populations of western and southern Greece, distinguished by their dialect and alleged energy from the softer but allegedly more sophisticated Ionians whom the Dorians had chased from Greece to Anatolia and the Athenians now claimed to lead. It was a distinction that could from time to time still serve, at least in Sicily and at Sparta, to rationalise those chosen to be friends and enemies.)[5] The people who had been expelled from Syracuse by the dynasty were returning to that city and its remaining supporters moved to Messina. Syracuse was a large and expanding place made prosperous by trade and tribute from within Sicily itself, and after the tyranny had become to an extent democratic.[6] Davies invokes Diodorus to say that by the beginning of the 430s the Syracusans had 'a hundred triremes and doubled the number of their cavalry; they also developed their infantry forces and made financial preparations by laying heavier tributes upon the Sicels who were now subject to them. This they were doing with the intention of subduing Sicily little by little' (12.30.1). But the new leaders in Syracuse were not known to have arrived at any understanding with the Peloponnesians or to have harboured designs on other Greeks; their attentions beyond Sicily were directed to Carthage, which the previous regime had repelled from Sicily in 480 and they knew they might have to contend with again. There did not appear to be anything in Sicily that the Athenians needed to defend themselves against.

Their interest in the island, Thucydides says, was in their own power; in the possibility, as he puts it, of bringing affairs there under their own control (3.86.4). George Cawkwell wondered whether Pericles might not already have been suggesting that the Athenians might in time think about taking on the east and the west: 'with the naval power you now possess there is no one to stop you sailing the world's seas – neither the great king of Persia nor any other people on earth' (2.62.2). In recommending himself to the Spartans in the winter of 415–414 Alcibiades was to say that Athens intended to extend the city's dominion to the western Mediterranean and North Africa (6.90.2). Dover wondered whether the Athenians might have disdained the western Greeks. But apart from the fact, if it was a fact, that most Athenians had a poor grasp of the

---

[5] It is not clear how much the contrast between Dorian and Ionian mattered in the later fifth century, Hornblower *CT* I: 142. At *CT* II: 226 Hornblower sensibly suggests that one might conclude that 'it was possible for rhetorical purposes either to assert or deny the importance of the racial factor', as Hermocrates was to do in trying to unite Siceliots behind him in 424 on grounds of common interest against Athens (4.61). Also Ch. 12 below.

[6] Doubts about how 'democratic' Syracuse was when, Lewis, 1994: 125–6.

size of Sicily and the challenge it might present (6.1.2), Pericles can be over-interpreted; Alcibiades, as I mention in Chapter 12, may well have invented his ambition for the moment; and one can wonder whether even the most arrogant of Athenians would have regarded disdain for the western Greeks to be sufficient grounds for war. Yet Thucydides' more material explanation for Athens' interest in Sicily, that it wanted to stop grain being exported to the Peloponnese (3.86.4), seems equally improbable. Sparta could largely provide for itself, and if Sicilian wheat was going to Corinth one can imagine that it would have been easier to try to impede its reaching Corinth's own few ports than to try to stop its export from the many scattered round Sicily.[7] Nonetheless, although the Athenians may not have thought hard about why they wanted what they did, they did respond to a request for protection from Leontini in the summer of 427, despatched twenty ships to Sicily and from their base in friendly Rhegion went to war with the Leontinians' enemies. One can only suppose with Thucydides that they did so because they could. Having power can tempt a state to use it if the costs are not too great, and although at this point in the war the Athenians had good reason to conserve their resources, they do not seem to have been too concerned to do so – unless they believed that Sicily could augment them.

They despatched their expedition despite the fact that in 427–426 Athens was again to suffer from the 'plague'. Thucydides reports that at the end of this second outbreak a third of the hoplite ranks, 4,400 out of 13,000, had died, together with nearly a third of its cavalry (3.87); we may suppose that tens of thousands of others had also gone. But the Athenian force that was away in Sicily seems not to have been affected, perhaps because it had left before the outbreak, and with its own ships and some support from Rhegion attempted to secure command of the Messenian straits and, although it was soon to lose it, to capture Messina itself in the following summer (3.87–8). In 426, however, the Athenians were saved from having to decide whether to respond to yet another Peloponnesian march on Attica at the start of the fighting season in 426; earth tremors prompted Archidamos' son Agis to turn back almost as soon as he had assembled at the isthmus (3.89.1). Yet despite the difficulties presented by the plague, about which Thucydides says no more, or perhaps as in 430 because of these, the Athenians despatched thirty ships to sail round the Peloponnese and a further sixty with 2,000 hoplites under Nicias'

---

[7] Hornblower *CT* I: 335–6 quoting George Cawkwell on Pericles. Alcibiades' scheme, Dover in *HCT* IV: 363. Disdain for western Greeks, Dover 1980: 31–2. Grain to Corinth (Th. does ambiguously talk of imports rather than exports) Hornblower *CT* I: 493. Lendon 2010: 212–13.

command to take the island of Melos in the southern Cyclades. It was intended perhaps to get men out of Athens or make a show of force. It may have been both. Melos had a connection with Sparta; it is known to have made two contributions to the Spartans' war fund around this time, perhaps in 427,[8] and to take it might make a point to the Peloponnesians. When the Athenians were trying to subjugate it ten years later, they said that 'Melos' independence could suggst to others that their dominion was weak' (5.95); I come to this in Chapter 11. But as that attempt in 416 makes clear, Nicias did not succeed in taking it in 426. He may not have tried very hard to do so; he was soon required to take his forces back to meet an army that was marching from Athens to meet him in Boeotia, where he and another general were to proceed to march on the city of Tanagra and do some wasting along the coast (3.91).

Athens already controlled the island of Euboea off this coast. But it had made no attempt to conquer any territory in Boeotia since its defeats there in the middle of the century and Sparta had been absent from the area since razing Plataea. In 426, however, the Spartans decided to found a colony at Heracleia, 2 miles inland from the head of the Maliaen gulf, not far from the old battle site at Thermopylae. It was an unprecedented move, and Thucydides makes a point of remarking that Spartans went to Delphi to seek the god's approval for it. It was again opportunistic; peoples in the area wanted protection from troublesome neighbours, and having initially thought of asking the Athenians, had decided that these were not to be trusted and approached the Spartans instead, to whom 'the city seemed... well placed for their war with Athens: a fleet could be made ready there for an attack on Euboea with only a short crossing to make'. The place would be useful also for access by land through Thessaly to Thrace (3.92.4). (Brasidas later used it for this purpose, which has led some commentators not very persuasively to speculate that he may have been party to the colonisation even before he was chosen to command the later expedition.) But the founding was not a success. The Thessalians did not welcome Sparta's presence, the Spartan governors (who included Alcidas) were clumsy, the population drifted away, and fearing that the place might be captured by Athens, the Boeotians were in 419 to appropriate it for themselves (5.51–5.52.1).

Spartans and Athenians continued to be tempted by others into adventures on the mainland to the north and west of the Corinthian gulf. Thucydides does not need to repeat that as in 429 the invitations came from peoples in the region who thought that they might use one or other of the large powers to gain advantage over each other. While Nicias' sixty

[8] Meiggs 1972: 328.

ships were engaged at Melos, the thirty that had sailed round the Peloponnese had reached Leucas off the western mainland, a Corinthian ally that had provided ships to Sparta. When they arrived, the Acarnanians urged the Athenian commander, Demosthenes, to wall the place up and besiege it. But Messenians who had been settled along the gulf in Naupactos after the end of the siege at Ithome in the 450s arrived to urge Demosthenes to go for the inland Aetolians instead. These, they said, were 'a great and warlike people, but they lived in unwalled villages, scattered over a wide area, and since they were only lightly armed they should be easy to subdue before they could combine' (3.94.4). To do this, the Messenians argued, would not only remove a threat to Naupactos itself; it would also allow the Athenians to advance east to Boeotia. It was an extravagant suggestion, and though Thucydides makes no comment, would seem to have made little military sense; Boeotia was more readily accessible from Attica itself. But Demosthenes, keen perhaps to show that Athens could deploy force on land as well as sea, agreed. The Aetolians responded by mobilising across to the Maliaen gulf. The Messenians urged Demosthenes not to be deterred, and he was not. Indeed he was so confident, says Thucydides, that he set off without waiting for javelin-throwers to arrive to help him against what he knew were the similarly lightly armed Aetolians he would encounter. These were indeed waiting for him, confounded his archers and killed 120 of his 300 hoplites. The survivors made their way back to Naupactos and thence to Athens; Demosthenes, fearing prosecution in the city, chose not to return with them (3.97–8). The Aetolians meanwhile had not been satisfied and asked the Spartans to recruit 3,000 hoplites to attack Naupactos itself and the Messenians and Athenians there. Demosthenes was helped at the last minute by Acarnanians (who in their anger at his refusal to besiege the city on Leucas had at first declined) and the Aetolian forces and their Peloponnesian allies were deterred.

It was nonetheless the Spartan commander Eurylochos who was now unable to resist temptation. No sooner had he retreated from his defeat to the west than Ambraciots approached him with the argument that if he were to use his force to defeat the Amphilochians and Acarnanians, then he would find it easy to bring the whole of Amphilochia and Acarnania over to Sparta. In the winter of 426–425, the Ambraciots proceeded by themselves to Amphilocian Argos; the Acarnanians wanted to prevent Eurylochos arriving to support them, and called on Demosthenes. He arrived with hoplites and archers, and twenty ships from Athens sailed in to station themselves in the Ambracian gulf. In the confrontation that followed, the Ambraciots and Peloponnesians were defeated and Eurylochos and his second-in-command killed. When the remaining

Spartan general asked for terms of retreat, Demosthenes tricked him and his men into appearing to abandon their allies, hoping thereby to make the Spartans look even less reliable than they did already. Meanwhile, a large number of Ambraciots who had set off to support their compatriots had arrived nearby. Demosthenes approached them quietly after dark, attacked them at first light the next day, and as Aetolians had done to his own forces in the summer, his men chased many to their deaths in ravines. An Ambraciot herald arrived on the following morning seeking permission to remove the bodies and was surprised to see how many there were. Someone asked him how many of his side he had thought had died:

> 'Some two hundred.'
> 'But these are not the arms of two hundred men – more than a thousand, surely?'
> 'Then they don't belong to the men who fought alongside us.'
> 'Yes, they do, that is, if you are the ones who fought yesterday.'
> 'But we didn't fight anyone yesterday. That was the day before yesterday, in the course of the retreat.'
> 'Well, there were certainly the men we fought yesterday, the ones coming up to support you from the city of the Ambraciots.'
>
> [3.113.3–4]

Thucydides reports that after this exchange (one of only two that he writes in this way) the herald was so shocked that he left without making the arrangements he had come for. Perhaps forgetting Plataea, he writes that this was the greatest disaster for any political community in (one presumes) the ten-year war. He also remarks that the 120 hoplites whom Demosthenes had previously lost to the Aetolians were 'surely the best of all that died in this war from the city of Athens' (3.98.4).

He has no need to explain the ironies in the outcome of these campaigns. The Acarnanians, Amphilochians and Ambraciots together swore a hundred-year treaty by which each would restore the territories it had taken from the others, the Ambraciots agreed not to join the Acarnanians against the Peloponnesians, the Arcananians agreed not to join any Ambraciot campaign against the Athenians and they would all defend each other from future attacks. Having nonetheless avoided a second Athenian defeat, Demosthenes did now feel able to go back to Athens, which kept control of Naupactos and the support of the Messenians there. But neither of the large powers had gained anything in the region, and both had now lost allies there. The Corinthians, whom one presumes had not been included in the treaty, quietly took an opportunity to station a small garrison of their own in Ambracia, though with what in mind, Thucydides does not say (3.100–2, 3.105–14).

In the summer of 425, Agis did manage to complete a march into
Attica and the Spartans despatched sixty ships to support the faction that
favoured Corinth in a now famished Corcyra. At the same time the Athenians sent forty ships to help those already in Sicily to recover Messina
and take command of the straits. The ultimate purpose is unclear, but
Demosthenes sensed an opportunity. He had asked to travel with the
fleet and make use of it on its journey round the Peloponnese. It can
seem surprising that he was allowed to do so, but he was now a private citizen and one presumes that those in Athens who acceded to his
request (Thucydides is again silent about the *boule*) would have trusted
the fleet's commanders to decide whether he should be allowed to act
on it. The action he was able to take, initially against the commanders'
will, provides Thucydides with one of his most dramatic set pieces: one
whose consequence, which not even Demosthenes could reasonably have
expected, had a decisive effect on how both sides were to pursue the rest
of the ten-year war and though he does not say so, will have decided
Thucydides to write it at length.

He explains that when the Athenian fleet was off Laconia and learned
that the Peloponnesian ships were already at Corcyra, the commanders
were for pushing on, but Demosthenes asked that they should stop at
Pylos, in the south-western Peloponnese, to do 'what was needed' there
(4.3.1); to do, that's to say, what Demosthenes thought was needed. The
commanders refused, but a storm drove the whole fleet into the bay.
'Demosthenes immediately recommended that they fortify the place'
on high ground overlooking the small northern channel to the sea and
Thucydides now and rather casually remarks that this is exactly what
he had had in mind. He pointed out to the commanders 'that there
was ample timber and stone there and that the location was naturally
strong and was uninhabited, as was much of the surrounding region'.
The commanders retorted that if he was determined to bankrupt the
city there were plenty of empty headlands in the Peloponnese to occupy.
But Demosthenes thought that this place had a particular promise: it
was in Messenia, only 45 miles or so south-west of Sparta, there was
a harbour in the large bay close by 'and the Messenians, who were the
original inhabitants and spoke the same dialect as the Spartans, could
inflict the maximum harm on them from this base and would at the same
time form a reliable garrison there' (4.3). The commanders were still
not persuaded, but the poor weather kept the ships confined, the men
became bored, and to occupy themselves, Thucydides explains, they
began to reinforce an old fort to protect the place. This they did in six
days, by which time the weather had improved and the fleet was able to
leave for Corcyra. Having accepted that Athens might after all be able

to gain something in the place, the commanders left Demosthenes with five ships and men to guard it. The Spartan army was away with Agis in Attica and Spartans in Sparta itself were enjoying a festival and did not think (or did not want to think) that the threat was serious. Agis however saw that it might be, abandoned his campaign in Attica, which itself had been in difficulties because of the bad weather, marched quickly back, recalled the sixty Spartan ships from Corcyra, and with these, his own troops and others in the area who were loyal to Sparta, went to Pylos to resist. Demosthenes meanwhile asked the Athenian commanders, who for some reason had got no further north than Zacynthos, to bring their ships back.

Thucydides' topographical ambiguities do not make it easy to grasp what the Spartan defenders had in mind.[9] The large bay at Pylos is wide enough for a wind to make it as choppy as the sea, but it is partially blocked by a long steep island, Sphacteria, that runs from north to south across it. As Thucydides says, the entry past the northern end of the island is narrow, that past the southern end wide, too wide in fact to allow what he says were the eight or nine triremes intended to close it (it is suggested that he may have meant to write eight or nine stades); too wide therefore for the Spartans to have been able to realise their objective of blocking both entries and safely stationing troops on Sphacteria in order to besiege the fort at Pylos itself. But this was not Demosthenes' immediate problem. The Spartans had set about attacking the promontory on which Pylos itself stood, just inside the northern entry; they were coming from land and sea and outnumbered him, and he had no retreat. He exhorted his men not to stop to think about the fix they were in, take courage and act.[10] In the event, the Spartans were defeated both by the tactical difficulties (in the account of which Thucydides, using what Hornblower well describes as 'the whole paint-box', gives an arresting account of Brasidas leading a sally and yelling at the trierarchs to run their ships to pieces onto the shore to enable the men to land and fight) and by the Athenian fleet arriving from Zacynthos. The Athenians

---

[9]   Hornblower *CT* II: 159–60. Gomme *HCT* III: esp. 482–8 is generally more informative on the topography and the practicalities of the episode. Mynott *TWPA*: 254 has a considered map. Pylos was the Athenians' name; the Spartans called it Coryphasium (4.118.4). There is a forthcoming study of the campaign by William Shepherd. The large bay was the site of a battle between British, French and Russian ships and those of the Ottoman Empire on 20 October 1827, during the Greek war of independence, after which the British commander was criticised for destroying the Ottoman fleet and thereby making it easier for Russia to make a play for the Mediterranean. The Russians erected a monument to the occasion on Sphacteria.

[10]   As Mynott *TWPA* illustrates in a note, in prose that would have surely been self-defeating if he had spoken as Th. writes him to have done.

disabled a satisfactory number of the Spartan ships and proceeded to sail some of their own round the island to isolate 420 men, Spartiates and their accompanying *perioicoi*, who had landed there (4.8–4.14.1).[11]

As Thucydides says, this, for the Spartans, was a disaster. They could not help their troops on the island, but because some were of high standing in Sparta itself (and there was already some anxiety about the city's manpower, which he does not mention) they did not want them to be overwhelmed, and they could not leave them to be killed. Having been able to secure a truce with the Athenians which allowed them under supervision to send food to the island in return for handing over their ships at Pylos and in the rest of Laconia until there was a more enduring settlement (Laconia was a city state in Spartan territory), they sent envoys to Athens (4.14.2–16). These spoke eloquently and at unusual length, a fact to which they drew to their audience's attention, but they were diplomatically almost as clumsy as the Spartans had been in Athens in 432; not that Thucydides, who might himself have heard what they said, makes any comment. He simply writes them in direct speech to have declared that Sparta was pre-eminent still among the Greeks; to have suggested that the Athenians should forsake the convention of favouring friends and harming enemies for the honour they would gain in agreeing an end to a war that most Greeks could no longer understand; to have presumed that if the Athenians were to do this, Athens would welcome a share in the domination of Greece; to have expected that the Athenians would be as be as keen now on a settlement as they had appeared, at least rhetorically, to be in 432; and to have taken it for granted that if they did not agree to settle, they would fear the Spartans' lasting anger. In the spirit of what they described as 'a gentle reminder of what good counsel consists in, directed at those who can appreciate it', the envoys suggested that the Athenians should not make too much of one unexpected advantage (4.17–20).

The Athenians saw things differently. Disregarding the Spartans' argument that 'there is no reason for you to suppose that because of the present strength of your city and its acquisitions you will always enjoy the same good fortune', Thucydides reports that they 'reasoned that while they were holding the men on the island, they could have a truce with the Spartans at any time they wanted to arrange one and . . . were grasping for something more' (4.17.4, 4.18.3, 4.21.2). Cleon, who may have urged this response, insisted that the trapped Spartans should

---

[11] On the fighting, Hornblower *CT* II: 166. Plutarch remarks on Th.'s ability to make his readers visualise a scene, Mynott *TWPA*: 599–600. The *perioicoi* ('dwellers around') were inhabitants of Spartan territory (sometimes urban and sometimes moderately prosperous) who had limited rights but not full citizenship of Sparta itself.

surrender their weapons and be held in Athens until Sparta itself was willing to release the territories that the Athenians had conceded in the peace of 446–445. The envoys would have had neither the wish nor the authority to agree to this, but said nothing at the assembly and suggested that negotiations should proceed in private. Cleon publicly ridiculed this and the assembly voted against the suggestion (though one vote did reportedly have to be taken three times).[12] Seeing the mood at Athens and aware of the danger in its becoming known that they were prepared to abandon their allies – despite what they said, they are not likely to have believed that the peace they were proposing would be honoured by other Greeks – the envoys left (4.17–22, the Spartans' claim of honour at 4.20.4). The truce was thereby ended but having decided to charge the Spartans with having made an attempt on Demosthenes' fortifications at Pylos while it was still in force, the Athenians said that they would not now return the Spartan ships and brought in more of their own. The two sides then settled into a stalemate. The only movement was that of Spartans sending helots on the promise of liberation across to the island at night to take wheat, cheese and wine to the men there; some, to avoid detection, even swimming with skin-bags of poppy-seed, linseed and honey in tow (4.26).

An opportunity had been seized. But the stand-off began to worry the Athenians. The Spartans were inactive, the Athenian troops at Pylos did not have access to good water and it was difficult to see how they could reliably be supplied with anything else through the winter. In Athens meanwhile, Cleon was being criticised for guiding the assembly to reject the Spartans' offer of peace. Unable, says Thucydides, to go on denying the bad news from Pylos, he eventually 'gestured at Nicias son of Niceratus, who was a general and also a personal enemy of his, and taunted him saying that if the generals were men it would be easy enough with a proper force to sail there and capture [the Spartans] on the island; and that was what he would do himself if he was in charge' (4.27.5). Nicias immediately offered to resign, and when he would not retract, jeers made it clear to Cleon that he would have to go himself. But he was no fool. He knew that Demosthenes had a plan to land on the island, and announced that he would retain him as his partner. He also realised that a capture would require peltasts and archers rather than hoplites, and recruited both. It would all be done, he announced, the men on Sphacteria killed or brought to Athens, in twenty days. There was surprise and laughter and what Thucydides describes as 'wiser heads' (some hear a sneer) saw that if he were to fail they would be rid of him and that if he did not, Athens might have invaluable hostages (4.27–8). But Cleon doubtless had his supporters too, and may have had the last laugh; Thucydides does not suggest as much, but knowing what he did about Nicias' pride and Demosthenes' plan, he may have engineered the confrontation to enhance his own reputation.

He certainly knew that Demosthenes' men at Pylos, 'suffering from the privations of their position and feeling more besieged than besieging', as Thucydides puts it, were eager to face whatever risks there might be (4.29.2). But the island was covered with brush and small oaks. It reminded Demosthenes of what he had suffered from the Aetolians; the Spartans might see him before he saw them, and being now familiar with the place, succeed in beating him off. One can wonder whether, as the Aetolians had done, he even thought of starting a fire. In the event, one of his men cooking on the shore accidentally did so. That enabled Demosthenes literally to see what he had to do, and having confirmed that the Spartan commander on the mainland would not surrender, he proceeded to do it. Thucydides devotes his formidable powers of description to the ensuing events. The Spartan hoplites had no defence against the Athenians' lightly armed troops, and when they had been backed onto rising ground at the north end of the island and could go no further, a Messenian scout found a way to go behind them. 'To compare small things with great', remarks Thucydides, they 'were in the same predicament as the men at Thermopylae' (4.36.3). But unlike the Persians in that battle, Demosthenes did not attack; he and Cleon wanted prisoners and proposed a truce. The Spartans asked if they might seek orders from the mainland about how to proceed, and heralds were despatched. These returned to say that 'the Spartans instruct you to make your own decisions about yourselves as long as you do nothing dishonourable' (4.38.3). Few if any would have thought that this could extend to surrender, but that is what the men decided on. Formalities were observed, and of the 420 who had gone to the island the surviving 292 (including 120 Spartiates) were taken to Athens and chained (4.30–9, 4. 41.1). As he had said he would be, Cleon was back in the city in twenty days.

'Nothing in the war', says Thucydides (he may again have meant the first ten years), surprised the Greeks more. He captures the humiliation and the irony. One of the prisoners was asked in Athens whether those who had died on the island had been 'good men and true'; the man replied it would have been a clever arrow (not being an archer, he used a demeaning synonym) that distinguished the brave;[13] and anyway, the Spartans who had gone to the island had been chosen by lot (4.8.9,

---

[13] Herodotus reports a Spartan fighting against the Persians at Plataea in 479 to have lamented that he was dying by arrow rather than a 'deed worthy of himself', 9.72.2.

4.40.2). The Athenians, announcing that the prisoners would be executed if the Peloponnesians were to invade Attica again, were themselves
now free to attack at will. Nicias and two other generals duly took eighty
ships, 2,000 hoplites and 200 cavalry to fight Athens' first set-piece land
battle of the war on the Peloponnese itself (the only one that Athenians
were to fight there on their own), on the eastern side of Corinth. They
managed to confine the Corinthian forces and established a fort on a
headland near Epidauros (4.42–5).

The ships at Pylos had meanwhile resumed their journey to Corcyra to
deal with the enemies of 'the people' there. Notwithstanding the Athenians' threat to take any who attempted to escape from the island, the
people tricked some into believing that they would be supported if they
did; a few made the attempt and were caught, and since the Athenians
were keen to get on to Sicily and did not want the trouble of having to
take them to Athens, they handed them over to the people. Thucydides,
struck once again by gratuitous suffering, dwells on the horror. Rebels
who were not killed by their opponents killed themselves, and 'hardly
anything worth mentioning' of the revolt remained (4.46–4.48.5). On
the mainland Acarnanians, evading the spirit of the treaty they had made
with the Amphilochians and Ambraciots, combined with Athenians to
remove a Corinthian settlement in the far west (4.49). And in the winter,
the Athenians ordered the Chians to take down their walls; Thucydides
does not say, but perhaps they wanted to make sure that Chios (which,
unusually in their dominion, was not a democracy) did not go the way
of Mytilene, some of whose fugitives were now making trouble in north-
western Anatolia (4.51, 4.52.2–3).

Athens was nevertheless worried about the continuing expense of the
war, and in 425 appears to have decided to increase the tribute from its
subject states. In what historians used to regard as a serious omission,
Thucydides does not mention this, but recent scholarship suggests that
the decree was not enforced.[14] An Athenian officer collecting money at
Eion in Thrace in the winter of 425–424 may only have been engaged on
one of the several more immediate attempts in these years to raise funds
from the subject states. We know that he was there because Thucydides
reports him having arrested a Persian carrying a letter to Sparta which
complained that Spartan emissaries to Persia were not being clear about
what they wanted. The Athenians were understandably interested to
learn what was being discussed, but the Persian King died before they
were able to do so. What seems reasonably sure, though Thucydides
does not mention it, is that the Athenians themselves were to reaffirm

[14] Kallet-Marx 1993: 160–70.

their peace with Persia in the following year. Meanwhile, they made a move under Nicias and two other generals on the island of Cythera off Cape Malea in the south-eastern Peloponnese, set up a garrison there and imposed a stiff tribute (4.53–4, 4.57.4).

Looking back – as Thucydides does not – to the ventures in these years, it would be too sweeping to say that the few from which one side or another emerged with success were devoid of intelligence, or that none was of any consequence. Demosthenes' guile had enabled him to succeed against the Ambraciots and his imagination and determination, ably supported by Cleon, brought success at Pylos. Notwithstanding their differences, the Acarnanians, Amphilochians and Ambraciots had made a practicable treaty with each other. And Nicias and his fellow generals had dealt effectively with Corinth and Cythera. It would similarly be too sweeping to say that the defeats came from mistakes, although Demosthenes had initially been reckless in the west and the Spartans cannot have been thinking very carefully when they stationed men on Sphacteria without being able to block the southern passage from the sea to the bay. But none of these outcomes was planned. There is no single sense to be made of their conception, execution or outcome, no 'meaning' to be drawn from them beyond saying that in the absence of strategies, protagonists on both sides were seeking whatever advantage for themselves and disadvantage for others they could see, hoping that some benefit of some kind might follow; and Thucydides does not attempt to make any such sense. The one lasting consequence was of the Spartans' error in opening their men to capture at Pylos, which as he says later was 'unexpected and calamitous; both Pylos and Cythera were now in enemy hands, and on all sides [the Spartans] were encompassed by a war that was developing rapidly and in ways that it was difficult to prepare for'. 'They were less confident about giving battle; their morale had been undermined because of their previous inexperience of adversity and they now thought that every move they made would end in failure' (4.55.1, 4.55.4). This is entirely plausible. The question was what use Athens or Sparta itself could now make of the fact.

9   Necessities 424

Thucydides writes what has come to be called 'the Archidamian war' in years that start at the beginning of spring and close at the end of the following winter. By the end of the seventh year, in the late winter of 424–423, the Spartans, as he says, were in despair. Some 292 men, 120 Spartiates and 172 *perioicoi* who had been with them at Pylos were in custody in Athens, and the Spartan fleet had been confiscated. The Athenians by contrast, in 'their current run of good luck . . . felt the right to expect that nothing could go wrong for them, but that they could accomplish the possible and the impracticable alike, no matter whether with a large force or a weaker one. The reason for this attitude was the success of most of their undertakings, which defied rational analysis *and so* added to the strength of their hopes' (4.65.4, my emphasis). And hope, as Thucydides writes Pericles, Archidamos and Diodotos all to have observed, was dangerous – as dangerous, indeed, as despair. It is not therefore surprising that one notable reading of the text has detected 'recurring structural elements of event sequences' of confidence, reversal and remorse and concluded that in Thucydides' story man in general 'defines himself as incapable of grasping himself within the limits of his own current situation'.[1]

Such sequences however are belied by the ventures into which Athens and Sparta had been tempted in the mid 420s. The Aetolians were certainly confident at the start of the campaigns on the western mainland in 426 and the Ambraciots by the end in despair. The Ambraciots may also have felt regret, an attitude towards oneself. But they will not have suffered remorse, which is an attitude towards others.[2] And the significance of the sequence does not stop there, for the sequence itself did

---

[1] Stahl 2003: 129–57, 169–70, the last on the Melian dialogue (Ch. 11 below), which in combining hope and its foolishness in one instant is for Stahl the thematic climax of the work. His commentary was first published in 1966; the English edition contains a new chapter on books 6 and 7.

[2] The distinction between regret and remorse may not be sharp, but is real. Konstan 2010 argues that in a pre-Christian society there may have been no move from remorse

not. The Ambraciots had gone on to join the Aetolians in a new alliance with their former enemies the Arcananians against their former friends the Spartans as well as the Athenians. Demosthenes also will have been confident at the start of his campaigns in the area, but he was set back by the Aetolians. He may have regretted his tactical carelessness and chose to avoid impeachment in Athens, but he also is unlikely to have suffered any remorse, and such regrets as he may have had will have been short-lived, for he went on to defeat the Ambraciots. He will have been equally confident at the start of the siege of Sphacteria until he and those in Athens saw that they might not be able to sustain it through the winter; that was a reverse, and some Athenians had begun to regret not having accepted the Spartans' offer of a settlement. But a majority, we suppose, had felt no remorse about proceeding to attack the Spartans on the island and imprisoning those who survived. The Spartans by contrast had experienced more reverses and were later to suffer both regret and remorse at not having tried harder to prevent war when they could have done (7.18.2). Yet they cannot be said to have had much confidence in the first place; Archidamos had hesitated, Sthenelaidas had blustered, and those who sent envoys were trying to negotiate a way round the votes that their own assembly and the Peloponnesian league had taken. Even if one can agree that few men at any time anywhere are capable of understanding the limits of their current situation, the sequences of this kind that there are in Thucydides' story are altogether more fitful and incomplete than Stahl's generalisation suggests.

Stahl nonetheless extends it into a 'tragic view of the place of man in the historical process', a sorrow in Thucydides at what he describes as 'the de facto inevitability of what appears from rational hindsight to have been avoidable': 'not merely the tragedy of Athens but in a much broader sense the tragedy of humanity itself: of human beings who make themselves and others into the victims of their vast plans'. This, Stahl claims, is the significance of the offer of peace from Sparta after the surrender and imprisonment of their men in 425: arguably the first occasion in the war on which each side found it had what he calls a 'free choice' about whether to continue, an opportunity which the Athenians had neither need nor reason to reject yet gambled away and were later to regret that they had.[3] But as Cleon saw, Athens had no good reason at that moment to accept the kind of settlement that the Spartans were offering, and quite apart from the Spartans' extravagant suggestion that the two powers might rule

to seeking forgiveness, which on the strongest reading might be thought to require a transformation of character; cf. Williams 1993: 91.

[3] Stahl 2003: 143, 10, 151–2.

Greece together, the failures of the peace and alliance that they were to swear in 421 make one doubt whether anything they might have agreed in 425 could have held; the envoys had been unwilling to speak openly at Athens for fear that their allies might suspect betrayal, and this is exactly what Sparta's allies did later suspect. The greater gamble for each side in 425 would have been to agree to something rather than not. This aside, it is not clear that either had 'vast plans' for the war; or if they did, that these amounted to anything more definite than the fantasy of a lasting victory or a wish to return to something like the stand-off that had emerged in the thirty-year peace of 446–445.

There are also deeper and more important muddles in the notion of de facto inevitability and in what Thucydides might have thought might in 'rational hindsight' be seen to have been avoidable. De facto inevitability is empirical necessity, and this, in human action, is compulsion. Whatever others may have believed at the time, Thucydides does not suggest that men are compelled to act in one way rather than another by gods or as we would say, other supernatural entities; as Francis Cornford said, he is an agnostic.[4] Nor does he give any sign of believing that men's actions were determined by chains of antecedent causes of a more mundane kind or compelled towards predetermined ends. He knew that others thought in this way and that, like the Corcyreans, Corinthians and Athenians in their self-justifications at Sparta in 432 (4.98.6, 5.105), were prone to explain themselves in talk of need. This is not to say that he rejects all thought of the unavoidable. *Ananke*, 'necessity', the condition of being bound and its related forms, occurs 161 times in the text, and nearly a hundred times in his own voice.[5] To him, men can be bound by what they believed themselves to be in their own or someone else's eyes, compelled by the real or perceived power of others, and impelled by their own.

Individuals and collectivities alike will often accede to the power of others. But if they see a risk in so doing of being disabled or as the Greeks were prone to say 'enslaved', deprived of all room to act and at the limit extinguished, they strive to confront it. This much is obvious.[6] So also is the fact that confronting power can be difficult to engineer and dangerous. The Athenians and Spartans found this to be so in the first ten

---

[4] Cornford 1907: 70–1.

[5] Ostwald 1988: 74. Stahl agrees that 'inevitability' is borrowed from our philosophy of history and has no place in Th., 137n, 154 n. 31.

[6] It has been put to me that this is a Schmittian point (Schmitt 1996: 53–5) and for this reason contentious. It is certainly Schmitt's, not Th.'s. But it is also an elementary truth that Th., I believe, would have accepted.

years of the war, and like the United States and the Soviet Union between the late 1940s and late 1970s, allowed themselves instead to be tempted by third parties into visions of advantage to themselves and disadvantage to the other that were often not well-judged. In Megara and then Boeotia in 424, the Athenians were to succumb yet again. Their run of successes, Thucydides observes, had made them careless. The Spartans by contrast had had a run of failures, and become more hesitant. They nonetheless believed that unless they were able to negotiate the release of their fleet and the prisoners in Athens, they might lose their standing altogether. In Sicily, Hermocrates, the leading man in Syracuse, was more difficult to read; either he believed what he was saying about the Athenian threat to the island or he was using it as a pretext with which to advance the power of his own city.

After the collapse of the dynasty in Syracuse under Gelon and his brothers in 466, the smaller Greek cities in Sicily had drifted into two loose groups of mutual antagonism. These could favour the identities of 'Dorian' and 'Ionian' and, sacrificing symbolic purities for practical success, each sought help from the 'barbarian' Sicels, ertswhile enemies whose own association had collapsed after the death of its leader in 440–439. Thucydides does not say anything directly about what Syracuse's interest now in the island might have been. The Sicilian historian Diodorus, looking back from the end of the first century BC, said that when Hermocrates' protegé and son-in-law Dionysios established a new tyranny over much of Sicily and southern Italy in 405, his purpose was simply subjection (12.30.1), and that might have been what Hermocrates wanted also.[7] Athens' interest appeared to be more modest. The ships that had stopped at Pylos and Corcyra in the summer of 427 went on as intended to offer support to the 'Chalcidean' cities in the north-east.[8] But Hermocrates and those around him were not so sure that this was all that the Athenians had in mind for the island. In the summer of 424, when the Athenian fleet had been at its base in Rhegion for the whole of the previous winter, Hermocrates addressed representatives who had come from all the cities in Sicily to a meeting at Gela.

---

[7] An excellent brief account in Davies 1993: 129–32, 187–97. More fully on Dionysios, Lewis 1994, persuasively more sceptical of him as a strategist than Davies. A nasty moment of the personal kind which Th. generally avoids was when Dionysios' wife, Hermocrates' daughter, committed suicide after being maltreated by Syracusans who were furious with Dionysios for abandoning a fight with Carthaginians at Gela in 405, Lewis 1994: 134 from Plutarch, *Dionysius* 3.

[8] 'Chalcidean' from Chalcis in Euboea, from which their founders had come some 300 years before (6.3). Full discussion by Dover in *HCT* IV: 198–210, supplemented by Hornblower *CT* III: 272–8.

Thucydides himself would by this time have been taking up his first and only posting at Thasos, 700 or so sailing miles away in the northern Aegean, and unless he had heard about this meeting in the winter of 424–423 when (and if) he returned to Athens to be tried for his failings, he will only have heard accounts of what was said there some time after it had been. Commentators detect his hand in the speech he writes for Hermocrates, and his admiration also. He has Hermocrates repeat the word: it was 'sensible'. It was also political. 'I represent the most powerful city here, more likely to think of aggression than defence. But as I contemplate this future I conclude that my city should reach some compromise: we must avoid harming our enemies in such a way that we are the more damaged ourselves, and we should avoid persuading ourselves, in some stupid fit of ambition, that we are as much the masters of fortune, which we do not control, as we are of our own plans; instead, we should make whatever reasonable concessions we can' to each other (4.64.1). The conflicts between cities in Sicily and the *staseis* within them, he said, could only make it easier for Athens to take them all. That is why Athenian ships were still in the vicinity. 'The Athenians you can forgive for such a policy of aggressive self-interest; the people I blame are not those who want to rule but those who are too ready to submit; for it has always been human nature to dominate those who yield and to protect oneself against attack' (4.61.5). What he collusively described as 'we Sicilians' must therefore come to an agreement, however temporary, to resist what was coming. He did not go on to suggest what the resistance should consist of, how it would be arranged, or under whose auspices. His audience would have known which city he had in mind, and Thucydides leaves it for readers to infer.

He mentions no debate at this gathering. In 415, a Syracusan democrat was to challenge the need for a united defence of Sicily, but though that man may have been right to say that this happened to suit his city's desire for dominion, he did not help his case by mocking the thought that the Athenians might sail across when they were actually on their way (6.38). Thucydides does not anticipate, and merely reports that the representatives at Gela accepted Hermocrates' argument, those from the cities which were allied to Athens sending for the Athenian commanders at Rhegion to explain that Athens was expected to be a party to a peace between all the cities on the island, Siceliot and other, and to respect the commitment to a common defence. In a notable success for Hermocrates, the commanders agreed and left for home. But the Athenians in Athens, as Thucydides has said, were now convinced 'that they could accomplish the possible and the impracticable alike' (4.65.4), and were not pleased to be told that they had been made party to the peace.[9] For the want perhaps of a better charge, Eurymedon was convicted of taking a bribe and fined for leaving Sicily when the Athenians, says Thucydides, believed that it was Athens' for the taking, and his fellow commanders were exiled. Hermocrates' success, however, was short-lived. Not long after the agreement was made, the leaders of Athens' ally Leontini, a day or two's march inland from Syracuse, decided to expropriate some of the city's land. Having asked the Syracusans to help expel the 'common people', those who had lost their land removed themselves to Syracuse itself, where they got into some sort of trouble, returned to Leontini, and caused it to divide. In 422 the Athenians sent a man (without force) to resolve the dispute. He achieved little at Leontini itself but did manage to persuade the leaders at Acragas, Sicily's second city, and those at Locri in Italy to declare allegiance to Athens (5.4–5).[10]

Nothing appears to have necessitated the Athenians' interest in Sicily. They may have had a fantasy of controlling it, but no power there was a nuisance to it, much less a threat, and the argument for stopping shipments of grain to the Peloponnese, as I have said, does not ring true. Megara was a different matter. This state was on the isthmus that connected Attica and the Peloponnese, and with Corinth to its west and south, could command the land route between the two. In 446, it had also moved out of Athens' orbit into the Peloponnesian league. Only now does Thucydides reveal that the Athenians had been failing to bring it back or at least to neutralise it not once but twice every year since 431. In 431 itself, they had gone in with 13,000 troops, the greatest land force they were ever to assemble in the war. That, he points out, was before the first outbreak of plague (2.31.2). He does not say how many they deployed against Megara in later years and whether their incursions had repeatedly failed or were meant to be no more than threats. In 424 however, there was a promise of actual capture. Internal strife in Megara had brought leaders of 'the people' to power, and these men had exiled their opponents to Pegae across on the Corinthian gulf, a dozen or so miles away from the city of Megara itself. But the exiles were sending raiding parties to the city, and it was becoming hard for the leaders to deal with these and the Athenians; needing support from one of these threats against the

---

[9] Gomme in *HCT* III: 526–7 has careful and illuminating remarks on the likely generals in Athens and their dispositions in 424; related to events later in this chapter, also at 528 on what might be inferred about the politics of Megara (below).

[10] In 425, Aristophanes (*Acarnians*, 606) had already described Sicily as a place where expensive and useless ambassadors go. As so often in Aristophanes, one can take this in more than one way.

other, they chose the exiles they knew over the Athenians they feared. Those in the city who favoured the exiles were naturally pleased, but so, to the surprise and alarm of the leaders, were 'the people' themselves. The leaders decided that the Athenians might be the less bad option after all, and quietly approached Hippocrates and Demosthenes for support.

The two generals were attracted, put men into Megara and frightened away Peloponnesian troops who had been stationed there from a garrison that had been established at nearby Nisaea to resist an Athenian attack from the sea. By dawn on the following morning (or so it can seem from what Thucydides writes) 4,000 Athenian hoplites and 600 cavalry were assembled outside the gates of Megara. All was set for an occupation. But the leaders were betrayed and the exiles' supporters in the city persuaded a sufficient number of citizens that it would be dangerous to let more Athenians in. The Athenian commanders took their force to Nisaea instead, where they closed the walls, expelled the population and disposed of the Spartan garrison, hoping that those opposed to them in Megara might be intimidated and concede.

What Hippocrates and Demosthenes did not know was that Brasidas was passing to the south of the city on his way to Corinth to recruit men for a Peloponnesian expedition to the north. Learning what was happening on the isthmus and being too late to recapture Nisaea, he decided to send 300 men to Megara itself to ask if they could enter the city and secure it, thinking that it would be possible to recapture Nisaea later (4.66–70). 'The rival factions felt apprehensive', writes Thucydides, 'the one side concerned that he might bring back the exiles and drive them out instead, the other that the people, fearing precisely this, might attack them and that the city, then at war with itself and with the Athenians lying in wait nearby, might face destruction. They therefore refused him, both sides thinking that they should stand aside and see what would happen. Each was expecting that a battle would take place between the Athenians and the relieving force and that it would therefore be safer for them not to join whichever side they favoured until it had actually won' (4.71.1–2).

Brasidas had had the foresight not to rely on his force alone and invited the Boeotians to send troops. Leaders in Boeotia had already been thinking that the Athenian danger was getting rather too 'close to home'. For this reason they assembled on the site of Plataea and were able at once to despatch 2,200 hoplites and 600 cavalry. Brasidas now had 6,000 hoplites at his disposal and positioned them with horsemen to face down the Athenians. He saw no reason to attack; if the Athenians wished to engage, he could beat them, if they did not and were to leave, he could relieve the city. Hippocrates and Demosthenes did decide to leave. They thought that they could lose too many valuable hoplites to a commander who had reserves to draw on. In any event, Thucydides remarks, they calculated that 'most things had gone their way so far' (4.73.4). In this they may have been deluding themselves; or they may have believed that Megara did not matter that much, though if this was so, one wonders why Athens had been marching troops into its territory for what Thucydides suggests had been seven successive seasons; or they may simply have been putting a good face on things to preserve their strength for a campaign in Boeotia that they already had in mind for later in the year. The Athenians who were still inside Megara departed with them and the people's leaders invited the exiles to return, having bound them 'by the most solemn oaths not to nurse past grudges but to consider only the best interests of the city' (4.74.2). The exiles, acting on their own interpretation of what the city's best interests were, immediately arranged for the execution of the hundred or so citizens who had supported the Athenian invasion and set up 'an extreme form of oligarchy'. Never, remarks Thucydides in one of his favourite formulations, was there 'a change of constitution arising from internal conflict that was brought about by so few and lasted so long' (4.74.4). In the twenty years that he records, it was certainly the closest we know to a very perfect coup. The Athenians had brought about exactly what they least desired.

With one immediate exception, their relatively small force at Megara in 424 was larger than any force that they were able again to muster on land; they were to send only 1,000 hoplites to join the force challenging Peloponnesians at Mantinea in 418, and only 2,200 Athenian hoplites to Sicily in 415.[11] The plague as well as war was having its effect. The exception was what Thucydides calls the comparatively small 'full force' of 7,000 Athenians, 'citizens and metics and any other visitors present too' that Hippocrates was able to call up for the campaign that he and Demosthenes had in mind for Boeotia (4.77.1, 4.90.1).[12] Megara was an understandable irritation. Boeotia was not. The Boeotian federation of states was part of the Peloponnesian league and did border Attica, but though unfriendly, it had so far shown no inclination to act against Athens. There was accordingly no necessity there; merely, once again, temptation. Hippocrates and Demosthenes had been talking to men who wanted to introduce an Athenian kind of politics in some of the Boeotian cities and could not resist interceding on their behalf. Their plan was for Demosthenes to sail from Naupactos to Siphae in the eastern Corinthian

---

[11] On Sicily in 415–413, Hornblower *CT* III: 1061–6; it is not easy to estimate how many more Athenians arrived in the second wave.

[12] This suggests that Hippocrates was the senior general, agreed by some, Hornblower *CT* II: 255, disputed by Gomme in *HCT* III: 539. Metics were long-term resident aliens with limited political rights but liable for taxes and military service.

gulf, the port for the Boeotian city of Thespiae, to support dissenters in Thespiae itself and encourage those in the Chaeronea, in north-western Boeotia, where dissenters were more numerous; and for Hippocrates to march up from Athens to establish a fort near the shrine at Delion to the east, near the coast. The pair believed that they would thereby surprise the Boeotians on two fronts on the same day and divide the federation, and that when Chaeronea and other cities also came over, which the conspirators in these places were unsurprisingly predicting, they would be able to divide it further (4.76). Gomme followed an earlier German scholar in imagining that Demosthenes and Hippocrates might have been inspired by Athens' capture of Pylos and Cythera, the idea of garrisons from which dissidents could be mobilised and the enemy attacked without the need for a large force, and he may have been right.[13]

But everything went wrong. Demosthenes turned up at Siphae earlier than had been agreed; more consequentially, the Athenians' conspiracy had been discovered even before he did so, a Boeotian force arrived, the conspirators decided not make a move and Demosthenes withdrew. Hippocrates had given himself two days to build a fort at Delion; seemingly out of contact with Demosthenes, he was unaware of the failure at Siphae; not himself expecting to be confronted by Boeotian forces, he had begun to send the men he thought he would not need back to Athens. But troops from cities in Boeotia, including some who had gone to Siphae, were now assembling on the border. Ten of the eleven boeotarchs, representatives of the cities in the federation, thought it prudent to allow Hippocrates' men quietly to cross back into Attica. But the eleventh was a Theban, Pagondas, and he happened to be the leading man. Attack, he argued, was the necessary defence, and Hippocrates was compelled to make the same case to his own men; Thucydides gives both speeches. The forces engaged first on foot, the Theban hoplites at the centre of the Boeotian formation, fighting no less than twenty-five rows deep against the Athenians' eight. The Athenians were battered, and when they saw Boeotian cavalry riding out from behind a hill, imagined that another army was arriving and ran.[14] Some 2,000 Corinthians then arrived and, with Megarian help and troops from the now evacuated Peloponnesian garrison at Nisaea, mounted an ingenious and frightening fire machine, burned down the wood and brush walls that Hippocrates had put up and chased away those Athenians who had not already been burnt alive. The fighting had lasted for seventeen days; 500 Boeotians and a number of

---

[13] *HCT* III: 538–9.

[14] Scholars argue about how hoplite battles were fought; Wheeler and Strauss 2007: 202–13 is a balanced review.

accompanying lightly armed troops and baggage-carriers had been killed against 1,000 Athenians, including Hippocrates himself. Demosthenes attempted to divert the Boeotians south by moving ships and troops against Sicyon, but he was repelled (4.89–4.101.2). Thucydides as usual makes no comment, but it is difficult not to conclude that it had from the start been an unwise venture.

The Spartans were still worried about their men imprisoned in Athens and their impounded fleet and realised that if the Athenians would not freely agree to negotiate, they must be forced to do so. Once again, but in this instance thinking well, they turned to a third party. Perdiccas, they discovered, though not at this moment openly hostile to Athens, was worrying about the Athenians' apparent strength. As Thucydides explains, the Spartans had also learnt that the cities in Chalcidice and Bottiaea which had rebelled against Athens in the late 430s were anxious lest the Athenians should intervene when they realised that some of their number were going over 'in secret' to the Peloponnesians. The Spartans accordingly invited envoys from Macedonia and the northern cities to talk about diversionary action (4.83.4). Perdiccas instructed the Macedonian envoys to say that he would do his best to bring the Greek cities over to the Spartans if the Spartans would help him reduce Arrhabios, the king of the 'barbarian' Lyncestians who were being a nuisance to his west. Perdiccas and the dissidents in Chalcidice together promised to meet the Spartans' costs, and the Spartans, Thucydides adds, were attracted by the possibility of sending helots on a distant expedition and thereby dispersing those amongst them who might otherwise think of taking advantage of the Athenian presence at Pylos and Cythera to revolt against Sparta itself (4.80.1);[15] that would also avoid putting Spartiates themselves at risk again.

The Spartans would have had no reason to believe that they could sustain a foothold in 'the Thraceward region',[16] and we do not have any reason to think that they would have wished to. They simply needed to have 'places available to transact in mutual exchanges' with Athens

---

[15] To force the point, Th. relays a story of Spartans having at some unspecified time offered freedom to helots who claimed to have distinguished themselves in battle, garlanded 2,000 who said they had and, presuming these to be the most courageous and thus most likely to revolt, quietly had them done away with (4.80.3–4). On Grote's fulmination and a characteristically ironic reaction, Gomme in HCT III: 548, more reflectively Hornblower CT II: 266–7. Hornblower doubts its truth on the grounds that it would have been difficult to do away with 2,000, a number which is anyway suspiciously common in Th. and Herodotus. One might also wonder (Paul Cartledge suggests to me too sceptically) whether it was not an ancient, perhaps more particularly Athenian, 'urban myth' that escaped Th.'s caution about such tales.

[16] On which Th. expands at 1.56.2.

and thus relieve 'pressure on the Peloponnese from the war' (4.81.2). One supposes that they believed that the prisoners were an asset the Athenians would rather bargain with than waste, saw no problem in expending helots and foreign mercenaries and could see no more feasible alternative. What is certain is that they put Brasidas in command. They knew that he was a man who could get things done, he was keen to go and his reputation with others was high; Chalcidiceans indeed had expressly asked for him (4.79.2–4.81.1). He was given 700 helots and money to hire other troops from members of the Peloponnesian league.

Thucydides does not explain all of this, and what he does he mentions later. He writes for narrative effect, making it possible to see how things might have been seen at the time and leaving the reader to guess why things happened the way they did. As with several other campaigns, he takes the expedition in stages, alternating his account of its beginnings with Athens' moves against Megara and Boeotia. There are chronological grounds for this, although both Gomme and Hornblower have wondered whether in this instance he is not also using the alternations to draw attention to the contrast: the Spartan expedition to the north was much the more considered of the two.[17] Contemporary readers would have known that in the short term, at least, it succeeded, and they may already have come to think of it as Brasidas'; those in his force who survived it are said to have taken pride in being known as his men. Thucydides certainly writes it to highlight his qualities; in no other episode does he focus quite so much on one man or so often do so through the focus of others.[18]

This however is Thucydides, and nothing is what it might at first seem. Brasidas' first speech on reaching Chalcidice late in the summer of 424 was at the notionally pro-Athenian city of Acanthos. Some Acantheans were keener than others on the idea of an alliance with Sparta, but afraid of losing their grape harvest, which was still outside the gates, all agreed to let him in. Not speaking badly, says Thucydides, for a Spartan (4.84.2), Brasidas declared that 'I have not come here to harm the Greeks but to liberate them, and I have bound the Spartan authorities with the most solemn oaths to guarantee absolutely that those whom I win over as allies will keep their autonomy. Moreover, I have come not to add you to our list of allies either by force or by fraud, but on the contrary to offer ourselves as your allies in your fight against enslavement by the Athenians' (4.86.1). We do not know if what he said about binding the authorities in Sparta

---

[17] Gomme in *HCT* III: 540, Hornblower *CT* II: 257.
[18] Admirably illuminated by Rood 1998: 73–4.

was true; if it was, the promise was not to hold for long. Brasidas also bent truth and reason in claiming that although the Athenians had had a larger force at Nisaea, they had been afraid to engage him there, which showed that they would not come north to do so; this also proved to be mistaken. In any event, he added, he wanted to be clear: if the Acanthians were to reject his protection he would ruin their land and compel them (4.85.7, 4.87.2). Thucydides is careful to mention that notwithstanding the threat, there was a long debate in Acanthos, in which the fate of the grapes remained a lively concern. In a secret ballot, a majority eventually agreed that he could bring his army into the city if he would swear that its autonomy would be secure (4.88.1–2).

Brasidas had marched his 700 helots and the 1,000 mercenaries that Thucydides says he had hired up through Thessaly. The Thessalians had long been well disposed to the Athenians but, because as Thucydides puts it they had 'traditionally been governed by powerful ruling groups rather than enjoying equality before the law',[19] Brasidas, as a Spartan, did not find it difficult to get permission to pass through their country (4.78.2–3). Unlike Spartans whom we know of before him (Pausanias had been the last on his own initiative to go further north than Heracleia, where Alcidas was now making a difficult situation worse) he could be diplomatic; as Thucydides repeatedly says, he also moved with speed. Once out of Thessaly, he met with Perdiccas' Macedonian force and marched on to confront Arrhabios. At least, that is what Perdiccas expected him to do. But Arrhabios indicated that he would prefer to avoid a confrontation and asked Brasidas to mediate. 'Perdiccas told Brasidas that he hadn't brought him in to act as an arbitrator in their domestic disputes but rather to do away with anyone he, Perdiccas, designated as an enemy, and since he was the one providing maintenance for half of Brasidas' army Brasidas would be wrong to get together with Arrhabios' (4.83.5). Brasidas persisted. The Chalcidiceans had already asked him not to become embroiled in Perdiccas' problems, and he wanted to go on to their cities. He accordingly withdrew his army and an understandably cross Perdiccas reduced his funding from a half to a third; in not reducing it further he probably saw, shrewd as he was, that he might want help from Brasidas later. Brasidas himself had gone on to Acanthos.

Acanthos was on the eastern peninsula of Chalcidice, most of which was subject to Athens. Athens also had authority over the southernmost

---

[19] Mynott *TWPA* notes that 'the contrast in the Greek is between *dunasteia* and *isonomia*, which may amount in practice to the difference between oligarchy and democracy but doesn't quite say that'.

part of the central peninsula, where Torone was the most important city, and over much of the peninsula in the west, including the cities of Mende and Scione. It was these cities, Torone, Mende and Scione, that Brasidas was later to take and the Athenians, when they arrived, to defend. But Brasidas' priority was Amphipolis, which he wanted to capture before the Athenians could reach it. This, one supposes, is why he had gone first to the eastern peninsula; Amphipolis was most easily reached from there. This city, the former Nine Ways, had been re-founded by Athenians in 437 and was an important source of timber for masts and for revenue also (perhaps directly in gold, present in many of the watercourses that ran into the Aegean from the north and east, for it seems not to have paid a cash tribute). A large lake (since drained) impeded movement to its north, and it commanded the land route to the east. Eion, 3 miles down the river Strymon, and the island of Thasos, half a day's sailing to the east, commanded the route by sea.

The Spartans may have had Amphipolis and Eion in mind from the start and conceivably Thasos also (where they had promised to intervene in the 460s); Brasidas had certainly worked on his tactics in the two months and more he had been in the region. He expected to have support from dissidents from Argilos, a town near Amphipolis, and as so often in these ventures, from those who were 'involved' with dissidents in Amphipolis itself, together with others who had been alerted by Chalcidiceans and Perdiccas (4.103.3). He set off soon after his declaration at Acanthos, marching his men for 30 miles, stopping for supper at a place with fresh water, pressing on for a further 15 miles through a stormy night and snow (it was now December) to Argilos, not stopping until his force had covered the last few miles to the bridge over the Strymon at Amphipolis. Quickly disposing of the guard and meeting sympathisers from the city he crossed the river and was in control of the area outside the walls by dawn. His motley force had been on its feet in foul weather for more than twenty-four hours. The move was testimony to his powers of command.

There was consternation inside Amphipolis and no little confusion. People said that Brasidas could have taken it straight away, but his men needed to plunder and no doubt get warm and rest. An Athenian general, Eucles, was in the city, and managed to close the gates and get a message to Thucydides at Thasos. This worried Brasidas. Although neither of the Athenian generals had a force to hand, he knew that Thucydides was rich, that he had influence with leading men on the mainland, and might quickly be able to raise men from the places around. He accordingly announced that everyone in Amphipolis itself who wished to stay could do so, 'retaining their property with fair and equal rights',[20] and that those who did not should take what they could and leave within five days (4.105.2). The few Athenians in the city, realising that Eucles had lost authority and that help was unlikely to arrive soon, were happy to go, and the rest of the citizens were relieved. Necessity now descended on Thucydides who, writing of himself in the third person, explains that he took half a day to sail the seven ships he had from Thasos to Eion, arrived just after Brasidas had taken his vote in the city, and was able only to deter an attack on Eion (4.106). Whether he was then impeached in Athens for failure (or believed that he would be if he returned to the city) he went into exile for twenty years. Had he not, we might not have had the text we do (5.26.5–6).

The capture of Amphipolis was an important moment. When the cities in the north that were still subject to Athens learnt of the terms that Brasidas was offering and the 'easy manner' (4.108.3) of the man,[21] they were excited at the thought of change. They were encouraged also by the Athenian defeat in Boeotia and 'the seductive but misleading assertions of Brasidas when he said that the Athenians had been unwilling to engage with him at Nisaea when he was there just with his own army'. They all wanted to be the next to secede, asked Brasidas to intervene and assumed that this would be easy. 'They felt there was no cause to fear', Thucydides writes, 'though this later proved to be an underestimation of Athenian power on the same scale of magnitude as the power itself. They preferred to make their judgements on the basis of wishful thinking rather than prudent foresight, as men often do when they indulge in uncritical hope for what they want but use their sovereign powers of reason to reject what they would prefer to avoid . . . Above all, they were ready to take any sort of risks because they felt a rush of excitement in their present situation and were for the first time about to have some demonstration of what the Spartans could do when strongly aroused' (4.108.4–6). The Athenians sensed this and 'sent out garrisons to the cities, doing the best they could at such short notice and in the wintry weather'. Brasidas tactfully proceeded to reconstruct a shrine to Athena at the edge of Amphipolis, made preparations for triremes to be built on the Strymon (4.108.3–7), and went off before the winter ended to take the eastern peninsula in

---

[20] Mynott *TWPA* notes that '*ise kai homoia* ("the equal and the same") seems to be a sort of formula, of which we also get an echo in 4.106.1 (which reads literally "not being deprived of the city (*polis*) in the equal (*iso*)"'.

[21] Mynott *TWPA* notes that this is Th.'s only use of *praoteta*, which could be translated as 'gentleness'. Hornblower *CT* II: 42–9, 276–8 remarks on the distinctiveness of Th.'s language more generally on Brasidas.

Chalcidice and the city of Torone, where in the face of more resistance than he had met in Acanthos or Amphipolis he assured the inhabitants – many of whom, Thucydides engagingly observes, had had no idea of what was going on – that they had not wronged the Spartans but had themselves been wronged by the stronger power. He also asked Sparta for reinforcements (4.109–4.116.3).

Thucydides does have the notion of 'being bound'. But the 'things done' in 424 show that he was wise to deploy it sparingly. One can suppose that in the anxiety and agitation of a war that was proving so difficult to pursue, all were impelled to use their power where they could. The Athenians however had no military or political need to take Megara; at the very least, they had no more evident need to take it in 424 than they had in 431. Nor did they need to conquer Boeotia; in doing so indeed they might well have opened a front on which they could not be sure of victory and, as it was, they suffered losses and one supposes no little humiliation also; their failure certainly helped Brasidas to reach the north. Hermocrates and his associates in Syracuse also appeared to believe that they had to act. The Athenians, they said, were preparing to attack, and in hindsight, can be seen to have been right. But in 424, the threat was not immediate, and the Athenians who were in Sicily itself readily accepted peace. If Hermocrates and his associates felt bound to move as they did, it was because they had reasons for preferring to do so now rather than later, when it might be too late to retain Syracuse's own initiative and pre-eminence. The Spartans certainly thought it essential to recover the prisoners at Athens and also their fleet, and one can see why. The Athenians had had them in a vice. The opportunity offered by Macedonia and the Greek cities in the north to threaten Athenian control at no expense was accordingly too good to resist, and there seemed to be no practicable alternative. The problem now for the Spartans was quite different: the success of their venture north might defeat their interest in sending it.

10   Interests 423–421

There is no exact equivalent for our concept of interest in ancient Greek and it is not an altogether satisfactory term of art in politics now. The word seems not to have appeared in English political writing until the later sixteenth century, and by the end of the twentieth, had often come narrowly to connote a regard for self and indifference to others. But this does not have to be so, and there is no more satisfactory term.[1] Its explanatory force in English, as in the Greek, lies in what is to someone's advantage, and even if advantage in politics may not always include other people, it will invariably be formed in relation to them. And it is not always simple. 'What's thy interest in this sad wreck? How came it? What is it? Who art thou?', the Roman tax-collector asks what he does not know to be the sexually disguised daughter of the king of the Britons who, in the gathering complications of Shakespeare's *Cymbeline*, has just woken on the headless body of an enemy whom she has mis-identified as a former ally and lover (4.460–1). Thucydides saw that complications arise at every point: in just how clear an interest is, who has it, its nature and how it comes to be formed and informed (or misinformed) as it is; in the differences between the interests people admit and those they might be thought truly to have; in the relations between their interests and those of others; and in how all these things are affected by circumstance, including the passage of time.

The most persistent interest in his story, as in all politics and war, was in power: *dunamis*, the raw property; *arche*, command, by extension empire or dominion; and *cratos*, rule (as in *aristocratia*). It was, we might say, a 'real interest', *aitia*, what Thucydides' translators often call a 'true reason', although 'reason' can understate its genesis. In the less moralised politics of the Greek fifth century, as again in the Renaisssance, men were

---

[1] The Athenians' reference to fear, honour and *interest* at 1.75.3 is often translated thus; but some (Thucydides 1907 and Hornblower *CT* I: 120) prefer 'advantage', Hobbes (Thucydides 1989) 'profit', Blanco (Thucydides 1998) 'gain'. In modern political (and legal) conversation, interest appears in a wide range of sometimes tendentious rhetorics (such 'the public interest').

more ready than those in the theatres of modern democratic politics to admit to pursuing it.[2] This is not to say that they were above dissembling when it suited them to do so. 'We accepted an empire when it was offered', Thucydides had Athenians say to the Spartan assembly in 432 (1.76.2). We just happen to have the upper hand, he has others say to Melians in 416 (5.105.2). But they were more often frank. The power of Athens' dominion or 'empire', the Athenians had explained in their speech at Sparta (to an audience that would surely have known), enabled them to allay their fears, maintain their honour and pursue their 'self-interest' in material gain (1.75.3). It was in the wider interest of retaining this dominion, Cleon explained to Athenians in the Mytilene debate, to do away with subjects who had freely decided to revolt, an interest that Diodotos shared but did not think was most wisely pursued in that way (3.40.4, 44). Dominion is 'like a tyranny', Pericles had explained, 'which it seems wrong to take but perilous to let go' (2.63.2). We use power, the Athenians were to explain to the Melians, 'knowing full well that you and anyone else who enjoyed the same power as we do would act in just the same way' (5.105.2) No one can be blamed for pursuing it, Hermocrates had said at Gela; it is those who fail to resist it who should be (4.61.5).

All these men knew of course that without power, nothing was possible, though as always, there was a question about where it lay, what to use it for and how to deploy it. It could lie in the authority of custom, law or office; in force; even occasionally in the force of the better argument.[3] It could be used to affirm solidarity, as the Spartans used it with the Thebans at Plataea; to inflict punishment, as the Athenians used it at Mytilene; to make a conquest, as the Athenians aspired to use it in Sicily; to exert restraint, as Archidamos and Pericles had argued it should be and Nicias was to suggest to Athenians who were keen to go to Sicily (6.11.4); or, as Pericles had hoped, to deter. As so often, it was not always possible to wield it alone; those with whom one shared it might share theirs with others, and enemies could do the same. Facing the threats one knew of was bad enough; not knowing where to turn made things worse. This was the prospect facing the secondary states in Greece who found themselves

---

[2] I use 'real interest' to refer to one that people may actually have, not that suggested by some theorists, which people may only be able to see when they have perfect information and can deliberate freely (well explained by Geuss 1981: 45–84).

[3] A once much-discussed conception is of power as the effect of any action on any other action, not necessarily confining or destructive or wielded by an obviously political subject, Foucault 1980: 140. The qualification has force, but the more general point makes power uninterestingly coterminous with all social relations (as in comparably simple interpretations of Nietzsche, Pippin 2010: 6 n. 8). Foucault himself tended to abandon this conception after the 1970s, but it lingers. Other difficulties concisely exposed by Detel 1998: 6–21.

excluded from a peace and alliance that Athens and Sparta were to swear in 421. And like anyone with power, those leading these states knew that retaining what they had required them either to use it or credibly threaten to do so, for otherwise it could vanish.

For all Greeks affected by the war, 421 was to be the most perplexing year. The argument in Sparta in the winter of 424–423 had been about what power to use for what end. Brasidas' campaign in the north and the praise that he gained for it there had become an object of envy to 'the principal leaders' in Sparta itself. But it was not envy alone, Thucydides explains, that gave these men pause. What did was the campaign's success. Leaders in Sparta were thinking that if Brasidas took the Spartans on 'to yet further successes and brought about a more equal balance of power' they stood to lose what they wished most immediately to gain: the Athenians might retaliate by executing the prisoners and refusing to return the confiscated ships. The Spartans concluded that 'even if in carrying on the fight [on what would now be a more] equal basis, they would have a better chance of final victory', it would be better now to desist (4.117.1–2). Their interests in the return of the prisoners and their fleet came first.[4]

They may have deceived themselves in imagining that a final victory could be theirs. One can be reasonably sure that no Athenian in the spring of 423 would have envisioned that. But the Athenians had their own reason for wishing to stop Brasidas. They wanted time, says Thucydides, 'to organise things properly'. Each side now therefore was interested in a truce. Envoys came from Sparta to discuss terms with the Athenian council (in the early spring, at the time of the Dionysia, where they might have found some entertaining relief),[5] and in their presence one of the Athenian *strategoi* explained to the assembly the terms that both sides were proposing. Thucydides interestingly (and to literary scholars intriguingly) transcribes the formalities. Each side would have access to the pan-Hellenic shrine at Delphi, envoys would be allowed to move freely, no state would accept slaves or other fugitives from the other, all disputes would be taken to arbitration, and the parties would explore terms on which the war itself could be ended. In the manner of many terms of possible agreement then and since, the last was usefully ambiguous. It might seem to have been a provision in bad faith, and perhaps it was;

---

[4] Th.'s gloss on the Spartans' reasoning is contested; the possibilities are discussed by Gomme *HCT* III: 594–6 and Hornblower *CT* II: 361–2, both of whom decide (with attention to various possible readings of the Greek) along the lines I suggest here.

[5] Gomme *HCT* III: 603, who mentions that at this festival, which drew people from outside Athens in some numbers, they may well have seen three comedies.

politics often is.[6] It allowed for the war to be resolved in a more enduring agreement or in further fighting, and there were disagreements on both sides about which to choose. But the Athenian assembly approved the terms as they were set out, and these were solemnised by two Corinthians, two Sicyonians, two Megarans, an Epidaurian, three Spartans and three Athenians, the last acting on behalf of both Athens itself and its 150 or so subject states (4.118.11–4.119).

Brasidas had not learnt of the truce when leaders in the city of Scione announced that they were coming over to him. He went to the city at once, travelling overnight in order to be able on the following morning to repeat what he had said at Acanthos and Torone and congratulate the Scionaeans for having 'of their own free will come forward to claim their freedom rather than timidly waiting to be led by some external compulsion to do what was so evidently in their own interests; . . . that was clear proof that they would bravely endure even the severest challenges. He said that if he could now settle matters in the way he planned he would truly count them as the most loyal of Sparta's friends and would pay them every other honour' (4.120.3). As Thucydides has already said (4.65.4), what Brasidas claimed was in the Scionaeans' real interest may not have been: the Scionaeans, like those in other cities in Chalcidice, were overlooking Athens' capacity to resist. As it was, they gave Brasidas a hero's welcome 'and publicly crowned him with a golden crown as the liberator of Greece, while individuals among them came up and decorated him as if he were an athlete' (4.108.4, 4.121.1). His reputation was rising, and it was a good moment for him to try to bring over Mende and Potidaea also.

As he was about to leave his base at Torone to raise troops to do this a ship arrived to announce the truce. An Athenian official explained that all the cities in the north could retain the allegiance they had had when the truce had been solemnised but that these did not include Scione, which had declared for Sparta two days later. Brasidas contested this, but the leaders in Sparta overrode him and offered to take the matter to arbitration. The facts favoured the Athenians, yet it was they who refused. For even though he had not been elected *strategos* that spring, Cleon was able to seize the moment to persuade the assembly to decree that all Scionaeans should be executed; Thucydides does not say, but one supposes that he argued as he had for the elimination of the Mytilenaens, taking a different view of Athens' longer interest, as he saw it, from that

---

[6] Price 2001: 263–73 who unpersuasively suggests that Th. writes it as such. Price nevertheless, and rightly, admires Rood's excellent discussion of Th.'s ironies in his account of the subsequent peace and alliance and their consequences to 418, Rood 1998: 78–108.

of those who had agreed the truce. Not, one supposes, having heard of what Cleon had in mind for the Scionaeans, the Mendaeans declared to Brasidas that they wanted to come over too. Notwithstanding the terms of the truce, the wish in Sparta itself to observe these terms and the force that he was himself expecting to arrive from the south to enforce it, Brasidas accepted their offer, had their women and children and those in Scione also moved to safety, and decided to use the time it would take for an Athenian force to arrive to help Perdiccas subdue Arrhabaios. Thucydides does not say why he did this; perhaps he wanted to settle things with Perdiccas in order to make sure of the contribution that the Macedonian might still be willing to make to his costs; perhaps he hoped that if circumstances should make it useful to do so, he could call on the Macedonian army for purposes of his own; it was very probably both.

But Arrhabaios was holding back, and since Illyrians from further west had promised to come to help the Macedonians against him, Perdiccas thought it safer to wait until they had arrived. Brasidas resisted. He was concerned that an Athenian expedition might now be nearing Chalcidice and wanted to get back there as quickly as he could. The two were still arguing when Perdiccas learnt that the Illyrians had decided to help Arrhabaios instead. The Macedonian troops panicked – it can happen, remarks Thucydides, in any large army – and Brasidas woke the next morning to find them gone (4.124–4.125.1). He had no choice but himself now to retreat from the advancing 'barbarians'. He told his troops that although the Lyncestians and Illyrians would be a noisy and frightening sight ('all that empty brandishing of weapons in the air looks very threatening') they had none of the Greeks' discipline, and being as willing to flee as to fight, had no honour either. Nor should his men fear their numbers, he said, 'for you come from a political system where the many rule the few, not one like theirs where the minority rule the majority, a minority that has acquired its privileged position solely by virtue of success in battle' (4.126.2), an argument whose force (indeed whose sense, for Spartans) is still disputed.[7] He managed to out-manoeuvre his pursuers trying to out-manoeuvre him, and when he was back in

---

[7] Hornblower *CT* II: 398–9; like Hornblower, I think that Gomme's common sense is right, *HCT* III: 614–15. With Athens in mind, it is not usual to think of Sparta as almost a democracy, though Brasidas was presumably alluding to its moderately corporate oligarchy; with Sparta in mind, however, it is easy to see the Lyncestians and Illyrians as peoples ruled by unaccountable clans; there is an allusion in the Greek to ruling families. This aside, none of Brasidas' troops would have been Spartiates, and one wonders how well they could have grasped what Th. has him say and how Th. himself had discovered what this was.

Perdiccas' territory, allowed his men to slaughter the oxen and pillage the carts that Perdiccas' troops had left behind.

It was then, remarks Thucydides, that Perdiccas began to think of Brasidas as an enemy and 'nursed a lasting hatred of the Peloponnesians'. This hatred, Thucydides goes on to say, given his bad relations with the Athenians, was against Perdiccas' 'natural instincts'. Perdiccas nonetheless ignored what Thucydides regards as 'the inevitable consequences for his own best interests' and worked as quickly as he could now to reach a new understanding with the Athenians (4.125.2–4.128, 4.132.1). These are puzzling observations. Perdiccas reveals as sharply and consistently as anyone in Thucydides' story and perhaps understood more acutely than any the intricate and shifting relations between necessity, interest, circumstance and opportunity. He had always had a reason for changing sides, even if he had not always quite done so, which was itself usually in his interest; he had been thought still to be favouring the Athenians when he had first asked Brasidas to help him against Arrhabaios. One may ask whether his temper now might have got the better of him. The Athenians would not have been impressed by the assistance he had given Brasidas in securing the area around Amphipolis and one can think that he could not be certain that the Athenians would help him where Brasidas might not against Arrhabaios and the Illyrians. But only weeks before, his brother-in-law Seuthes had succeeded to the kingship of the Odrysians to the east and thus to the control of Odrysian Thrace. This kingdom was an ally of Athens', Seuthes had a large army at his disposal and the Athenians controlled the sea. Thucydides may not therefore have been correct about 'the necessary consequences for Perdiccas' own best interests' as Perdiccas himself understood them.[8]

The Athenians meanwhile arrived to enforce Athens' interest in the truce. Nicias and Nicostratos, who had worked well together in taking Cythera in 424, had brought fifty ships with 1,000 hoplites and 600 archers and a further 1,000 mercenaries 'and other peltasts' from Thrace. The troops on Brasidas' side (Thucydides does not make it easy to determine how many there were) were weaker, and his authority in

---

[8] As it turned out, Seuthes was unable to hold Thrace together. In the winter of 418–417, after the Spartan victory at Mantineia in 418 and probably realising that Thrace was a safe ally no longer – not least because there was no longer one Thrace – Perdiccas joined a new alliance between Sparta and Argos (5.80.2). He did not think it necessary to break openly with Athens until the winter of 417–416, when the Athenians accused him of having pre-empted an expedition of theirs to the north in the previous summer, and gave him no choice (5.83.4). It is a tribute to Perdiccas' skill as well as luck that he died in his bed and still in power in 413. If the Mediterranean monarchy of Macedonia can seem to us 'a sort of ancient banana republic' (Morris 2011: 268), it can suggest that then, as now, political skill is not the prerogative of the more conventionally civilised.

Mende was not enhanced when one of his officers assaulted a recalcitrant citizen. Nicias and Nicostratos reclaimed Mende with ease. Having calmly told the citizens 'to go on managing their political affairs (*politeuein*) as they were used to doing and to pass judgement among themselves' on anyone they thought responsible for the revolt in Brasidas' favour (4.129–4.130.7), they proceeded to establish a garrison at Scione and then went home. In response perhaps to this intervention, the Spartans in Sparta now decided to send troops themselves. But like those that Brasidas had brought, these would have had to come up through Thessaly, and Perdiccas, who had connections there, persuaded the Thessalians not to let them pass; he knew that Nicias wanted proof of his renewed adherence to the Athenian cause, wanted to keep in with the Thessalians – and now also with Odrysian Thrace – and no longer had any interest in having Peloponnesians in his area.

The following winter was quiet. At its end, still acting against the terms of the truce, Brasidas made an attempt on Potidaea, but his ruse for getting over its walls was exposed and he had to retreat. A few Spartans who had been sent to manage the Spartan successes did reach him, and in a new kind of move for Sparta, which had not been used to overseas administration, two of these men were assigned to govern Amphipolis and Torone (4.131–2, 4.133.4, 4.135). The truce was for some reason extended into the summer of 422, and nothing more was to happen in the north until it expired. As soon as it did, Athens sent another expedition; as Thucydides more exactly puts it, Cleon persuaded the assembly to send another, and having now been elected *strategos*, took command. He stopped at Torone and with clever tactics and in the absence of Brasidas (the Spartan could not reach the city in time) he took it; in contrast to the tact that Nicias and Nicostratos had displayed at Mende he sold the women and children into slavery and sent the surviving men to Athens. He then went on to Amphipolis and Brasidas followed. Brasidas knew that although his force was no smaller than Cleon's, it might be less good, and he decided to wait inside Amphipolis' walls rather than confront Cleon in the open. Brasidas expected him to approach to reconnoitre, and hoping that he would think the place undefended, conceived a surprise attack. Most of his own troops came from places other than Sparta, and he encouraged them with the thought – attractive perhaps to Thucydides, who relished cunning and appreciated irony – that it is 'tricks and tactics which bring the greatest glory, when you completely deceive the enemy and thereby most benefit your friends' (5.9.5).

The tactic succeeded. Brasidas arranged for a small party of men to rush out of one gate to chase the Athenians along the outside of the walls and for the rest to rush out of another to catch them, and Cleon's force turned and fled. Those who share what they take to be Thucydides' dislike of the man recoil at Cleon's belligerence, and assuming that he was one of the populists whom Thucydides accuses of having divided Athens against itself (2.65.10), are inclined to blame him for the defeat.[9] He did at a crucial moment leave a flank exposed and was said ignominiously to have been struck from behind, but he had not previously been a notably incompetent commander and was never a coward. In the event, he and Brasidas were killed, Cleon not knowing that he had lost, Brasidas living just long enough to learn that he had won. Brasidas was buried with ceremony in Amphipolis, and 'ever since then', Thucydides writes (we do not know when), the people there 'make blood-sacrifices for him as a cult hero and have instituted games and annual offerings in his honour'; expecting the Spartans to remain the power in the city, they also tactfully re-dedicated its foundation (5.6.3–5.11.1). Now that the truce was over, another force had been coming up from Sparta to support Brasidas; one can only suppose that the Spartans had some reason to believe that the Athenians would not after all execute the prisoners from Pylos. But when this force learnt that the Athenians had lost and that Brasidas was dead, it turned back without waiting to discover if Perdiccas would again intercede to impede it. It had also learnt that Sparta was inclined now to move from a temporary truce to lasting peace (5.12–13).

This peace, we might say, was over-determined. The Athenians had already been defeated in Boeotia and now lost Amphipolis; they were uncertain about how their subject cities would continue to regard them and Thucydides writes that they 'no longer had the confidence that comes from assured strength, a confidence which had previously led them to reject the chance of a treaty when they thought they could ride their good fortune to final victory' (5.14.1). The Spartans were still anxious about appearing weak to their allies and their own subject peoples around Sparta itself, and no doubt still worried about their prisoners and ships. They were also afraid of what the Argives might do when the treaty they had with them expired in 421; they could not take on Argos and Athens together and did not want cities in the Peloponnese to seek Argive protection. The politics within each city had also changed. Brasidas and Cleon had been opposed to peace: Brasidas, says Thucydides, because of the standing that success in war had given him, Cleon 'because in time

---

[9] One of the more recent and extreme of commentators, in just two pages describing Cleon as 'revolting', 'repellent', 'appalling', 'loathsome' and 'evil', is Lendon 2010: 382–3. Gomme *HCT* III: 652–4, 659 makes a careful case for him, also Woodhead 1960.

of peace his misdeeds would be more transparent and his slanders less credible'. But what Aristophanes called these two pestles in war's mortar were now dead.[10] Circumstances favoured a different course of action, and different men were in a position now to press it. Interests in the two cities had changed. The Spartan king Pleistoanax had returned from the exile into which he had been sent for allegedly taking bribes in Attica in 446 and wanted no setback for which he could again be blamed. Nicias likewise wanted to find 'immediate relief from [the Athenians'] troubles both for himself and for his fellow citizens and to leave behind for the future the reputation of a man who lived his whole life without ever failing the city in any way' (5.16.1).

In the negotiations that followed, the Athenians once again spoke for their subject states and the Spartans for themselves; their Boeotian, Corinthian, Elean and Megarian allies, having no interest in agreeing to what they feared would be a joint dominion of large powers over them, refused to take part. Once the Spartans had ceased to intimidate the Athenians 'by sending word round the cities to prepare to build a fort in enemy territory' and other squabbles had been resolved, and despite the refusal of the Spartan allies to be party to it, peace was agreed. Thucydides again provides the text. 'The treaty shall be in force for fifty years between the Athenians and their allies and the Spartans and' – notwithstanding their refusal – 'their allies without deceit or intent to harm and shall have effect by land and sea.' The last would allow the Spartans their ships. The powers agreed also to return the prisoners and places they had taken from the other, including Pylos, Cythera, Amphipolis and (Sparta here acting on behalf of the Boeotians) Panacton, a fort on the border between Boeotia and Attica which had been captured by Boeotians during the recent fighting in the north. In a further annulment of Brasidas' campaign, it was agreed that Athens could do what it liked with Torone and Scione (there was no need now to mention Mende) and that other cities in the north would be free providing that those that had previously been paying tribute to Athens would continue to do so. More unsurprising in the run of such agreements, but fanning the suspicions of the Spartan allies who had wanted no part in it, was a clause allowing Athens and Sparta together to make any change in its terms they might jointly see fit (5.17.2–19).

The two powers drew lots to decide which of them would make the first move to implement the terms. The Spartans lost and immediately failed. Even when the Spartan carrying the order to return Amphipolis to

---

[10] *Peace*, 270–82. This play won the second prize in the Dionysia in 421, just a few weeks before the agreement on peace.

the Athenians had got back from Sparta, where he had gone to check that it really was an order, the people in the city refused; the man himself did not want to impose it and perhaps could not have done. The Spartans again asked their allies to accept the new terms, and again they refused. Then Argos declined to renew the treaty it had had with Sparta. These refusals impelled the Spartans to bind the Athenians more tightly by turning the agreement into a fifty-year alliance. The Argives would be no threat without support from Athens, and an alliance with Athens would stop members of the Peloponnesian league playing off one side against the other in their own interests; in fact it would not now matter if smaller states in the Peloponnese were to turn to Athens. Athens may have won the war as Pericles had envisaged it, but Sparta would not be seen to have lost.[11] Not only would it have no reason any longer to fear Athens; it need not be frightened of its helots either, for Athens was now also bound into helping suppress any revolt.

The Spartans' interests in the new accords are no puzzle. But what of the Athenians'? Commentators looking at the terms from Nicias' point of view argue that the peace and alliance allowed Athens to retain most of its overseas dominion and achieve the dual hegemony over Greece that Cimon had wished for in the 460s and which had in practice been accepted in the peace of 446–445; others argue in a different idiom that Athens' honour was satisfied and some of Sparta's saved.[12] Nicias, who was proud and sensitive to popular opinion, though not always skilled in using it to his personal advantage, would have been aware also that after so much fruitless fighting, peace was desired; the drift of Aristophanes' *Peace* and the enthusiasm after 420 for a shrine on the Acropolis to Asclepios, the god of healing, some of the surviving dedications to whom are to those wounded in war, suggest that it was. And even if the fracture of the Peloponnesian league might have made it possible for Athens to override the agreement and at last decisively take the war to Sparta, the Athenians might have been pleased to be relieved of ten years of trying to do so. The Athenians did return the Spartan prisoners as soon as the treaty came into force. But in a passage that he will have written later, Thucydides explains that confidence was short-lived. The Corinthians and some cities in the Peloponnese did their best to try to destabilise the agreements, and the Spartans began to arouse the suspicions of the Athenians by not acting – in the case of Amphipolis, not being able to act – on some of the provisions they had agreed to. 'For six years and

---

[11] On the view that Athens won the Archidamian war, Lewis 1992a: 432, who does not add that Sparta could claim not to have lost.
[12] Hegemony, Kagan 1981: 27–8. Honour, Lendon 2007: 367.

ten months the two sides refrained from invading one another's territory, but elsewhere the truce failed to hold firm and they inflicted as much damage on each other as possible; and then were finally driven to break the treaty . . . and reverted again to open warfare' (5.25.3).[13]

None of the secondary powers would seem to have had much materially to fear. Currencies do not seem to have been a problem. Among the more sizeable states only Sparta appears not to have had a monetised fiscal system by this time and, although there was a multitude of denominations issued by others, it is assumed that the willingness of markets to accept specie by weight would have allowed for easy exchange. At some point in the 420s Athens did try to impose its own coinage (and its weights and measures) on its dominion. That would probably have favoured its terms of trade and the value also of its tribute, but it is not known how successful the decree may have been. Little is known about the other costs of trade in the fifth century, but there is no reason to suppose that the kind of embargo that Athens had imposed on the Megarians was already widespread or likely to spread further, although Athens was imposing levies on ships passing through the Hellespont. One can certainly imagine that with the end of fighting, it would have been a relief not to have one's land open to the risk of repeated ravaging.

Looking back from modernity, where ideologies of one kind or another have mattered in politics, one could suppose that the powers that were not party to the accords might have been puzzled and conceivably dismayed by an agreement between what in the increasingly common terms of the later fifth century would have been described as a democracy and an oligarchy. But political arrangements at the time were more varied than these terms suggest, and the categories themselves appear to have carried less force than they tend to do now. Cities like Corinth and Sparta, commonly regarded as oligarchies, had assemblies; Sparta's politics were complicated by the existence of a double kingship and a degree of separation between elected powers; and Athens' democracy had until recently been directed by aristocratic oligarchs. It is safe simply to say that under Athens' dominion and in much of the Peloponnesian league cities enjoyed a degree of self-rule, usually but by no means always to an extent that suited the power whose 'protection' they enjoyed (1.19); that with varying degrees of conviction (and a few exceptions) they tended to approach democracy in the one and oligarchy in the other; and that smaller settlements, *komai*, would be under the authority of the nearest

---

[13] Th.'s reference to 'six years and ten months', whenever one dates it from, does not end in any event we know. But his general point stands.

city.[14] In what might have been thought of at the time as democracies as well as oligarchies, 'the people' frequently resented the *oligoi*, 'the few', those who defined themselves as *kaloi k'agathoi*, 'the good men and true', and in what might have been thought of as democracies the few commonly looked down on the many. Then as now, the general characterisations were as much crude and loose terms of approval and disapproval as descriptions of clear constitutional fact, and where they did not prove useful in internal strife were of more interest and concern to those whom we would now think of as intellectuals. For most of the time, political entities in Greece were driven by the wish to rule themselves. Unless there was a threat from a larger power or the possibility of invoking one of these powers to support a party in internal war, 'they did not want to be enslaved under either an oligarchy or a democracy', as Phrynichos was to observe in the last phase of the war, 'but to be free, whichever of these they ended up having' (8.48.5). The first allegiance, even of opposing factions, was almost always to their local place: their interests were in being ruled by their local kind and avoiding 'enslavement', accepting alliances, if they had to, for protection (5.69.1). Megara was indicative; in the dilemma that the leaders of 'the people' faced there in 424, they had initially opted to recall their internal enemies rather than accept support from Athens.

Thucydides follows the convention of referring to political communities by the name of the city from which they were governed, giving those who lived in the city and round about it that name also and, where the entity is unclear or does not matter to him, referring to the *ethne* in the area, to 'Thracians' for instance, or 'Illyrians'. But names in the agonistic politics of the Greek fifth century were rarely neutral. At the extreme, they could be all but erased. Sparta and Thebes had hoped to obliterate Plataea and Cleon may have wished that Athens could obliterate Scione (though that was in fact to remain the name of a place in which refugees known as 'Plataeans' were later to be settled (5.32.1)). Now that the treaty and alliance between Athens and Sparta were threatening joint dominion over all by the two most powerful powers, anxieties were acute. Thinking that they could no longer use one or other of the large powers to safeguard what they had from the other, the excluded states

---

[14] Power and self-government, Hansen 1998. Hansen's demographic reconstruction suggests that in the fourth century there were about 7.5 million people in the wider 'Greek city-state culture', extending through the eastern Mediterranean and up to the lands around the Black Sea, and that about 40 per cent of these lived in the largest 10 per cent of cities, Hansen 2006b. It is striking to learn that the population in 'the Greek homeland' in the fourth century BC was significantly larger than that in the second part of the nineteenth century AD.

had to look to themselves; and if the joint dominion should fail, they would need insurance against the consequences of that also. The question therefore for these places after 421 was not whether one or more new alliances for mutual security should be made, but how and with what confidence.

The Corinthians were the first to try. Soon after the treaty was agreed, they went to Argos to try to persuade the leading Argives that now they were free of their tie with Sparta, they should take the initiative by inviting any city that was so inclined to join them in mutual defence. The Corinthians asked only that until the idea became an agreed reality, it should be kept from 'the people' in Argos, who might reject it. The Argive leaders, says Thucydides, were not unsympathetic. They had contempt for Sparta's present weakness, saw themselves being able one day to command the Peloponnese, and were anticipating a war. Notwithstanding the Corinthians' request, they did ask their people, who agreed, and duly issued the invitation that the Corinthians had asked for. The Mantineans, who Thucydides says were also democrats, were the first to accept, and he reports that others, suspecting that the Mantineans might know something they did not, soon followed. Spartans went to Corinth to protest, but the Corinthians, having carefully asked representatives of the other states to join the discussion, offered what Thucydides forbears to point out was a pompous and self-refuting defence and refused to revoke the move. (Thucydides does mention that although they did not raise the matter at this meeting, the Corinthians were particularly annoyed by the fact that the peace treaty made no provision for the restitution of two places which they regarded as theirs.)

Those whom Thucydides refers to as 'the Chalcidians in Thrace' and the citizens of Lepreon in the western Peloponnese also accepted the Argives' invitation, but the Boeotians and Megarans were not willing to commit, and the Tegeans, who were in the geographical centre of the Peloponnese, openly refused. These were significant states, and the Corinthians, who tried and failed again with the Boeotians, began to lose heart. The Spartans meanwhile unilaterally attacked an ally of Mantinea's and resettled the survivors of Brasidas' former helot force in Lepreon. They even deprived the released prisoners from Pylos their rights for a while, fearing that they might also foment dissent in Sparta itself. They were plainly not confident of being able to hold to their accord with Athens. The Athenians meanwhile were annoyed. The Spartans had not managed to return Amphipolis or made any discernible effort to get the Boeotians or Corinthians to accept the new agreements. The Spartans repeated that they had no power over Amphipolis, but they did promise to try again with the Boeotians and Corinthians. They also asked to have Pylos back or, at the very least, for the Athenians to withdraw the Messenians and helots from there as the Spartans had withdrawn their people from Thrace. The Athenians, muttering about the mistake they had made in so quickly releasing the prisoners from Pylos, did withdraw the men the Spartans had asked them to, but were careful to hold on to Pylos itself, and did so until 409 (5.27.2, 5.35.2–8). And 'so', concludes Thucydides in his best lapidary manner, 'for this summer there was peace and there were these diplomatic missions between the two sides' (5.35.8). The Athenians had lost little apart from Amphipolis; if the Corinthians and Mantineans were now to make an alliance with Argos, the Spartans stood to lose much more. Tim Rood detects the emergence of an ancient trope: one's fate will be sealed by attempts to avert it.[15] But this was politics, not epic or drama; there was no certain fate, and the ironies that Thucydides relishes were to turn, several times.

They did so in a series of events that ended in something approaching farce. This was of little lasting consequence and Thucydides' detail can try a reader's patience; but he presents it with the zest of a true aficionado.[16] It also vividly indicates the kind and degree of political anxiety that Sparta and the other states were experiencing in a moment of radical uncertainty. All believed that whatever their interests were – and to most, beyond their immediate security, these were not clear – they could not be assured of realising these without an alliance with at least one other state; and could not then be assured that the alliance they made would not excite opposition from yet another and thereby undermine the purpose they had in making it.

New ephors had been elected at Sparta in the winter of 421–20. Two of these were opposed to the accords with Athens and invited Corinthians and Boeotians and other allies to Sparta, with Athenians, to discuss the situation. As the visitors were leaving, they took the envoys from Boeotia and Corinth aside to suggest that they consider an alliance with Argos which Sparta could later join. The ephors did not want a war between Sparta and Argos in the Peloponnese, and they believed that the war that might recommence beyond it would be more effective if the Peloponnese were united. They asked only that the Boeotians return Panacton to the Athenians in order to make it easier for the Athenians to return Pylos to them. On their way back to their own governments, the men from Boeotia

---

[15] Rood 1998: 80–1.

[16] The most efficient short account I know is Westlake 2009, although this does not examine the deeper political problem, and on some particulars, arrives at judgements with which I differ, for example Westlake's reading of Agis at 310 and mine in Ch. 11 below.

and Corinth were intercepted by 'two very high-ranking Argive officials' who suggested much the same to the Boeotians, hinting that the alliance they had in mind need not initially include Sparta. The Boeotians heard this to be what the two Spartan ephors had just proposed, which it was not quite, and were delighted. When they told their boeotarchs, these too were pleased, and promised to send envoys to Argos to pursue the idea. The men who had been to Sparta and talked to the Argives then went directly to the councils in Boeotia, the bodies above the boeotarchs which decided the federation's policy, to propose that Boeotia, Corinth, Megara and the cities in Thrace should swear mutual assistance. The boeotarchs however had neglected to tell the councils that this was what Spartans themselves had proposed, and the councils decided that since the Corinthians had split from Sparta over the agreements with Athens, they should not offend Sparta by including both in another. The proposal accordingly stalled and because it had, no Boeotian returned to Argos, 'and the whole business, explains Thucydides, 'became beset by distraction and delay' (5.36–8).[17]

Meanwhile, Spartans went directly to ask the councils in Boeotia to hand Panacton back to the Athenians. The councils were still innocent of what had been proposed in Sparta and discussed in Argos and replied that they would only return Panacton if Sparta were to make a separate treaty with them. The Spartans knew that this would be against the agreement with Athens but were keen to have Pylos back, and accepted. The Boeotians then destroyed the fort at Panacton. The treaty between Boeotia and Sparta alarmed the Argives, who had still heard nothing directly from Boeotia itself. They even began to wonder whether the Boeotians were not now being included in the alliance between Sparta and Athens and started to imagine the awful possibility of being at war with Spartans, Athenians, Boeotians and Tegeans all at once. Argive envoys accordingly hurried to Sparta in the hope that they could come to an agreement of their own. Having secured an exception that seemed as bizarre to the Spartans as it can to us, allowing the two states to fight over a disputed territory on their borders, in effect a licensed duel between friends, the two states agreed a fifty-year treaty of their own, subject once again to approval by 'the people' in Argos. Meanwhile, the Spartans, who had been charged with returning Panacton and prisoners in the fort there to Athens, discovered that the Boeotians had destroyed it. The Boeotians explained that they had long ago sworn with the Athenians that each of them could have use of the land at Panacton, and it was the land that

[17] 'The whole story gives us a very poor impression of the management of the Boeotian Foreign Office', Freeman 1893, quoted by Jeffery 1988: 359–60.

they would now be handing over. The Spartans were not pleased and the Athenians, as they had feared, were in uproar, all the more so when they discovered that the Spartans had agreed a separate treaty with the Boeotians, thereby ignoring the agreement they thought they had with the Spartans to coerce allies into the treaty they already had with each other (5.39–42).

Thucydides is as unsmiling as ever in the face of these politicians appearing, disappearing and reappearing in various combinations and degrees of sincerity, duplicity, bewilderment and panic. The situation was indeed serious. Five alliances had been proposed in little more than a year since Athens and Sparta had made their agreements. The three that would have been multilateral – one proposed by Corinth between Corinth itself, Argos, Mantinea, the Lepreates and 'the Chalicidians in Thrace'; and two, first proposed by some Spartans and then by the Argives, between Boeotia, Corinth, Argos and Sparta – had not materialised. The two that were bilateral – one between Boeotia and Sparta, the other between Sparta and Argos – had. Multilateral agreements are always more difficult but, even if Sparta had not been the inspiration of either of those that were bilateral, the fact that it was party to both showed how divided what Thucydides called 'the authorities' there were about the state of affairs. This might not have mattered if a sufficient number of effective men in Sparta and Athens had been convinced that ten years of war had wasted too many men and resources, both directly and in fruitless campaigns with allies who had been using the powers to press interests of their own; if a sufficient number in each had been willing, the Athenians on land, the Spartans at sea, to accept that they had no strategy for winning outright; and if a sufficient number in each had sincerely intended to bind their states and be as determined against opposition within and beyond as their predecessors had been during the first ten years of the peace that had been agreed in 446–445. Then the agreements might, for a time at least, have held. But none of these conditions obtained.

The leading men in Athens and Sparta may have been anxious about their capacities for continuing war – funds were not unlimited, Athens had lost many active men from plague and, for what appear to be reasons of economy and of birth and death itself, the Spartiates were not reproducing themselves – but the Spartans were already at odds with each other over the peace and alliance and Athenians were very soon to become so. On neither side did those who wanted to continue fighting show any sign of acknowledging that they had no strategy for defeating the other; and Sparta, not least because of the reappearance of an unbound Argos, was at this moment the more nervous of the two and continued perversely to place its hope in the allies that had excluded themselves from the treaties in 421. Some on each side, after so much uncertainty, were craving security; others, after so much failure, victory. The interests that had appeared for a moment to converge in Sparta and Athens in 421 were again diverging, and the secondary states felt less secure. Thucydides makes it clear that in the disarray feelings everywhere were rising.

11   Emotion in deed 420–416

Dionysius of Halicarnassus delighted in 'the old-fashioned wilful beauty' of Thucydides' writing, its 'solidity, pungency, condensation, austerity, gravity and terrible vehemence', and he was right to say that it 'above all' affected the emotions.[1] Yet although Thucydides was fashioning his prose when the advent of writing was hastening moves in Greek to abstraction, he nowhere indicates that he himself thought of the emotions, feelings, *pathe* or *pathemata* as a class. He uses neither word for the generality and has no very elaborate lexicon in which to convey the particulars; he says less than one might expect about desire, pleasure, envy, pity, sadness, inner disturbance or shock; he writes often only of fear and hope and of *orge*, mood or disposition, the more definite connotation of which, when there is one, is anger rather than feelings of a calmer or more positive kind; and he barely mentions any other. On motive itself, he tends simply to mark its existence in the verb *hormo*, to be eager for something or be motivated to bring it about.[2] His skill lies in conveying the emotion in the deed.

As I mentioned in Chapter 1, it was this that attracted Nietzsche. Thucydides precedes what Nietzsche sweepingly describes as the Platonic and Christian (and we can now see also post-Christian) inclination to separate intentions from the motives that give rise to them and separate

---

[1] Dionysius in Mynott *TWPA*: 594–9.

[2] Abstraction in Th., Allison 1997, the possible effect of writing, 100. Hussey 1985 suggests that it can be illuminating to read Th. against his more abstract contemporary Democritos, who urged a balance between mind and *psuche* (which Hussey translates as 'emotion') in the individual and the *polis*. The language may be interesting, but although Th. might have agreed, Democritos' point is rather banal and on none of the four occasions on which Th. uses the word can *psuche* be read as emotion. Another piece of Democritos' conventional wisdom, Ch. 5 n. 14 above. A considered comparison between Democritos and Th. (not bearing directly on this question), Farrar 1988: 192–264. I am indebted to Mynott's understandings of Th.'s use of relevant words and his explorations in Schrader 1998; Th. mentions hope seventy-six times, fear (*deos* or *phobos*) seventy times, *orge* forty times, *hedone* seventeen times and the other particular emotions less often. Macleod 1983f: 135 nicely appropriates, for Th., a remark made about Michaelangelo: 'he says things, and you say words'.

both from the actions to which motives and intentions contribute. One can read him to incline to what a philosopher might now describe as a non-separability thesis on motive, intention and action and a non-isolability thesis on motive, intention and action and their context; to the view that one may analytically distinguish between motive, intention and action, but cannot in practice always separate them; that one may be able analytically to distinguish between motive, intention, action and their contexts, but cannot in practice always isolate these. Nietzsche put the point more strongly. 'There is no "being" behind doing, effecting, becoming; "the doer" is merely a fiction added to the deed – the deed is everything.' Robert Pippin persuasively reads this to suggest that we have pre-volitional, pre-reflective commitments to one or another state of affairs, commitments that we can discover in what we and others think and how we and they act; foundations, if one can describe them so, on which we all argue; and that in fashioning our arguments and forming intentions from these commitments we more often than not embellish, qualify or transmute them and so hide them from ourselves and each other; which is why it can follow that the best evidence on why we do what we do may lie not in what we say or think but in how we act. ('Obras son amores y no buenas razones', say the Spanish. Actions speak more truthfully than words.) If we are honest with ourselves (something that is ironically made easier, Nietzsche agreed, by insisting on the autonomy of reason and its separation from motive) we will acknowledge that the impulse to act is the wide Greek sense of the word, often erotic. It would be a mistake, the kind of mistake that Pericles made when he told citizens that they should love the city (2.43.1), to suppose that we can *decide* to do so. Like desire and love themselves, and hate, our commitments happen to us.

The philosophical questions are for Nietzsche.[3] Thucydides was not philosophically inclined, or if he was, he did not make his inclination explicit. And if he did accept something like the picture that Nietzsche draws, he will not have been aware that there was anything remarkable in so doing. But if he did have this picture, it would account for his tendency to examine what men thought (often expressed in speeches to others) in the light of what they did. It would explain the distance he keeps from matters of principle and the purity of motive. And it could go some way to resolve the puzzle of a writer who though evidently alert to the force of

---

[3] Quotation from Nietzsche, *On the Genealogy of Morality*, first essay, section 13; I take the translation by Pippin 2010: 74. The interpretation of Nietzsche also from Pippin, who suggests the philosophical terms of art and summarises some of the questions we might ask at e.g. 83–4; also Williams 1993, Pippin n.d., Geuss 2008: 11–13. Pericles also Ch. 5 n. 12 above.

emotion in men's commitments, spent so little time considering it apart from how they acted.

One does however have to ask about the emotions themselves. Thucydides' declaration that the effects of war will always be what they are 'while human nature remains what it is, though the degree and kind of the damage may vary in each case according to the particular circumstances' (3.82.2) is not unambiguous, but most read it to say that there are enduring truths about humans, not least in the feelings they have. If what he says about the pride, humiliation, resentment, vindictiveness, extremism and moderation in politics and war in fifth-century Greece are constant features of what he calls 'the human condition', *to anthropinon* (1.22.4), we might believe that what he conveys of these is what we might find everywhere and always. But this is too simple. One does not have to subscribe to a strongly cognitive view of the emotions to accept that they are always directed to things in the world, to what circumstantially there is and how the culture in question tends to view it. Few moderns are presented with the circumstance of slaves, helots or aristocrats who matter. Few in steadier places will have been faced with violence from neighbouring settlements or their own. Few will have known large assemblies or popularly constituted courts of law. And what many moderns do encounter will not usually be shaped by fifth-century Greek notions of honour, shame, justice and revenge. Thucydides may have believed that he was writing a 'possession for all time', but he was not an anthropologist in reverse, trying to make strange his own experience of the 'human condition' in order to make it familiar to readers whose understandings and misunderstandings he could not have imagined. One may reasonably presume that for late fifth-century Greeks, as for us, if emotions do not matter, nothing does. But we cannot unthinkingly presume that those embedded in the pre-volitional, pre-reflective commitments of the people Thucydides is writing about are those that we might feel now or even immediately grasp.[4]

---

[4] Arguments about 'naturalist' *vs* 'cognitive' or 'constructivist' views of emotions in classical Greece in Konstan and Rutter 2003; Konstan 2001 is a constructivist review. Emotions mattering, Elster 1999: 403, who gives a 'naturalist' account; a recent expression of the contrary case, that what matters to people is given not by emotion but by a non-metaphysical, non-naturalist, normative cognitivism (roughly, reason), Parfit 2011: 426–63 and *passim*. An informative survey of Greek conceptions, largely but not entirely from the fourth century, Dover 1974. The argument that if we are to escape from scepticism about others' states of mind and feelings, we have no choice but to believe that there is a sufficient number of ways in which their experience and emotions resemble our own (Davidson 2001) is plainly sensible, not least for daily life; but it can be too swift for those whom we have not met or never will. A sketch of the moral considerations, Dunn 1980: 110–11.

'Hubris' is an interesting instance and an important one. It was an emotion recognised by the Greeks, whose name for it we use, and was as significant and pervasive in ancient Greek politics as it is in our own. But the Greeks' *hubris* was not quite ours. It did describe action that crossed a line, but the line was differently defined. In Christian conceptions (and readings of Greek texts that have been infused with such conceptions) it connoted an offence that offends the divine, and we can moralise it still in a secular way. In a study of twentieth-century American presidents and British prime ministers it is described (in what the authors claim is a medical language) as seeing the world as an arena in which one can achieve glory in power; express messianic zeal and exaltation; show a disproportionate concern for the presentation of one's self and 'image', conflating this often with a collective entity; exhibit excessive self-confidence and contempt for others; and accept accountability only to a higher court. Hubris nowadays, it is said, is characteristic of those who are restless, reckless and impulsive, allow their rectitude to disregard or override considerations of a practical kind and can at the limit altogether lose touch with what the more restrained take to be reality.[5] For fifth-century Greeks, by contrast, *hubris* was a deliberate act, the direct and amoral practice of demeaning others for the sheer pleasure of doing so; of disrespecting or dishonouring them, treating them perhaps as slaves, yet not always thereby honouring oneself. Thucydides uses the term as a noun or in its verbal form on just fifteen occasions, usually reporting what he has learnt from others: in three instances of Corinthians imputing it to Athenians and one other of Spartans doing so; in three instances also, of Spartans or Athenians rejecting the imputation; and in two, of Cleon and Diodotos imputing it to the rebellious Mytileneans. Scholars suggest that in Athens at least, *graphe hubreos* was a suit for a public offence of emotional resonance, and although they can disagree, the so-called Old Oligarch (whose views on democracy I mentioned in Chapter 5) hints that cases were not uncommonly brought to court.[6] But Thucydides does not dwell on judicial matters. His other reports of the accusation, in which he is again 'focalising' others, are instances of sacrilege: of Athenian soldiers using water at the shrine at Delion for the

---

[5] Owen and Davidson 2009.

[6] The Greek understanding of *hubris* from Fisher 1992, who emphasises the disposition to dishonour but, as Cairns 1996 argues, underrates the accompanying disposition to high spirits which I mention at the end of this chapter. Aristotle classed *hubris* with anger, Konstan 2001: 46, 73. A 'weighty offence' of 'emotional resonance', Cohen 1995: 120. Frequency of cases, which is disputed, in the so-called Old Oligarch 3.5, Gagarin and Woodruff 1995: 143. A further brief discussion of the civil offence (with special but not exclusive attention to rape), Harris 2006: 316–20.

things that soldiers use water for (4.97.2–4) and of miscreants mutilating statues of a god in the streets of Athens (6.28.1). Nonetheless, *hubris* was a central quality of many of the actions he describes, and nowhere more evidently so than after the failure of the peace in 421.

It was Alcibiades, writes Xenophon fifty years or so later in a pointedly ethical piece, a man of 'insolence, incontinence and high-handedness', who was 'the most hubristic of those who lived under the democracy'.[7] Introducing Alcibiades' intervention in Athenian politics in 420, Thucydides simply observes that he was 'still of an age that would be thought young in any other city', that's to say about thirty, was 'highly regarded by others because of his ancestry' and had a 'considered view' of what the city should do following the peace and alliance that had been agreed in 421. Although Thucydides does not mention (as seems likely) that Alcibiades had not been elected *strategos* until the spring of 420, he does say that he had been piqued at not having been consulted on the moves to peace by either Nicias or Laches in Athens or the Spartans, with whom his grandfather had had a close association ('Alcibiades' was in origin a Spartan name) and for whose prisoners from Sphacteria he had shown concern (5.43.2).[8] Alcibiades' 'considered' view, which appears not to owe anything to the slight he had suffered over the moves to peace but was in 420 nevertheless self-serving, was that Sparta could not be trusted. He used the authority of his new office to urge leaders from Mantinea and Elis to ask Argos to invite all three states into a new, alternative alliance that Athens could subsequently join. The Argives were keen, reflecting, so Thucydides says, 'that if it came to war they would have in Athens a city fighting alongside them that had ancient ties of friendship with them and was governed by a democracy, as they were, and moreover had great power at sea' (5.44.1).

Alcibiades is commonly contrasted with Pericles and Nicias. It is less often noticed, not least by Thucydides who nevertheless makes it clear in what he writes, that he shared much with Cleon. The two came from different parts of Athenian society; Cleon was the son of a tanner, Alcibiades the son of an aristocratic general who had died in battle in the 440s and through a family connection arranged for his son to be a ward of Pericles. Alcibiades also had personal attractions that Cleon did not. But as Thucydides writes them, both were driven by a restless desire for personal power; both were compulsively competitive and prone to jealousy;

---

[7] Xenophon, *Memorabilia*, 1.2.
[8] Alcibiades perhaps elected *strategos* in 420, Andrewes *HCT* IV: 69. He had fought at Potidaea in the late 430s, where Socrates is said to have saved his life, and at Delion in 424–423, Plato *Symposium*, 221e and perhaps relying on Plato, Plutarch, *Alcibiades*, 7.

both were confident operators; and in contrast to Pericles and Nicias, both can seem to have been unusually free of anxieties about their own honour. *Hubris* came easily to them. Cleon had demeaned the envoys from Sparta who came to Athens to try to resolve their difficulties after Pylos in 425, and Alcibiades now was to do the same. Having learnt in the summer of 420 that the Athenians were minded to make an alliance with Argos and that they had invited Argives, Mantineans and Eleans to Athens to discuss it, the Spartans had at once sent envoys of their own to Athens to settle the differences that had appeared since the peace. They had said that they had full powers to negotiate, the council was persuaded, and Alcibiades feared that the assembly in Athens might be persuaded also. To avoid this, writes Thucydides, he told the envoys that if they were to explain to the assembly that they did not in fact have full powers and thereby appear to be attractively flexible, he would be able to persuade the Athenians to return Pylos to Sparta and resolve other out-standing differences between the states. 'His motive was both to distance the envoys from Nicias and to enable him in the assembly to discredit the Spartans for having dishonest intentions and for never saying the same thing twice, and thereby to effect the alliance with the Argives, Eleans and Mantineans. And so it turned out' (5.45.3–4). The Spartans did as Alcibiades asked, the assembly's suspicions were aroused, the envoys from Argos, Mantinea and Elis were called in, and it was only the fact or omen of a sudden earth tremor, Thucydides says, that prevented a treaty with them being agreed there and then.

It is alas an improbable story. Several commentators have wondered how in all the to-ings and fro-ings, multiple suspicions and pervasive leaks of one party's intentions to another, the Spartans could not already have suspected Alcibiades and, even if they did not, how they could so readily have fallen for his ruse. Others have wondered just how full the Spartan envoys' powers could have been. And one can ask why the Athenians who had already talked to Spartans in the council did not intervene in the assembly. But the story does reveal how Alcibiades was seen by others and how he might himself have wished to be. (Indeed Thucydides may have heard the story from Alcibiades himself and, as Andrewes hinted, been seduced by his predilection for tales of trickery.)[9] In the event, in

---

[9] Andrewes *HCT* IV: 51–2. If so, Plutarch was diverted also; his version of the tale is slightly different but similarly inclined, *Alcibiades* 14. Hornblower *CT* III: 106 is curiously casual. Alcibiades himself as the possible informant, Brunt 1993b. It is also (just) conceivable that Alcibiades colluded with at least one of the Spartan envoys, Endios, whose patronym was Alcibiades and who was a hereditary *xenos* or guest-friend of Alcibiades' family. Th.'s remark that the Spartans had sent 'men they thought likely to be appropriate for the Athenians' (5.44.3) may (just) mean more than appears.

the assembly the next day Nicias was able to take the initiative. He told the Athenians that to postpone the resumption of war would enhance their standing and be an embarrassment to the Spartans and that the situation in which they now found themselves 'was a very satisfactory one and their best course was to preserve their success for as long as they could, while the Spartans were suffering misfortunes and urgently needed to risk everything on a lucky break' (5.46.1). It reveals much about the dispositions of the Athenian assembly that a majority was now swayed by this and agreed to send Nicias with others to ask the Spartans to abandon the treaty they had made with the Boeotians, undertake to return Panacton in good condition, and thereby observe the conditions of the peace.

But Nicias found the Spartans unable to accept and feared for his honour; he feared also for his authority against Alcibiades and others who distrusted the Spartans and of being accused of naivety if he went home empty-handed. He accordingly asked the Spartans formally to reaffirm their existing oaths. This they did, though the avowal meant little, and on his return Nicias was powerless in the face of the assembly's anger and Alcibiades. The envoys from Argos, Mantinea and Elis were recalled and the Athenians agreed a hundred-year treaty of full military alliance with them.[10] Nicias would have been able to take comfort only from the fact that neither of the large powers actually renounced their oaths to the other and the fact also that 'the Corinthians, Argive allies though they were, did not join in this sworn treaty – indeed they had not joined the Eleans, Argives and Mantineans earlier in making their full alliance to be at war and peace with the same people – but said instead that they were satisfied with their first limited alliance' (as they had not been when the Athenians had proposed a similar alliance with the Corcyraeans) 'whereby they helped each other defensively but did not join in campaigns to attack third parties. In this way the Corinthians distanced themselves from their allies and were turning their attention again to Sparta' (5.46–8, 5.50.5).

Alcibiades was not alone in taking pleasure in diminishing the Spartans. The Eleans were to do so in front of all the Greeks at the Olympiad later in the summer of 420. Olympia was in Elean territory and it was an Elean body that ruled on procedure for the games. It judged that in the face of the truce that was always observed between states during the festival,

---

[10] Th.'s specification at 5.47.9 of the authorities who formally swore to the treaty in each state is tantalising; connoisseurs of constitutional forms in Greece would very much like to know more about those in Mantinea and Elis and those he calls 'administrators' at Argos.

Sparta had attacked Lepreon, on the border of Elis, and that Spartans should therefore be banned from the games. It is not clear how far this truce did extend before the Olympiad and what kind of attack Sparta (or one of its proxies) had in fact mounted. The Spartans protested and refused to pay a fine immediately; when the Eleans agreed that they could instead come to the altar of Olympian Zeus at Olympia itself to swear to do so at some future time, they refused again; to have accepted would have been to acknowledge their fault. Things deteriorated further when a prominent Spartan was whipped for falsely entering his winning chariot and four as Boeotian. The 'whole gathering', says Thucydides, was terrified that this would prompt an attack at Olympia itself, but the festival passed without further incident. One presumes that the Spartans had decided not to risk their reputation in front of all the Greeks (5.50.1–4).[11] They did not however leave Lepreon, and their humiliation was to continue.

At the end of the year, 'neighbouring tribes' attacked the Spartans' fort at Heracleia and killed men there, including the Spartan military commander, Xenares, who was perhaps the same Xenares (Thucydides does not say) who was one of the ephors who had opposed the peace and alliance in 421. The Boeotians dismissed the Spartan governor for his poor leadership and took possession of the site at the end of the winter; they were afraid that with the Spartans occupied in the Peloponnese, the Athenians might decide to capture it. And in the following spring, at the start of what was now the thirteenth year of the war, Alcibiades took it upon himself to demonstrate the new alliance he had secured with Argos, Mantinea and Elis by taking a force into the Peloponnese. Gomme observed that it was striking 'for an Athenian general at the head of a mainly Peloponnesian army to march through the Peloponnese, cocking a snook at Sparta when her reputation was at its lowest. Its daring, theatricality and small practical value were characteristic of Alcibiades.'[12] It had a practical value for Alcibiades' own political ambitions, but was again an act of *hubris*.

Argos had meanwhile decided to invade Epidauros, claiming that dues had not been paid on a shrine of theirs in Epidaurian territory. 'Even without that excuse it seemed a good idea to Alcibiades and the Argives to attach Epidauros to the alliance if they could, both to keep Corinth quiet and to offer the Athenians a shorter route from Aegina' (5.53).

---

[11] The various questions about the episode are discussed by Hornblower *CT* III: 124–35.

[12] Sensitive as always to the political geography, Gomme asked how Alcibiades might have entered the Peloponnese. The isthmus would have been hostile, and he probably went first by sea to Argos, *HCT* IV: 69–70.

A Spartan force set off; no one that we are aware of, including Thucydides, knew for where, perhaps it was to intervene against this incursion, only to turn back when the customary sacrifice on the border produced omens that were inauspicious. The Spartans then asked their allies to prepare for a joint expedition to Epidauros at the end of the coming month, which was sacred to Dorians and not an appropriate time to fight. Hearing of this, the Argives suspended their calendar so as not themselves to cause offence by fighting at a sacred moment and were able to forestall the attack. The Epidaurians appealed in turn to their allies, but the allies, citing the standing calendar, either excused themselves or marched only as far as the Epidaurian border.

In what might have been a countermove by Nicias, though Thucydides does not say so, the Athenians had meanwhile invited a number of cities to a meeting in Mantinea to consider restoring peace in the Peloponnese more generally. A delegate from Corinth said that it was idle to be talking of peace when Argos and Epidauros were fighting. Others agreed and the meeting was suspended in order to try to persuade each side to stop. Neither would, and the delegates reconvened only to disperse. A Spartan force set off once more to intervene against the Argives, only to turn back once again in the face of unsatisfactory omens. The Argives were thus easily able to waste a third of Epidaurian territory and to go home without waiting for the 1,000 hoplites under Alcibiades that were on their way from Athens to help them. 'And so the summer passed' (5.54–5). In the following winter, there were merely local skirmishings. But Alcibiades, alert to any opportunity to humiliate the Spartans further, ordered an inscription to be added to the foot of the stele in Athens that recorded the peace of 421, declaring to all for all time that Sparta had broken its oaths.

The emotions in play in 420–418 were not just those of a few ambitious and influential individuals.[13] When a culture configures an emotion and people find a common object for it, it will spread. All Sparta's enemies were impelled to demean the Spartans when they were down, and in the summer of 418, they did try to recover their standing. We hear nothing now of omens, good or bad, as Agis was despatched to combine against Argos with armies from Tegea in the central Peloponnese, cities in Arcadia to the north and Corinth, Sicyon, Megara and Boeotia. When the troops met to the north of Argos, Thucydides says that it was obvious to those present that this was 'the finest Greek army ever assembled up to this time' (an odd remark, since few of those present would have seen

---

[13] Aristotle, considering *hubris* in *Politics* V, tends to concentrate on the actions of individuals.

many others), all 'picked men . . . who looked capable of taking on not only the Argive alliance but that and another such too' (5.60.3).

Agis however was an unusual commander, and he presents a striking contrast to the Athenians of the moment. He may have shared the caution that his father had displayed in 432. But he exhibited none of what might be seen as the *hubris* that Archidamos and other Spartans had shown at Plataea. And events now suggest that he may have been playing a longer game against the dispositions of ephors and others in his own city. He evaded an initial Argive advance and, moving south, divided his army in order to be able to surround the enemy on three sides above the plain of Argos, on which the Argives, cut off from their city and lacking the cavalry that Athens had promised, had regrouped. He was in a strong position, and without consulting others in their ranks two Argive generals approached him with a proposal of truce and a treaty of peace. Consulting just one other on his own side, Agis agreed. His men were disgruntled; they were sure that they could have inflicted a defeat. With rather less reason the Argives believed that they could have done so themselves, and were equally cross. On their way home they stoned one of the two generals who had proposed the truce; he escaped with his life but had to forfeit his property; in Sparta, Agis was merely censured.

Meanwhile, cavalry from Athens had arrived. Alcibiades, now ambassador rather than *strategos*, upbraided those in Argos who had agreed to a truce with Agis and thereby violated the terms of the alliance that he had brokered with Elis, Mantinea and Athens itself. He insisted on the matter being taken to the Argive assembly, which he attended, arguing in the presence of Eleans and Mantineans that the Argives were obliged to pursue war with Sparta, and managing to persuade them to authorise a force to recover hostages that the Spartans were holding in a small town in Arcadia. This angered the already furious Spartans in Sparta even more, and they turned their censure of Agis into a punishment; the assembly agreed to fine him 100,000 drachmas (if Thucydides is correct, a remarkable sum) and have his house demolished. One presumes that it was only his kingship that enabled him successfully to plead that he would answer their criticisms on a future battlefield and to escape by agreeing that before withdrawing from any future engagement he would consult advisers whom the ephors would appoint (5.57–63). Neither Thucydides nor any other source explains why he had acted as he had on the Argive plain.

Yet he was to do the same again. Having heard from sympathisers in Tegea in the central Peloponnese that that city would soon secede to the Argives and their alliance unless the Spartans at once intervened, he was again sent hastily north to stop it doing so. He reached Tegea with a few allies, others promising to come as quickly as they could. The Argives backed onto a hill and Agis advanced. He was not in a good position. One of his men shouted that he was 'curing one ill with another' (5.65.2); it was foolish to have come down to the plain to meet the Argives on the first occasion, and it would be foolish to attack them uphill now. Whether in response to the jeer or because he shared the opinion, Agis drew back and removed his army to the plain south of Mantinea. Thucydides does not explain this or mention the reactions in Sparta to his having done so; the kings did have discretion in the field, and we hear nothing now of advisers. But Agis can be seen to have been moving to a better place. The Argives went down to the plain on the following morning to confront him. In the battle that ensued, Agis' left wing was drawn out by having to keep facing the Argive army's right; the hoplites from Mantinea in the Argive army had been succumbing to what Thucydides describes as the common tendency of phalanxes to drift, each man being inclined to seek the protection of the shield of the man on his unshielded right. The result in this instance, Thucydides observes with unusual sharpness, was 'a complete and utter failure in tactical skill' (5.72.1); it caused a gap to open in the middle of the Spartan line, which now stretched for perhaps a mile, and when Agis ordered two Spartiate polemarchs to round up men to fill it, they refused. This appeared now to be a complete and utter failure of Agis' authority. But he himself took the initiative, led 300 Spartiates into the gap, turned left to rout the Mantineans on the Argives' right and then back to scatter the rest of the Argive force. Most of the contingent of Athenian hoplites and cavalry, being on the Argive left, managed to get away, but not their generals, Laches and Nicostratos, who died (5.64–5.75.2). The battle went to Sparta.

The Spartans had had doubts about Agis after his first decision not to engage the Argives. On the second occasion, Thucydides' story of the sceptic's shout suggests that his standing with his own men was not high; it is the one moment in the text when one can hear Spartans laughing. On the third, Agis allowed a gap to open in his line and his order to officers to close it, in what Thucydides has taken care to explain was a formally unambiguous line of command (5.66.3–4), was refused.[14] But the Spartans had not sent their other, older king, Pleistoanax, putting him in command only of a supporting force to Mantinea which turned out not to be needed. And Agis had won. He remains an enigma. Either

---

[14] Th.'s remark that Agis headed this command 'in accordance with legal custom' (5.66.2) should probably not be read as irony. He would have been writing for Athenians who knew little about Spartan arrangements.

he did not want to engage unless he thought he could win, or he did have a longer plan. Since he could have won on his first encounter and perhaps his second, and since on the third, in the battle at Mantinea, he had actually taken a risk in circumstances he had worked to avoid, one could infer that he had been working all along to bring Argos back to the Spartan side, colluding to this end with sympathisers in Argos, which would explain the private agreement he had made with two Argive generals to withdrew from the first encounter, and that he was waiting until he could be sure of getting the result he wanted.[15] In not telling the ephors what he had in mind, not being the indecisive coward that some (including some of his own men) had thought, and resisting the temptation to shame the Argives, he was cool indeed, arguably less susceptible to the emotions around him – and perhaps also to his own – than anyone else in Thucydides' story. His success allowed those who wanted to end the existing regime in Argos to do so. They persuaded the assembly to renounce the city's treaty with Elis and Mantinea, made a treaty with Sparta instead, and with Spartan help proceeded to end the democracy in the city and establish what Thucydides calls an oligarchy (5.76.2–5.81.2).[16]

It was a short-lived victory. In the following summer, 417, the fifteenth year of fighting, after yet another of the internal disputes that Thucydides had said were incited by the wider war, the leaders of 'the people' in Argos reimposed their will. Agis went to do what he could in the winter to reverse the change, but he failed to find sufficient support in the city and in the summer of 416, Alcibiades had the 300 leaders of the former oligarchy there transported to islands under Athenian control (5.82.2–5.84.1). Nonetheless, Sparta had at last inflicted a defeat on Athens, albeit at a moment of nominal peace, at the geographical centre of the war. Thucydides explains that this 'wiped away the stain of the charges the Greeks had been holding against them at that time – of cowardice [surrendering] over the disaster on the island, and more generally of indecision and slowness'. The Spartans 'were now thought to have been the victims of a chance misfortune but to be still the same men in spirit that they always were' (5.75.3).

---

[15] Diodorus 12.79.6–7 writes that Agis was prevented from slaughtering the elite Argive force, which may have been less willing to negotiate with the democrats in Argos, by an appointed adviser. Th. does not mention this, and only one commentator (Kagan 1981: 131–2) gives it credence. If it is true, I am wrong.

[16] In an interesting but frustratingly vague aside on oligarchies, Th. also mentions that the Spartans went on to institute an arrangement at Sicyon 'to favour the oligarchs *more*' (5.81.2, my emphasis).

What Thucydides does not so explicitly say is that the Spartans' relief at last from the *hubris* of others, in part as a result of Athenian miscalculation, in part perhaps as a result of Agis' abilities, was the beginning of humiliation for the Athenians. They had for the first time engaged the Spartans in the Peloponnese itself and been seen to lose, and they were now to show their pain. They did so at Melos. The inhabitants (or the leaders at least) of this island in the south-western Cyclades held to an historic connection with Sparta but had been formally neutral at the start of the ten-year war (2.9.4) and remained so, although they had prudently contributed to Sparta's war chest. As I mentioned in Chapter 8, Nicias had tried, not very hard, to take the place in 426. It was not a strategic priority for Athens then and would seem to have been less of one now that the Athenians controlled both Cythera, off the coast of Laconia, and Thera, east of Melos.[17] In the summer of 416 Athens nonetheless sent two generals with thirty ships of its own, six from Chios and two from Lesbos, together with 1,200 Athenian hoplites, 20 mounted archers and 300 on foot, with about 1,500 more hoplites from its allies. The force camped on the island, did some ravaging, which was itself an act of *hubris*, and its generals sent envoys to talk to the leaders of the Melian oligarchy. The envoys appreciated that the Melian leaders did not want their people to hear a long and persuasive speech which they might not be able effectively to challenge, and offered to deal with the issues in private (5.84–5).

The Melian dialogue, as it is known, has been one of the three or four most remarked upon of all passages in Thucydides. It is unprecedentedly stark and direct. The form is unusual and has invited comparison with tragedy, philosophical dialectic and texts on rhetoric. Readers see significance in the fact that it comes immediately before Thucydides' long account of the Athenians' expedition to Sicily. (For Rawlings, imagining that Thucydides planned to write ten books, it would have come half way through the text and been matched at the end of the work by an exchange between the Athenians and Spartans after the defeat of Athens in 404.) The seeming political point of the exchange, that when power has an interest it will do what it can to press it, has been taken by students of international relations as the quintessence of what has come to be described as a 'realism' about the relations between states, by some classicists as revealing the true thrust of Athenian imperialism and, in

---

[17] Cythera had not been returned to Sparta after the peace of 421. Thera (now Santorini) had been independent in 431 but may have been paying tribute to Athens since 429 or 428, and had certainly been doing so since 426, Meiggs 1972: 321–2, Lewis 1992a: 409 n. 110.

post-imperial times, has excited disapproval. Some have even wondered what it reveals about Thucydides himself and the 'lesson' he might have been intending to impart. But the Athenians' motive at Melos has been understated.

One has first to ask why the Athenians acted at Melos, of all places, and why they did so when they did. Melos, they conceded, was one of the weaker islands in the Aegean (5.97); it was not particularly rich and as I have suggested, had little strategic significance. There does not appear to have been any fighting in the Cyclades or the southern Peloponnese after the Athenians took Cythera in 424, and Melians had not been involved in the political manoeuvres after the peace and alliance between Athens and Sparta in 421. The Athenians did say that they were concerned to forestall any threat from an island they did not control (5.99). But since Melos was unlikely to present one, this cannot have been their central concern. Nor, despite telling the Melians that 'your enmity does us less harm than your friendship – that would be taken by our subjects as a sign of weakness on our part, while your hatred is a sign of our strength' (5.95), was their reputation likely to be. It is difficult to imagine who beyond Melos itself would have thought the island in any way important. Except the Spartans. 'Our dispute here is not with them', the Athenians said (5.91), and that was correct. But they would appear to have been the Athenians' intended audience. The Spartans had defeated the Athenians among others in the allied force at Mantinea, thereby demonstrating their superiority still on land in the Peloponnese, and their long-standing reputation had been restored. The Athenians wanted to demonstrate their superiority in moving at sea. In presenting the choice they were now offering to the Melians, to submit or risk extinction, they were taking no risk in showing this superiority to anyone who cared to be looking and directly insulting the Spartans, who might be. It was pure *hubris*.

As Thucydides reconstructs the exchange – or perhaps invents it, for there is not likely to have been a written record and we do not know which of the Athenians present, if any, he might have talked to – it certainly took a reasoned form and avoided what Thucydides has the Athenians call the 'fine phrases' of rhetoric and 'long and unconvincing arguments'. The Melians at once saw the choice they faced, to win the case for justice and suffer war, or to submit and be 'enslaved'. The Athenians replied that justice was not an issue where the contending parties were unequal. The Melians made little effort to challenge this claim and turned to what might follow for the Athenians in acting on it. The Athenians said that they were not concerned with criticism or retribution from others in the future but with their subjects now. Of course, they continued, there can be arguments and counter-arguments, but if fear is not to prevail, power must. In what can seem in the circumstances to have been an exaggerated reply to the question of whether they were not now afraid of making enemies, they repeated that what they feared were subjects already 'smarting under compulsions' who might commit some irrational act and plunge everyone into a situation that could have been avoided. In response to the Melians' suggestion that it would nonetheless be courageous and honourable for them to resist, the Athenians said that the only issue was the Melians' self-preservation. In response to the Melians' further suggestion that there was always hope in hope, in general and for rescue by the Spartans, the Athenians ridiculed both, adding that the Spartans acted as expediently as any when it was in their interest to do so. 'Surely', they went on, reverting to the Melians' sense of themselves, 'you will not be drawn into that sense of shame which is quite fatal when it is danger and dishonour that are staring you in the face. For many people, even though they can see the dangers they are being led into, are still drawn on by the seductive power of a name – this thing we call "dishonour" – and, victims of a word, in fact fall of their own accord into irreversible disaster and so bring on themselves a dishonour all the more shameful because it comes more from their folly than their misfortune' (5.86–5.111.3). The Melians' arguments were the more forceful at the start of exchange, the Athenians', as this last remark reveals, at the end. But both had known from the start that the only question was the Melians' survival, and that the outcome was not in doubt. All who read the exchange are in Dionysius' phrase 'above all' affected by the Athenians' cool ruthlessness and contempt. The reasoning, good and bad, is mere form. The Melians did not concede, the Athenians besieged the city and, after some resistance, which required a second expedition after most of the men on the first had left, secured a surrender; they killed all the men that they had arrested, enslaved the women and children and 'at some later time', sent 500 settlers from Athens itself (5.114, 5.115.4–5.116).[18]

---

[18]   There is a large literature. The reasoning is taken for what it appears to be and lavishly reconstructed by Alker 1996. Morrison 2006: 82–99 also takes the arguments for what they appear to be and concentrates on the 'lessons' he believes Th. is intending to impart, regretting only that Th. is not more explicit about these. Hussey not inaccurately describes the exchange as 'a symmetry of unreason', Hussey 1985: 127. Macleod 1983b remains close to the text, and reflects on how the Melians' rhetoric failed in the face of power. Bosworth 2009 agrees with Hobbes, who wrote that 'I see no reason why the generals had to enter into disputation with [the Melians], whether they should perform their charge or not, but only whether they should do it by fair or foul means; which is the point treated in this dialogue.' The charge was what it was, to take Melos; the question was whether the Melians would accept the necessity and survive, or not. To Bosworth this, together with the privacy of the encounter, can suggest that neither the Spartans nor anyone else at the time need have known what transpired, and that Th. was making a point to his readers about what Bosworth mischievously describes as

If what students of modern international relations call 'realism' in relations between states means acting on one's interests in the light of the
best knowledge of the circumstances and an intelligent appraisal of the
likely consequences, Athens' action on Melos was not realistic. Beyond
exacting some tribute and being able to settle colonists, they had no
substantive interest in the island. The circumstances were certainly pro-
pitious; they were confident the Spartans would not intervene. But their
consideration of the consequences, as the Melians revealed, was remark-
ably casual. If 'realism' means using power when one has it, this was an
instance. But 'realism' in this sense is at best half true. As Pericles had
seen after 445 and the Spartans, notwithstanding the Corinthians' jibe
(1.69.4), had appreciated, the effective possession of power can consist
in a credible threat to use it rather than actually doing so; indeed to
use it can reveal a weakness. (And if 'realism' is the claim that states
will sometimes pursue their advantage and sometimes not,[19] there can
seem to be little reason to bother with the doctrine at all.) What the
exchange does show is that on the Athenians' own inadvertent admis-
sion that 'the best recipe for success is to stand up to equals, defer to
superiors and be moderate towards your inferiors' (5.111.4), it was at
once politically unreasoned and not so much immoral as devoid of any
moral or expedient consideration at all. Thucydides offers no comment
of his own, and his account would have been less powerful if he had. It
reads as an act of rage and *hubris*, intended to salve the pain of Mantinea,
humiliate the Spartans, and impress citizens, one suspects, in Athens
itself.[20]

Nietzsche remarked on Thucydides' 'unconditional will not to be
fooled and to see reason in *reality*, – *not* in "reason", and even less in
"morality"'.[21] The political reality of *hubris* in fifth-century Greece did
not lie in the considered pursuit of an interest in defence, *autonomia* or
domination. Nor, except in so far as it was defined as a violation of the
rights of citizenhood within the state, was it a fact of moral attitude; to
be reduced to slavery or worse was just bad luck. In the actions of Alcibiades and the Greeks at Olympia as well as of the Athenians at Melos,

Athenian 'humanitarianism' and Melian foolishness in the face of necessity. The action,
one might reply, was there for all to see.

[19] Argued from the Melian case by Monten 2006: 16–20, drawing on Waltz 1979.

[20] Macleod 1983b: 62 argues that 'the Athenians' "ruthlessness" should not be confused
with *hubris*, if that term implies an overweening conviction of superiority, because they
are at pains to stress that their actions conform to the normal pattern of men and even
of gods'. But they are conforming to the pattern of the powerful, who in virtue of their
power, above all when this is unchallengeable, are superior and will take pleasure in
showing that they are.

[21] Nietzsche 2005: 225, his emphases.

it was theatre, the demonstration to others and oneself of one's power to demean and an expression of the pleasure in doing so. In the wars of the crumbling Yugoslavia in the 1990s, one could hear the frightening laughter. One might imagine it also at Melos in 416.

12   Purposes and decisions 415

Not everything in politics and war is necessity, interest or the thrill of doing down opponents. In agonistic times there can also be a restlessness, a diffuse and unfocused disposition to find something to act against. So it can appear to have been with the Athenians in the sixteenth year of this conflict. Frustrated in Greece itself, they were more strongly inclined than they had been 'to sail to Sicily and subjugate it if they could'. Few in Athens, Thucydides says, had much sense of the island or realised that if they were to try to conquer it they would be 'taking on a war on almost the same scale as that against the Peloponnesians' (6.1.1). He knew himself that Syracuse was as large as Athens (7.28.30). But even he may not have appreciated that Sicily contained a fifth of the 3 million or so Greeks against no more than a further fifth in Athens' dominions to the east and a tenth in Attica, or that Sicily had twice as much land under cultivation as the whole of the rest of 'Hellas'.[1] One can nevertheless believe him when he says that those who voted for another expedition to Sicily did not see themselves to be starting a large war; suggests, without quite saying so, that they would not have seen themselves to be starting a war at all; suggests that most of them did not know quite what they had in mind. Apart from Nicias and perhaps a few others, 'Athenians' may in some sense have wanted to subjugate Sicily. But it would be too strong to say that they were determined to do so and too strong to say that they weren't. They were, one might say, in a mood to see.

Their purposes were certainly not well defined. Majorities in the early spring of 415 voted in successive assemblies in Athens for an expedition

---

[1] Th.'s extended account of the settlement of Sicily at 6.2–5 may not be as consequential for the Athenians' 'unawareness' as he implies, Dover *HCT* IV: 198–210, supplemented by Hornblower *CT* III: 262–99; it may merely but not uninterestingly be one of Th.'s demonstrations of fact against hazy memory and slack supposition. A comparison of 'footprints' (against which Th. himself warns, 1.10.2) suggests that Acragas was of a similar size to Syracuse; other sources in Hornblower *CT* II: 432. Phaeax had brought Acragas over to Athens in 422 (5.4.6) but the city remained neutral in the subsequent campaign (7.33.2, 7.58.1).

to support two allied cities in Sicily and pursue the city's 'best interests' there (6.8.2). Alcibiades was to say that 'we are forced to take active initiatives against some cities [in Sicily] and keep our grip on the rest because there is a danger that if we do not take others into our empire we shall fall into theirs' (6.18.3). Thucydides himself, writing about the Athenians' first engagement with Syracusans in the following winter, says that they were 'fighting' – he may mean that they believed themselves to be fighting – 'to make a foreign country their own and to save their own country from the damage of defeat' (6.69.3); it is not clear whether they thought the one was a means to the other. An envoy from Athens, the nicely named Euphemos, was more diplomatic in telling the wavering citizens of Camarina in Sicily a few weeks later that 'we exercise our rule over Greece to avoid subjection to another power there, while in Sicily we promote freedom for your cities to avoid being harmed by them here' (6.87.2). From Syracuse itself, by contrast, Hermocrates had set out to alarm the Siceliots into believing that the Athenians wanted simply to acquire the 'good things' of Sicily (4.61.3).[2]

The power of Syracuse itself was not a new consideration for Athenians. Herodotus (7.157–62) mentions that Spartans and Athenians had in 481 asked Gelon, then leader of the city, to use it to help the Greeks against an attack from Persia. (Gelon refused when they declined to give him one of the supreme commands.) I have already mentioned that the Athenians had by mid century sworn alliances with Halcyae, possibly then also (but possibly later) with Egesta, and by the 430s with Leontini and Rhegion. In 422 Phaeax had been asked to see if there was any prospect of gathering these and other allies to fight what Thucydides describes as 'the growing power' of Syracuse (5.4.5). But there is nothing in the text to suggest that Hermocrates thought that Syracuse would or should fight Athens in the east, and even Alcibiades was not to claim that the Syracusans might wish to. Hermocrates was to owe his political survival to Sparta and Corinth in the course of Athens' attack in 414, but even then he sent no more than twenty ships to support the Spartan fleet in the Aegean in 411 (8.26.1). As Macleod observed, all who claimed that the Syracusans would go to the aid of Peloponnesians had reasons of their own for doing so.[3]

---

[2] Material ambitions, Cornford 1907: 50–1, Green 1970: 11–35, Cartledge 2011: 89–90. Dover on Greece as 'an essentially predatory economy', notwithstanding his warning against imputing explanations that Th. himself does not mention, *HCT* IV: 230. The only evidence for suggesting that the Athenians were trying 'to break the deadlock of the Peloponnesian war' (Davies 1993: 128) came later, and from Alcibiades, Ch. 13 below.

[3] Small reasons to doubt the number of Syracusan ships in 411, Andrewes *HCT* V: 61; Selinus sent two more, Macleod 1983d: 82. Cawkwell 1997: 78–80, endorsed by Hornblower *CT* III: 327, asks whether there may nevertheless been an ungrounded fear of

It is possible that having been away from Athens for nine years and probably not having visited Sicily, Thucydides simply knew too little about thinking in either place by 416–415; that he was generalising after the event about what 'the Athenians' wanted, and insufficiently informed of their vagueness or ambivalence – on this matter perhaps relying too much on what he had heard from Alcibiades.[4] Possible, but unlikely. He insists that he always did his best to check what he had been told and this part of his story was important to him. If there had been more to discover about what he would have called the Athenians' 'true reasons' for going to Sicily and how they arrived at them, one supposes that he would have discovered it; that since he didn't, perhaps there wasn't; and that his insistence on their poor sense of the place marks the fact.

What a majority of Athenians did at first assent to was a request to defend an ally. Their inclination to accept this, the insistence with which Alcibiades incited them to do so, Nicias' hapless attempts to discourage them and their more generally excited state together explain why they sent a large expedition. Egesta was an originally Elmyian city in western Sicily in dispute with the nearby Siceliot city of Selinus 'over some issues about intermarriage and disputed territory' (6.6.2), and Syracuse had sent a force against it.[5] The Elmyians aspired to be taken as Greeks and envoys from Egesta came to Athens in 416 to warn that if the Syracusans were to succeed against it they would also capture Leontini, gain control of the whole of Sicily and go on to support the Spartans and their allies in defeating Athens itself (6.6.2). Like Alcibiades and Euphemos in the months ahead, they gave no reason for thinking this. But they did say that they would meet the costs of an Athenian expedition to help them now. Envoys sent from Athens to see if they had the wherewithal to do so returned in the spring of 415 with Egestans carrying sixty talents of uncoined silver, sufficient to keep sixty Athenian triremes in active service for a month. 'The Athenians held an assembly and listened to the Egestan envoys and their own telling them various things that were both enticing and untrue, in particular that there was plenty of money available in the temples and the public treasury' in their city (6.8.2), and the Athenians wanted to believe. They voted to send sixty ships with Alcibiades,

<hr/>

Sicily in Athens. Th. reports that Athenians were to be afraid that the Syracusans might attack the Piraeus *after* the defeat in 413, 8.2.2.

[4] Th.'s knowledge of Sicily, Dover *HCT* IV: 466–7. Alcibiades as a possible informant, Brunt 1993b: 28.

[5] The Elmyians in the west were one of the three 'indigenous' (that's to say pre-Phoenician and pre-Greek) peoples of Sicily, originating perhaps in Anatolia (Th. says Troy). The others were the Sicani in the centre of the island and the Sicels in the east.

Nicias and Lamachos as the generals in command with full powers of decision.[6]

Diodorus suggests that the three generals decided one thing straight-away. 'Sitting in secret session with the council, [they] discussed what disposition they should make of Sicilian affairs if they should get control of the island. They agreed that they would enslave the Selinuntians and Syracusans and impose an annual tribute on others' (13.26). Scholars observe that where it is possible to trace Diodorus' sources, he more often than not proves to have kept closely to them; he certainly repeats Thucydides almost word for word on other events leading up to the expe-dition to Sicily. If his source for this story was sound and what he says is true, some Athenians were indeed imagining that they might conquer the island. But Diodorus was a Sicilian patriot and admitted that he was pleased to distribute praise and blame after the event. There is no record of a comparable meeting before any other Athenian venture in these years (though Thucydides rarely mentions the *boule*, the Athenian council of 500);[7] it would have been imaginative indeed of the Athenian generals to believe that they could readily 'enslave' Syracuse and Selinus; and if they did meet in council to decide to do so and to impose tribute on the rest of the island – the decision seems inherently unreal – it is difficult to believe that Nicias, the most senior amongst them, would have agreed that it was sensible even to think of doing so. For although he had been appointed to go to Sicily, he did not think it wise, and in an assembly that was called four days later ostensibly to decide on the resources with which to do so, he took the opportunity to say why (6.9–14). Alcibiades replied (6.16–18), and Nicias tried again (6.20–3).

This was the high politics of Athens on a matter on which speakers were to disagree more widely than on any other since before the start of the larger war – any other, that's to say, that Thucydides lets the reader see. As always, 'no statement or prediction or factual implication in these speeches', as Dover remarked, 'can be taken at its face value; everything is coloured; everything is exaggeration, insinuation or half-truth'; it may not have been the way in which moves were proposed in Athens but it was in good part how they were decided, and for this, persuasion was

---

[6] Aristophanes *Lysistrata*, 390–2, put on in 411, says that one Demostratos (an 'ill-fated fool'), later a commissioner of 'the ten' (Ch. 15 below) was pre-eminent in arousing the Athenians' enthusiasm for an expedition. Plutarch, *Nicias* 12 repeats the story. Th. makes no mention of Demostratos, and if he did speak, we do not know whether he did so at the first assembly in 415 or the second or both.

[7] Once at 5.41.1 and then not until the events of 411 at 8.67.3, 92.6 and 93.1. Discussed by Hornblower *CT* III: 23–31, who suggests that Th. may have thought that giving it its place would have reduced the drama with which he wanted to write Athens' politics.

all.[8] Dover did not add that Nicias was bad at this, and in Thucydides' reconstruction of what he said one can hear him failing from the start. 'I know your temperament, and I know my arguments would be powerless if I tried to persuade you just to look after what you have and not put present possessions at risk for uncertain future ones; but I shall at least seek to show you that your haste is untimely and that your ambitions are not easy to achieve' (6.9.3). He reminded the Athenians that the peace of 421 had not held and that Athens was not secure at home; the parties to the peace might start to fight again, and the Spartans might be tempted to strike. Even if the Athenians were to conquer the Siceliots, they would be unable to sustain rule over so many cities so far from home. It would be better, he argued, if the Syracusans were to conquer the Siceliots themselves. If the Athenians were to go to Sicily at all, they should simply display their power and leave. That would avoid taking what would otherwise be the greatest risk in the city's history. Empires, he rather casually observed, do not fight empires. The Athenians should at most ensure that the Siceliots stayed within their present, uncontroversial boundaries and let the Egestans themselves solve the problems they had created; they had done nothing for Athens and notwithstanding their opinion of themselves, were barbarians.

If a speaker intended to attack an adversary, it was usual for him to do so at the end of a speech, and Nicias did. Even then he did not mention Alcibiades by name, but he made it clear that in the previous assembly the case for an expedition had been made by someone voicing the unattainable interests of self-interested youth (6.12.2–6.13.1). Others spoke, Thucydides says, most of them against rescinding the first vote, before Alcibiades rose to defend himself and restate the case for not doing so.[9] He insisted that he was not only entitled to hold a command; he deserved to do so. His victories in the chariot races at Olympia had brought prestige to Athens, and it was he who had mobilised the forces at Mantinea after which the Spartans, though not defeated, had failed, he said, falsely, to recover their confidence. 'I know', he said, 'that successful people of this kind and all those who have stood out as pre-eminent in some way are resented in their own lifetimes, in the first place by their

---

[8] *HCT* IV: 229.
[9] Th. inserts a chapter (6.15) to reintroduce Alcibiades. Like 2.65, which it does something to explain, this was plainly composed after the end of the Peloponnesian war: its judgements, which are not self-evidently clear or even consistent with each other, only make the sense they do in the light of Alcibiades' actions and political reception after 411. Excellent discussions by Dover *HCT* IV: 242–5 and V: 423–7, also Chs. 13 and 14 below. As with 2.65, one can regret that Th. included this chapter, at least where he did. In addition to *HCT* and *CT* on all three speeches, Macleod 1983d on Alcibiades' rhetoric.

peers and then by others they associate with; but their legacy is that later generations claim a relationship with them, even where none existed, and their countrymen, from wherever they come, feel a sense of pride in them and hail them not as foreigners or offenders but as their own home-grown heroes' (6.16.5). Against what Nicias had claimed, it is all to the good that such men are young, energetic and ambitious. (Neither Alcibiades nor Thucydides mentions Nicias as an Athenian 'guest-friend', *proxenos*, at Syracuse. Diodorus, who does, may be mistaken (13.27.3). If he is not, this could have been a motive for Nicias' opposition to the expedition and for some of his hesitation when he found himself in command there.) As for the Siceliots, Alcibiades went on, they were a divided 'rabble', and many Sicels, who were hostile to them, might come across to the Athenians. In any event, he said, it is in the Athenians' nature to act. They had succeeded against the Persians when they had troubles at home, and they would put themselves and their empire at risk if they failed to act now. Even if they did not manage to add Sicily to their dominion and rule over all the Greeks, they would damage the Syracusans. I have youth, Alcibiades insisted, and Nicias (as his name and record would have suggested) has 'a winning touch'; young and old must unite. A city that is divided and inactive 'wears itself out from within, just like anything else, and all its knowledge will diminish with age; but when it is exercised in adversity it will keep adding to its experience and will acquire the habit of defending itself not just by argument but by action' (6.18.6).

It was a striking performance. Alcibiades aligned his energy with the Athenians' own, elided its promise with Athens' dominion, alluded to the unity of the democracy, and excited the larger part of his audience to admire and identify with them all. More completely even than Pericles and with at least equal effect, he made his self-flattery theirs, and they were enchanted. Apart perhaps from the popular and to some aristocrats at least, offensive Hyperbolos – whom (Thucydides does not mention) Alcibiades, Nicias and Phaeax had conspired to have ostracised at some point before 415 – no other politician we know of in Athens in the last thirty years of the century was so openly daring. None, certainly, was so effective.[10] Egesta's temptation is the first part of the explanation for

[10] Plutarch, *Alcibiades*, 13, *Nicias*, 11. Also Connor 1992: 79–84, Rosenbloom 2004. Plutarch sees the battle to be one between age and youth, Hyperbolos *vs* Nicias, Rosenbloom as one between a lower- and upper-class politician, Hyperbolos *vs* Alcibiades. Ostracism, claims Rosenbloom, was a 'manifestation of a political culture, a symbol-laden activity and decisive act of self-definition' (57), what one may more prosaically describe as a means of showing which man (and of what kind) was top demagogue. Forsdyke 2005 more charitably regards it as democracy's answer to destructive conflict within the political elite. Nicias' victory in the ostracism of Hyperbolos, Rosenbloom

the Athenians deciding to go to Sicily as and when they did. Alcibiades' rhetorical feat is the second.

As many have remarked, Nicias made it easy for him. And the Egestans and Leontines also who were present at the assembly did not make it easy for Nicias. They reminded the Athenians of their 'sworn oaths' of support and were well received. Nicias persevered. He conceded that the Athenians had already made up their mind but he insisted on explaining what an expedition from Athens would face, believing that they knew little of Sicily. 'We shall be taking on cities, as I understand the reports, which are large and which are not subject to one another; nor are they in need of change of the kind people might welcome in order to exchange an enforced subjection for some easier status, nor are they likely to embrace our rule in place of freedom' (6.20.2). Of the nine cities on the island only two, Naxos and Catana, could be thought to be friendly. The others were not, and what he now identified as Athens' two targets, Selinus, which was annoying Egesta, and Syracuse, which was annoying Leontini, were particularly well defended. They had money, hoplites, archers and javelin throwers; they possessed triremes and men to crew them; and they could call on horses for cavalry and grain of their own. Athens would need more than what Nicias bravely described as its weak naval force: infantry to get around the cavalry, reliable supplies, which would be difficult over such a distance, and good communications within Sicily and with Athens itself, which would be more difficult still. 'You must think of us as founding a city in the midst of alien and hostile peoples, and on the very day the invaders land' – he said now but signally failed to act on when the time came – 'they must immediately become masters of the field, in the sure knowledge that if they fail they will find every circumstance hostile to them' (6.23.2). A good outcome for Athens, in short, would depend on good fortune alone.

Thucydides writes that Nicias had hoped either to deter the Athenians from the expedition or to ensure that, if they were determined to go, they would be fully prepared. They chose to take what he said as encouraging advice and became even more enthusiastic. 'Everyone alike had fallen in love with the voyage: the older men believing that either they would overwhelm the places they sailed against or that so great a force could at least suffer no disaster; the young men of military age yearning to see these far-off sights and spectacles, full of good hope for their safe return;

suggests, licenced the mutilation of the Hermes and upper-class pantomiming of the Mysteries later in the year. Th.'s disparagement of Hyperbolos on the occasion of his death, 8.73.3. Hyperbolos' class and character, of course, were separate matters, even if they were elided in the polemics.

and the mass of common soldiery seeing an opportunity to earn some money in the short-term and to acquire a power that would be an endless source of earnings in the future' (6.24.3) Those who had reservations decided that it would be wise to stay silent, and the second assembly ended with a reaffirmation of the vote at the first. Nicias was pressed to elaborate on what was needed, and Thucydides remarks that with the coming of age of a generation that had escaped the plague and, in knowledge of the funds that had been accumulating during the recent peace, it was easy to satisfy most of those who heard him.

The belief in further money from Egesta, the force of Alcibiades' rhetoric, which Nicias had inadvertently served to strengthen, and the promise of pay and profit might together have been sufficient to impel a majority to mount an expedition. But the Athenians seem to have been in an excitable state since they had reasserted their power at Melos in the previous summer and destroyed it in the following spring. This is the third, more encompassing explanation of why they responded so eagerly to calls to go, and the democracy allowed their fervour to prevail. Their excitability, however, was not without anxiety. During the night of what we would identify as 25 May 415, almost all the small statues of the god Hermes in the city – 'the square-cut ones in the local style which stood everywhere in the doorways of private houses and in temples' – were defaced, and other mutilations and manifestations of a more private profanity came to light in the flurry that followed (6.27–8). Whatever their religious import, these were taken to be public acts.[11] Hermes was believed to protect travellers and the mutilations were a bad omen for the expedition. As the aristocrat Andocides was later to confess, the profane pantomimings of the Eleusinian mysteries may have been performed in gatherings of one or more of the upper-class political clubs, *hetaireiai*. They were taken to indicate 'a conspiracy for a political uprising and the subversion of popular rule', which made it easy for those opposed to 'tyranny' to implicate Alcibiades (6.27.3, 50.2).[12] He declared himself innocent and ready to stand trial. But his prospective prosecutors knew, as he probably did himself, that his arrest would not go down well with the troops and those who had welcomed the support that he had obtained for the expedition to Sicily from Mantinea and Argos; speakers were accordingly put up to suggest that he be allowed to sail in the

---

[11] A magnificent examination of the event and its chronology by Dover *HCT* IV: 264–88, expanded and brought up to date by Hornblower *CT* III: 367–72, who notes more recent scholarly attention to the religious significance of the events.

[12] The *hetaireiai* at 3.82.5 and 8.48.3. Cf. the more politically practical *synomosiai* (8.54.4), Hornblower *CT* III: 916–20.

expectation that he would be recalled when the campaign was under way and a case had been prepared against him (6.29).

The impulse to go had become a decision, the decision had been reaffirmed, and preparations had to be made. When asked to say what these should be, Nicias had suggested one hundred triremes, including troop carriers, and 5,000 hoplites, with more of each to be obtained from allies; he added archers and slingers, but oddly in view of what he had said about the Siceliots' advantage, made no mention of cavalry. The full force, which was eventually to assemble for the journey at Corcyra, included 134 triremes from Athens, forty of which were troop carriers (adaptable perhaps for fighting), together with two old-fashioned pente-conters (single-decked ships with twenty-five oarsmen on each side) from Rhodes, and 5,100 hoplites, 2,200 of whom were from Athens, the rest from allies, together with nearly 1,200 allied troops of other kinds and a boat for thirty horses. As Thucydides notes, this was no larger than the force the Athenians had taken to Epidauros and then to Potidaea in 430, but in view of the distance and likely length of a campaign in Sicily, which required boats also for builders, masons and bakers and grain itself, it would have been more expensive to equip (6.25.2, 6.43, 6.31.2). Even so, one can ask whether it was the most that Athens could muster at the time. The city had sent thirty ships to support Argives in the Peloponnese in the previous winter, and if these had returned in time to be dried out and refitted for Sicily, thirty more were available to help Argives again in the summer of 414 (6.7.2, 6.105.1). Moreover, although ninety-four fighting ships would have been a sizeable force for a short campaign in the Aegean or Adriatic (thirty-eight triremes and 3,000 men had gone to Melos, which had no navy, in 416) it was small for a venture of unknown dimensions to the west.

Thucydides writes that practically the whole of the rest of the population of Athens, native and foreign, went down at dawn to the Piraeus on a day in June 415 to see the expedition off. 'At that moment, when amid all [the] impending dangers they were about to take their leave of each other, the perils of their situation came home to them more forcibly than they ever had when they were voting to make the voyage. Nonetheless, they took courage again at the evidence before them of their present strength, the sheer quantity of every kind of resource they could see with their own eyes. As for the foreigners and the rest of the crowd, they came for the extraordinary spectacle, finding the whole conception of the thing quite remarkable and incredible.' Thucydides is not right to say that this was 'the longest voyage from home ever yet attempted' by the Athenians (6.31.6); he forgets the expeditions to Sicily in 427 and 425 and Pericles' expedition with Lamachos to the northern shore of the Black Sea in the early 430s,[13] but one can believe him when he says that it carried 'the most disproportionate hopes of future gains compared to their present possessions'. One can certainly see why 'it all looked more like a public display of power and wealth aimed at the rest of the Greeks rather than a preparation for war with their enemies' (6.31.1–6). Modern commentators have remarked on its wastefulness, but that is beside the point. Melos, which had excited the Athenians, was an exercise in shaming the Spartans, demonstrating Athens' continuing power at sea and parading their dominion. This was the first attempt in living memory to extend that dominion. The Athenians were affirming to themselves what Athens could once again be.

I suggested in Chapter 7 that although it was a change of mood in Athens in 427 rather than the force of argument that prevented the destruction of the Mytilenaeans, the occasion of a debate did then at least allow the change to prevail. In Athens in 415, it had served to galvanise the existing mood. In Syracuse by contrast, it appeared at first to have no discernible effect at all. This may be why Thucydides reports or reconstructs a debate there at length; the political ironies were too strong to resist. Although Hermocrates, he writes, the first man in Syracuse, was 'of outstanding intelligence', 'capable in terms of practical experience', 'conspicuous for his courage' and determined not to let the Syracusans 'give in to the course of events' (6.72.2), he failed against the force of disbelief and hostility in his city and the power of a majority of the other generals there.[14] Nothing of what he recommended – to seek support from the Sicels, the Carthaginians, who had their own anxieties about Athens, and the Peloponnesians, who might help by drawing the Athenians back to the war in Greece itself, and for the Syracusans to sail out immediately to frighten the Athenian fleet into retreat – was acted on. His adversary, one Athenagoras – 'comparison with modern parliaments', remarked Dover, 'is not wholly to the disadvantage of Syracuse, but comparison with other men whom we meet in the pages of Thucydides is very much to the disadvantage of Athenagoras'[15] – ridiculed the thought that Athenians were coming, accused Hermocrates of saying they were in order to concentrate his power and proceeded to offer the most convincing defence of democracy by any speaker (including Pericles) in Thucydides' whole story (6.36–40). He too was all but ignored.

It is a further irony that this defence of democracy should come from a city about to go to war with Athens. 'It will be said that a democracy

---

[13] Plutarch, *Pericles* 20.
[14] Hermocrates' qualities of command are also described by Xenophon, *Hellenica* 1.1.30.
[15] *HCT* IV: 301.

is neither wise nor fair', Athenagoras began, 'and that those who own property' – in contrast to what Pericles had called 'the many'; Thebans, 'the worse sort' (2.37.1, 3.65.3) – 'are the people most likely to rule well'. Athenagoras had no wish to dispute the claim. 'But I say first', he went on, 'that "people" is the name of the whole and "oligarchy" the name of only a part, and secondly that while the rich are the best guardians of property, the wise would be the best counsellors, and the majority the best judges of what they hear; and all these . . . have an equal share in a democracy.' An oligarchy shares dangers with the people but 'wants more than its share of the benefits. It actually wants to take and keep them all' (6.39). 'The people' may not be best fitted to decide on matters of state, but they should do so; oligarchic governments rarely rule in the people's interest, the habit of decision makes for a better person than the habit of ignorant obedience, and those who stand to lose everything should be allowed to decide whether they want to take the risk of doing so.[16] But this was not a moment for speech. When Athenagoras had finished, a general stood up and declared that 'it was unwise for speakers to exchange personal insults with each other or for their audience to tolerate this'. The city should concentrate on defending itself against invaders, should they come, and, even if they did not, it should be pleased to have provided itself 'with horses and weapons and all the other glories in which war rejoices'. There would be no harm in sending missions to other cities 'for observation and any other purposes thought useful'. The generals, he concluded, could safely be left to arrange all this, and they would keep the city informed (6.41.2–4).

It has been said that Thucydides is preparing the reader to see Syracuse as a 'close analogue' of Athens. Both were powerful, as Nicias had remarked, both were imperially inclined (6.11.3) and within each there was open political contest. But though the voting habits of the Greek electorate being what they were, the well-to-do, as Dover remarks, were usually elected in both cities, their politics were at this moment working in rather different ways. After sixteen years of war, Athens was governing itself in an ever more unsteady manner. Whatever its internal differences, Syracuse at this moment was not. And one can wonder whether Thucydides was not pleased to draw attention to the contrast between the practical effectiveness of the city at this moment and the ineffectiveness there of public speech.[17]

---

[16] Dover on parliaments, *HCT* IV: 301; his nonetheless splendid gloss on Athenagoras, on which it is impossible to improve, 305.
[17] Th. presenting Syracuse as an analogue of Athens, Connor 1984b: 168–76. Th. is explicit, though very general, at 8.96.5. Voting habits, Dover, *HCT* IV: 430.

On arriving in the west Nicias, Alcibiades and Lamachos had expected to be able to gather support at Rhegion and to rest there while they waited for the return of three ships they had sent to fetch funds from Egesta. To their surprise the Rhegines refused them, saying that they wanted to talk to other cities in Italy before committing themselves. A further surprise to Alcibiades and Lamachos, though not to Nicias, was that the advance party returned from Egesta to say that the Egestans had been dissembling; they only had thirty talents (6.42–6). Nicias used the news to suggest that the expedition should set the limit of what he now described as its sole purpose: to stay just long enough to persuade or force the Selinuntines to come to terms with the Egestans, sail round Sicily to demonstrate Athens' power and its support for its other allies and then go home. Alcibiades disagreed. It was shameful to have come so far with so much and do so little. He suggested that they should first make sure of Messina, at the straits and a good base for their operations, gather more allies, including Sicels, open negotiations with the cities they could and then, unless Selinus had meanwhile come to terms with Egesta and Syracuse with Leontini, attack them both. Lamachos took a different view again. The Athenians should attack Syracuse at once; this would surprise its inhabitants, many of whom would be caught working in the fields outside the city, cause a panic and encourage the Sicels to side with the Athenians. The Athenians themselves should then make a base at the conveniently uninhabited harbour of Megara Hyblaea to the north of Syracuse (6.47–9).

Grote had no doubt. 'The plan of Lamachos was by far the best and most judicious.' A Demosthenes or Brasidas, he fancied, would have embraced it at once; Alcibiades by contrast showed himself 'superior in military energy to one of his colleagues [and] no less inferior to the other'. But Lamachos, a military man with no political standing, deferred to Alcibiades and by two to one the generals adopted Alcibiades' plan. Dover wondered whether Lamachos might not have seen that the differences between them would become known ('the Greeks had only a rudimentary conception of military discretion') and that if his own plan, the most risky of the three, were to fail, he would look foolish and like others before him be impeached.[18] As Lamachos saw and Grote and many since have repeated, Alcibiades' plan gave the Syracusans notice to prepare. Alcibiades went himself to Messina but failed to persuade leaders there. Two of the three Athenian generals (Thucydides does not say which) then took sixty ships from the temporary base they had established outside Rhegium to Naxos, which admitted them, to Catana, which did not, and

[18] Grote 1862: 168, Dover in *HCT* IV: 313.

went on to Syracuse to proclaim their intention to restore the Leontines to their city. The Catanians, they had thought, might be persuadable, and the generals made their case to an assembly in the place. While Alcibiades was speaking, Athenian soldiers broke in, the inhabitants who were sympathetic to Syracuse fled and the Athenians were allowed to make a camp. Reports of sympathy had now come also from Camarina, but these proved to be mistaken. The Athenians then had an unfruitful skirmish with Syracusan cavalry on the way back, a portent – though it is not Thucydides' inclination to point to any such thing – of difficulties to come. It had not been a notably successful start (6.50–2).

And a new difficulty awaited them. The state ship *Salaminia* had arrived at Catana with an order to escort Alcibiades home. An informer in Athens had given names on the mutilation of the Herms and some had already been sentenced to death. People in Athens were still 'in a constant state of fear, regarding everything with suspicion' (6.53.3). But the mocking of the mysteries remained unsolved. The Athenians were sure that there had been 'some conspiracy involving oligarchy and tyranny' (6.60.1) and they thought they knew how the tyranny of the Peisistratids in the city some hundred years before had led to oppression. It was being said that Alcibiades was behind a small force of Spartans who had happened to arrive at the isthmus ostensibly to talk to Boeotians, and that his associates in Argos were planning an attack on 'the people' there. Having been excited by Alcibiades' promise of leadership and enthusiasm for extending Athens' tyranny overseas, Athenians were now being incited to panic about the prospect of him tyrannising them. He would clearly be in danger if he returned.

At this point, Thucydides famously interrupts his story with a long digression on the end of the Peisistratids (6.54–60). It is quintessentially Thucydidean. He parades the care with which he has checked the facts, turns an accepted account of events on its head, revises a popular opinion of tyranny itself, makes a shrewd point about the current panic in Athens, and then refrains from saying what his point is.[19] He begins by explaining that Peisistratos was succeeded on his death in 527 not by Hipparchus 'as is commonly supposed' (if not by Herodotus (5.55)) but by his elder brother Hippias. 'These tyrants were in general not oppressive in their exercise of power towards the people at large but managed their authority

---

[19] A much debated passage. Lewis 1988 includes an excellent summary and notes other ancient sources and comment. The issues are reviewed by Hornblower *CT* III: 433–53. Forsdyke 2005: 121–6 notes that Peisistratus was unusual in his time in refusing to exile his opponents and acknowledging the opinion of non-elite Athenians. Connor 1984b: 178–80 and at greater length Ludwig 2002: 159–67 (whom Hornblower does not mention) consider the connections between *eros*, political commitment and unreason.

without arousing resentment; and compared to other tyrants they set the highest standards of behaviour and good sense. Indeed, although they exacted from Athenians only a twentieth of their income they kept their city in good order, fully supported their wars and provided sacrifices for the temples. The city remained free to observe all the laws previously in place, except in so far as the tyrants took care to ensure that one of their people always held office' (6.54.5–6). There was a plan to assassinate Hippias, but only because he was the prominent brother of Hipparchus, who had publicly demeaned the sister of a young man he desired who was the lover of another. In the event, the two assassins, this other and the woman's brother, thinking that their plan to kill Hippias had been discovered, chanced across Hipparchus and killed him instead. Hippias, hearing of the original plan, then instituted a repression. He was deposed three years later by Spartans and exiled members of the Alcmaeonid family, went over to Persia and was said to have led the Persians to fight the Greeks at Marathon in 490. Thucydides can be read with characteristic indirectness to be saying that tyranny-and-oligarchy – a common hendiadys of the time, Hornblower suggests – is not invariably to be feared, and that when it is, the causes can lie in the passions of an 'erotic circumstance' which embraces the political and the personal rather than any quality of tyranny itself. In Athens in 415, the citizens were in an excited and nervous state, passionately or as they might put it erotically committed to their sense of themselves in the city (6.59.1). They had been fervently in favour of a potential tyrant – not necessarily a bad thing, Thucydides can be read to be suggesting, either in general or for Athens at this moment – only with equal fervour to have come to be made hostile to the man. It would not be surprising if Alcibiades were to decide to pursue his ambitions elsewhere.

This he did, slipping away with companions when his ship and the *Salaminia* stopped off at Thurii on the way back, and in his absence the Athenians sentenced him to death. Nicias and Lamachos rearranged the expeditionary force into two divisions from the three that they had created with him, and appeared more or less to revert to the plans that each had had after arriving.[20] Nicias took men to Egesta to collect the thirty talents, acquired a further 120 from selling into slavery captives he had taken on the way, ignored Selinus and, after a tactical failure at another place, returned to Catana. There, Lamachos may have been the decisive voice,

---

[20] Dover saw a 'much closer accord' with Alcibiades' plan to communicate with all the Siceliot cities except Selinus and Syracuse, win over the Sicels and then attack Selinus and Syracuse, *HCT* IV: 339. But this doesn't fit with Nicias ignoring Selinus, and it is difficult to see why he and Lamachos should now have bothered with Alcibiades' suggestion.

for in 'the following winter the Athenians made immediate preparations for an assault on Syracuse' (6.63.1). At the same time, the Syracusans were preparing to attack them. This is the most disappointing moment in Thucydides' account of the expedition. It is impossible to discern from what he writes whether one side decided to attack before the other, or each accepted that it could not avoid a confrontation with the other or each believed that it could pre-empt a confrontation altogether. He does say that the Syracusans had been surprised that the Athenians did not attack them straight away, and that when they saw Nicias embroiled in what they regarded as a fruitless venture in western Sicily, they 'became all the more dismissive . . . and urged their generals, as a mob will in a rush of confidence, to lead them against Catana' (6.63.2). On this occasion the generals demurred, but were subsequently tempted by a man who came from Catana to say that if the Syracusans were indeed to send a force there, sympathisers would arrange for them to enter the city, kill the sleeping Athenians, burn their ships and destroy their camp. The Syracusans duly sent a force but the Athenians, who had them-selves put the man up, had already left Catana under darkness for a site south of Syracuse, just inland from the middle of the bay of the large harbour there. It was a place that enabled them to attack the city while the Syracusan forces were away, and one that they were later to use as a base.

The Syracusans managed to rush back in time. Nicias found no plea-sure in the engagement that followed. Frank as ever, he told his troops that it would not be easy. As they would have seen for themselves, the Siceliots may have more bravado than skill, but 'they are being told that the battle will be for their own country; I tell you' (as his troops also surely knew) 'that it will not be in your own country but in a place where you must win or else face a difficult exit, with their cavalry all over us in numbers' (6.68.3). The Athenians and their now dispirited allies were forced to fight with inadequate means and no easy exit, facing exactly the unenviable choice that Nicias had anticipated in speaking against the expedition before it sailed. In the event, the Athenians just managed to prevail over the disorderly Syracusans, losing fifty men against their enemy's 160 and forcing their adversaries back. It was nonetheless appar-ent, says Thucydides, that to continue in Sicily they needed active support from within the island, funds and grain from Athens and, above all, cav-alry, 'to avoid being completely outmatched in this respect' (6.71.2), as they had just been. The Syracusans on their part accepted Hermocrates' argument that their indiscipline had been caused by a confusing struc-ture of command, reorganised themselves, worked on the city's defences and now sent envoys to Sparta and Corinth to ask these powers either to help in Sicily or to act to divert Athens in Greece itself. The Athenians, discovering that on his journey out Alcibiades had worked to turn Messina against them, sent an embassy to Camarina to seek what they thought they had reason again to believe would be support there, and Hermocrates, who was afraid that after what had been Syracuse's first defeat they might succeed, followed them with an embassy of his own.

Few if any moves in the long war, I have been suggesting, turned on an argument in debate; the better argument, that's to say, as that might have been thought to be by those involved at the time. (Pericles' arguments may have been a partial exception, but Thucydides does not let us hear those that were made against him.) What one might describe as an 'external' reason to act will provide a motive only if it fits an 'internal' reason for doing so, and such 'true' reasons, as Thucydides called them, often turn out to be pre-commitments that are not reasoned at all.[21] As I suggested in Chapter 7, Thucydides himself was sceptical of *logoi* in politics whose plausibility lay more in rhetoric than truthfulness. As at Syracuse therefore, so now at Camarina: he could have simply summarised the debate and observed that the outcome owed more to the situation in which the Camarinaeans found themselves than to what they heard. But whatever the causal force of political argument, argument was part of politics, and the speeches that Hermocrates and one Euphemos, a 'good speaker', from Athens gave on this occasion are some of the most purely political in the text (6.76–87). The real reasons on each side were plain. Now that the Athenians had engaged, Hermocrates was even more urgently of the view that a firm alliance of Siceliot cities was necessary to defeat them. Euphemos, realising what the Athenians now found themselves committed to on the island, believed that they had to get as many of these cities on their side as they could. The Camarinaeans were equally transparent. They did not want to fight, in part because they had alliances with both Syracuse and Athens, in part no doubt because they lacked any appetite to; but if they had to, they wanted to be on the winning side.

Hermocrates apologised at the end of his speech for having explained what the Camarinaeans already knew, but few may have been able to put it so well. He began as he had on previous occasions. The Athenians' actions since the end of the Persian war left no doubt about their wish to dominate the Greeks, and they would find it easier to dominate a Greek Sicily that was divided against itself. The Camarinaeans, he went on, should not suppose that the Athenians' object was Syracuse alone and that they could therefore be safe; they would be safer fighting alongside the Syracusans. Nor should they in fear or anger believe that they could

---

[21] The language of internal and external reasons in Williams 1981a.

let Syracuse suffer but not so much as to make the Syracusans unable to protect them; no one can manage the future that finely. And if they should think that they were obliged by right to favour Athens over Syracuse they should remember, as had the Rhegines, that the treaty they had sworn obliged them to help Athens when it was attacked, not when it was itself the attacker. If they should decide instead to stay neutral, they should realise that they would incur the wrath of winner and loser alike.

Euphemos announced that he had come to renew Athens' alliance with Camarina, but having heard Hermocrates, saw that he should first explain his city's larger purpose. He was disingenuous to a degree. After the Persian war, he said – at variance with what Athenians had claimed at Sparta in 432 (1.75.2) – Athens had done what it had to do to protect itself against the domination of the Spartans. It had also had another purpose, not incompatible with this but distinct. What he referred to as 'the Ionians and the islanders' had in the earlier war 'joined the Persians in attacking us, their mother-city, and they did not have the courage to revolt and to sacrifice their homes, as we had to when we abandoned our city. They willed their own enslavement and wanted to impose the same thing on us' (6.82.3–4). The Athenians were in Sicily now, he continued, for a different reason again. If you Camarinaeans 'are safe and strong enough to offer some resistance to the Syracusans, then we are protected against their sending a force to help the Peloponnesians' (6.84.1). In empire and tyranny, he continued, bracketing the two with ease, expediency dictates and trust is the only bond (in the Greek, 'nothing is illogical that is expedient, nor is anything kindred that is not trusted'). 'Circumstances determine who is friend and who is foe, and in our situation here our advantage lies not in harming our friends but in weakening our enemies through the strength of our friends' (6.85.1). The Athenians, in short, were in Sicily to protect their own interests. 'We treat each of the allies we lead in Greece according to their utility', said Euphemos, and we treat you in the same way. We have no need for finer words. We could not defend ourselves against a united Sicily, and you could not defend yourselves against any power that united it. Euphemos did not draw the parallel, and nor does Thucydides, but commentators have been unable to resist: the Athenians were now claiming to be to the Syracusans what the Spartans had claimed to be to the Athenians. 'We exercise our rule over Greece to avoid subjection to another power there, while in Sicily we promote freedom for your cities to avoid being harmed by them here' (6.87.2).

The Camarinaeans were suitably sceptical. Whatever Euphemos claimed, the Athenians, being Athenians, might come to subjugate them; or else the Syracusans might come out on top without Camarina's help.

Not wishing to set themselves against either, they decided that since the Athenians had won the first encounter they would offer the Syracusans the 'modest help' of a few cavalry and otherwise give the same formal answer to each side: 'since this was a war between two parties, both of whom happened to be their allies, they thought the best way to honour their oaths was to give help to neither' (6.88). The embassies departed and the two powers proceeded with their preparations. The Athenians returned to their camp at Catana, secured promises from Sicels in the hills, those on the plain staying loyal to Syracuse, explored the possibility of help from Carthage and Tyrrhenia, asked Egesta for horses, and devoted the rest of the winter to preparing for a siege of Syracuse itself. The Syracusans sent envoys to seek support at Corinth, asking Italian cities on the way for help also, and being pleased that the Corinthians 'immediately took the initiative and voted to commit themselves in every way', the envoys went on to Sparta (6.88.1–8).

If in 415 the Athenians did want to subjugate the whole of Sicily, they could not be said already to have formed a firm purpose to do so. It was at best a vision, present already in the 420s, excited by Melos and the insistent and duplicitous demands for help by the Egestans, and given what shape it had by Alcibiades. It is not easy to decide whether without Alcibiades' ambition, there would have been the political will to move. Thucydides is silent about what Nicias thought of the Leontines' difficulties; but he was clearly hostile to the self-interest of what he regarded as the alien and meddlesome Egestans. And there is no reason to believe that any other politician would at this moment have encouraged the Athenians to make so considerable a move. As it was, Alcibiades gave direction to their mood and Nicias' opposition served to strengthen it. The creation of a considerable force, moreover, would have increased the desire to go, and although some had come to fear Alcibiades' ambition in Athens – a fear, Thucydides has hinted, that was unjustified, for a decent tyranny might have served the city better than an impulsive democracy – it had become politically impossible to prevent him sharing the command. Yet if we discount Diodorus' reference to a conference of generals before the expedition departed, there had been no decision to do more than offer support to Egesta and Leontini; if there had been, Diodorus appears not to have appreciated, Nicias, Alcibiades and Lamachos would not have needed to discuss what to do when they arrived. But Athenagoras was probably wrong to suppose that Hermocrates was merely pretending to believe that the Athenians were hoping to conquer the island and that Syracuse could be their first object. The Syracusan generals were certainly taking the threat seriously. Nicias did continue for some months to act on his conviction that the Athenians should limit themselves to giving modest assistance to Egesta; he ignored Selinous and seems not to have been concerned about Leontini at all. The Syracusans however became convinced that the Athenians intended to attack their city, and Thucydides' narrative suggests that Nicias and Lamachos came to see that they had to do so; they might otherwise be defeated, and as Nicias admitted, they had no easy exit. The decision to attack Syracuse was forced upon them.

Whether this would be in what had been described in the resolutions in the spring as Athens' 'best interest' was not now relevant. Nor was the question of whether the Athenians might conquer the whole island. They had propelled themselves into a distant venture the purposes of which had been poorly defined and for which, almost whatever they intended, their own resources were inadequate, local support lacking, the opposition formidable and their leadership uncertain. Only clever tactics and luck could redeem it.

13 Character and circumstance 414–413

Thucydides says nothing about the early years of the men in his story or their lives outside politics; he allows Pericles and Archidamos, two of the most prominent, to die outside his text; and unlike other ancient writers, he uses none to make a moral point. The strictest reading of the strictures that he can seem to place on himself is that he writes individuals simply to signify their *politeia* in action. It has been said that some are more fully realised in the later parts of the text; that they have more individual character and produce effects that are more distinctively theirs. Some argue that this is a corollary of Thucydides' increasing interest and attentiveness, others that it reflects the changing nature of events later in the war.[1]

It is not easy to decide. The events as we know them are in large part the events as Thucydides describes them. Nonetheless, the last year and a half of the Sicilian campaign and the two years that followed did stretch Athenians as they not been stretched before; in part, one can suggest, because the politics of Athens in the later fifth century more generally opened themselves more to the vagaries of individual character than those of any other political community in Thucydides' story, in part because the city was for four months in 411 divided against itself. No *politeia* would have been immune to the circumstances of war over three decades. But in Sparta and perhaps also in Corinth there were restraints of a constitutional and institutional kind (a distinction that was less sharp at this time than it came to be) that were not to be put in place in Athens until after the war. And in places like Macedonia, where power

---

[1] Westlake 1968: 308–19 argues for a change in Th. He considered twelve men, Pericles, Phormio, Cleon, Nicias, Demosthenes, Archidamos, Cnemos, Alcidas, Brasidas, Alcibiades, Gyllipos and Astyochos, a Spartan commander in 411; a thirteenth, Hermocrates, in Westlake 1969. Emphasising the significance of the change in events, which Westlake also allows, Gribble 1999, Kallet 2001: 288–9 and *passim*. Individuals as 'filters' for their *politeia* or 'political community', n. 20 below. Th. names 431 individuals in all, seven of whom are women; these do not include those mentioned only when endorsing a formal agreement.

was between kin and decided by character alone, we know too little to say anything very much.[2]

The relative ease with which men were able to take power in Athens after the early 420s could not very paradoxically prompt some to try to change the rules of rule themselves and cause others to fear that they might. This explains the charge of 'a conspiracy against the people' against those alleged to have been party to the destruction of the Herms and profaning the Eleusinian mysteries in 415. It also explains why Alcibiades was able to turn this charge around, choosing to think, or at least to say, that it was his city that had abandoned him, not he the city, and make little secret of his determination to return to lead it, if need be under new rules of rule. That he could conceive of this and use Spartans and Persians to help him achieve it says much about his nerve. That he could secure support in Athens itself and after the defeat in Sicily nearly succeed says much about the regime there and the room for ambitious men within it.

After he and his associates had slipped their escort at Thurii they went to Elis, Alcibiades himself, says Plutarch, going on to Argos to send a request to Sparta for asylum.[3] Envoys from Syracuse and Corinth were already at Sparta when he arrived, and they addressed an assembly together. 'I do not think of myself now,' Alcibiades declared, 'as attacking a city which is still mine so much as reclaiming one which is mine no longer. The true patriot is not the man who holds back from attacking the city he has had unjustly taken from him, but the one who in his passion for it makes every effort to get it back' (6.92.4). In seeking support for Syracuse and urging diversionary attacks on the Athenians in Greece, the envoys from Syracuse and Corinth could speak with the authority of their states (6.93.1, 7.18.1). Alcibiades had no choice but to speak with his own. To an audience most of whom may not have known that his family had a historic connection with Sparta, he explained that he had sought to revive the connection in trying to make sure that the prisoners from Pylos came to no harm. He explained also that he had urged the confrontation at Mantinea because it had been demeaning of the Spartans to make peace with Athens without involving him. Should any Spartan suspect him of favouring the *demos*, he would remind them that it had been his family and Spartans together who had deposed the Peisistratids, and that it was only because resistance to tyranny was a popular cause that 'we' – in Athens – 'have retained the leadership of the masses'. (His mother and

---

[2] It would nevertheless be wrong to equate 'democracy' with the invention of politics itself, wisely Bodéüs 2000, cf. Meier 1990: 20–5 and Farrar 1988: 15–43.

[3] Plutarch, *Alcibiades*, 22–3; also Dover *HCT* IV: 360.

Pericles' wife were both Alcmaeonids.)[4] And 'while the city was operat-
ing as a democracy', he went on, 'it was necessary for the most part to go
along with the way things were. Amid the prevailing indiscipline . . . we
did try to behave with greater moderation in our politics, though there
were others, both then and now, who led the mob into worse habits – and
these were the ones who banished me.' Spartans above all would understand that it was 'right to preserve the form of constitution we inherited in
which the city enjoyed its greatest power and freedom' and that although
the democracy in Athens was an 'acknowledged folly', 'we' were not going
to change while you Spartans 'were almost on top of us' (6.89.4–6).

His value to Sparta now, Alcibiades continued, lay in the intelligence
he could bring. The Athenians were hoping to encircle the Peloponnese.
(Thucydides mentions (2.7.3) that they had envisaged this in 431, but
if Alcibiades knew he did not say so; to do so would have weakened his
claim to revelation.) Athens' plan, he explained – it is only elsewhere
attested by Thucydides himself writing after he knew what Alcibiades
had said (6.15.2) – was to capture Sicily, Italy and Carthage and with the
resources these conquests would provide to return to surround Sparta.
But the Syracusans had lost the first engagement in Sicily and were now
weak. They needed Spartan support and, he tactfully added, a Spartan
commander. And soon. Rather than invading Attica again, as they were
thinking of doing, and apart from helping the Syracusans in Sicily itself,
the Spartans should prosecute the war in Greece 'in a more conspicuous
way' and establish a fort in the area. Deceleia, he suggested, 13 miles
or so north of Athens in the direction of Boeotia, should be the place;
he may have known that Spartans had long favoured it (6.90, 7.19.2).[5]
In fact, they did not fortify Deceleia for another year, and although they
did now appoint a commander for Sicily, the envoys from Syracuse and
Corinth will have been at least as effective as was he in prompting them
to do so. Alcibiades was persuasive, but one should not overestimate his
effect at this moment.[6]

---

[4] He may not have known that the Spartans had once reminded Athenians of a curse on
the family, 1.126–7, although it was always Alcibiades' inclination to ignore inconvenient
facts. On this family, which gave Alcibiades such a decisive start and had been important
in the change of rule at Athens, Hatzfeld 1940: 1–26.

[5] Deceleia's past relations with Sparta, Herodotus 9.73, who adds that Sparta spared it in
the Peloponnesian invasions in the 430s. The Corinthians had floated the idea of a fort
in enemy territory in 432 (1.122.1) and to concentrate Athenian minds, the Spartans
themselves had suggested it to their allies in the winter of 422–421 (5.17.2).

[6] Open, like many such assessments, to argument: cf. Dewald's claim that 'Alcibiades
alone is responsible for the Peloponnesian decision to support Syracuse with arms, and
he is the determining factor in their decision to fortify Decelea' with her own salutary
observation that Th. 'did not try to simplify or overinterpret what he saw', Dewald 2005:
153, 21.

In Sicily itself, meanwhile, the protagonists were proceeding as one might expect. For all Athenians except Nicias it was still just one more campaign and demanded nothing unusual from them. To remedy their lack of cavalry, they had received 250 horsemen and thirty equestrian archers from Athens, together with 300 talents for horses and more. In the early spring of 414 their officers took troops onto the upland called Epipolai, at the northern edge of Syracuse, to try to wall the city off from that direction. The Syracusans failed to forestall them and when they attacked were driven back down (6.96–103). They returned to try to foil the Athenians with a cross-wall of their own but failed and went back down again to stop the Athenians besieging the city. Lamachos, as Grote remarked perhaps the most capable commander of the original three, was killed in a skirmish, but things were going the Athenians' way, and they were now attracting support from those who resented the Syracusans in western Sicily. Moreover 'supplies for the army were arriving from all over Italy. Many Sicels, who had previously been watching the turn of events, now joined the Athenians as allies and three peneteconters arrived from Tyrrhenia. Other things also were progressing just as they hoped. The Syracusans no longer expected to prevail by force of arms since no help had reached them, even from the Peloponnese; indeed all the talk amongst themselves was of coming to terms, and they were saying this also to Nicias, who now had sole command.' In their dismay, they appear to have dismissed Hermocrates and two of their other generals (6.103.2–4).

The commander the Spartans had appointed, Gylippos, may have been chosen because his father had had a connection with Italy.[7] He was no Cnemos or Alcidas (or Astyochos, who was to lead the Peloponnesian force in the Aegean in 412–411); he was able and could work well with others. He had already reached Leucas, off the western coast of Greece, where the word was that Syracuse was already lost. But he believed that something might still be done to stop the Athenians taking Italy and hurried on across the sea with two ships of his own and two from Corinth; fifteen more from Corinth were to follow. Nicias, not wanting perhaps to frighten his men, or hoping to persuade himself, or believing it to be so, dismissed them as privateers. On arriving in Italy, Gylippos learnt that Syracuse had not completely been walled off. But it could only safely be approached now from land and, needing to augment his forces, he decided initially to avoid it, sail along the northern coast of Sicily and return with more men to enter Epipolai from the west (7.1).

[7] Hornblower *CT* III: 535.

Thucydides, now thoroughly into the dramatic narrative in which he excels in book 7, is for a moment carried away. The Syracusans, he writes, were actually 'on the point of holding an assembly to discuss getting out of the war' (7.2.1) when news of Gylippos' imminent arrival came from one Gongylos ('Tubby'), who had been on the first of the Corinthian ships to arrive from Leucas. The Syracusans went out at once to find that Gylippos and his augmented force were already at the western end of Epipolai or perhaps (it is not clear) already up there. This is improbable. It would have taken Gylippos days if not weeks to recruit the 1,100 Siceliots and 1,000 Sicels that Thucydides says he managed to add to the 700 he had brought from Leucas. Either he had arrived in Sicily well before Gongylos, who had not known that he had, or Thucydides is wrong about when Gongylos arrived himself. The Syracusans moreover knew which way Gylippos was approaching the city, something which Gongylos could not have known and which the Syracusans themselves could only have been aware of in news from Gylippos himself or someone else along his route from the west. It suggests that the Syracusans' despairing assembly might have been held a little earlier. Thucydides may therefore exaggerate when he now declares, as he had of the Mytileneans in 427 when a second ship arrived at their city just in time to stop the order given to the first to kill the men there, 'so close did the Syracusans come to disaster' (7.2.4, 3.49.4). There is no reason though to doubt that the Syracusans and Gylippos did appear on Epipolai just as the Athenians were about to complete their final stretch of wall to the sea.

Gongylos, one suspects, is dramatic licence.[8] Alcibiades' resurrection was not. No one writing about these events could have ignored it, and Thucydides could not have invented such a singular event. But his narrative can otherwise suggest that the decisive moves in the first part of the Sicilian campaign were not unexpected. There was nothing in the motion for the expedition on which the Athenians had voted to suggest that they should attack Syracuse first; had there been, Nicias, Alcibiades and Lamachos would not have needed to discuss what to do when they arrived. The Egestans had deceived the Athenians and no other city in Sicily had initially been willing to commit itself to the Athenian campaign. But the generals had not been inactive. They had foiled a pre-emptive move on their base at Catana, and although they achieved a victory of a kind in the battle that followed, Nicias' reading of the circumstances was that they could not be sure of doing so again. The Athenians did send additional resources, Nicias and Lamachos did start to build a wall on

---

[8] I should say that Green 1970: 213–14 and Stahl 2003: 210–16 appear to see no difficulty in the timing.

Epipolai and the Syracusans did fail to remove it. But the Peloponnesians had responded and their force and advice had restored the Syracusans' confidence. Nicias may have been too quick to dismiss the first Peloponnesian flotilla, but he might not have acted very differently if he had not done. His part in the conduct of the campaign, after the initial discussion on how to pursue it, had been sound. His reputation as a lucky commander had been grounded in fact. But Alcibiades had gone, Lamachos was dead, and he was now to make his first serious mistake.

The Syracusans were determined to make the Athenians' walls useless and prevent a siege of the city. Gylippos' first attempt to fend off the Athenians on the upland had failed – he had erred in not allowing his cavalry and archers space in which to fight effectively and actually apologised to his troops for not having done so – but his second attempt succeeded and made it pointless for the Athenians to go on building.[9] One can imagine that even if the Peloponnesians had not arrived and the Syracusans had not opted for a truce, they would themselves have attempted something similar against the Athenian walls; just as Nicias had decided that although it would difficult to prevent the Syracusans' wall overtaking his own, not to try to do so would be to give up on extending the campaign (7.6.1). As it was, Gylippos' effective deployment of forces on land had convinced Nicias that the Athenian campaign had to be won on the sea, and Nicias had accordingly begun to transfer a large part of his force from the inner part of the large harbour at Syracuse to Plemmyrion, a headland at the harbour's southern point. This was nearer by sea to the Syracusans' naval base in the smaller harbour to the north, and would allow him more effectively to protect ships arriving with supplies from Athens and Italy. But he seems not to have realised that his men would need to go inland for fresh water and so open themselves to attacks from Syracusan cavalry; Thucydides goes so far as to assert that his move was 'the start and major cause' of the deterioration of the Athenians and their ships (7.4.6). Gylippos was meanwhile continuing to recruit, a few more triremes had arrived from Corinth and the morale of the Syracusans, who were demonstrating their seamanship off Plemmyrion in the way that Nicias himself had hoped that the Athenians might find it sufficient to do, was rising. Nicias was not happy, and, fearing that his reflections might be misrepresented by an oral messenger, he decided to write to Athens (7.3.7–10).

His letter arrived there at some point in the winter of 414–413 and was read to an assembly. Its textual interest lies in the fact that it was a letter;

---

[9] Details of the topography and the complications of the various walls in maps in Mynott *TWPA*: 448, and Dover *HCT* IV: 466–84.

Thucydides includes nothing else like it, although written despatches from campaigns abroad were not unknown and Nicias alludes to some that he had previously sent. Its substantive interest lies in what it says about the state of the Athenian forces more than a year after they had arrived and about Nicias himself. Besieging Syracuse, Nicias explained, was not now possible. His ships, he claimed, had had to stay afloat in case of attack and were waterlogged.[10] The crews were tired. The mercenaries and conscripts and others who had come on the expedition because they 'thought that they would be making money rather than war' were deserting, and he was unable to recruit more. Supplies from Italy were essential, and if these were cut, it would be the Athenians who would be under siege. He realised that people in Athens did not like bad news, but presenting much the same kind of alternative as he had presented to the assembly in the spring of 415, he said that they must either double their support or let his force come home. As on previous occasions, he assured the Athenians that he had served them well. But in his own interest and what he presumably thought was Athens' also, he added that whichever path it now chose, Athens should replace him. (He did not mention Lamachos' death; news of that must already have reached the city.) He was ill, and wished to be recalled (7.11–16).

One can speculate on how the letter might have been received. Indeed one has to, for Thucydides only reports the outcome. Nicias was not replaced. The city instead ordered two men who were already serving with him to share the immediate burden of command and Eurymedon and Demosthenes to go from Athens to join him; Eurymedon just as soon as he could with ten ships and 120 talents, Demosthenes later, when he had assembled more. Meanwhile, ships would be sent round the Peloponnese to frustrate any that might be intended for Sicily. Thucydides mentions no dissent or even discussion in Athens (7.16). Pride and love of victory, *philonikia*, as he puts it later, must have committed the Athenians to conquering Syracuse, which was now clearly the first purpose of the expedition; and one can only presume that they decided that Nicias' anxieties, being Nicias', could be discounted and countered by reinforcements. One might nevertheless expect there to have been some discussion of the demands of war in Greece itself. It is difficult to believe that Athens had not heard that the Spartans had been encouraged by the envoys from Syracuse and Corinth and by Alcibiades to divert Athenians there with a fort, or that the Spartans had regarded an Athenian venture into the

---

[10] 'Disingenuous moonshine' says Green 1970: 238, who could not believe that Nicias would have needed more than one hundred ships at any one time to block the large harbour.

southern Peloponnese (which I mention in a moment) as the first clear violation of the terms of peace in 421 (6.105). Spartan morale, Thucydides remarks, was once again high, and notwithstanding the news from Sicily, one can only suppose that the Athenians' was also (7.18). Yet it is curious that even if most of those involved in the decision now in Athens thought that the Spartans could be safely contained and the campaign in Sicily vigorously pursued, no one, so far as we know, said that it would be sensible to relieve a sick and demoralised Nicias. One does not need hindsight to see that not to have done so was to take an unnecessary risk.

Even so, although the next engagement in Sicily did reveal the mistake that Nicias had made in basing himself at Plemmyrion, it did not all go the Syracusans' way. At the beginning of the spring of 413 the Spartans had collected 1,600 hoplites for Sicily and arranged for Corinthian ships to divert Athenian attention from the transports that were leaving for the west. In the move that had in the Spartans' view decisively broken the terms of the peace, though it is striking that they should now complain of this, Demosthenes had taken 1,200 hoplites and other troops from Athens' subject states via Laconia, where another Athenian general was engaged after having attempted to raise troops in Argos. Gylippos meanwhile had arrived back at Syracuse with the troops that he had recruited in Sicily itself (7.19–7.21.1). He suggested that the Syracusans should now attempt a battle at sea.

Hermocrates must have recovered his standing, for he now joined Gylippos in assuring assembled Syracusans that the Athenians were not invincible. He agreed that the Athenians were experienced on the water, but they had once been landbound; what mattered was the spirit in which they were confronted. Gylippos however did not only have a sea battle in mind. His object was Plemmyrion; the Syracusans would attack the Athenian forts from the sea, he from the land. He took his infantry to the area by night, and eighty ships were ordered to arrive to coincide with his attack. In fact, they arrived before him, and when at dawn Gylippos' troops advanced on the forts, they found that many Athenian soldiers had already got out of bed and gone down to the shore to see the spectacle. The Syracusans' spirits were high, but their expertise was wanting. Their ships crashed into each other in the bay, and the Athenians took eleven for the loss of only three of their own. Nonetheless, the material victory went to Gylippos. In the course of destroying one of the forts on the headland and garrisoning the others, his men seized the Athenians' stores, including a deal of food, three triremes, the sails and tackle for forty more and perhaps some money also. Thucydides remarks that this was 'one of the greatest and most serious blows suffered by the Athenian army. No longer was it safe to sail in to deliver provisions, since the Syracusans would have their ships lying in wait there to stop them, and ships bringing in supplies now had to fight their way through. In other respects too the capture of the fort brought general alarm and despondency' (7.21–4, these remarks at 7.24.3). Perhaps Nicias and his fellow-commanders had not been able to persuade his soldiers to stay at their post; he had intimated in his letter that discipline was difficult. Gylippos' move had been the obvious one to make, and he had made it well.

Events now started to build rapidly through the summer of 413 to the disaster that every reader of Thucydides will have known was to overcome the Athenians in September. Some read him to be writing in anticipation of it, but he was not, and it was not predetermined. Here as always, he writes from where the protagonists found themselves. His account of the early months of 413, it is true, does suggest that the Athenians' prospects were not good. They had failed to complete their siege wall on Epipolai; their commander, though experienced, was ill and appeared to be alarmingly short of will; he had lost a base and important stores; and it was not going to be easy for his forces to continue to be supplied. Moreover since March, Athens itself had been suffering the occupation of the hill at Deceleia. The Spartans had sent what Thucydides describes as their 'whole army' there with Agis to stay and command operations. These were quickly to cost the Athenians control of a large part of the Attic countryside, their livestock and draught animals, and the flight of perhaps 20,000 of 100,000 or so slaves. The destruction of property and the loss of life, Thucydides suddenly writes in a sentence that sounds as though he inserted it later, was another of 'the principal factors in their demise' (7.27.3). The Spartan presence at Deceleia also meant that all supplies for Athens itself had now to come by sea (though from Euboea that may have been no slower or more expensive than bringing them overland) and the city became a fortress that had exhaustingly to be guarded day and night. The situations at home and in Sicily were grim.

Thucydides is as surprised as were the Syracusans and Spartans that the Athenians were able to continue at all. They were 'conducting two wars at the same time, and they brought to them a competitive spirit that had to be seen to be believed. It was incredible that when they were themselves under siege from a Peloponnesian fort in their own country they should not even then withdraw from Sicily but should in turn be besieging the Syracusans in just the same way, inhabitants of a city which was itself as big as that of the Athenians; incredible too that in their display of power and daring they could so confound the Greeks – some of whom at the start of the war had thought the Athenians would survive one year, some two, but none more than three years, if the Peloponnesians invaded their country; and now, against all reasonable expectation, in the seventeenth year after the first such invasion, and already war-worn in every way, they should go to Sicily and undertake another war on the same scale as the one they already had with the Peloponnese' (7.28.3). Driven though they continued to be, the Athenians were short of funds (though they had not yet touched the 1,000 talents that Pericles had insisted they put aside against an attack on Athens itself (2.24)). A new assessment of tribute was due in 414, and one infers from Thucydides that Athens pre-empted it by substituting a 5 per cent duty on everything that its subjects were sending by sea. If the city was able to collect this, it might have brought in more than 900 talents in a year (7.28.4).[11]

After Plemmyrion the Syracusans again sent a ship east to encourage their allies to intensify the war in Greece, destroyed most of a convoy of eleven ships that were bringing supplies to the Athenians from Italy and worked hard to place underwater obstacles in the way of any Athenian ships who might try to reach Syracusan vessels in the shipyards in the small harbour. Intending no doubt to impress other Siceliot cities with the support they were receiving from beyond, they also sent a delegation of Corinthians, Ambraciots and Spartans across the island to ask for men and ships to pre-empt the reinforcements they knew that the Athenians would be sending. Demosthenes was in the Peloponnese trying (as it happens fruitlessly) to gather these, including, he had hoped, helot refugees, for whom he had fortified an isthmus 'just as at Pylos', from which he could send raiding parties inland (7.24–5).[12] Eurymedon returned from Sicily to bring the bad news about Plemmyrion and assist him. In Sicily itself, the Syracusans had raised 2,300 men, though 800 of these were killed on their way to the city by Sicels whom Nicias had recruited for the purpose; Gela and Camarina provided another 1,900. Almost all the Siceliot cities were now with Syracuse, and a battle in the Corinthian gulf changed nothing (7.34).

Knowing that reinforcements were coming, the Syracusans wanted to test the Athenians in the restricted space of the harbour, and they modified their ships to make them effective in ramming head-to-head in a way that the Athenian triremes, designed to row round an enemy in the open sea, were not (7.36). Gylippos was again favouring an attack also by land, and took men up to Epipolai. This surprised the Athenians, who expected a confrontation only in the large harbour. That came, and they put out seventy-five ships against the Syracusans' eighty. The first

---

[11] Dover in *HCT* IV: 408; it is thought that Athens never succeeded in reimposing tribute, Hornblower *CT* III: 594–6.

[12] 'Some anonymous noodle had got it into his head that if you put Demosthenes ashore in a deserted part of the Peloponnese and encouraged him to play bricks, remarkable results were guaranteed', Green 1970: 250–1.

day's fighting was inconclusive. On the second, a Corinthian steersman thought of arranging lunch for the Syracusan crews on the shore. When the crews broke to eat the Athenians took them to be breaking for the day and were unprepared when they came back out. The Athenians had taken the precaution of preparing for an escape and came away with only small losses. Nonetheless, it was a victory for the Syracusans, who were much encouraged by, as they saw it, having defeated a large Athenian fleet; they began at once to prepare a new combined offensive (7.37.3–7.42.1).

But the pendulum swung again. Demosthenes and Eurymedon arrived with no less than seventy-three triremes, 5,000 hoplites and a number of javelin-throwers, slingers and archers. 'The immediate reaction of the Syracusans and their allies was one of great consternation at the thought that there was no final deliverance from danger in sight, since they saw that despite the fortification of Deceleia a further invading army as large or nearly as large as the first one had now arrived and that the scale and reach of Athenian power seemed endless. The effect on the original Athenian force, by contrast, was some strengthening of morale after their earlier troubles' (7.42).

Demosthenes had to work with his fellow-commanders. But the initiative appears now to have been with him, and he took it in the way he had before disappearing from active service after the defeat at Delion in 423. Thucydides is dramatically exact. 'On his very first day' Demosthenes realised that he must not repeat the generals' mistake when they had first arrived in Sicily. The Syracusans should be attacked at once. They had managed to build only one wall across the Athenians' on Epipolai, and with the advantage of surprise, this should not be too difficult to cut. 'He was therefore eager to try this offensive and thought it the shortest way for him to end the war – since either he would be successful and take Syracuse, or he would take his army home and both the Athenians serving with him and the city as a whole would be spared pointless waste' (7.42.5). Foiled in his first attempt by day, he decided to try again at night with two of the other Athenian generals, leaving Nicias and the fifth general to look after the fortified area that the Athenians had unwisely established more than a year before in a marshy area near the shore of the large harbour.

Hornblower regards Thucydides' attention to the person of the new arrival as simply his 'way of dramatising Demosthenes' delusional dynamism'.[13] It is true that from what we know of Eurymedon's actions

---

[13] Hornblower *CT* III: 622. There is much debate on whether what is expressed here is Demosthenes' view or Th.'s; Dover *HCT* IV: 419–21 argued that the grammar is consistent with Th. expressing both; also Dover 1988.

in the past and the condition of Nicias now, neither would have been likely to attempt a new attack on the Syracusan wall, and Nicias' other fellow-commanders may not have had the authority or the nerve to try either. And the charge of delusion is not misplaced. Neither Demosthenes himself nor Thucydides explains how, when the Athenians had broken the wall, they might at all quickly proceed to 'take Syracuse'. They might have been able to besiege the city from the north, but the Syracusan cavalry would have continued to frustrate an approach by land from the south, and the Athenians were not now in uncontested command of the sea. In any event, a siege would be a long affair, and the point that Nicias had made in both of his speeches in Athens in the spring of 415 – that it is one thing quickly to bring a distant city under one's control, quite another to keep it so – was a good one. This aside, an attack on enemy forces at night was unusual. This one was a fiasco, and Thucydides writes it brilliantly.

The Athenians quickly took the Syracusan wall. But they rushed on to try to make sure that none of the enemy remained to fight back. The orders about who should be where and doing what were not clear; it was difficult to see who was who; as the night went on, men going in one direction met others they could not reliably identify coming back; accents were no guide; passwords were parroted; and because the paeans of some of their allies were indistinguishable from those of the enemy, many Athenians could not tell who was cheering on whom. They were eventually pushed back by some Boeotians. Many got lost on the way down to the plain, many more abandoned their arms, and when those who had recently arrived on the island did get down they were unable to find their way back to camp and wandered the countryside until Syracusans rode out in the morning and picked them off (7.43.3–7.45).

The morale of the Syracusans rose again, and that of the Athenians fell. Many of Nicias' men, camped on marshland in high summer and probably not well nourished, were ill. Demosthenes was not now deluded; he said that the force should go home. It had sufficient ships, their sheer number would make it easy for it to fight its way out, winter would come, and Athenians would be better employed attacking those 'establishing bases in their own countryside' (7.47.4), as at Deceleia, than in settling down for siege in Sicily. Nicias disagreed. As so often, he was pessimistic. He did not want the enemy to discover how weak the Athenians saw themselves to be; if they were to do so, they would obstruct an escape. 'Besides, the situation of the enemy – and he had more inside information about this than his colleagues did – still gave some reason to hope that their position would become even worse than their own if the Athenians persisted in the siege; they would exhaust the Syracusans by starving them of resources, especially now that the Athenians, with the support of their present fleet, were far more the masters of the seas. There was also a party in Syracuse that wanted to surrender to the Athenians and they were getting messages to him urging him not to withdraw' (7.48.1–2). One might think that by this point in the war any commander would be wary of the siren-songs of dissidents in enemy cities; but Nicias may have had reason to be convinced.

Nonetheless, says Thucydides, he was in two minds. Privately, he could see the case now for leaving. (One naturally wonders how Thucydides knew.) But to his colleagues, he argued the opposite. He said that the Athenians in Athens would only approve withdrawal if they were to vote for it themselves, which he did not think likely; they would not see things as those in Sicily did, and clever men in the city could always twist an argument and turn a decision. The troops, it was true, were fed up. But Nicias knew the Athenian character. If they were to leave Sicily now, they would say that they had been bribed to go, and he had 'no wish to be unjustly put to death by the Athenians on some dishonourable charge; but would rather take his chance and die at the hands of the enemy on his own terms'. In any event, the Syracusans were running short of money and could not withstand a long siege. The Athenians should stay (7.48–7.49.1, remark at 7.48.4). Demosthenes replied that if they did, they should move north, to Thapsos or Catana, from where they could use infantry to harass the country inland and deploy their ships in the open sea. Eurymedon agreed, but Nicias continued to object and the others wondered whether he knew something they did not about the situation in Syracuse itself; they may also have wondered, as may we, about his position as *proxenos*. 'And so it was that the Athenians continued to procrastinate and stayed on where they were' (7.49.4).

It was certainly not predetermined that they would do so. The question is what else might have been possible to these men in that place. Demosthenes had shown himself once again to be a restless and tactically inventive man who did not think far ahead. He would have known that he was taking a risk in attempting a battle with a force that was not in an advantageous position, at night, and in which there was no one with experience of that kind of venture; and he gave no idea (that we know) of how he thought that if he were to succeed in restoring Athens' wall and securing it the Athenians could take Syracuse in any reasonable time. Not to have tried would have saved morale, which before the defeat on Epipolai had been high. It would also have saved a confrontation with Nicias who might then not so starkly have seen the choice to be between going home or staying put. Even after the defeats, it is true, Nicias was still talking of a siege, but if Demosthenes had not been so keen on one, the force might have moved north; it might have survived any likely encounter on the open sea; and the question of what then to do might have been a question that could be answered on Athenian rather than Syracusan terms. As it was, Nicias was driven into a state of indecision. Despite his contacts with dissidents in Syracuse, he had his doubts about staying. But if Thucydides is right, he did not state them, and the arguments he did offer were not noble; Dover, always sharp but not given to overstatement, was of the opinion that his 'pride and consequent cowardice in the face of personal disgrace led him to put forward as disgraceful a proposition as any general in history'.[14] In fact he sounds like nothing so much as a sick and miserable man who was angry with the position in which he found himself; the city that had put him there; the men he commanded and his fellow-generals, who were now questioning his authority; and tormented by what he regarded as his sense of responsibility. He may have known that he was failing.

Gylippos had meanwhile arrived at Syracuse with more men, and he and the Syracusans were thinking of a new combined operation. Even Nicias now realised that the Athenians should leave and ordered arrangements discreetly to be made to do so. 'Then', on the night of 27 August, in a moment that appears to have owed little to Thucydides' taste for the dramatic turn, 'just when everything was finally ready and they were on the point of leaving, there was an eclipse of the moon, which was then on the full. The majority of Athenian troops reacted strongly to this and urged the generals to hold back; and Nicias (who was rather too much given to divination and that kind of thing) refused even to discuss the question of an earlier move until they had waited the "thrice nine days" the soothsayers prescribed.[15] So this was the reason why the Athenians prolonged their delay as they were on the point of departing' (7.50.4). The ironies in Nicias deciding to stay when he had at last agreed to go, acceding to a new fear in himself and a fear among the men he had so recently been traducing, are almost too obvious to mention.

The Syracusans were not susceptible to the eclipse and took advantage of the delay. Not wanting the Athenians to disperse in the countryside and cause trouble there, they decided to force them into a battle in the large harbour. This they won, but not decisively, and they saw that they had to

---

[14] *HCT* IV: 426. Dover's note (438–9) on Nicias' 'superstition' (next paragraph) in the face of an eclipse, however, is informative and sensible.

[15] Plutarch says that Nicias' usual 'diviner' had recently died, that he had on this occasion to consult another, and that another still might have said that lowering light at night was just what risky undertakings needed, *Nicias*, 23. Green 1970: 297–8 allows himself to wonder whether the Syracusans, knowing Nicias' susceptibilities, had bribed the man he consulted.

confine the Athenian fleet and try once more. The Athenian generals and
the navarchs, who were now very short of supplies, agreed that they had
no option but to fight with virtually every man who could stand and every
ship that could float; if they won they could take the fleet to Catana and
if not, hope to escape to friendly territory on foot. Macaulay regarded
Thucydides' account of what followed, an old-fashioned land battle on
the water (cf. 1.49.1), as his finest piece of war-writing, and many have
agreed (7.59.2–7.72.2). The Syracusans won again, this time decisively,
and when the Athenian generals suggested (now without Eurymedon,
who had made a mistake in the previous battle and been killed (7.52.2))
that with their remaining sixty ships (of an initial 110) against the enemy's
fifty, they could make a break for the open sea at dawn and return to
Athens, their men refused; they were shattered by their defeat, Thucydides says, and no longer believed they could win (7.72.3–4). Leaving
the badly wounded and the unburied dead, the surviving force – 40,000,
says Thucydides, which even including attendants and others, many of
whom had already deserted, may be an overestimation – left on foot and
most were eventually overtaken and killed or captured.

The end of the affair was appalling for the troops. It was grisly also
for the two Athenian commanders. Demosthenes believed that he had
secured a safe surrender for his men and Nicias gave himself up to Gylippos, whom he trusted. But despite what Thucydides reports as Gylippos' wish to take them both back to Sparta, Demosthenes as the villain of
Pylos, Nicias as more of a friend in virtue of his work for peace in 421 and
the release of the prisoners at Athens, their throats were cut and their men
sold or placed in quarries. Thucydides writes that it was rumoured that
the dissidents in Syracuse who had been in contact with Nicias feared that
they might become known to their fellow citizens;[16] and that Corinthians
were afraid that someone able to reimburse the enemy's costs, as Nicias
had said he would if the Syracusans would release his men, might be able
to buy his own release also.[17]

For the first time, writes Thucydides in a short chapter that shows signs
once again of having been inserted later, the Athenians had in Syracuse
come up against a city like their own: a rich and democratically inclined

---

[16] On the possibility that it might have suited Th. not to mention that Nicias had been
proxenos for Syracuse in Athens, if he was, Trevett 1995. Th. however, not given to
gratuitous detail about individuals, might have decided that mentioning his contacts in
Syracuse itself was sufficient.

[17] Diodorus 13.19–32 has Gylippos arguing against Hermocrates and another that both
men should be executed.

place whose internal divisions they could not exploit (7.55).[18] This is broadly true, and the symmetry does have a certain historical as well as literary appeal. As Thucydides indicates at the beginning of book 6, it explains why those who argued for the expedition might have done well to think harder. But it does not in itself explain why the Athenians were defeated. Their 'misfortune', as Thucydides describes it (7.86.5), was strictly circumstantial. Many have identified points at which, once the campaign was under way, things could have gone differently, and commentators disposed to lay blame have echoed Dover rather than Thucydides in pointing to Nicias.

It is impossible not to imagine that those in Athens who considered Nicias' letter in the winter of 414–413 might have relieved him. If they had replaced him with Demosthenes or Eurymedon or both in a joint command and that Demosthenes might still have decided to try to demolish the Syracusan wall on Epiolai at night, a disaster there might still have been likely; and Eurymedon had never shown any particular courage or skill as a naval commander. But unlike Eurymedon, who had good reason to fear a hostile reception in Athens for not trying harder (4.65.3), Demosthenes, though he had himself declined to return to the city after a previous defeat (3.98.5), plainly did not share Nicias' anxiety about that now. He might either with Eurymedon have been able to bring the expeditionary force home or to take it to Thapsos or Catana or the deserted Megara Hyblaea, from where its ships would have been able to fight to advantage, though it would not have been easy, even if possible, then to take Syracuse. Finally, if Nicias had remained in command and when he at last accepted the case for leaving had not been 'given to divination and that kind of thing', or despite that, had been willing and able to overrule his men – who by then, says Thucydides, whatever their fear of omens, did want to leave – the final battles would not have had to be fought.

This, however, is to focus too closely on the months between Nicias' letter and the final defeat. Thucydides writes more cleverly. The fact that Syracuse together with Sparta, Corinth and their allies had the will and capacity to resist the power of Athens in Sicily was geopolitical and determined long before 415. (Listing the states that fought on each side in Sicily, Thucydides observes that they did so 'not so much on the grounds of principle, or even kinship, as on various contingent factors of self-interest and necessity' (7.57.1, his list at 7.57.2–11).) Nicias' political tact and moderation and Demosthenes' military vigour together with the

---

[18] A possibly late insertion, Hornblower *CT* III: 650. Th. actually writes '*cities* like their own'; this raises interesting questions which are not of great relevance here.

relatively good luck that both had enjoyed in the previous ten years or so had served Athens reasonably well when its power could not so easily be resisted; or when it was, did not not so seriously jeopardise its capacities. In Sicily, where its power was at the limit, Nicias' moderation became weakness of will and near-paralysis, and Demosthenes' risky vigour, until he saw that the Athenians should leave, became rashness; they had little luck; and the consequences for Athens were more serious than at any time since the 440s. Each was the same man in all the circumstances in which he found himself; Machiavelli may have been right to wonder whether anyone can change their political character.[19] But as extreme circumstances tend to do, the last year and a half of campaigning in Sicily brought out extremes in the character of both. Some circumstances of the kind could bring out aspects of character that met the need of the moment, like those in which Pericles found himself until he came to give his last speech in 430 and those that Brasidas created for himself to the moment of his death in 422, in this respect like the circumstances in which Demosthenes found himself after a winter at Pylos in 426–425, and which Nicias enjoyed in Athens after Cleon's death and Pleistoanax's return to Sparta in 421. Those in which Nicias and Demosthenes increasingly found themselves in Sicily did not.

Thucydides says no more about Demosthenes. Nicias, he writes in his only appraisal of a whole career, was 'a man who of all the Greeks in my time least deserved to meet with such misfortune, since the whole conduct of his life had been regulated by virtuous practices' (7.86.5). This was a conventional expression of pity for someone whose suffering was not merited, and it would be still. And in so far as it relates to one aspect of Nicias' excellence (*arete*), what one might loosely call his goodness, it is unexceptionable, even if Nicias was not above putting his reputation before the well-being of his men. But although a person's goodness in this sense and his luck are relevant to an assessment of his life as a whole they bear no relation to each other – beyond the fact, appreciated more perhaps by Greeks than many moderns, that the capacity for goodness may itself be seen as a matter of luck. In so far as Thucydides' judgement relates to Nicias' excellence as a politician and soldier, it is incomplete. He was a politically constructive and moderate man; his work for peace appealed to Athenians and Spartans alike, and he was more tactful with the defeated than most of his compatriots. But what can appear to be his responsibility to the past decisions and prospective will of the *demos* can also be construed as an excessive concern with his personal standing. He had been right to argue the foolishness of embarking on the expedition

---

[19] Machiavelli, *The Prince*, Ch. 25.

to Sicily and right again in what he said in his letter in the winter of 414–413, but quite apart from his mistake in moving the larger part of his force to Plemmyrion, his concern for his reputation and by the end of the campaign for his very skin did contribute to the nature and extent of his city's defeat there.[20] Alcibiades, one hardly needs to explain, was exactly the opposite. He was confident that his reputation would be raised by his exercise of initiative rather than be put at risk by it, and he had no hesitation in evading his city when he had to and setting out to create a circumstance in which he might return to lead it.

[20] Mynott remarks that Th.'s judgement is hard to translate. 'The literal sense and word-order is "on account of the whole for virtue [*arete*] having been observed practice [of his life]"; but the relationship of the key words is unclear, and perhaps deliberately ambiguous, and there may be a sense that he practised the conventional virtues as well as regulating his life by virtuous practices.' It is important not to elide this opinion with Th.'s regret at the disappearance in conflict of that 'simplicity of spirit, which is such an important part of true nobility' (3.83.1). On the relations between luck and moral assessment, Williams 1981b, qualified by Nagel 1982, refined in Williams 1995; and on Williams deploying Nietzsche's distinction between virtue (intrinsic goodness, worth etc.) and responsibility, Clark 2001: esp. 117. On the complexities of Th.'s assessment of Nicias and an argument that Nicias 'functions as a filter' for Athens in the text, Rood 1998: 183–201. One might more cautiously say that rather like Friedrich Paulus at Stalingrad, committed to a campaign that he'd come to believe he couldn't win, being ordered not to leave, and not knowing what more he could do, he functions as a filter for an aspect of his state at that moment.

14   One war 413–411

It would be striking indeed if Thucydides is right to say that the *whole* of Greece 'experienced an immediate surge of elation' after Athens' defeat in Sicily: that even 'those who were aligned with neither side were thinking that even if no one invited them to join in they should no longer stand aside from the war but should of their own accord move to attack the Athenians, each of them reasoning that the Athenians would have done the same to them had they met with success in Sicily; and that they calculated that the rest of the war would be short-lived and that it would be a fine thing to have played some part in it'. It would suggest that the Hellenes felt themselves to be one. But it is easy to believe in the 'eagerness' of Sparta's allies to be released from the 'great hardships' of war and that 'most important of all, the subjects of Athens were now ready to revolt from her, even beyond their means to do so, because they were judging the situation in a mood of high emotion and could see no case for believing the Athenians would survive through the following summer' (8.2.1–2). All sides, says Thucydides, were preparing for conflict 'as though they were only now beginning it' (8.5.1). The 'first war' as he had thought of it had ended in 421 (5.24.2). This was in effect the start of 'another' (7.28.3).

   It is not always easy to see what the protagonists' ambitions might have been in the previous eighteen years, not least because they did not always seem themselves to be sure. But now they were. The Athenians wanted to save themselves and what they could of their dominion, and the Peloponnesians and disaffected parties in Athens' subject states wanted to end it. But the subject states could not be sure of succeeding alone and neither of the two leading powers was confident of achieving what it wanted to with its own resources. Each accordingly sought support from Persian satraps in Anatolia, who were themselves being pressed to raise revenues from the Greek settlements that had been ceded to them in 449. The politics therefore were simpler than before. Clear interests made each party in Greece more transparent to itself and others, and, except in the dealings between Greeks and Persians, there was less need to dissemble. The politicking itself however was both more complex and more intense; events were moving quickly, the connections between them were more immediate, and there was greater urgency on all sides. Politics may have few rules, but it is a competitive game. When it is what it was in Greece and the western provinces of the Persian empire in 413–411; when those involved can often be competing as fiercely with each other as they are with their enemies; when its combats and combinations can reveal what I described in Chapter 1 as its full range of passion, ambition, imagination, calculation, caution, courage, cowardice, cunning, deception and stupidity, together with the usual mixture of good luck and bad, its richness and pace can be hard to convey. Thucydides writes the politics of these two years with brilliance, and in what for him is a discernibly new way.

When other scholars were still asking why book 8 was not in their view as stylistically accomplished as the ones before, Wade-Gery was wondering whether Thucydides might not have been deliberately forsaking his 'compromise between drama and chronicle' in favour of a more 'organised' narrative. Macleod picked up the thought. 'If book 8 is in some ways odd and exceptional', he said, most obviously though not only in the almost complete absence of speeches written as speeches, 'that is partly because the historian had to find a way of beginning again after so triumphantly concluding his work'; 'its more tentative and less dramatic style may indicate not so much that he had not thought through his material, as that he was seeking new ways of presenting it'. Carolyn Dewald had meanwhile been demonstrating the change from 'a journal-like format' in which he wrote the war, incident by separate incident, to 'a more flexible, integrated, and ongoing narrative' in which he sees that he has to make the connections between 'superficially different movements'. Macleod thought that Thucydides may simply have found this a more effective way in which to write. Cratippos, a younger contemporary and perhaps an admirer, was said to have said that Thucydides had discovered that readers disliked the speeches, though this might have been speculation after the event. For whatever reason, because he was simply taking pleasure in a new style, because the events were indeed more concentrated and connected, even perhaps because he had more detail, Thucydides writes now in a more fluid fashion.[1]

---

[1] Wade-Gery 2012, from 1949. Macleod 1983e: 141 from a lecture given in 1981. The last full defence of what had standardly been regarded as the 'unfinished' nature of book 8, Andrewes *HCT* V: 361–83, the assumptions of which were criticised by Connor 1984a. Dewald 2005, from a dissertation prepared in the 1970s, quotation at 159. On Cratippos, Gomme 1954, who thought the remark attributed to him foolish. A radical

The Athenians, he remarks, recovered quickly from Sicily. Within weeks of venting their anger on those who had urged the expedition – 'as if they had not voted for it themselves', he says – as well as on 'the oracle-mongers, seers and all those whose divinations at the time had raised their hopes', they put together a new fleet, 'gathering timber and money from wherever they could', and agreed to make economies elsewhere. In order one presumes to put a stop to the competitive demagoguery that had led them to disaster in 415, they also appointed a board of elders 'to oversee current business as might be required'. 'In the panic of the moment', observes Thucydides, they were 'ready to accept good discipline in everything, as the people (*demos*) tend to do in such circumstances' (8.1).

The moment was comparatively short-lived. The government of elders was not to last and within two years a number of citizens, including some who had been irritated by the city's politics long before the decision to go to Sicily, were to decide that the democracy was no longer a regime with which to attract the Persians and pursue the war. Not least because of what appeared to be his close Persian connection, they also found it convenient to accept Alcibiades' reversion to the city's cause. But they were divided over Alcibiades himself, the new regime they created and how to deal with the opposition to it in the city itself and from its soldiers and sailors stationed on Samos. So far as one can see, the Spartans' internal politics were steadier, but they were to have problems with their commanders. Neither power was finding it easy to see how to achieve what it wanted to; each, when it acted, created hazards for itself elsewhere; neither inspired much confidence in those who looked to it for support; and both were, to a degree, at odds with themselves.

Thucydides does not say in so many words that the initiative after Sicily lay with the Spartans. But it did, and it shaped the actions of others. He writes these with all the particularity that politicking demands. It would not have been propinquity alone that prompted Euboeans to be the first to go to Agis' new base at Deceleia in the winter of 413–412 to discuss breaking with Athens. They knew their material importance to the Athenians and will have known that the Spartans knew it too.[2] But envoys from Lesbos went to Agis soon after, and because they were backed by Boeotians promising ten ships in addition (so it seems) to the one hundred that Agis had already been given the authority to requisition,

---

but not widely accepted view of the editing of Th.'s text, which bears on book 8, Canfora 2006.

[2] Th. emphasises the significance of Euboea to the Athenians at the start of book 8. On its importance as a source of food, Moreno 2007: 77–143. Also 8.95.2 and 8.96.2.

he put their wishes first. Envoys from Chios and Erythre on the Ionian mainland went directly to Sparta with an envoy from Tissaphernes, the Persian satrap in Ionia, to offer support against Athens. This was more attractive still. Chios' navy was important to Athens, and Tissaphernes, who was being pressed by his king to put down a certain Amorges, a rebellious Persian in Caria to his south, offered to pay the Peloponnesians to maintain a force that might help him do so; the Peloponnesians thought they could use this for their own purposes.[3] Tissaphernes' counterpart Pharnabazos, in the Troad to the north, sent two Greeks to suggest that the Spartans should go directly to him. This also was tempting; Pharnabazos' responsibility extended to the Hellespont, through which the crucial supplies of wheat from the northern shore of the Black Sea came to Athens each summer. But the Spartans could not go everywhere at once, and soon after the end of the winter of 413–412, they met with their allies at Corinth and decided that it would make sense first to gather resources at Chios and proceed from there to Lesbos and thence to the Hellespont. Agis was accordingly persuaded to hold back on Euboea and Thucydides says that he was content to do so (8.5–8). What he does not say is that had the Peloponnesians paused to reflect on the likely reactions of the Athenians to their plan, on the ambitions of the secondary states, and on the interests of the Persian satraps, they could be seen at last to have had a considered strategy.

The Corinthians were crucial to this, but at the start of the spring of 412 they were celebrating the Isthmian festival and unwilling to take any action until that was over. The festival occasioned a truce, Athenians attended it and had their suspicions about Chios confirmed. But the rebels there had not revealed their hand, and they were starting to worry that a Peloponnesian force would not arrive in time. One had in fact set out from the isthmus, but Athenians had chased it into an abandoned harbour in the north-eastern Peloponnese and blocked its escape. The intention had been to send five more ships from Sparta itself with Alcibiades and one of their own, Chalcideos, to meet the first ships at Chios, and Alcibiades insisted that these should still go; he optimistically argued that news of the blockade would take time to reach Chios, and he needed to use the influence he had to persuade Greeks on the Ionian coast to support the Peloponnesian move. He also explained privately to the Spartan ephor Endios, a family friend, that if he were to go at once he would be able to deny the prize of Chios to Agis, with whom

---

[3] Hornblower *CT* III: 798–9 calculates that the Chians could provide upwards of forty ships, the crewing of which would have been made possible by the unusually large number of slaves there.

he was 'having his differences' and whose powers at Deceleia, one can add, Endios himself may well have resented.[4] Alcibiades prevailed, and Thucydides rather implausibly suggests that to make sure that news of where they were going did not get out, he and Chalcideos arrested everyone they met on the way. They had arranged with the conspirators for the council at Chios to be in session when they arrived; they explained that more men would be coming and did not mention that these had been blockaded. Most of those on the council were taken by surprise; but believing that the Athenians would not be in a position to resist and that other subject states would follow, they agreed to change sides. The Erythreans on the mainland to the east did so at once (8.9–14, 8.24.4).

This was serious. Chios was the Athenians' largest and most powerful subject state – 'the Chians', remarks Thucydides, 'along with the Spartans, were in fact the only people known to me who managed to be both successful and prudent at the same time; the greater their city grew, the more they cared for its good order and security' (8.24.4) – and its defection would send a signal to others. The Athenians now released the 1,000 talents they had set aside in 431 against an attack on Athens and sent a general, Strombichides, to Chios (8.15.1). But Alcibiades and Chalcideos were ahead of him and leaving their own sailors to defend Chios itself, had gone on with a force of Chians to capture Miletus, to the south of Erythre, a subject state of Athens' that the Persians wished to repossess. This prompted the first of three treaties that Sparta was to make with Tissaphernes. The parties agreed that 'whatever territory and cities are in the possession of the King and were in the possession of his forefathers, these will belong to the King', that the war against the Athenians would be pursued by the Spartans and their allies and the Persians together and not ended without agreement between them, that no money would be allowed to pass to the Athenians and that each would help the other against any state that might revolt from either (8.15–18). Thucydides does not need to explain that the Spartans were abandoning any advantage they may have hoped to gain in promising to 'liberate' Greek settlements in Ionia or anywhere else in Anatolia. They were plainly in need.

Having been too late to stop the move to Chios and Miletus, Stromichides went on to Samos. The government there will have been more congenial to the Athenians than the more oligarchic arrangement at

---

[4] Th. is restrained. Plutarch retells a fourth-century story of an affair between Alcibiades and Agis' wife, of which Agis had learnt and which produced a son, *Alcibiades*, 23. It was the kind of story that people told about Alcibiades, which is not to say that it may not have been true.

Chios. But it appears to have been in the hands of excessively greedy or otherwise imprudent men, for 'the common people', taking advantage of the general situation and Strombichides' arrival, replaced it. They took the city, killed 200 of the richer citizens, exiled a further 400, distributed the land and houses that were vacated, and in withdrawing the rights of the landed classes went so far as to forbid 'any future marriages in either direction between them and their own people' (8.21). On what one assumes to have been the advice of Strombichides himself, a notable democrat who was to be killed in resisting the post-war dictatorship of the Thirty in Athens, the Athenians took the rebels to be 'reliable' and went so far as to grant the island its autonomy (8.21). It is not clear whether they saw that Samos would be the vital base it became. But Strombichides would have been aware that they could not afford to lose it.

The Spartan ships that had been blockaded by Athenians in the Peloponnese had meanwhile managed to escape and a new commander for the Peloponnesian fleet, Astyochos, went from Sparta to Chios with four more. The Pelponnesians' plan was still to go on from there to Lesbos, and Astyochos found that the Chians had in fact already taken thirteen ships to raise revolts in Methymna and Mytilene (8.22). But Athenians from Samos quickly recovered both places, and Astyochos, presuming that he had insufficient force or simply losing his nerve, drew back and even refused requests from Chios for support against Athenians who had landed there. Peloponnesians who had already started to march up to the Hellespont to execute the third part of the plan that had been agreed at Corinth were ordered back to their cities,[5] and in a scuffle near Miletus, Chalcideos was killed.

Athens was becoming an unexpected impediment. In the early autumn of 412 forty-eight more of their ships arrived at Samos and at once went across to Miletus. The men landed, won a fight with the Milesians and their allies, including some of Tissaphernes' mercenaries and (more surprisingly) his cavalry, and began to wall off the city, thinking that if they brought it over, others on the Ionian coast would come across also. Their momentum was short-lived. On the evening of the day on which they started their wall at Miletus, they learnt that fifty-five more ships destined for Astyochos' command, twenty-two from Syracuse under the command of Hermocrates, the rest from Sparta itself under one Therimenes, had

---

[5] Th. has not previously mentioned this expedition. Andrewes *HCT* V: 53–4 remarks that it seems to be 'a clear instance of [his] starting to write before he obtained information which he knew he would need'. It could alternatively be an example of his frequent practice of not mentioning an event until the narrative required it, Rood 1998: 22 and *passim*.

arrived just out of sight of Miletus itself. Alcibiades at once galloped out to where the men from these had camped to tell them that 'if they did not want to ruin their initiative in Ionia – and indeed their whole cause – they should go quickly to the aid of Miletus and not just stand by while it was walled off' (8.26.3). They agreed to do so in the morning.

It was the Athenians now who hesitated. The officers wanted to engage. Their ships were nearby, the balance of forces was not unfavourable – they had sixty-eight triremes against the Peloponnesians' eighty – and imagining that Athens still inspired fear on the water, they thought that victory could easily be theirs. But their commander, Phrynichos, was not so sure. He agreed that the larger part of the Peloponnesian navy could be destroyed and the campaign in the Aegean won. But after the recent disasters, he argued – he will have been thinking of Sicily – 'the city could barely afford to take further initiatives anywhere, even deliberately and after making sound preparations, except in a real emergency; much less should they be rushing into dangers of their own choosing when there was no compulsion to do so' (8.27.3). The Athenians could be beaten and another campaign lost. To the annoyance of his officers and of Argive troops who were with him, he accordingly ordered a retreat to Samos; the Argives went home. Thucydides leaves the reader to reflect on his decision, and there can be arguments still about it. But in what is for him an unusual anticipation, Thucydides does observe that Phrynichos had 'gained a reputation as a man of intelligence' – *sunesis*, for Thucydides a term of high praise – 'not only now or in this matter, but just as much later and in whatever else he was involved in' including, one infers, the coup against the democracy in Athens in the following summer.[6] Tissaphernes was pleased. The Athenians' retreat freed Peloponnesian forces to go down to Iasos in Caria and capture the irritating Amorges, with whom Thucydides later reveals the Athenians had some sort of understanding. He observes that the Syracusans were distinguished in this move, as Hermocrates himself was also soon to be in insisting to Tissaphernes that he should keep his promise to pay the Peloponnesian crews (8.28.2, 8.29.1–2). These men were no doubt pleased to be able to cart off most of Amorges' wealth, transfer his mercenaries (many of whom had come from the Peloponnese) to Chios and take their ships back to Miletus.

---

[6] Phrynichos exemplifies Th.'s complex characterisation of individuals: praised here for his intelligence, if not his action, unfavourably described as one of the more extreme leaders of the coup in Athens in 411 (8.90.1–2); cf. a simpler view on Phrynichos, coloured perhaps by a modern ideology, Shear 2011: 26–9.

In the following winter, Astyochos was unable to persuade the Corinthians in his fleet or Pedaritos, the Spartan who had been put in charge at Chios, to make a fresh attempt on the cities in Lesbos (8.32–5). He nevertheless felt secure at Miletus. The inhabitants were supportive, and he and Therimenes decided that they could negotiate a more favourable treaty with Tissaphernes. In the event, the agreement the two sides arrived at strengthened the Persians' claim on lands they had previously held by stipulating that the Spartans should not seek tribute from these. And although Tissaphernes was willing to agree that 'whatever forces shall be in the territory of the King on the summons of the King, the King shall meet their costs', the condition 'on the summons of the King' was open to interpretation. For a reason or reasons we can only guess, Thucydides mentions that when the agreement was concluded, Therimenes handed the Peloponnesian ships over to Astyochos and sailed off in a small boat, 'never to be seen again' (8.36.2–8.38.1). This may have deepened Astyochos' disinclination to help Pedaritos on Chios, who was now facing an Athenian occupation along the coast there, and the unwillingness of the Chians and Pedaritos' own mercenaries to respond to that. Pedaritos reacted in what may have been the only way he knew, which was to tighten his political control of the island and send a formal complaint about Astyochos to Sparta.[7] Astyochos was also now refusing to be drawn into battle with the Athenians themselves (8.38.2–4).

In the previous summer, the Spartans had recalled the force that they had sent marching up to the Hellespont; they may have realised that they could not be sure of being able to support it at sea. But the Hellespont remained their objective and they now despatched twenty-seven ships to assist Pharnabazos against the Greek settlers there. These ships were to go first to Miletus, where the decision on when and how exactly to deploy them would be made. In light of the complaint that Pedaritos had made about Astyochos and perhaps of the treaties that Astyochos had made with Tissaphernes, they carried eleven advisers. Clearchos was placed in charge, 'and if they so decided the eleven were to remove Astyochos from the overall command' (8.39.2). The ships put in first at Melos, which notwithstanding Athenian control was apparently still open to Spartans,

---

[7] Andrewes *HCT* V: 84 has an interesting detail and an entertaining story about this complaint. The detail is that the (almost certainly Athenian) author of the *Hellenica Oxyrhynchia* mentions Pedaritos on Chios as an instance of private empire-building by Spartan commanders. The story, from Plutarch, is that Chians who happened soon after to be visiting Sparta were quizzed by Pedaritos' mother, who was not pleased by what she learnt and wrote to her son to say that he should do better or not come home. On women 'policing' men's behaviour in Sparta, Figueira 2010.

and there encountered ships from Athens. There was a skirmish, and fearing that the Athenians who escaped it would tell their compatriots at Samos that they were on their way, the Spartan commanders decided to divert to Crete, calling in first at Caunus, on the southern Anatolian coast, north-west of Rhodes. Once there, however, they abandoned their diversion and asked Astyochos to send a convoy to escort them to Miletus.

Astyochos received their request when he had at last decided that he had to go to help Pedaritos, who with Chian leaders had been continuing to urge him 'to come with his whole fleet to help them resist the blockade and not stand by and watch the largest of the allied cities cut off by sea and devastated by raiding parties on land' (8.40.1); the large number of slaves on the island had gone over to the Athenians and knew the place as the Peloponnesians did not. But Astyochos could not refuse the Spartans who had come to assess him or be seen to put their fleet at risk on the journey they now wished to make to Miletus, and went instead to Caunus to meet them. Having been warned, as the Spartans at Melos had feared they would be, that the twenty-seven ships were on their way, Athenians came out from Samos to intercept them. There was a battle, but the weather was poor and neither side was decisive against the other. The Peloponnesians managed to get to Cnidos, west of Caunus, and the advisers and Tissaphernes, who joined them there, set about considering the 'matters already negotiated' and how to proceed in order 'to serve both their best interests' (8.41–8.43.2).

The considerations did not go smoothly. One of the advisers, Lichas, a man of standing in Sparta and fame beyond – he had defied the ban on Spartan participation at the Olympiad, gone on to win the four-chariot race there and in 418–417 negotiated for Sparta at Argos – voiced his anger. 'It was outrageous, he said, that all the territory the King and his ancestors had ruled in the past should be deemed to lie under their control now too; that would open the way for all the islands to be returned to slavery as well as Thessaly, Locris and everywhere as far as Boeotia; and what the Spartans would then be conferring on the Greeks was not freedom but Persian rule' (8.43.3): he wanted a new treaty. We do not know what territories Tissaphernes had in mind in the agreements he made; he may not himself have had a very exact sense, and Lichas may have been exaggerating. But Thucydides reports that Tissaphernes left in a temper and that the Spartans, needing the kind of support that the Persians might not now provide, went to Rhodes where 'the most powerful men' had shown an interest in their campaign.[8] They levied a tribute there

---

[8] Mynott *TWPA* notes that 'there are similarities, but also small variations, in the language used to distinguish the different groups here at Rhodes (*dunatoi* and *polloi*), those at Chios

which would have been sufficient to support their fleet for a month or
so, and drawing ships onto the shore, stayed doing nothing for the next
two-and-a-half. Thucydides says no more for the moment about Sparta's
expectation that the advisers would send ships on to Pharnabazos and
the Hellespont. And although Astyochos may have been excluded from
the exchange with Tissaphernes at Cnidos, the advisers appear not to
have pursued Pedaritos' complaint against him.

At this point, for a reason that scholars have not been able to agree, but
perhaps because he thought it impractical in a single narrative to try to
capture so many connected events moving so quickly in so many places,
Thucydides takes the reader back.[9] He explains that Tissaphernes' temper, which may to a degree on this occasion have been feigned, and the
Spartans' inaction had almost certainly had another cause. The Spartans had for some time been suspicious of Alcibiades and after the death
of Chalcideos and the battle at Miletus, had ordered Astyochos to do
away with him. This order and the reason for it, if it was sent at all, are
unclear; it may have been invented by Alcibiades himself to cover the
escape he was now planning from the Spartans, although Thucydides
does not think so.[10] What Alcibiades had been doing was to use what
Plutarch was to describe as his famed capacity to take on the colouring of
those from whom he wished to gain something to persuade Tissaphernes
'not to be too keen to bring the war to an end'.[11] It would be in the
Persian interest, Alcibiades argued, to keep the Athenians on the sea and
the Spartans and their allies on land. That way, the Persians would not
face an enemy in control of both and be able to play each off against
the other. He urged Tissaphernes 'to wear down both sides and then,
after curtailing the Athenians as much as possible, finally to get the Peloponnesians out of his territory'. Thucydides himself believes that 'as far
as it was possible to infer from what he was doing', Tissaphernes took
the advice. He reduced his financial support for the Spartans, refused to
continue to let them to fight at sea, allowed their fleet to go out of condition, placated them with the promise that he would be able to mobilise
Phoenician ships that were the king's to deploy from the eastern Mediterranean to the Aegean 'and in other respects made it only too evident

(*oligoi* and *polloi*, 9.3) and at Samos (*dunatoi* and *demos*, 21), though it is unclear in all
these cases what, if any, formal sense of organised oligarchic or democratic "parties" is
implied'.

[9] 8.45–54. This has been much discussed, not least by those who argued that book 8 is a
draft that Th. would have intended later to revise. Hornblower reviews the arguments
in *CT* III: 883–6.

[10] Andrewes *HCT* V: 95–6 is wisely unsure.

[11] Any colour, adds Plutarch, except white, *Alcibiades*, 23.

that he had little enthusiasm for collaborating with them in the war'
(8.46).

Alcibiades was clearly freeing himself to return to power in Athens. He
had persuaded the Athenian army at Samos that he had influence with
Tissaphernes, that he would be willing to return to Athens if 'there was
an oligarchy there rather than the iniquity that had cast him out', and that
they should make Tissaphernes their friend. 'Even more on their own initiative', says Thucydides, the naval captains who were stationed at Samos
had themselves wanted to overthrow the democracy in Athens and their
enthusiasm spread to the city on the island; men who wanted money
from Persia and power for themselves there had gone to the Ionian mainland to talk to Alcibiades (8.47.2, 8.63.3).[12] On their return, they had
formed a conspiracy and told the soldiers that the king would befriend
them and give money if Alcibiades were to be restored and Athens was
no longer governed by a democracy. The common soldiers had not been
happy with the suggestion but were quietened by the expectation of pay,
and the conspirators proceeded to discuss the prospect with members of
the upper-class political associations in Athens, who agreed that it was
both 'viable and credible' (8.48.1–3, 8.49.1).

Phrynichos had again been sceptical. Alcibiades, he guessed, 'had no
more wish for oligarchy than for democracy nor any consideration other
than finding a way of being recalled'. And the last thing Athens needed
was the internal division that his return would incite. In any event, the
Persian king would have nothing to gain. The Spartans and their allies
were still a presence on the sea and in lands that he regarded as his.
It would be easier, Phrynichos thought, for him to make friends with
them than align himself with the Athenians, whom he did not trust.
Nor were the subject states likely to remain any more loyal to Athens if
it were to become an oligarchy. In Phrynichos' opinion, they cared as
little for that as they did for democracy; what mattered to them (as the
Athenians, he did not mention, had already acknowledged at Samos) was
their autonomy. The 'best people', moreover, those who would exercise
power in an oligarchy, would be just as oppressive as others. It was they
who had already profited from the subjection of the smaller states, and
they who were more likely than democrats to put people to death without
trial. That, he concluded, was what Athens' subjects would have learnt in
their subjection, and he was sure that it was what they still believed. But
Phrynichos' arguments failed to move the conspirators, whom he was
later himself to join. They reaffirmed their view and prepared to send

---

[12] There is a question about who knew what at this point in Athens itself; Th. does not
make it clear: Andrewes *HCT* V: 108.

an erstwhile demagogue and target of comedy, Peisander, with others
to Athens to negotiate the return of Alcibiades, to destroy 'the popular
cause there and to establish the friendship between Tissaphernes and the
Athenians' (8.48.4–7, 8.49.1).[13]

Phrynichos, Thucydides has said, was intelligent; his scepticism indeed
was not unlike Thucydides' own. And he was determined to discredit
Alcibiades. He had accordingly sent a letter to Astyochos at Miletus,
explaining that Alcibiades was now working for an alliance between Tissaphernes and the Athenians and thus ruining the Spartan cause. Astyochos had immediately gone inland to Magnesia in Anatolia to show
the letter to Tissaphernes and Alcibiades. Alcibiades promptly wrote
to those in authority at Samos telling them what Phrynichos had done
and demanding that he be put to death. But Phrynichos, though now
'alarmed', says Thucydides, 'and in the most extreme danger because of
the information against him', kept his head. He wrote again to Astyochos,
telling him he thought it dishonourable to have shown a 'secret letter' to
the other two and cleverly adding that he and Tissaphernes should anyway realise that Samos was not well defended and could easily be taken.
Having learnt that Astyochos was betraying him and having the wit to see
that a letter from Alcibiades revealing his second betrayal would be on its
way to Samos, Phrynichos pre-empted this by himself being the one to
tell the army there that the Peloponnesians intended to attack, explaining
that Alcibiades and Tissaphernes knew that the island's defences were
poor and that it was important that the Athenians and Samians should
immediately set about strengthening them. The result was that when
Alcibiades, as Phrynichos had expected, did write to Samos to say that
Phrynichos had betrayed the army there and that the Spartans and Tissaphernes' forces were about to attack, he was taken simply to be slandering
Phrynichos in revenge for the critical speech that Phrynichos had made
about him (8.50). For connoisseurs of the political game, it is a delightful
story; the difficulty has been in knowing whether it was in fact Phrynichos
who sent the first letter or Alcibiades (or an associate of his) who had said
that he did. Each had their motives, Phrynichos to discredit Alcibiades
and Alcibiades, in his move to weaken support for the government in
Athens, to discredit Phrynichos and ingratiate himself with the Athenians on Samos. Most have assumed that Thucydides, careful in sifting
his sources, was correct. But whatever one believes about the first letter,

---

[13] 'That's why Peisander and the rest set their sights on power/Created turmoil everywhere – to cover up their thieving', Aristophanes *Lysistrata* (produced in 411), 490–1;
also *Peace* (produced in 421), 395, and *Birds* (produced in 414), 1556. On profit from
Athens' overseas dominion, n. 18 below.

Alcibiades had for once been outwitted.[14] In the event, as Thucydides explains (8.56.2), Tissaphernes had become more afraid of the Spartans than of the Athenians. If they succeeded, they could threaten his territories; if they did not, they would make claims on him that he would not be able to meet. By the time of Lichas' outburst against him, he was already distancing himself from them.

Peisander and the envoys travelling with him from Samos had reached Athens in late December 412 or January 411. Having first discussed their moves with the political associations in the city, they emphasised to an assembly that 'by bringing back Alcibiades and modifying the form of their democratic government it was possible for the Athenians both to have the King as an ally and to prevail over the Peloponnesians'.[15] Thucydides says that there were 'dissenting voices on the subject of the democracy, and that Alcibiades' enemies were protesting loudly that it would be a terrible thing if he should come back after what he had done in trampling on the laws'; priestly groups also 'testified about the affair of the Mysteries which was the cause of his banishment, and invoked the gods in opposing his recall. Peisander then came forward and in the face of widespread opposition and abuse he challenged each of the objectors in turn and asked them this question. In a situation where the Peloponnesians had at least as many ships as their own lined up against them at sea, where the Peloponnesians had the larger number of cities in their alliance, and where the King and Tissaphernes were supplying the enemy with money while the Athenians no longer had any themselves – what hopes did the Athenians then have of saving the city unless someone persuaded the King to change over to their side?' Thucydides records no answer, which if true, is striking, for there was as yet no terror in

---

[14] A summary in Hornblower *CT* III: 202–7. The character of both men would almost certainly have been known to Th.'s readers. In *Frogs*, 688–70, which was produced in 405 but here refers to 411, Aristophanes mentions Phrynichos' 'wrestling moves' that can trip the unwary; this may have been a play on the name, for a different Phrynichos (our man having been murdered in 411) was a contemporary comic poet and rival of Aristophanes'.

[15] Andrewes *HCT* V: 131, 187–9, on the *synomosiai*, 128–31. On these also Ch. 7, n. 16 above. Andrewes convincingly claims that Th. does not satisfactorily sort out the chronology of Peisander's visit to Athens. Not only is it difficult to believe that Peisander would have suggested suspending the democracy before talking to the political associations and seeing what other support he could rely on. It is also the case that in *Lysistrata*, which was first performed in February 411, Aristophanes makes no reference to anything that could be described as 'not the same form of democracy'. The omission would have been strange if Peisander had proposed what Th. reports him to have done by then. And it is difficult to believe that the terror which followed in Athens (8.66) could have been sustained for the relatively long period that would be implied by Peisander having no further reason to remain in the city. But see Hornblower *CT* III: 910–11. Th. says that he stayed for three months or so.

the city, and those who might have thought that Peisander had quite
different motives might have spoken. As it is, Thucydides writes him
to have answered for himself. 'This is not going to happen unless we
govern ourselves more prudently and restrict office to fewer people than
now, so that the King comes to trust us; unless we stop consulting more
about our constitution than about our salvation in the present situation
(we can always make some changes later if there is anything we don't
like); and unless we recall Alcibiades, who is the only man alive able
to bring this off' (8.53.1–4). Perhaps angry, as the soldiers at Samos
had been, but perhaps also frightened and silent, the majority voted to
allow Peisander to negotiate with Tissaphernes and Alcibiades. Knowing
that Phrynichos' poor opinion of Alcibiades would be an obstacle to
such negotiations, Peisander had him dismissed as general, invoking what
Thucydides, freer in his judgements now than he has been, calls the
'slander' of being responsible for not having defeated the Spartan fleet at
Miletus when he could have done, thereby losing the port of Iasos and
the support of the Persian Amorges.

Thucydides resumes his main narrative as matters began to turn again.
Alcibiades now inflicted a defeat on himself. He had known that Tissaphernes feared that the Spartans might turn against him and insist that
the Greek cities under Persian control should be free. Lichas, with whatever sincerity, had reasserted that ambition. Alcibiades also knew that
Tissaphernes, whose own forces were few, was taking his advice to let
the Spartans and Athenians wear each other down. 'My own view', says
Thucydides, 'is that Tissaphernes wanted the same result too' (8.56.3).
Alcibiades guessed that Tissaphernes would not therefore want to come
to any agreement with Athens but wanted it 'to seem to the Athenians
that it was not that he was unable to persuade Tissaphernes, but that
the Athenians, after he' – Tissaphernes – 'had been persuaded and was
willing to take their side, were not making sufficient concessions'. This
required a delicate manoeuvre, and even Alcibiades could not manage
it. Speaking formally for the Athenians but in fact for Tissaphernes, he
managed concession after concession on the first two days, getting the
Athenians to agree that Persia could have all of Ionia and 'the outlying
islands', such that by the third, he was driven to ask them also 'to allow
the King to build ships and sail his own coast whenever and with as many
ships as he wished'. This was not necessary; Tissaphernes had already
secured this advantage in gaining Ionia and the islands in the king's name
in a previous agreement, but Peisander and the other Athenians, apparently not appreciating the fact, did now balk. One of the provisions in
the so-called Peace of Callias that had marked the end of the earlier hostilities between Persia and the Greeks in (perhaps) 449 had been that

the king's ships would not again enter the Aegean.[16] That would have been very important to Athenians, Peisander and his envoys may well have remembered it, and it was a line they could not bring themselves to cross. Realising that Alcibiades had been dissembling, they returned in anger to Samos (8.56.2–4).

The strategy that Alcibiades had recommended to Tissaphernes required Tissaphernes to hide his intentions from the Spartans also. 'Immediately after this', therefore, Tissaphernes set out to bring the Peloponnesians 'back to Miletus and, after making a further agreement with them on such terms as he could get, to offer them maintenance and avoid an all-out conflict'. Thucydides explains that it was not that Tissaphernes was afraid of the Spartans being forced to fight the Athenians on the sea. He did not want them to find their ships left without crews, which would allow the Athenians to win without his help and escape his power; above all, he did not want defeated Spartans hungrily ravaging his own territories (8.57.1). The third agreement was sufficiently ambiguous to meet Lichas' objections to the second, but was even more favourable to Persia. The king was to retain all the territory that was his, the Spartans all that was theirs, and neither was to attack the other. Until the arrival of the ships that Tissaphernes was promising, the Persians would pay for the Spartan fleet; and if the Spartans needed further funds, they would be offered a loan. It was further agreed that when the king's ships did arrive, the Persians and the Spartans should 'act jointly ... in prosecuting the war, in whatever way may seem best to Tissaphernes and the Spartans and their allies. And if they wish to bring the war to an end they shall end it jointly' (8.58.2–7).

In the following summer Tissaphernes did take Lichas down to the southern coast of Anatolia ostensibly to fetch the promised 147 ships; but even if he had had the King's authority to do so, which we do not know (and nor did Thucydides), he almost certainly had no intention of bringing them into the Aegean; if he had done so, he could have finished the war with consequences that would not obviously have suited him. As Thucydides repeats in a commanding piece of analysis (8.87), Tissaphernes was indeed preferring to let the Athenians and Spartans wear each other out. Meanwhile, the two Athenian commanders who had been appointed to replace Phrynichos and another man went down to try to contain the Peloponnesian fleet at Rhodes and attacked Chios. Some Peloponnesian ships, leaving Rhodes for Chios, were diverted by Athenians to Miletus, Chios itself was retaken and Pedaritos was killed.

---

[16] Andrewes *HCT* V: 132–5. The Peace of Callias, see Ch. 2 n. 10 above.

'So the winter ended, and with it the twentieth year of the war Thucydides wrote' (8.60.3).

The Spartans were nonetheless intent on their original plan. In the early spring of 411 a Peloponnesian expedition by land and sea did reach the Hellespont and there brought two Athenian subject cities over to Pharnabazos, though one of these was soon recaptured by Strombichides, who had hurried up from Chios. At Chios itself, the man who had replaced Pedaritos attempted to break the Athenians' siege and managed not to be beaten at sea. These were modest successes, but were sufficient to encourage Astyochos to advance on Samos. At about this time or a little earlier, however, the democracy at Athens had been overthrown. The Athenians, now suspicious of each other, were disinclined to fight (8.60–8.63.3), and Astyochos' journey to Samos proved not to be necessary. In contrast to distant Thasos – where those opposed to popular rule were to see no reason to accept an 'aristocracy' imposed by Athens when Athens no longer had the power to impose anything and instead established a 'moderate' government of their own, 'the opposite of what those Athenians establishing the oligarchy had wanted, just as it was, I suppose', Thucydides remarks, 'in many of the other subject states' (8.64.5) – Peisander had already persuaded 300 of the rebels on Samos to rebel again and oppose the democracy in Athens.

The new rulers in Athens believed that they faced a simple choice: Athens had either to get support and protection from Persia or to make a new peace and alliance with Sparta; perhaps, remembering the failures of 421, with other Peloponnesian states also. Thucydides does not go into the last possibility; he may have assumed that an agreement with Sparta had to be secured first. What he has been criticised for is not explaining what Hornblower calls the new rulers' 'intellectual or "ideological"' argument for changing the rules of rule. This may be because there was none.[17] They wanted if possible to maintain the city's autonomy and what remained of its overseas dominion and to secure Persia's support for this; and the Persians, they thought, would not be willing to support a democracy. 'The fickle Athenian public' (8.70.2) must be fickle no more. Indeed the instigators of the coup, whose phrase this was, may

---

[17] Hornblower *CT* III: 945, 1035. Hornblower's suggestion that Th.'s silence might be filled with the *Athenaion Politeia* (*Athenian Constitution*) from the 330s, formally attributed to Aristotle, a document that relies on a range of sources, including Th. himself, is not persuasive. This is more constitutional than political, and to infer putatively principled (or 'ideological') positions from constitutional proposals can overlook the possibility that such proposals were informed by more immediate political interests, in this instance many years later. There is a thorough examination of 'sources for the revolution' by Andrewes *HCT* V: 184–256, his conclusion on Th. at 251–6.

have assumed that Persia did not want to hear from the Greek public at all, and they were probably right. Some, like Aristarchos (8.90.1), had had no taste for the democracy anyway; this may have been no more (but also no less) than a manifestation of that higher-class disdain for those beneath that has pervaded most modern democracies for most of their history. Others among the instigators may merely have believed that the regime had not served the city well in war. That also would not have been new. Some such belief had already been evident in Pericles, who had said that his greatest fear was of the mistakes that the Athenians themselves might make; evident also in different ways in Cleon, Diodotos and Alcibiades; and evident in a good number of citizens themselves after the calamity in Sicily (2.40.2 and 1.144.1, 3.37 and 3.43.3–5, 6.89.6, 8.1.3–4). The difference now was that even more urgently than in 413, some Athenians had an external reason, however well considered it might have been, to act on their convictions.[18]

It would certainly be wrong to say that the men behind Peisander were not able. Antiphon, perhaps the sophist known from the fragments that survive under the name and perhaps not, was in Thucydides' notably generous view 'second to none among the Athenians of his day in his qualities and his powers of thought and expression' in court and on paper, distrusted by the citizens (and perhaps also by some of his peers) for this reason and his reluctance to take part in public politics.[19] Thucydides has already remarked on Phrynichos' intelligence. And Theramenes (whose soldier-father Hagnon had been one of the ten elders appointed to supervise the city's business in 413) was also a man 'of considerable eloquence and judgement'. But even for clever men, one can believe Thucydides when he says that it was no easy matter to deprive the Athenian people of their freedom when none among them would have had any memory of being ruled by others (8.68.1–4).

The instigators of the coup had been shrewd to choose Peisander to speak for them, and for a moment at least, they succeeded. They cancelled all payment for civic service and announced that no more than 5,000 men 'with the most to contribute both materially and personally' should participate in the management of affairs, meaning, Thucydides makes clear, that they themselves would run things; we hear no more of

---

[18] Grene 1950: 45–9 suggests that 'conservatives' were willing to tolerate Athens' democracy for so long as the city's dominion profited them and turned against it when it weakened and ceased to do so. Notwithstanding Phrynichos' statement to the contrary, Finley 1978: 123 remarked that 'we are unable to specify how the upper classes could [ever] have been the chief beneficiaries' of the overseas dominion, though he concedes that one or two had substantial holdings; also Morris 2009: 149.

[19] Hornblower *CT* III: 954–6.

the body of elders which had been set up two summers before. Dissenters met mysterious deaths, for which charges were not brought, and the rest of the population, not knowing who among them might be favouring the coup (Thucydides says that these included some whom no one would have expected to do so) were frightened into silence (8.65.3–8.66). When Peisander returned from Samos and his tour of other subject states, the junta appointed ten 'secretaries' or commissioners to draft proposals on how the state should henceforth be governed and at a special assembly outside the city, moved that all existing offices should be abolished and 400 men be chosen to rule 'as they judged best' with full authority in a reconstituted council with the power to convene the appointed 5,000 when they thought it appropriate to do so (8.67).[20]

One of the junta's first moves beyond the city was to discover whether Agis was willing to agree a peace with Sparta. Agis himself, more wary of tempting dissenters than many before him on both sides had been, reasoned that they might not yet be in full control of the city, and decided to bring an army to Athens' walls to test his advantage. His men were attacked and he went back. But the junta persisted, and he agreed to receive its envoys at Deceleia. More immediately pressing for the junta was Samos; a large part of the army and the whole Athenian fleet was there. It is remarkable that Thucydides should express no surprise at the fact that the instigators had made a coup in the city without being in effective command of the larger part of the Athenian forces. And indeed, after Peisander had persuaded 300 Samians to come over to his side, Leon and Diomedon, Athenian generals at Samos; Thrasyboulos, a trierarch; and Thrasyllos, a hoplite; together with the crew of the *Paralos*, one of the two Athenian state triremes, combined to urge the people to resist. Thirty of Peisander's 300 were put to death and the rest offered amnesty, and in ignorance of what had happened in Athens, the *Paralos* went to the city to explain. Its men were understandably ill-received, and one who managed to get back to Samos gave an excitedly lurid account of the state of affairs in the city. Thrasyboulos and Thrasyllos, knowing that they were taking a risk but also knowing that since the defeat in Sicily it had been the forces on Samos that had been holding Athens' dominion together, now succeeded in bringing the soldiers and sailors and the people on the island to swear resistance to the coup. It was they, the two men argued, who were upholding Athens' 'ancestral laws' (8.76.6), they who were in a better position to exclude Athens from the sea than Athens was to exclude them, they who through Alcibiades

---

[20] There is a more charitable account of how the 400 were appointed (forty from each of Cleisthenes' ten 'tribes') in the *Athenian Constitution*, 31.1.

could secure Persian support; and if they were to fail, they had the ships and men necessary to go off and settle somewhere else in Greece.[21] Athens, as Thucydides nicely puts it, was trying to force oligarchy on the armed forces, Samos to force democracy on Athens. Envoys despatched to Samos by the 400 were wise to decide not to complete their journey (8.72–7).

Meanwhile, the Peloponnesian sailors at Miletus were becoming restive. Tissaphernes was showing himself to be increasingly unreliable, and Astyochos had still not engaged the Athenians. When he did change his mind, the Athenians retreated; then, when the Athenians acquired the reinforcements they were expecting from Strombichides in the Hellespont, it was Astyochos who drew back. In accordance with his standing orders from Sparta, he decided instead to go to Pharnabazos, who had been asking him to. Only ten of his ships got through the bad weather on the way, but these were sufficient to take the small city of Byzantion, which prompted the Athenians to send a similar number to the area themselves (8.78–80).

Back at Samos, Thrasyboulos had decided to act on his faith in Alcibiades. He fetched him from Tissaphernes, and Alcibiades impressed an assembly in Samos more than he clearly did Thucydides. He announced that Tissaphernes had given a solemn undertaking that if he could trust the Athenians they would not lack for sustenance, even if that meant 'selling off his own bed', and that he would deliver the Phoenician ships he had promised which were now waiting for them, not the Peloponnesians; but Tissaphernes, Alcibiades said, had added that he could only trust the Athenians if Alcibiades himself was safely restored to power and able to act as his guarantor (8.81.2–3). The assembly, carried away as so many before had been by Alcibiades' ability to present his own confections as fact, at once elected him general. 'There was not one of them', says Thucydides, 'who would exchange for anything else his present hopes of safety and of revenge on the 400. Indeed, on the basis of what they had been told, they were ready there and then to make light of their present enemies and sail against the Piraeus'. Alcibiades himself restrained them; he pointed out that they had an enemy still at Miletus and that he should now go to Tissaphernes to plan the next move. As Thucydides explains, he was using Tissaphernes to intimidate the Samians and Athenians, and hoping to intimidate Tissaphernes with them (8.82.1–2).

---

[21] Shear 2011: 41–9 explains that all sides in the argument at Athens were appealing to the idea of an 'ancient constitution'. As she says, Th. appears to have thought this less interesting than the events themselves.

Tissaphernes himself was still having trouble at Miletus. Men in the Peloponnesian force there suspected that he was collaborating with Alcibiades and undermining their cause, and were angry about not being paid. Relations deteriorated further when Astyochos, defending Tissaphernes, struck the commander from Rhodes. The Milesians themselves then attacked a fort that Tissaphernes had constructed there. (And later, though we do not know how much later, when Lichas, who had himself turned to reminding the locals of their obligations to Tissaphernes, fell ill and died, the Milesians prevented the Spartans from giving him the burial they asked for.)[22] Now also – perhaps by previous arrangement, perhaps in response to the political difficulties that his command had been thought to create, Thucydides does not explain – the Spartans decided to replace Astychos and recall him. He took an envoy from Tissaphernes to reassure the Spartans of the Persian's continued support and thus, one presumes, to strengthen his own position, which in turn prompted Hermocrates, at odds with Astyochos over pay for the sailors and other matters (and now exiled from Syracuse), to go to Sparta himself to explain Tissaphernes' double dealing (8.83–5).

The Spartans and Corinthians had had a strategy in the spring of 412, but had not succeeded in pursuing it. The Athenians had recovered from Sicily, Tissaphernes was letting the Spartans down, the Spartan commanders in the Aegean were at odds and a people used to taking orders from each other at home had corroborated the long-standing view in Athens that Spartans had not mastered the art of persuading others. The Athenians had had no strategy of their own other than responding to the Spartans', which they nonetheless did with effect. Tissaphernes had been letting them down also, but they were better at campaigning and, as they had shown at Samos, Chios and Lesbos, more practised in dealing with others. Yet it was the Spartans who, despite their setbacks in the Aegean, were able to sustain their internal politics, the Athenians who were dividing. It would be too simple to say that Alcibiades had caused them to do so – others might have approached the Persians and galvanised opposition to the democracy – but he played no little part in exacerbating the division. Yet in a further political twist it was he now who 'for the first time and to a greater extent than anyone else', says Thucydides, was to perform 'a real service' to Athens (8.86.4).

---

[22] An inscription from Thasos published in 1983 referred to one Lichas son of Arkesilaos as *archon* there in 398–397. If Th.'s Lichas son of Arkesilaos is the same man, his 'later' must be later than this, and can suggest that Th. was still alive then. But nothing corroborates this. Hornblower *CT* III: 995.

The envoys from the junta who had initially thought it unwise to press their case at Samos eventually arrived to do so. The occasion was noisy; the envoys said that the stories of persecution and death in the city were not true, and the soldiers, who did not believe them, called for an attack on the Piraeus and the deaths of those who had made the coup. Thucydides believes that only Alcibiades could have restrained them again, and he did so. He pointed out that if the men went to the Piraeus, the enemy would be able to seize Ionia and secure the Hellespont. He therefore asked the envoys to tell the junta that he would not prevent the 5,000 from ruling but that it should 'get rid of the 400 and reconstitute the council as it had been before, a body of 500; and if there had to be any cutbacks in the interests of economy, which would result in better pay and provisions for the men on active service, then he applauded that. Otherwise, they should hold firm and concede nothing to the enemy. If the city was kept safe there was every hope that they could also reach agreement amongst themselves; but once one or other party faltered, either those at Samos or the Athenians at home, then there would be no one left to be reconciled with' (8.86.1–7) – and no one therefore, Alcibiades was no doubt thinking, for him to return to lead.

Whether or not he knew that it would do so, his suggestion, Thucydides reports, appeared to reassure most of those in Athens itself who were 'involved with the oligarchy'. They 'were already feeling troubled and would gladly have got rid of the whole business any safe way they could'. Indeed they were themselves now starting to gather and 'find fault with the state of affairs. Their leaders were men who were very much part of the oligarchy and held office within it, such as Theramenes son of Hagnon, Aristocrates son of Scelias and others. They . . . were now seriously afraid, they said, of Alcibiades and the army in Samos . . . They thought they should dispense with the excessively narrow oligarchy they had, and should instead demonstrate that the 5,000 existed in reality and not only in name and establish the constitution on a more equal basis.' Yet this, Thucydides explains, was pretence. They were not in fact conceding. Each was 'contending to establish himself as the foremost champion of the people' (8.89.1–2, 8.89.4).[23] Antiphon, Phrynichos, Aristarchos and Peisander, realising that Alcibiades' strength would

---

[23] In the middle of this account (8.89.3), Th. inserts what Andrewes *HCT* V: 301 rightly describes as the reckless generalisation that in an oligarchy leaders compete with each other to be first whereas in a democracy they can console themselves with the thought that defeat is by the people's vote. Mynott's suggestion that Th. is here thinking of selection by lot is ingenious, but it's not clear that it saves the claim. Shear 2011: 60–7 suggests that Th. based his distinction between the more and less extreme instigators of the coup on evidence presented at subsequent trials.

threaten their own, decided that Antiphon and Phrynichos would go with others at once to Sparta to seek peace on any terms, and that the walls at the Piraeus would be rearranged to make it more difficult for the forces from Samos to enter.

Thucydides reports that the Euboaeans meanwhile had asked the Spartans for support and that forty-two ships (including vessels from Italy and Sicily) were preparing to go there. Thinking that the embassy to Sparta had returned without an agreement, Theramenes 'and his circle' within the junta were convinced, or said that they were convinced, that the rearrangement of the walls was intended to allow the Spartans in rather than keep the men from Samos out. Thucydides thinks that this was not unfounded. Antiphon and others would have liked to retain control of Athens 'and rule over the allies too, but failing that they hoped at least to keep their ships and fortifications and be independent; and if that too was denied them, then at any rate they had no wish to become prime candidates for certain destruction at the hands of a resurgent populace' – and soliders from Samos – 'but would actually bring in the enemy, giving up their walls and ships, and agree the fate of the city on any terms at all, provided that they saved their own skins' (8.89–92).[24]

Neither side took any action when on his return from Sparta, Phrynichos was assassinated in the market square. But when the Peloponnesian fleet stopped at Epidauros and overran Aegina, which was not obviously on the route to Euboea, Theramenes became convinced, says Thucydides, that it was heading for the Piraeus, and thinking that the work on the walls was indeed intended to make it easier for it to take the place, tacitly approved what appears to have been a spontaneous move by the hoplites constructing the walls to take them down. Aristarchos and his associates were angry but managed to silence the builders by promising to reveal the list of the 5,000 and in an emergency meeting of the 400 conceded that the 400 themselves would henceforth be drawn from this larger number. That had the desired effect, despite or more probably because of the fact that no one was sure who the 5,000 might be. The junta then agreed to the suggestion of an assembly in a few days' time in the sanctuary of Dionysos (rather than on the more usual site of the Pnyx), ostensibly to discuss the question of unity in the city. Just as the pandemonium was dying down however – Thucydides recounts it in

---

[24] Moreno 2007: 121–6, noting Th.'s observation that the junta had instructed that all grain for Athens, local and imported, was to be stored in the warehouse at the walls (8.90.5), suggests that his hostility to the junta had got the better of his judgement; but whoever was in the city would have to eat, and no sensible set of rulers would have wanted to risk riots over food. Nothing unfortunately can be decided from Th.'s puzzling account of the walls themselves, *HCT* V: 303–6.

great and pacy detail – it became known that the Spartan fleet had left
Megara and would soon be sailing past Salamis, which was very close
to the Piraeus indeed. All now were convinced that Theramenes had
been right, and there was a scramble to man the ships and the existing
walls. In the event, the Spartans did sail on to Euboea. Athenian ships
pursued them, but being unprepared and in some disarray, were out-
manoeuvred. Twenty-two were lost, Athenians who sought sanctuary in
what they supposed would be the friendly city of Eretria on Euboea were
murdered, and the Spartan commander was quickly able to secure the
island (8.91.2–8.92.2, 8.92.3–8.95).

Nothing, Thucydides declares, not even their defeat in Sicily, had
scared the Athenians quite as much as the loss of Euboea. He has said
his sort of thing before – when Spartans had landed on Salamis in the
winter of 429–428 (2.94.1), when the Athenians had been routed at
Syracuse in 413 (7.71.7), and about the aftermath of the defeat in Sicily
(8.1.2) – and although it may be far-fetched to suggest that he intended
to dramatise a sequence of rising reactions,[25] it is easy to believe that
the Athenians were more given than ever to despair. 'How could they
not have had good reason to feel cast down', he asks, 'when the army
at Samos was in revolt, when there were no more ships to be had nor
crews to man them, when they themselves were divided and there was
no telling when they might break out in open conflict with each other.'
And Euboea mattered more for their food than the countryside of Attica
itself. 'What caused the greatest consternation of all was the threat so
close to home, and the fear that the enemy might be emboldened by
their victory to go straight on to attack the Piraeus now that it was bereft
of ships. Indeed, they thought they were as good as there already. In fact',
continues Thucydides in his own voice, looking back in a way he has not
done earlier, 'had the enemy been bolder they could easily have done just
that and they would then either have deepened the divisions in the city
still further by standing off Piraeus or, if they had stayed and settled into
a siege, they would have forced the fleet in Ionia, despite their hostility
to the oligarchy, to come to the rescue of their own relatives and the
city as a whole; and in the process the Hellespont would have fallen into
enemy hands – and Ionia, the islands and everything as far as Euboea –
in fact you could say, the whole Athenian empire' (8.96.1–4). Athens'
thalassocracy would have been over.

Thucydides writes this counterfactual as his own. But it is the one
with which Alcibiades had frightened the men at Samos when they had
wanted to attack the Piraeus, and is equally dubious. Alcibiades then,

---

[25] Hornblower *CT* III: 1029–30, also Rood 1998: 272 n. 82.

perhaps deliberately, and Thucydides now were forgetting that even if the Spartans might manage to occupy the Hellespont, the Persians would have been unlikely to accept their doing so. The Spartans were anyway being more cautious. Agis had decided that it was sensible to retreat when he had approached the walls of Athens, and Agesandridas, who commanded the fleet that had taken Euboea, may have been similarly careful now; as Thucydides himself suggests, 'it may well be that [he] had been hanging around Epidauros and that area under some prearranged agreement, but it is also likely that he stayed there of his own accord with an eye to the current disturbances in Athens in the hope that he might arrive there at a critical moment', and decided that such a moment had not come. Not for the first time, remarks Thucydides in the manner of the Corinthian speakers at Sparta more than twenty years before, the Spartans were the most convenient of enemies (1.70, 8.96, 8.94.2). What he does not suggest is that Agesandridas can be seen to have acted in Sparta's better interests, and that some at least of the 400 would have seen that too.

The scare had nevertheless been salutary. Or so it appears. For after the loss of Euboea, the Athenians, Thucydides writes in disappointing generality and haste – one would like to know which Athenians, and how, though they will have included some members of the junta – convened an assembly and held it on the Pnyx. This decided to hand powers to the 5,000; to put a curse on anyone who received pay for public office, which was a strange thing to affirm unless there would be someone in position again to offer it; to arrange other matters in later meetings; and to recall Alcibiades (who was in fact not to return to Athens until 407). 'For the first time, in my life at any rate', Thucydides remarks from the distance of exile, the Athenians 'appear to have enjoyed good government, with a moderating balance between the few and the many' (8.97.2).

The characterisation is tantalisingly loose, and has been much debated.[26] If Thucydides is referring to a constitution, this would have been somewhere in the space between the extremes of oligarchy and democracy. If he is referring to an actual government and its politics,

---

[26] It is a prime instance of the difficulties that can arise in translating Th. Mynott explains to me that the relevant clause can be rendered as 'There was a moderate mixture between the few and the many' and 'There was a moderate as between the few and many mixture.' The senses are different. And other translations and authorities, including Paul Cartledge in private communication, can favour 'blend' over 'balance', which in modern English has a distinct political connotation. Hobbes, the most politically committed of translators, writes of a state of affairs 'which consisted now of a moderate temper, both of the few and the many', a different emphasis again (Thucydides 1989: 560–1). Examined previously by Andrewes *HCT* V: 322–40 and more briefly in the light of later literature by Hornblower *CT* III: 1033–6.

these were either led by the discretion of an elected few or, if the franchise was wider, may have balanced the interests of the few and the many, or indeed both. If the 'few' were the 5,000, but the 5,000 were 'all those who could provide their own hoplite armour', the fact that as Andrewes suggested the number who could do so would be in excess of 5,000 can indicate that 'the five thousand' had become a convenient phrase with which vaguely to indicate something more than the 400 but short of all the citizens; if this was so 'the few' would have been many, though less than 'the many'. These considerations apart, if Thucydides really meant to say that this was the first time in his life that the Athenians had enjoyed good government, he will have thought it superior as a constitution or a politics to that of the 430s, which does not sit easily with his retrospective praise of Pericles at 2.65. In any event, even though the new arrangement was to last for just nine months, it did mark the start of a solution to the internal problems that the Athenians had had after Sicily. When all but three of the more extreme members of the junta had fled to the Spartan fort at Deceleia – Phrynichos was dead, Aristarchos had gone to betray the border fort at Oenae to the Boeotians, only Antiphon stayed to face trial in Athens – it marked the end of the *stasis* (8.97–98, 8.68.2). That had only lasted for four.

Having recovered themselves politically, the Athenians' morale was to be further improved later in the summer of 411 by Alcibiades managing to strengthen their position in the Hellespont; victories that Thucydides recounts with his usual vividness. The Spartans had accepted that Tissaphernes would not deliver what he had promised; their new commander at Miletus, Mindaros, had acted on Pharnabazos' repeated requests for help against the Athenians in his area; and Thrasyllos had pursued him there from Samos. Tissaphernes – annoyed by what appeared now to be Pharnabazos' success with the Spartans, on whom Pharnabazos had embarrassingly spent less than he had, and by the Spartans' own interference in several places under his command – went north to reaffirm his promises. Thucydides' text ends in the middle of a report of his journey there (8.99–109).

As I have said, his account of these years has disappointed many of those who admire the first four books and his description of the Sicilian campaign in the sixth and seventh. Book 8 has none of the drama of word and deed in the one and nothing of the climax that has given an all but irresistible meaning to the other; indeed there is no ending at all. But it is Thucydides' most sustained and compelling exposition of practical politics. The Peloponnesians did have a strategy but gave little sign of thinking in advance about how others might react to it. Their caution in pursuing it, in Astyochos at least, is not always easy to distinguish from loss of nerve – the Spartans were slow to see this and correct it – and their commanders had not worked well together. Alcibiades, when he was acting for Athens, had at crucial moments been more constructively agile than the army and navy on Samos or any collective entity perhaps could have been, and those on Samos were less careful than he. The greatest concentration of clever men may have been in those who made the coup in Athens, but it was a concentration also of political stupidity; they were uncunning in pursuit of their own interests and if it is said that events were outrunning them, that was in good part the consequence of their making a coup without having made sure of armed support for it. Luck may have favoured the Athenians when the Spartans were held up on their first moves to Chios, the Spartans when Phyrnichos decided not to engage them at Miletus, Alcibiades if Astyochos had in fact been instructed to kill him and failed to act and Astyochos himself when the coup in Athens removed the need to attack Samos; but there was no turn of fortune that compared in its likely consequence with those in the Archidamian war or the campaign in Sicily. The conflicts in this new war were more concentrated and the connections between events in it were closer; Thucydides may have had more detailed information than he usually had before and his new way of writing rose to the occasion.

The surviving accounts by others of events to the end of the war have less life. Sparta and its allies will have been frustrated by Athenian victories in the Hellespont later in the summer of 411; by Athens' refusal of an offer of peace after a victory in at Cyzicus on the Black Sea coast in 410, where Mindaros was killed; by another victory at Byzantion in 408; and yet another at Arginusae, east of Lesbos, in 406, after which the Athenians again refused the suggestion of peace. But the Peloponnesians will have been encouraged by the continuing differences in Athens itself that one supposes were in part the consequence of distrust after the events of 411, by evidence of the Athenians' want of funds, by a victory of their own at sea near Ephesos in 406 (in large part due to a mistake by Alcibiades' second-in-command) and by Alcibiades' own subsequent withdrawal from Athens, an extreme reaction, it has been said, to the welcome he had had from all sides there in 407, as though he were a Pericles returning and had disappointed the city as only a 'first man' could. But the Peloponnesians were becoming superior at sea, and as Thucydides explains in one of his late insertions (2.65.12), were able decisively to win when the king appointed his second son, Cyrus, satrap of Lydia and provinces to the east and commander of the Persian forces in Anatolia and through him financed a fleet that finally defeated the Athenians' own at Aegospotamoi in the Hellespont in 405.

It was an ironic end. Alcibiades, says one source, had advised the commanders of the Athenian fleet to base themselves at Sestos, 13 miles or so away from Aegospotamoi, where there was a proper harbour and the men could be readily supplied. But he was ignored. (He was by then living nearby and another source says that he had offered to provide fighters from the area if he were allowed to share the Athenian command.) Aegospotamoi did have the advantage of being directly opposite the Spartan fleet on the other side of the Hellespont, but it would have been sensible for the reputedly 30,000-strong force of Athenians to retreat to Sestos after having failed to incite the Spartan commander, Lysander, to engage at Aegospotamoi itself.[27] This was no more than a river mouth and beach from which the Athenians had to go inland to find food; Lysander had been careful in his reconnaisance and attacked the Athenian ships when many of their men were away from the place, all but literally out to lunch. The larger irony is that if the Athenians had not been defeated at this moment, reportedly losing all but ten of their 180 ships, Cyrus' support for the Spartans and their allies might well soon have been ended by the strain put on Persia by a rebellion against its dominion in Egypt in 404 and a dispute between Darius' sons. Athens might then have won the war by default. As things were, it was besieged and surrendered in the following spring.

One may be sorry that Thucydides did not complete the story. But it is not likely that if he had, he would have led one to a conclusion other than the one that I suggest in the next chapter. The Spartans felt themselves compelled to move against Athens in 431, and it would have been odd if they had not been impelled to do so again after Athens' defeat in Sicily in 413. In between, it was only Sparta, going to the northern cities to counter the Athenians' advantage after Pylos, and Syracuse, seeking the support of other cities in Sicily when the Athenians were coming, that had acted under what one might regard as necessity, and neither move proved to be decisive. Sparta withdrew from the north and agreed a peace, and the Syracusans were saved by Sparta and its allies. Of other ventures in the first eighteen years, some had of course been more likely, some less; not every possibility was equally probable at the moment in question. Yet as Thucydides allows one to see, things could have gone differently until the very last days. If Athens had prevailed and the Persians withdrawn their support for Sparta, one can suppose that it might have recovered

---

[27] An examination of what may have happened at Aegospotami and afterwards, Strauss 1983, who also explains likely divisions between the Athenian commanders.

some of its dominion; but funds to do so would have been wanting, no other power would have offered the kind of pretext for command that the Persians had presented in 478, the resistance would have been stronger and, even if it had managed to recover, the force that was to defeat Greece on land a little more than sixty years later might not have been deterred.

15   Back to the present

Thucydides, a literary theorist might say, 'sideshadows'; he writes from where the protagonists were, neither foreshadowing events they could not have known nor 'backshadowing' in hindsight. It is a device with which he makes it clear that in the first eighteen years or so of the conflict, no one was very sure what they were doing. Neither the Spartans nor the Athenians, having found themselves inadvertently at war, nor those relying on an alliance with the one or hoping to escape from the dominion of the other, were able to take the war to their enemies. They could only respond to opportunities to disadvantage others and gain what advantage they might for themselves, however notional that might be. The peace that the powers agreed after the first ten years of fighting, in effect a return to the balance in the treaty of 446–445, can suggest that the Athenians had won the war as Pericles had conceived it. But the Spartans had not lost, and it did not last. Powerful men in Athens and Sparta were not willing to accept it, Argos was not party to it, those in the Boeotian federation, Corinth, and other allies of Sparta feared it, and Athens' subject states had no say. The conflict resumed, and it was not until the Athenians themselves had been defeated in the ill-advised expedition to Sicily that the Spartans were to devise a strategy for winning and the Athenians to concentrate on not losing – strategies in which the Spartans hoped to persuade the Persians to support them and Athenians hoped to persuade them otherwise.

This is not to say that everything that everyone did in the first eighteen years of the war lacked reason in a way that what most were doing after 413 did not. Nor is it to say that most of what was attempted in the first eighteen years was to fail and that only the Spartans and their allies were later to succeed. It is however to suggest that the two most general readings of the way in which Thucydides writes the war were excessive. Jacqueline de Romilly long held the field. As her recent editors observe, she was less interested in what Thucydides thought about than in how he did so. But her answer to the one question did suggest an answer to the other. She argued that 'every human means' in the text 'is

subordinate to intelligence', by which she meant the 'rigour' of 'reason':
the reasoning of those about whom Thucydides writes, which continued
the preoccupation in poetry and epic with the typical, transformed this
into laws of the probable, refined these with the antithetic method of
the sophists and extrapolated; and that of Thucydides himself, which
she saw him deploying in the generalisations of his 'archaeology' and the
preceding 'fifty years' in book 1, his specification of the more proximate
causes and effects of 'things done' in the war itself and his depiction of
what John Finley had identified as 'the forces working themselves out in
the period which were beyond the control of any human agent'. Stahl
went to the other extreme. In exposing 'not merely the tragedy of Athens
but in a much broader sense the tragedy of humanity itself: of human
beings who make themselves and others into the victims of their vast
plans', he insisted, Thucydides shows them to have been defeated by
emotions that defy 'rational understanding and systematisation'.[1]

Much of course depends on what one means by 'reason'. It is certainly
too strong to say there were considered plans for most of the moves each
side made before 413. But even when there were, the reasoning was
usually more than the calculation of means for pre-given ends. Several
of those whose thinking Thucydides reveals (or reconstructs) in those
years – Pericles and Archidamos in the late 430s, Cleon and Diodotos
in 427, the Spartans after the surrender and imprisonment of the men on
the island at Pylos in 425, Hermocrates in Sicily in 424, Agis in 418 (and
again in 413), Alcibiades and Nicias in 415, and the generals on both sides
in the Sicilian campaign – were reflecting in more broadly reasoned ways,
some well, some not, on the situations in which they found themselves
and what might follow for what they should do. It is also too simple to
say that reasoning in the wider sense or the narrow was always defeated
by unreason. There were certainly occasions on which this was so. As
Thucydides writes them, Archidamos' arguments at Sparta in 432 and
Nicias' at Athens in 415 were almost at once overridden by the passion
of others, Pericles' in 430 and Cleon's in 427 were undermined by their

---

[1] De Romilly 2012: xiv, 104–5, 151, 183–4 and *passim*, first published in 1956 and carefully
examined in Gomme 1958; Finley 1942: 306–11, also 1967; the two were developing
their ideas independently of each other in the 1930s and 1940s. In an earlier work (1963,
first published in 1947), de Romilly had claimed to detect 'laws' of imperialism running
through a text which, ironically in the light of what I have been suggesting, she saw
fading only in the unfinished book 8. Stahl 2003: 60–1, 152. Dewald 2005: 15 restates a
more moderate version of de Romilly's thesis: 'in constructing the text, the historian as
narrator presents himself as using the same kinds of thinking – ... secular, pragmatic,
prudential – as do the most competent, intelligent actors in the account'. But no one
character in Th. (except perhaps Perdiccas) is consistently 'pragmatic' or 'competent' or
consistently not.

own, there is little sign of deliberation in many of the secondary states, and both Thucydides and his protagonists can make sharp remarks on the force of unreasoned hope throughout. The deeper question is about the place of reason itself. Thucydides was not what we or his contemporaries would recognise as a philosophical writer. But he can be seen implicitly to have held to what we can describe as a non-separability thesis on motive, reflective intention and action and a non-isolability thesis on all three and their contexts. These do not imply that each element can be seen as no more than an aspect of the other, reduced to it, or substituted for it. Each is distinct. It is to say that thought and action are guided by pre-rational commitments, that all three come together in ways that affect the facts of character, individual and collective, and that they together explain what people make happen, which can sometimes be nothing. Beyond logic, reason is never all there is; but nor usually, in most politics and war, is emotion.

This aside, it is not true to say that most actions failed. Perdiccas may have been the only man in the story always to succeed, or to manage with sufficient speed to recover from the threat of not being able to do so. But Pericles' decision not to resist the Peloponnesian invasions of Attica; Cleon's determination to capture the Spartans on Sphacteria and reject a suggestion from Sparta for peace; Athens' own attempt at a peace in 421, in contrast to Sparta's inability to bring its allies with it; Agis' decisions to act as he did and did not against Argos and later from Deceleia; Hermocrates' efforts to unite the Siceliots; the Spartans' attempts to agree terms with the Persians after 413; and Alcibiades' attempt to prevent the Athenian forces on Samos from attacking Athens cannot be said completely to have failed, and to insist that some were eventually to do so is to overlook the fact that few achievements in politics anywhere last.

In all these respects therefore, if not explicitly, Thucydides is suggesting complex explanations of actions and their outcomes and resists taking any one view of the outcomes themselves, nowhere more so than in the last book of the eight, which commentators were inclined to ignore. It was not until 413 that the Spartans and Athenians, the one acting more or less steadily, the other less so, had discernible strategies, and Thucydides excels in his account of how these were pursued. Book 8, as I have said, is the stuff of success and failure in politics and war. Yet even in the face of politics that were as exciting, tiring and at times unappetising as pure politics can be, he maintains his even-handedness. In remarking on the exercise of intelligence in the service of extremism, skill in the exercise of deceit, prudence in the pursuit of personal ambition and openly declaring his preference – regardless of time, place and kind of regime – for moderation (8.25.4, 8.97.2), he may be revealing his own inclination; but he continues carefully to explain why all those involved were attempting what they were. His passion for truthfulness is plain.

It was in this that he was most partisan and might himself be said, in two senses, to have been political. The first was in what might be called the politics of knowledge. Just as medical writers of the time were arguing that on matters of bodily affliction and how to alleviate them no one should prefer speculation to investigation; just as he was arguing that on the political past, 'no-one should prefer rather to believe the songs of the poets, who exaggerate things for artistic purposes, or the writings of the chroniclers, which are composed more to make good listening than to represent the truth, being impossible to check and having most of them won a place over time in the imaginary realm of fable'; so he can be read to be saying that on the recent past and near-present no one should prefer speech to facts that had been 'derived from the clearest evidence available' (1.21.1). In what he said at the funeral for Athen's first war dead, Pericles had taken the opportunity to present the city's politics as inclusive and participatory. But he did not accept the view of what might well have been a majority of its citizens when this was at variance with his own: 'what was in name a democracy was in practice government by the foremost man' (2.61, 2.65.9). Cleon accused the Athenians of having become 'used to being spectators of words and listening to deeds' (3.38.4). But he then immediately insisted that they hear what he had to say about the part 'the people' in Mytilene had played in the rebellion there. Brasidas assured the Acanthians that it would be safe to rebel because a large Athenian army had been afraid to engage a smaller force of his at Megara (4.108.5). But the force was not obviously smaller and this is not what the Athenian commanders or Thucydides himself had said; they were afraid that Brasidas could draw on larger numbers and were in a hurry to bring Boeotian cities over to Athens; anyway, they thought that 'most things had gone their way so far' in the encounter (4.73.4). Each man was dissembling. Pericles told a palatable half-truth about Athens' politics and subverted it, Cleon told an unpalatable half-truth and immediately made use of it, and Brasidas lied. It is interesting that Thucydides should remark that the politician who was 'second to none among the Athenians of his day in his qualities and powers of thought and expression' in what he wrote and spoke in the courts refused to speak politically at all (8.68.1). Speeches and their equivalents were an essential part of politics; but they were no more to be trusted on events in the present and what might follow for the future than were poems and chronicles on the past.

The second sense therefore in which it was political of Thucydides to write what was said in the light of what was done and vice versa was straightforwardly political. He portrays Pericles as clever but stubborn and eventually all but self-destructive, Nicias as 'virtuous' but weak, Alcibiades as a gifted rogue, Phyrnichos as shrewd and a traitor and all four as noticeably vain. It was Cleon, benefiting from the democracy but impatient with it and a bully to boot, who shared something of his own view of competitive speaking itself. (Pericles also might have agreed, but as far as we know did not say so (2.60).) Cleon was an able speaker who distrusted able speech; speakers could obscure the truth of 'things done' in order to shape what they wished to convey, and he used his own to do just that. As Thucydides wrote and Diodotos said, the 'common people' in Mytilene were not unequivocally inclined to revolt and, when they did, it was not for the reasons that Cleon gave. This is not to say that all speakers always deceived. The Athenians who addressed the Spartans in 432, Archidamos in the following winter, Pericles to the Athenians the next summer, Hermocrates to representatives of the Siceliot cities in 424 when the Athenians first showed an interest in the island, Nicias to the Athenians in 415 when they had decided to send an expedition to help Egesta and were thinking of attempting more, Phrynichos in private remarks about Alcibiades to fellow conspirators and political associations in Athens in the winter of 412–441: all were being truthful, if not completely so. Yet in refusing to compromise, Pericles, like the Athenians in their arrogance at Sparta in 432, was provoking Sparta to war, Archidamos was to lead an unnecessary attack on Plataea, Hermocrates was pressing the Syracusan interest in Sicily, Nicias was driven by anxiety over his present standing and future reputation and Phrynichos, though right about Alcibiades' self-serving ambition, turned out to be more determined than he to abandon the democracy in Athens and make peace with Sparta.

Thucydides writes Diodotos to have said of Athens that 'good advice honestly given has become as suspect as bad, and the result is that just as the person who wants to urge some dire proposal resorts to deceit to win over the people, so the person with better policies must lie to be credible' (3.43.2). Even so, only a few speakers in Thucydides' story – Pericles with the Athenians themselves after the start of the war, Hermocrates with the Siceliot states in 424, Alcibiades with the Argive assembly in 418, Peisander with the Athenians in 411 and Alcibiades with the Athenian soldiers and sailors at Samos later in the same year – succeeded with audiences that were undecided or confused. Others achieved what they wanted to with audiences who were already inclined to agree, including Diodotos himself (if indeed it was his speech that was decisive, which I suggested is doubtful). Political rhetoric was an art in which Thucydides took great interest and no doubt much pleasure, but for him to place it as he did in the text and thus expose it was itself a political act. The fact that like Antiphon, whose abilities he so admired, he was himself writing rather than speaking makes the point.

Meanwhile, there were all the other 'things done' to write truthfully about. It is too simple to say that the events which no one anticipated can all be attributed either to *tuche* – the wide meaning of which, 'chance' or 'luck', indicates the degree to which such attributions matter to the person who makes them – or to deep forces which, even if anyone had been able to understand them, were beyond control. Thucydides claims neither. It is not he but his speakers who talk of *tuche*, and only once does he say that war itself (war within a city, though exacerbated by war beyond) is a 'violent master'. One might be tempted to suggest, as readers have, that if an Athenian fleet had not had to shelter from a storm at Pylos, Demosthenes might not have been able to achieve what he did; that this was a chance occurrence with decisive consequences for the rest of the Archidamian war. But had Demosthenes not set out from Athens with the intention of stopping off somewhere on the Peloponnesian coast, he might not have seized the opportunity when it presented itself; and had he not had Cleon's support, he might not have been able to take advantage of the Spartans' error there. One might likewise be tempted to argue that no politician would have been able to constrain his opponents in Athens after the failure of peace in 421 and guide the *demos* more prudently through the angers and anxieties of the resuming war. But one cannot know that Alcibiades, if he had been able to stay in the city, could not have done so; or that even if the radical democrats were determined by some means or another to divert him, they might not have found it in them to do so in a way that did not prompt him to turn to Sparta. One might certainly argue that the Athenians were not predetermined to be defeated in Sicily. And one can imagine that if Thucydides had managed to write what in his 'second preface' he says he hoped to, he would in his indirect way have made it clear that having quickly recovered from Sicily and the interruption of the coup in 411 and despite the political turbulence of 410–406, which he does not write about, and the support the Persians at last decided to give Sparta, the Athenians were also not predetermined to be defeated in the Hellespont in 405 and thereby lose the whole war. The counterfactuals, as always, are debatable, but Morris is right to say that on these matters as elsewhere, they serve to question one's interpretations of fact, and Thucydides gives one the information with which to do so. Much of what happened in the course of his story did not happen either by chance or because it was unavoidable.

There might after all therefore be a 'meaning' in what he writes: that politics, as politics, is more likely than not to be agonistic; that although rhetoric is intrinsic to it and may express conviction, being rhetoric, and a part of politics, it is unlikely to be truthful or simply reasonable; that the intentions in human action are not always reasoned and that, when they are, the reasoning will usually have an unreasoned premise; that although all events have causes, these are many and varied, and they and their effects often occur in unexpected conjunctions with others; and that, except when subjected to the unassailable power of another, and sometimes even when they are, people are not bound to act in just one way. It is one thing to be able to get all this under control in a narrative, which Thucydides does, especially in book 8; it is quite another to argue, which he does not, that 'reason' either prevails or always fails. When he says that his work 'will have served its purpose well enough if it is judged useful by those who want to have a clear view of what happened in the past and what – the human condition being what it is – can be expected to happen again some time in the future in similar or much the same ways', one can hear him to be suggesting that *these* are the ways. The meaning that he can therefore be taken to convey (and if one favours the idiom, the lesson that he might be taken to be imparting) is not of the kind that has often been attributed to him. Except in the trite sense in which everyone who writes about the course of human affairs can find themselves tracing tragedies, he is not; even in his own account, some of what was said was true and wise, some things done did not turn out badly, some – if they did – were not bound to do so and men and states could recover. Nor can he said to have been gesturing at overarching theories, unless one wants in some loose sense to say that he is 'explaining' the inherent uncertainties of politics and war. In the form of a narrative written to reflect how men live their political lives, he is presenting what in later historiography might have been called an exemplar, what political scientists now might call a case study: an account of what it is to practice politics and make war that raises questions for other times and places but can answer them only for its own.

It may nevertheless be said that whatever one takes Thucydides to have been presenting, the modern study of politics and war is the study of modern politics and war, and he cannot be thought to be saying anything about these. Our politics and wars are played out in very different ways in very different kinds of arena. Most states now are more or less formally constituted by an impersonal law that is expected to bind the rulers as tightly as it does the ruled, governed through formally representative institutions, implemented by formally impersonal agencies and upheld by formally independent judiciaries. Our politics is thick with policies that Thucydides and his contemporaries could not have imagined, and attempts to implement these are made through incomparably more complex organisations with vastly more efficient technologies and more or less instant communication. Beyond states, moreover, there is now a large and expanding body of international law which although it carries no decisive sanction before the event or after, can require political leaders to justify themselves to others, an association of nations with a notionally overriding remit, many other associations with more specific purposes, and a large and proliferating number of non-governmental organisations and more informal networks that stretch across states. There is also an increasing number of media, formal and informal, public and private, through which to praise and shame them all. All but two or three of the most powerful states now and a few of the least, some of which are still involved in struggles to be states at all, are to a greater or lesser extent restrained by one or another of these things. It is true that outside the European Union and only to a qualified extent within it, there is no empowered legislature over a set of states, no set of binding general laws or any procedurally governed bureaucracy to execute whatever laws there might be, and no set of rights for citizens that can reliably be deployed to trump the discretions that states reserve for themselves. Many states are not now so quickly inclined as those in classical Greece to resort to violence, and even when their citizens are driven to direct action against them, the two sides more often now stop short of a fight to the death. But this is not universally true, and within and between all states, there have still to be credible threats of force.

Nonetheless, between states now and within them, many people do at least aspire to administrative rationality and generality, and the generalising disciplines of political science and international relations, together with universalising moralities and proposals for laws that will apply to all, reflect that aspiration. The modern world can appear to have the political, moral, legal and administrative sciences that it needs and the military sciences to draw on when these fail. Thucydides' perception of his time may be unsurpassed, and many of the people he writes about will have been politically as sophisticated as any modern, but his world is that of Sophocles and Euripides and, before them, of Homer, epic, and Aeschylus; a fifth-century world of hundreds of Greek political entities, most of them tiny; of an Athenian 'empire', a Peloponnesian 'league', and the less formal dominion of Syracuse in parts of Sicily; of simple monarchies in Macedonia and Thrace; and of other empires reaching out from Persia and Carthage, all very different in their self-conceptions and scope from anything we know now. These were places in which, if violence was not exactly endemic, it was plainly routine. Politics themselves, it is supposed, and ways of understanding them, have moved on. We cannot now see his world as he did; if by chance we happened to, we could not know that we had; and if we were to act as if our own was like his, we would condemn ourselves to political delusion, confusion, brutality, and failure.

Yet there are two arguments in favour of what Thucydides does allow us, as us, to see. The first is the more straightforward. We may agree that we live in a world that aspires to administrative rationality and generality and, in many quarters, to universalisable moral principles and a growing body of law by which states and their associations should be guided. But we have also to agree that this continues to be a world of political actors, trying more or less imaginatively to achieve what they want to do through the exercise of one or another kind of power; that, although these actors often have plans and may possess what we might now think of as distinctively political virtues, they are subject to the limits of mind and body, the fallibilities of character and agency, the force of habit, the unforeseen and unforeseeable, and other people; and that their public speech is not to be depended on. Modern politics may have more elaborate machineries than those devised by the ancients for attempting success and averting failure. But these do not run themselves and are not anywhere completely reliable. Even when they might be, people are always fighting over and within them. And there is more now to fight about and more counters, material and ideal, to fight with, not least encompassing commitments of religious affiliation that were absent in Thucydides' time. Politics remain and, as journalists and politicians themselves can often see more clearly than professional *politologues*, if we describe these in ways that do no more than mirror general aspirations and formal manifestations, or in the languages of the twentieth century as forces of a 'structural' kind, the exercise of 'rational choice' or the expression of a 'culture', they can be occluded. We need to be able to see them as politics, and in the clarity of an almost incomparably more elemental context, this is what Thucydides enables us to do – incomparably well.

Hence the second argument for recalling him. One might think that his resistance to illusion and obtrusively conclusive judgement could have been evident at almost any time anywhere in what we have come to call the West. But they almost certainly could not. Although Thucydides could trace a Thracian descent, he was in education and citizenship (he was registered in an Attic *deme* a few miles outside the city) a later fifth-century Athenian. It is true that the wilful complication and inventiveness of his language in compound words, abstract terms, and painful syntax; his invention of a genre of his own; and his fiercely personal impersonality can lead one to see him to be distancing himself from his context.

If there ever was such a thing as a typical aristocratic, wealthy, thinking, late fifth-century Athenian male, he is not it. Yet even in his splendid perversity, and in exile, he is of his place and time. Unlike the writers of epic as well as many of those about whom he writes, he has no patience with the gods. Nor, unlike Plato in the next century or even Aristotle, is he disposed to avert his eyes from the inherent uncertainties and general mess of practical politics, construct an ideal, and seek intellectual closure. In a long line from the fourth-century philosophers through republican writers in Rome and Christian and post-Christian thinkers, that inclination has continued: to press the thought that there is an imaginable and conceivably realisable state of affairs in which, as a result of the deliverances of reflection or the discovery of an inescapable empirical truth, we, whoever we are, can be at home, at one individually and collectively with the better part of our nature, in this world or another for the rest of time – or, in rejecting that inclination, to press a contrary cynicism. Later fifth-century Athens stands out as a moment of unillusion, a moment in which if one had the courage and the talent, and Thucydides very evidently had both, it was possible to look at human nature and the ever-changing complexities of the political world in the eye rather than divert oneself to the past or some hopeful future or another world altogether.

This is an extravagant generalisation, but it contains a truth. To the extent that it does, I like to think that it is not itself an illusion to suggest that what Thucydides allows us, requires us even, to see is how far we too, looking back at the bloody tatters of this or that compulsion and aspiration in the twentieth century and the first part of the twenty-first, are naked in our political condition, which is the condition that he portrayed: one which in looking forward, as one has to do, neither interest nor morality – nor mere reason in the service of either of them – can offer sufficient understanding or consolation, and before which the sensible stance is to be as realistic as one can be about politics as politics. There can be no resolution and, for reasons we may never know, Thucydides was saved from any temptation to arrive at one. Its absence could not be more fitting.

Synopsis of the text by book and year

The asterisked sections in this synopsis are those I do not discuss in any detail. Although not central to my argument, all contribute to Thucydides' narrative and some are of considerable historical, military and literary interest.

BOOK 1

Introduction [1.1–23.3]
Reasons for writing [1.1]
Early history of Greece [1.2–19]
Aims and methods [1.20–2]
Importance of this war [1.23.1–3]
Background to the war [1.23.4–46]
Causes of the war [1.23.4–6]
Epidamnos and Corcyra [1.24–55]
Potidaea [1.56–66]
First meeting of Peloponnesian league [1.67–88]
'Fifty years' of Athenian power [1.89–118]
Second meeting of Peloponnesian league [1.119–25]
Spartan ultimatum and Pericles' response [1.139–46]

BOOK 2

First year of the war, 431–430 [2.1–2.47.1]
Outbreak of war [2.1]
Thebans attack Plataea [2.2–6]
Preparations and alliances on both sides [2.7–17]
Peloponnesians invade Attica [2.18–32]
*Corinthians active in west [2.33]
Pericles' funeral speech at Athens [2.34–2.47.1]
Second year of the war, 430–429 [2.47.2–70]
Peloponnesians invade Attica [2.47.2]

Plague at Athens [2.47.3–54]
Spartan campaigns and Pericles' response [2.55–64]
Thucydides' assessment of Pericles and Athens' eventual defeat [2.65]
Campaigns in Zacynthus, Thrace and Ambracia [2.66–8]
*Athenians campaign in Peloponnese and Lycia [2.69]
Potidaea surrenders [2.70]
Third year of the war, 429–428 [2.71–103]
Peloponnesians attack Plataea [2.71–8]
Campaigns in north-east and north-west [2.79–82]
Athenian victories in Gulf of Corinth [2.83–92]
Peloponnesians make attempt on the Piraeus [2.93–4]
Thrace and Macedonia [2.95–101]
Phormio in Acarnania [2.102–3]

BOOK 3

Fourth year of the war, 428–427 [3.1–25]
Peloponnesians invade Attica [3.1]
Mytileneans revolt [3.2–6]
*Asopius' campaign around Peloponnese and west [3.7]
Mytileneans' request at Olympia [3.8–18]
Athenian expedition to Caria [3.19]
Plataea besieged [3.20–4]
Spartan approach to Mytilene [3.25]
Fifth year of the war, 427–426 [3.26–88]
Athenians debate and decide on action at Mytilene [3.26–50]
*Athenians attack Minoa [3.51]
Surrender, trial and execution of Plataeans [3.52–68]
Civil strife at Corcyra [3.69–85]
Athenians in Sicily [3.86]
Plague in Athens [3.87]
*Athenians intervene in Aeolia [3.88]
Sixth year of the war, 426–425 [3.89–116]
Peloponnesians invade Attica [3.89]
Athenians campaign in Sicily, Melos and Tanagra [3.90–1]
Spartan colony at Heraclea in Trachis [3.92–3]
Campaigns in the west [3.94–102]
*Athenians in Sicily and Italy [3.103]
*Delos [3.104]
Campaigns in the west [3.105–14]
*Sicily [3.115–16]

BOOK 4

Seventh year of the war, 425–424 [4.1–51]
Athenians in Sicily and Corcyra [4.1–2.3]
Demosthenes fortifies Pylos [4.2.4–6]
*Simonides in Thrace [4.7]
Spartans trapped at Pylos [4.8–23]
*Further action in Sicily and Italy [4.24–5]
Siege at Pylos, Spartans surrender [4.26–41]
Athenians attack near Corinth [4.42–5]
End of civil strife at Corcyra, Athenians to Sicily [4.46–8]
*Athenian and Acarnanian campaign in the west [4.49]
Athenians intercept Persian envoy [4.50]
*Athenians pressure Chios [4.51]
Eighth year of the war, 424–423 [4.52–116]
*Mytilenean exiles in Anatolia [4.52]
Athenians campaign in Cythera and *Laconia [4.53–7]
Hermocrates calls for Siceliot unity [4.58–65]
Athenians intervene in Megara, Spartans respond [4.66–74]
*Lamachos in Pontus [4.75]
Athenians intrigue in Boeotia and Acarnania [4.76–7]
Brasidas in the north [4.78–88]
Battle of Delion [4.89–101.4]
Sitalces dies [4.101.5]
Brasidas in Thrace, Amphipolis falls [4.102–8]
*Megarians raze long walls [4.109.1]
Brasidas takes Chalcidicean cities [4.109.1–4.116]
Ninth year of the war, 423–422 [4.117–35]
Athens and Sparta agree truce [4.117–19]
Brasidas assists revolts in Chalcidice, and attacks Lyncestians with
      Perdiccas [4.120–32]
*Events in Boeotia and Argos [4.133.1–3]
*Scione besieged [4.133.4]
*Mantineans and Tegeans fight at Laodicion [4.134]
Brasidas fails at Potidaea [4.135]

BOOK 5

Tenth year of the war, 422–421 [5.1–24]
*Delians expelled [5.1]
Cleon and Brasidas at Torone [5.2–3]
*Athenians intrigue in Sicily and Italy [5.4–5]
Battle at Amphipolis, Cleon and Brasidas killed [5.6–12]

Athenians arrive in Sicily and decide tactics [6.42–52]
Alcibiades summoned to face charges in Athens [6.53.1–2]
Events at the end of Peisistratid rule in Athens [6.53.3–6.59]
Athenians react to acts of sacrilege [6.60]
Alcibiades convicted, escapes [6.61]
Athenian activities along coast of Sicily [6.62]
Athenians attack Syracuse [6.63–71]
Syracusan reactions and debate at Camarina [6.72–6.88.6]
Alcibiades at Sparta [6.88.7–6.93]
Eighteenth year of the war, 414–413 [6.94–105, 7.1–18]
*Athenian offensives in Sicily [6.94]
*Military activity at Argos, Thyrea and Thespiae [6.95]
Syracuse beseiged [6.96–103]
Gylippos arrives in Italy [6.104]
*Spartans attack Argos, Athenians raid Peloponnese [6.105]

BOOK 7

Gylippos breaks siege at Syracuse [7.1–8]
*Athenian makes attempt on Amphipolis [7.9]
Nicias' letter to Athenians [7.10–7.17.2]
Corinthians agree to support Spartans in Sicily [7.17.3–4]
Sparta prepares to fortify Deceleia in Attica [7.18]
Nineteenth year of the war, 413–412 [7.19–87, 8.1–6]
Sparta fortifies Deceleia [7.19.1–2]
Peloponnesian reinforcements to Sicily [7.19.3–5]
Athenians raid Peloponnese [7.20]
Athenians win victory in Sicily but lose base at Plemmyrion [7.21–4]
Confrontations in Italy and at Syracuse [7.25]
Demosthenes to Sicily [7.26]
Athens suffers from Deceleia [7.27–8]
*Thracians massacre Mycalessos [7.29–30]
*Demosthenes' journey and further engagements [7.31–5]
Syracusans win sea battle [7.36–41]
Athenians fail on Epipolai [7.42–6]
Athenian generals confer [7.47–9]
Syracusan confidence increases [7.50–6]
*Catalogue of allies on each side [7.57–7.59.1]
*Battle in Great Harbour at Syracuse [7.72–87]
*Athenians withdraw and are defeated [7.72–87]

BOOK 8

Athenian reactions to defeat [8.1]

Preparations to resume war [8.2–8.5.3]

Chians and Persians seek help from Sparta [8.5.4–6]

Twentieth year of the war, 412–411 [8.7–60]

Chios and cities on Lesbos revolt from Athens [8.7–17]

First treaty between Spartans and Persians [8.18]

Fighting in Ionia and coup in Samos [8.19–8.36.1]

Second treaty between Spartans and Persians [8.36.2–8.37]

Fighting in Ionia and Aegean [8.38–44]

Alcibiades defects to Tissaphernes, seeks return to Athens [8.45–7]

Reaction at Samos; Peisander negotiates with Alcibiades, Tissaphernes and Athenians (Phrynichos resists) [8.48–54]

Fighting in Rhodes and Chios [855]

Third treaty between Spartans and Persians [8.56–9]

*Action at Oropos, Rhodes and Miletus [8.60]

Twenty-first year of the war, 411–410 [8.61–109: unfinished]

Fighting in Ionia, Aegean and Hellespont [8.61–8.63.2]

Reaction continues at Samos, rule of 400 at Athens [8.63.3–8.71]

Democracy re-established at Samos [8.72–7]

Peloponnesian disputes with Tissaphernes and Astyochos [8.78–80]

Alcibiades recalled to Samos [8.81–2]

Differences between Spartans and others in Peloponnesian force with Tissaphernes [8.83–4]

Mindaros replaces Astyochos [8.85]

Envoys from 400 at Samos, Alcibiades restrains Athenians there from attacking the Piraeus [8.86.7]

Alcibiades seeks advantage from Tissaphernes' equivocations [8.87–8]

400 in Athens lose confidence, replaced by 5,000 [8.89–98]

*Athenian conspirators disperse, movements in Ionia and Hellespont, Athenian victory at Cynossema [8.99–107]

Tissaphernes competes with Pharnabazos over support for Sparta [8.108–9]

Further reading

This is a selective note for those who might like to pursue one or another subject in this book. There is a full bibliography of the more recent writing on Thucydides by classicists in Rusten 2009: 479–513.

Among the many good short introductions to the Greeks, Dover 1980 is irresistible, not least but not only for his section on Syracuse. Cartledge 2011 vividly sketches the history of eleven cities, skilfully conveys the complexities, and is very informative. *The Oxford Classical Dictionary* (4th edition, 2012) is a convenient first source.

As I explain in the preface, my preferred English edition of Thucydides is Mynott's (Thucydides 2013); others I have consulted are listed in the references below. Hobbes' translation stands apart. It is a magnificent piece of writing in itself which exudes the spirit of the original and has many wonderful turns of phrase. It is presently available in Thucydides 1989; Hoekstra is preparing what will assuredly be the definitive edition for *The Clarendon Edition of the Works of Thomas Hobbes*.

Wade-Gery's introduction to the text (2012, first published in 1949) is a masterpiece of illuminating compression, containing all that most will need on the now largely abandoned question of the composition of the text and pointers to much else besides. On particulars, the two great section-by-section commentaries in English, Gomme, Andrewes and Dover 1945–81 and Hornblower 1991–2008, are indispensable. Gomme, Andrewes and Dover tend to concentrate on issues of language, history and topography; the political observations by Gomme in volumes I, II, and III and those by Andrewes and Dover – who extended Gomme's drafts for volume IV and wrote volume V – are invariably astute. Hornblower (*CT* II: 1–19, 2010: 16) explains that he pays more attention than Gomme, Andrewes and Dover to issues of religion and the literary character of the text, and otherwise devotes himself to those of a textual, archaeological, epigraphic, rhetorical, onomastic, philosophical and historical kind; he is also hugely informative on the more recent scholarship. To have these eight volumes to hand is to be engaged in a conversation of endless stimulation and enlightenment.

There is no one extensive consideration of how Thucydides has been read since the start of the fifteenth century or even since the eighteenth. The best short guide, concentrating on more recent work by classicists, is Rusten 2009: 1–29, and there are valuable collections of papers in Fromentin, Gotteland and Payen 2010 and Harloe and Morley 2012. Notable interpretations of what Thucydides can be thought generally to be suggesting are Finley 1942 and de Romilly 1963 (first published in 1947) and 2012 (first published in 1956 and carefully reviewed by Gomme 1958), and against these Stahl 2003 (first published in 1966). Hornblower 1994 is a vigorous prolegomenon to his commentary; Connor 1984b a selective reading of the text book by book which although concerned more with Thucydides' literary constructions and their effects on the reader, is shrewd on the politics; and Rood 1998 an elegant and sophisticated narratological analysis of the text with much of interest on what might follow for understanding its substance. The collection of essays in Rusten 2009 (many of which are otherwise difficult to access) is exemplary; this excludes the readily available pieces in Macleod 1983a, which are penetrating on the speeches and the way in which one might see what Thucydides writes as a tragedy (though Macleod makes no concessions to non-classicists). There is much of value also in Rengakos and Tsakmakis 2006.

Modern accounts of the war include the commanding narratives by Lewis and Andrewes in Lewis *et al.* 1992 and the relatively short book by Tritle 2010. As any has to, these depend largely on Thucydides himself; Tritle accompanies his with mention of what else was being written in Athens at the time and reflects on the experience of battle. Davies 1993: 117–33 is an excellent short introduction to events; he and Morris 2009 offer the most interesting 'strategic' interpretations. Morris also includes a concise survey of what is known about the Greek states and their societies and offers a careful argument for what might have followed an Athenian victory.

Farrar 1988: 126–91 and Ober 1998: 52–121, committed democrats in the American manner, interestingly diverge on what Thucydides might be taken to be saying about Athens' politics and by extension the promise of politics more generally. Students of the relations between states have suggested that Thucydides sees political entities deploying their power with little regard to law or ethics. Low 2007: 1–32, 212–57 is a superior set of reflections on reading the Greeks in general and Thucydides in particular in this way; Koskenniemi 2001: 413–509 is a persuasive explanation of the resurgence in the 1930s and 1940s of the so-called 'realism' that lies behind it. The most noted champions of this doctrine, E. H. Carr in Britain and Hans Morgenthau in the United States, barely mentioned Thucydides. Doyle 1990, distinguishing its 'minimalist', 'fundamentalist', and 'structuralist' variations, considers those who have; Monten 2006 examines the text in the light of the 'structural' variant, concentrating on the relations within what some can still think of as a 'system' of states; and Bloxham 2011 offers a brief and balanced account of how Thucydides was deployed in arguments about a foreign policy for the United States between the end of the Cold War and the 'war on terror'. Aron 1961, one of the wisest students of international politics and sociology in the twentieth century, drew attention to the importance Thucydides attaches to the *événementielle* and of individuals in it.

A very different kind of 'political realism' has been pressed against what has been regarded as the excessively abstract, other-worldly, and often apolitical character of much modern political theory. Williams 2005 makes an analytical case, Galston 2010 is a survey of what others were saying in the 2000s, and Philp 2012 is a set of sceptical reflections. If my own approach to political understanding were to have a name, realism would be it, though I have not been concerned in this book with the usual questions of political theory, modern or ancient, and I dislike labels.

References

EDITIONS AND TRANSLATIONS

Thucydides. 1907. *The History of the Peloponnesian War*. Trans. Henry Dale. London: Bell.

Thucydides. 1972a. *History of the Peloponnesian War*. Trans. Rex Warner. Intro. Moses Finley. London: Penguin.

Thucydides. 1972b. *Thucydide: la guerre de Péloponnèse*. Vol. VI Book 8. Ed. and trans. Jacqueline de Romilly, Raymond Weil, and Louis Bodin. Paris: Les Belles Lettres.

Thucydides. 1989. *The Peloponnesian War*. Ed. David Grene. Trans. Thomas Hobbes. Chicago University Press.

Thucydides. 1996. *The Landmark Thucydides: A Comprehensive Guide to the Peloponnesian War*. Ed. Robert B. Strassler. Trans. Richard Crawley. Intro. Victor Davis Hanson. New York: Free Press.

Thucydides. 1998. *The Peloponnesian War*. Trans., intro. and notes Steven Lattimore. Indianapolis: Hackett.

Thucydides. 1998. *The Peloponnesian War: A New Translation, Backgrounds, Interpretations*. Ed. Jennifer T. Roberts. Trans. Walter Blanco. New York: Norton.

Thucydides. 2009. *Thucydides: The Peloponnesian War*. Trans. Martin Hammond. Intro. and notes P. J. Rhodes. Oxford University Press.

Thucydides. 2013. *The War of the Peloponnesians and the Athenians*. Ed., intro. and trans. Jeremy Mynott. Cambridge University Press.

COMMENTARIES

Cameron, H. D. 2003. *Thucydides Book I: A Student's Grammatical Commentary*. Ann Arbor: University of Michigan Press.

Gomme, A. W., A. Andrewes, and K. J. Dover. 1945–81. *A Historical Commentary on Thucydides*. 5 vols. Oxford: Clarendon Press.

Hornblower, Simon. 1991–2008. *A Commentary on Thucydides*. 3 vols. Oxford: Clarendon and Oxford University Presses.

Rusten, Jeffrey, ed. 1989. *Thucydides, The Peloponnesian War, Book II*. Cambridge University Press.

OTHERS

Abrahams, Fred, Eric Stover, and Gilles Peress. 2001. *A Village Destroyed, May 14 1999: War Crimes in Kosovo*. Berkeley and Los Angeles: University of California Press.

249

Alker, Hayward R. 1996. 'The Dialectical Logic of Thucydides' Melian Dialogue'. In *Rediscoveries and Reformulations: Humanistic Methodologies for International Studies*. Cambridge University Press.

Allison, June W. 1997. *Word and Concept in Thucydides*. Atlanta: Scholars Press.

Andrewes, A. 1978. 'The Opposition to Perikles'. *Journal of Hellenic Studies* 98: 1–8.

1992. 'The Spartan Resurgence'. In *Cambridge Ancient History*, V: *The 5th Century BC*. Ed. D. M. Lewis *et al*. Cambridge University Press.

Aron, Raymond. 1961. 'Thucydide et le récit des événements'. *History and Theory* 1: 103–28.

Badian, E. 1993. *From Plataea to Potidaea: Studies in the History and Historiography of the Pentacontaetia*. Baltimore: Johns Hopkins University Press.

Bernstein, Michel André. 1994. *Foregone Conclusions: Against Apocalyptic History*. Berkeley: University of California Press.

Bissa, Errietta M. A. 2009. *Governmental Intervention in Foreign Trade in Archaic and Classical Greece*. *Mnemosyne* Supplements, History and Archaeology of Ancient Antiquity 312. Leiden: Brill.

Bloxham, John A. 2011. *Thucydides and US Foreign Policy after the Cold War*. Boca Raton FL: Dissertation.com.

Boardman, John. 1982. 'The Islands'. In *Cambridge Ancient History*, III.1: *The Prehistory of the Balkans; the Middle East and the Aegean World, Tenth to Eighth Centuries BC*. Ed. John Boardman *et al*. Cambridge University Press.

Bodéüs, Richard. 2000. 'The Statesman as Political Actor'. In *Greek Thought: A Guide to Classical Knowledge*. Ed. Jacques Brunschwig, Geoffrey E. R. Lloyd, and Pierre Pellegrin. Trans. Catherine Porter. Cambridge MA: Belknap Press of Harvard University Press.

Bosworth, A. B. 2009. 'The Humanitarian Aspect of the Melian Dialogue'. In *Thucydides*. Ed. J. Rusten. Oxford University Press.

Brunt, P. A. 1993a. 'Spartan Policy and Strategy in the Archidamian War'. In *Studies in Greek History and Thought*. Oxford: Clarendon Press.

1993b. 'Thucydides and Alcibiades'. In *Studies in Greek History and Thought*. Oxford: Clarendon Press.

Cairns, Douglas L. 1996. '*Hybris*, Dishonour and Thinking Big'. *Journal of Hellenic Studies* 116: 1–32.

Campbell, John. 1964. *Honour, Family and Patronage: A Study of Institutions and Moral Values in a Greek Mountain Community*. Oxford: Clarendon Press.

Canfora, Luciano. 2006. 'Biographical Obscurities and Problems of Composition'. In *Brill's Companion to Thucydides*. Ed. A. Rengakos and A. Tsakmakis. Leiden: Brill.

Cartledge, Paul. 2009. *Ancient Greek Political Thought in Practice*. Cambridge University Press.

2011. *Ancient Greece: A Very Short Introduction*. Oxford University Press.

Cawkwell, George. 1997. *Thucydides and the Peloponnesian War*. London: Routledge.

2011. 'Thucydides' Judgement of Periclean Strategy'. In *Cyrene to Caeronea: Selected Essays on Ancient Greek History*. Oxford University Press.

Clark, Maudmarie. 2001. 'On the Rejection of Morality: Bernard Williams' Debt to Nietzsche'. In *Nietzsche's Postmoralism: Essays on Nietzsche's Prelude to Philosophy's Future*. Ed. Richard Schact. Cambridge University Press.

Clausewitz, Carl von. 1984. *On War*. Ed. Michael Howard and Peter Paret. Princeton University Press.

Cohen, David. 1995. *Law, Violence and Community in Classical Athens*. Cambridge University Press.

Cohen, Edward E. 2000. *The Athenian Nation*. Princeton University Press.

Connor, W. Robert. 1984a. Review of Gomme, Andrewes and Dover, *A Historical Commentary on Thucydides V. Classical Philology* 79: 230–5.

   1984b. *Thucydides*. Princeton University Press.

   1992. *New Politicians of Fifth-Century Athens*. With a new preface. Indianapolis: Hackett.

Constant, Benjamin. 1988. 'The Liberty of the Ancients Compared with that of the Moderns'. In *Benjamin Constant: Political Writings*. Ed. and trans. Biancamaria Fontana. Cambridge University Press.

Cornford, Francis M. 1907. *Thucydides mythistoricus*. London: Arnold.

Crane, Gregory. 1996. *The Blinded Eye: Thucydides and the New Written Word*. Lanham MD: Rowman and Littlefield.

Darbo-Peschanski, Catherine. 2007. 'The Origin of Historiography'. In *A Companion to Greek and Roman Historiography*. Ed. John Marincola. Oxford: Blackwell.

Davidson, Donald. 2001. 'Three Varieties of Knowledge'. In *Subjective, Intersubjective, Objective*. Oxford: Clarendon Press.

Davidson, James. 2005. 'Adrift from Locality'. *London Review of Books* 27 (3 November): 10–14.

Davies, John K. 1993. *Democracy and Classical Greece*. 2nd edn. London: Fontana.

Detel, Wolfgang. 1998. *Foucault and Classical Antiquity: Power, Ethics and Knowledge*. Trans. David Wigg-Wolf. Cambridge University Press.

Dewald, Carolyn. 2005. *Thucydides' War Narrative: A Structural Study*. Berkeley: University of California Press.

Dolgert, Stefan. 2012. 'Thucydides Amended: Religion, Narrative, and IR Theory in the Peloponnesian Crisis'. *Review of International Studies* 38: 661–82.

Dover, Kenneth. 1974. *Greek Popular Morality in the Age of Plato and Arisotle*. Oxford: Blackwell.

   1980. *The Greeks*. Austin: University of Texas Press.

   1988. 'Thucydides' Historical Judgement: Athens and Sicily'. In *The Greeks and their Legacy: Collected Papers, II: Prose, Literature, History, Society, Transmission, Influence*. Oxford: Blackwell.

   2009. 'Thucydides "as Literature" and "as History"'. In *Thucydides*. Ed. J. Rusten. Oxford University Press.

Doyle, Michael. 1990. 'Thucydidean Realism'. *Review of International Studies* 16: 223–37.

Dunn, Francis M. 2007. *Present Shock in Late Fifth-Century Greece*. Ann Arbor: University of Michigan Press.

Dunn, John. 1980. 'Practising History and Social Science on "Realist" Assumptions'. In *Political Obligation in its Historical Context: Essays In Political Theory.* Cambridge University Press.

2006. *Setting the People Free: The Story of Democracy.* London: Atlantic.

Eder, Walter. 1997. 'Aristocrats and the Coming of Athenian Democracy'. In *Democracy 2500: Questions and Challenges.* Ed. Ian Morris and Kurt Raaflaub. Dubuque IO: Archaeological Institute of America, Colloquia and Conference Papers 2.

Edmunds, Lowell. 2009. 'Thucydides in the Act of Writing'. In *Thucydides.* Ed. J. Rusten. Oxford University Press.

Elster, Jon. 1999. *Alchemies of the Mind: Rationality and the Emotions.* Cambridge University Press.

Farrar, Cynthia. 1988. *The Origins of Democratic Thinking: the Invention of Politics in Classical Athens.* Cambridge University Press.

Figueira, Thomas J. 2010. 'Gynecocracy: How Women Policed Masculine Behaviour in Sparta'. In *Sparta: The Body Politics.* Ed. Anton Powell and Stephen Hodkinson. Swansea: Classical Press of Wales.

Finley, John H. 1942. *Thucydides.* Cambridge MA: Harvard University Press.

1967. 'The Unity of Thucydides' History'. In *Three Essays on Thucydides.* Cambridge MA: Harvard University Press.

Finley, M. I. 1978. 'The Fifth-Century Athenian Empire: A Balance Sheet'. In *Imperialism in the Ancient World.* Ed. P. D. A. Garnsey and C. R. Whittaker. Cambridge University Press.

Fisher, N. R. E. 1992. *Hybris: A Study in the Values of Honour and Shame in Ancient Greece.* Warminster: Aris & Phillips.

Flory, Stewart. 1988. 'Thucydides' Hypotheses about the Peloponnesian War'. *Transactions of the American Philological Association* 118: 43–56.

1990. 'The Meaning of τò μὴ μυθωδες (1.22.4) and the Usefulness of Thucydides' History'. *Classical Journal* 85: 202–8.

Fornara, Charles W. 1993. 'Thucydides' Birth Date'. In *Nomodeiktes: Greek Studies in Honor of Martin Ostwald.* Ed. Ralph N. Rosen and Joseph Farrell. Ann Arbor: University of Michigan Press.

Forsdyke, Sara. 2005. *Exile, Ostracism and Democracy: The Politics of Exclusion in Ancient Greece.* Princeton University Press.

Foster, Edith. 2010. *Thucydides, Pericles and Athenian Imperialism.* Cambridge University Press.

Foucault, Michel. 1980. *Power/Knowledge: Selected Interviews and Other Writings, 1972–1977.* Ed. Colin Gordon. New York: Pantheon.

Freeman, E. A. 1893. *The History of Federal Government in Greece and Italy.* London: Macmillan.

Fromentin, Valérie, Sophie Gotteland, and Pascal Payen, eds. 2010. *Ombres de Thucydide: la réception de l'historien depuis l'Antiquité jusqu'au début du xxème siècle.* Actes des colloques de Bordeaux, les 16–17 mars 2007, les 30–31 mai 2008, et de Toulouse, les 23–25 octobre 2008. Pessac: Ausonious Editions.

Gagarin, Michael, and Paul Woodruff, eds. 1995. *Early Greek Political Thought from Homer to the Sophists.* Cambridge University Press.

Galston, William A. 2010. 'Realism in Political Theory'. *European Journal of Political Theory* 9: 385–411.

Geuss, Raymond. 1981. *The Idea of Critical Theory: Habermas and the Frankfurt School*. Cambridge University Press.

2008. *Philosophy and Real Politics*. Princeton University Press.

Golden, Mark. 2000. 'A Decade of Demography: Recent Trends in the Study of Greek and Roman Populations'. In *Polis and Politics: Studies in Ancient Greek History Presented to Mogens Herman Hansen on his Sixtieth Birthday, August 20 2000*. Ed. Pernille Flensted-Jensen, Thomas Heine Nielsen, and Lene Rubinstein. Copenhagen: Museum Tusculanum Press, University of Copenhagen.

Gomme, A. W. 1954. 'Who Was "Kratippos"?'. *Classical Quarterly* 4: 53–5.

1958. Review of Jacqueline de Romilly, *Histoire et raison chez Thucydide*. *Gnomon* 30: 15–19.

Green, Peter. 1970. *Armada from Athens*. London: Hodder and Stoughton.

Greenwood, Emily. 2006. *Thucydides and the Shaping of History*. London: Duckworth.

Grene, David. 1950. *Man in his Pride: A Study in the Political Philosophy of Thucydides and Plato*. University of Chicago Press.

Grethlein, Jonas. 2010. *The Greeks and their Past: Poetry, Oratory and History in the Fifth Century BCE*. Cambridge University Press.

Gribble, David. 1999. *Alcibiades and Athens: A Study in Literary Presentation*. Oxford: Clarendon Press.

Grote, George. 1862. *A History of Greece*. V. 11 vols. London: Murray.

Hall, Edith. 1989. *Inventing the Barbarian: Greek Self-Definition through Tragedy*. Oxford: Clarendon Press.

Hamilton, Alexander, James Madison, and John Jay. 2003. *The Federalist, with Letters of 'Brutus'*. Ed. Terence Ball. Cambridge University Press.

Hammond, N. G. L. 1973. 'The Particular and the Universal in the Speeches in Thucydides with Special Reference to that of Hermocrates at Gela'. In *The Speeches of Thucydides: A Collection of Original Studies*. Ed. P. A. Stadter. Chapel Hill: University of North Carolina Press.

Hammond, N. G. L., and G. T. Griffith. 1979. *A History of Macedonia, II: 550–336 BC*. Oxford: Clarendon Press.

Hansen, Mogens H. 1998. *Polis and City State*. Copenhagen: Royal Danish Academy of Arts and Letters.

2006a. Review of Loren J. Samons, *What's Wrong with Athenian Democracy? From Athenian Practice to American Worship*. Bryn Mawr Classical Review 2006.01.32.

2006b. *The Shotgun Method: The Demography of the Ancient Greek City-State Culture*. Columbia MO: University of Missouri Press.

Hanson, Victor Davis. 2005. *A War Like No Other: How the Athenians and Spartans Fought the Peloponnesian War*. London: Methuen.

Harloe, Katherine, and Neville Morley, eds. 2012. *Thucydides and the Modern World: Reception, Reinterpretation and Influence from the Renaissance to the Present*. Cambridge University Press.

Harris, Edward M. 2006. *Democracy and the Rule of Law in Classical Athens*. Cambridge University Press.

Hatzfeld, Jean. 1940. *Alcibiade: étude sur l'histoire d'Athènes à la fin du Ve siècle.* Paris: Presses Universitaires de France.

Hawthorn, Geoffrey. 1991. *Plausible Worlds: Possibility and Understanding in History and the Social Sciences.* Cambridge University Press.

Heinzelmann, Martin. 2002. *Gregory of Tours: History and Society in the Sixth Century.* Trans. Christopher Carroll. Cambridge University Press.

Hobbes, Thomas. 1991. *Leviathan.* Ed. Richard Tuck. Cambridge University Press.

Hoekstra, Kinch. 2007. 'Hobbes on the Natural Condition of Mankind'. In *The Cambridge Companion to Hobbes' 'Leviathan'.* Ed. Patricia Springborg. Cambridge University Press.

2012. 'Thucydides and the Bellicose Beginnings of Modern Political Theory'. In *Thucydides and the Modern World: Reception, Reinterpretation and Influence from the Renaissance to the Present.* Ed. K. Harloe and N. Morley. Cambridge University Press.

Holder, Alan. 1964. 'T. S. Eliot on Henry James'. *Proceedings of the Modern Language Association* 79: 490–7.

Hornblower, Simon. 1994. *Thucydides.* 2nd edn. London: Duckworth.

1995. 'The Fourth-Century and Hellenistic Reception of Thucydides'. *Journal of Hellenic Studies* 115: 47–68.

2006. 'Herodotus in Antiquity'. In *Cambridge Companion to Herodotus.* Ed. Carolyn Dewald and John Marincola. Cambridge University Press.

2010. 'Introduction'. In *Thucydidean Themes.* Oxford University Press.

Humble, Noreen. 2002. 'Was Sophrosune Ever a Spartan Virtue?' In *Sparta Beyond the Mirage.* Ed. Anton Powell and Stephen Hodkinson. Swansea: Classical Press of Wales.

Hunt, Peter. 2006. 'Warfare'. In *Brill's Companion to Thucydides.* Ed. A. Rengakos and A. Tsakmakis. Leiden: Brill. 2006.

2010. *War, Peace and Alliance in Demosthenes' Athens.* Cambridge University Press.

Hunter, Virginia J. 1973. *Thucydides: The Artful Reporter.* Toronto: Hakkert.

Hussey, Edward. 1985. 'Thucydidean History and Democritian Theory'. In *Crux: Essays Presented to G. E. M. de Ste. Croix on his 75th Birthday.* Ed. P. A. Cartledge and F. D. Harvey. Exeter: Imprint Academic.

Irwin, Elizabeth. 2007. 'The politics of Precedence: The First "Historians" on the First "Thalassocrats"'. In *Debating the Athenian Cultural Revolution: Art, Literature, Philosophy and Politics 480–380 BC.* Ed. Robin Osborne. Cambridge University Press.

Jeffery, L. H. 1988. 'Greece before the Persian Invasion'. In *Cambridge Ancient History, IV: Persia, Greece and the Western Mediterranean, c.525 to 479 BC.* Ed. D. M. Lewis *et al.* Cambridge University Press.

Kagan, Donald. 1981. *The Peace of Nicias and the Sicilian Expedition.* Ithaca: Cornell University Press.

Kallet, Lisa. 2001. *Money and the Corrosion of Power in Thucydides: The Sicilian Expedition and its Aftermath.* Berkeley: University of California Press.

Kallet-Marx, Lisa. 1993. *Money, Expense, and Naval Power in Thucydides' History 1–5.24.* Berkeley: University of California Press.

Konstan, David. 2001. *The Emotions of the Ancient Greeks: Studies in Aristotle and Classical Literature*. University of Toronto Press.

2010. *Before Forgiveness: The Origin of a Moral Idea*. Cambridge University Press.

Konstan, David, and N. Keith Rutter, eds. 2003. *Envy, Spite and Jealousy: The Rivalrous Emotions in Ancient Greece*. Edinburgh University Press.

Koskenniemi, Martii. 2001. *The Gentle Civiliser of Nations: The Rise and Fall of International Law 1870–1960*. Cambridge University Press.

Lang, Mabel. 2011. 'Thucydides, first person'. In *Thucydidean Narrative and Discourse*. Ed. Jeffrey S. Rusten and Richard Hamilton. Ann Arbor: Michigan Classical Press.

Lendon, J. E. 2007. 'Athens and Sparta and the Coming of the Peloponnesian War'. In *The Cambridge Companion to the Age of Pericles*. Ed. Loren J. Samons II. Cambridge University Press.

2010. *Song of Wrath: The Peloponnesian War Begins*. New York: Basic Books.

Lewis, D. M. 1988. 'The Tyranny of the Pisistratidae'. In *Cambridge Ancient History, IV: Persia, Greece and the Western Mediterranean, c.525–479 BC*. Ed. D. M. Lewis *et al.* Cambridge University Press.

1992a. 'The Archidamian War'. In *Cambridge Ancient History, V: The Fifth Century BC*. Ed. D. M. Lewis *et al.* Cambridge University Press.

1992b. 'Mainland Greece, 479–451 BC'. In *Cambridge Ancient History, V: The Fifth Century BC*. Ed. D. M. Lewis *et al.* Cambridge University Press.

1992c. 'Preface'. In *Cambridge Ancient History, V: The Fifth Century BC*. Ed. D. M. Lewis *et al.* Cambridge University Press.

1992d. 'The Thirty Years' Peace'. In *Cambridge Ancient History, V: The Fifth Century BC*. Ed. D. M. Lewis *et al.* Cambridge University Press.

1994. 'Sicily, 413–368 BC'. In *Cambridge Ancient History, VI: The Fourth Century BC*. Ed. D. M. Lewis *et al.* Cambridge University Press.

Lewis, D. M. *et al.*, eds. 1992. *Cambridge Ancient History, V: The Fifth Century BC*. Cambridge University Press.

Livingstone, Ken. 2011. *You Can't Say That: Memoirs*. London: Faber.

Lloyd, Geoffrey. 2002. *The Ambitions of Curiosity: Understanding the World in Ancient Greece and China*. Cambridge University Press.

2012. *The Ideals of Ancient Inquiry*. Cambridge: Tarner Lectures (unpublished).

Loraux, Nicole. 1986a. *The Invention of Athens: The Funeral Oration in the Classical City*. Trans. Alan Sheridan. Cambridge MA: Harvard University Press.

1986b. 'Thucydide a écrit la guerre du Péloponnèse'. *Métis* 1: 139–61.

1991. 'Reflections on the Greek City in Unity and Division'. In *City States in Classical Antiquity and Medieval Italy*. Ed. Anthony Molho, Kurt A. Raaflaub, and Julia Emlen. Stuttgart: Steiner.

2009. 'Thucydides and Sedition among Words'. In *Thucydides*. Ed. J. Rusten. Oxford University Press.

Low, Polly. 2007. *Interstate Relations in Classical Greece: Morality and Politics*. Cambridge University Press.

Low, Polly, ed. 2008. *The Athenian Empire*. Edinburgh University Press.

Ludwig, Paul W. 2002. *Eros and Polis: Desire and Community in Greek Political Theory*. Cambridge University Press.

Macaulay, Thomas. 1889. 'The Romance of History by Henry Beele'. In *The Miscellaneous Writings and Speeches of Lord Macaulay*. London: Longmans.

2008. *The Journals of Thomas Babbington Macaulay*. Ed. William Thomas. London: Pickering and Chatto.

Macleod, C. W. 1983a. *Collected Essays*. Oxford: Clarendon Press.

1983b. 'Form and Meaning in the Melian Dialogue'. In *Collected Essays*. Oxford: Clarendon Press.

1983c. 'Reason and Necessity: Thucydides 3.9–14, 37–48'. In *Collected Essays*. Oxford: Clarendon Presss.

1983d. 'Rhetoric and History (Thucydides 6.16–18)'. In *Collected Essays*. Oxford: Clarendon Press.

1983e. 'Thucydides and Tragedy'. In *Collected Essays*. Oxford: Clarendon Press.

1983f. 'Thucydides on Faction (3.82–83)'. In *Collected Essays*. Oxford: Clarendon Press.

1983g. 'Thucydides' Plataean Debate'. In *Collected Essays*. Oxford: Clarendon Press.

Maehler, Herwig. 2012. 'Books, Greek and Roman'. In *The Oxford Classical Dictionary*. 4th edn. Ed. Simon Hornblower, Antony Spawforth, and Esther Eidinow. Oxford University Press.

Mann, Michael. 2012. *The Sources of Social Power*, III: *Global Empires and Revolution 1890–1945*. Cambridge University Press.

Marincola, John. 1997. *Authority and Tradition in Ancient Historiography*. Cambridge University Press.

Meier, Christian. 1990. *The Greek Discovery of Politics*. Trans. David McClintock. Cambridge MA: Harvard University Press.

Meiggs, Russell. 1972. *The Athenian Empire*. Oxford: Clarendon Press.

Moles, John. 1999. 'Anathema kai ktema: The Inscriptional Inheritance of Ancient Historiography'. *Histos* 3. www.dur.ac.uk/Classics/histos/1999/moles.html.

Monten, Jonathan. 2006. 'Thucydides and Modern Realism'. *International Studies Quarterly* 50: 3–25.

Moreno, Alfonso. 2007. *Feeding the Democracy: The Athenian Grain Supply in the Fifth and Fourth Centuries BC*. Oxford University Press.

Morley, Neville. 2012. 'Thucydides, History and Historicism in Wilhelm Roscher'. In *Thucydides and the Modern World: Reception, Reinterpretation and Influence from the Renaissance to the Present*. Ed. K. Harloe and N. Morley. Cambridge University Press.

Morris, Ian. 2009. 'The Greater Athenian State'. In *The Dynamics of Ancient Empires: State Power from Assyria to Byzantium*. Ed. Ian Morris and Walter Scheidel. Oxford University Press.

2011. *Why the West Rules – For Now: The Patterns of History and What they Reveal about the Future*. London: Profile.

Morrison, James V. 2006. *Reading Thucydides*. Columbus: Ohio State University Press.

Morson, Gary S. 1994. *Narrative and Freedom: The Shadows of Time*. New Haven: Yale University Press.

Nagel, Thomas. 1982. 'The Limits of Partiality'. *Times Literary Supplement*, 7 May.

Nicolai, Roberto. 2009. 'The Reception of Thucydides in the Ancient World'. In *Thucydides*. Ed. J. Rusten. Oxford University Press.

Nietzsche, Friedrich. 1997. *Daybreak: Thoughts on the Prejudices of Morality*. Ed. Maudmarie Clark and Brian Leiter. Trans. R. J. Hollingdale. Cambridge University Press.

2001. *The Gay Science*. Ed. Bernard Williams. Trans. Josefibe Nauckhoff and Adrian Del Caro. Cambridge University Press.

2005. *The Anti-Christ, Ecce Homo, Twilight of the Idols*. Ed. Aaron Ridley and Judith Norman. Trans. Judith Norman. Cambridge University Press.

Nozick, Robert. 1981. *Philosophical Explanations*. Cambridge MA: Belknap Press of Harvard University Press.

Ober, Josiah. 1996. 'The Athenians and their Democracy'. In *The Athenian Revolution: Essays on Ancient Greek Democracy and Political Theory*. Princeton University Press.

1998. *Political Dissent in Democratic Athens: Intellectual Critics of Popular Rule*. Princeton University Press.

2006. 'Thucydides and the Invention of Political Science'. In *Brill's Companion to Thucydides*. Ed. A. Rengakos and A. Tsakmakis. Leiden: Brill.

Orwin, Clifford. 1994. *The Humanity of Thucydides*. Princeton University Press.

Ostwald, Martin. 1988. *Ananke in Thucydides*. Atlanta: Scholars Press.

Owen, David, and Jonathan Davidson. 2009. 'Hubris Syndrome: An Acquired Personality Disorder? A Study of US Presidents and UK Prime Ministers over the Last 100 Years'. *Brain* 132: 1396–406.

Papagrigorakis, M. J., C. Yapijakis, and E. Baziotopoulu-Valavani. 2006. 'DNA Examination of Ancient Dental Pulp Incriminates Typhoid Fever as a Probable Cause of the Plague of Athens'. *International Journal of Infectious Diseases* 10: 206–14, comment 334–5, reply 335–6.

Parfit, Derek. 2011. *On What Matters*. II. 2 vols. Oxford University Press.

Parry, Adam. 1972. 'Thucydides' Historical Perspective'. In *Studies in Fifth-Century Thought and Literature*. Ed. Adam Parry. Yale Classical Studies V. Cambridge University Press.

1981. *'Logos' and 'Ergon' in Thucydides*. Salem NH: Ayer.

Pelling, Christopher. 2000. *Literary Texts and the Greek Historian*. London: Routledge.

Philp, Mark. 2012. 'Realism without Illusions'. *Political Theory* 40: 629–49.

Pippin, Robert. 2003. 'The Unavailability of the Ordinary: Strauss on the Philosophical Fate of Modernity'. *Political Theory* 31: 335–58.

2010. *Nietzsche, Psychology and First Philosophy*. University of Chicago Press.

n.d. 'Williams on Nietzsche on the Greeks'. http://home.uchicago.edu/~rbp1/publications.shtml.

Platias, Athanassios G. and Constantinos Koliopoulos. 2010. *Thucydides on Strategy: Grand Strategies in the Peloponnesian War and their Relevance Today*. London: Hurst.

Potter, Elizabeth. 2012. 'The Education Offered by Athens: Thucydides and the Stirrings of Democracy in Britain'. In *Thucydides and the Modern World:*

Reception, Reinterpretation and Influence from the Renaissance to the Present. Ed. K. Harloe and N. Morley. Cambridge University Press.

Pouncey, Peter R. 1980. *The Necessities of War: A Study of Thucydides' Pessimism.* New York: Columbia University Press.

Price, Jonathan J. 2001. *Thucydides and Internal War.* Cambridge University Press.

Raaflaub, Kurt A. 1994. 'Democracy, Power and Imperialism in Fifth-Century Athens'. In *Athenian political thought and the reconstruction of American democracy.* Ed. J. Peter Euben, John R. Wallach, and Josiah Ober. Ithaca: Cornell University Press.

Raaflaub, Kurt A., Josiah Ober and Robert W. Wallace. 2007. *Origins of Democracy in Ancient Greece.* Berkeley: University of California Press.

Rawlings, Hunter R. III. 1981. *The Structure of Thucydides' History.* Princeton University Press.

Rawls, John. 1971. *A Theory of Justice.* Cambridge MA: Harvard University Press.

Rengakos, Antonios, and Antonis Tsakmakis, eds. 2006. *Brill's Companion to Thucydides.* Leiden: Brill.

Rhodes, P. J. 2000. 'Oligarchs in Athens'. In *Alternatives to Athens: Varieties of Political Organisation and Community in Ancient Greece.* Ed. R. W. Brock and S. J. Hodkinson. Oxford University Press.

Richardson, John. 1990. 'Thucydides 1.23.6 and the Debate about the Peloponnesian War'. In *'Owls to Athens': Essays on Classical Subjects Presented to Sir Kenneth Dover.* Ed. Elizabeth M. Craik. Oxford: Clarendon Press.

Romilly, Jacqueline de. 1963. *Thucydides and Athenian Imperialism.* Trans. Philip Thody. Oxford: Blackwell.

1985. *A Short History of Greek Literature.* Trans. Lilian Doherty. University of Chicago Press.

2005. *L'Invention de l'histoire politique chez Thucydide.* Paris: Editions rue d'Ulm.

2012. *The Mind of Thucydides.* Ed. Hunter R. Rawlings III and Jeffrey Rusten. Trans. Elizabeth Trapnell Rawlings. Ithaca: Cornell University Press.

Rood, Tim. 1998. *Thucydides: Narrative and Explanation.* Oxford: Clarendon Press.

2006a. 'Objectivity and Authority: Thucydides' Historical Method'. In *Brill's Companion to Thucydides.* Ed. A. Rengakos and A. Tsakmakis. Leiden: Brill.

2006b. 'Rhetoric, Reciprocity and History'. In *III International Symposium on Thucydides: The Speeches.* Ed. Mariios Scortsis. Athens: n.p.

Rosenbloom, David. 2004. '*Poneroi* vs. *Chrestoi*: The Ostracism of Hyperbolos and the Struggle for Hegemony in Athens after the Death of Pericles'. *Transactions of the American Philological Association* 134: 55–105, 302–58.

Runciman, David. 2008. *Political Hypocrisy: The Mask of Power, from Hobbes to Orwell and Beyond.* Princeton University Press.

Rusten, Jeffrey, ed. 2009. *Thucydides.* Oxford University Press.

Rutherford, R. B. 1994. 'Learning from History: Categories and Case Histories'. In *Ritual, Finance, Politics: Athenian Democratic Accounts Presented to*

David Lewis. Ed. Robin Osborne and Simon Hornblower. Oxford: Clarendon Press.

Ste Croix, G. E. M. de 1954. 'The Character of the Athenian Empire'. *Historia* 3: 1–41.

1972. *The Origins of the Peloponnesian War*. London: Duckworth.

Salmon, J. B. 1984. *Wealthy Corinth: A History of the City to 338 BC*. Oxford: Clarendon Press.

Samons, Loren J. II. 2004. *What's Wrong with Democracy? From Athenian Practice to American Worship*. Berkeley: University of California Press.

Sarotte, Mary Elise. 2009. *1989: The Struggle to Create Post-Cold War Europe*. Princeton University Press.

Schmitt, Carl. 1996. *The Concept of the Political*. Trans. and ed. George Schwab. Foreword Tracy B. Strong. University of Chicago Press.

Schrader, Carlos. 1998. *Concordiana Thucydidea*. Hildesheim: Olms-Weidmann.

Schultz, Bart. 2004. *Henry Sidgwick, Eye of the Universe: An Intellectual Biography*. Cambridge University Press.

Scott, James C. 1998. *Seeing Like a State: How Certain Schemes to Improve the Human Condition Have Failed*. New Haven: Yale University Press.

Scott, Susan, and Christopher J. Duncan. 2001. *Biology of Plagues: Evidence from Historical Populations*. Cambridge University Press.

Shear, Julia L. 2011. *Polis and Revolution: Responding to Oligarchy in Classical Athens*. Cambridge University Press.

Sidgwick, Henry. 1962. *The Methods of Ethics*. 7th edn. London: Macmillan.

Skinner, Quentin. 1996. 'Reason and Rhetoric in the Philosophy of Hobbes'. In *Reason and Rhetoric in the Philosophy of Hobbes*. Cambridge University Press.

2002a. 'Hobbes and the *studia humanitatis*'. In *Visions of Politics, III: Hobbes and Civil Science*. Cambridge University Press.

2002b. 'Hobbes on Rhetoric and the Construction of Morality'. In *Visions of Politics, III: Hobbes and Civil Science*. Cambridge University Press.

Spence, Iain. 2010. 'Cavalry, Democracy and Military Thinking in Classical Athens'. In *War, Democracy and Culture in Classical Athens*. Ed. David M. Pritchard. Cambridge University Press.

Stadter, Philip A., ed. 1973. *The Speeches in Thucydides: A Collection of Original Studies*. Chapel Hill: University of North Carolina Press.

Stahl, Hans-Peter. 2003. *Thucydides: Man's Place in History*. Trans. David Seward. Swansea: Classical Press of Wales.

Strauss, Barry. 1983. 'Aegospotamoi Reconsidered'. *American Journal of Philology* 104: 24–35.

Strauss, Leo. 1964. *The City and Man*. University of Chicago Press.

Sullivan, Robert E. 2009. *Macaulay: The Tragedy of Power*. Cambridge MA: Belknap Press of Harvard University Press.

Süssman, Johannes. 2012. 'Historicising the Classics: How Nineteenth-Century German Historiography Changed the Perspective on Historical Tradition'. In *Thucydides and the Modern World: Reception, Reinterpretation and Influence from the Renaissance to the Present*. Ed. K. Harloe and N. Morley. Cambridge University Press.

Thomas, Rosalind. 1989. *Oral Tradition and Written Record in Classical Athens.* Cambridge University Press.

1992. *Literacy and Orality in Ancient Greece.* Cambridge University Press.

2003. 'Prose Performance Texts: Epideixis and Written Publication in the Late Fifth and Early Fourth Centuries'. In *Written Texts and the Rise of Literate Culture in Greece.* Ed. Harvey Yunis. Cambridge University Press.

Tocqueville, Alexis de. 2000. *Democracy in America.* Ed., trans., and intro. Harvey Mansfield and Delba Winthrop. University of Chicago Press.

Trevett, J. C. 1995. 'Nikias and Syracuse'. *Zeitschrift für philosophie und Epigraphik* 106: 246–8.

Tritle, Lawrence A. 2010. *A New History of the Peloponnesian War.* Malden MA: Blackwell-Wiley.

Urbinati, Nadia. 2012. 'Thucydides the Thermidorian: Democracy on Trial in the Making of Modern Liberalism'. In *Thucydides and the Modern World: Reception, Reinterpretation and Influence from the Renaissance to the Present.* Ed. K. Harloe and N. Morley. Cambridge University Press.

Vogt, Joseph. 2009. 'The portrait of Pericles in Thucydides'. In *Thucydides.* Ed. J. Rusten. Oxford University Press.

Wade-Gery, H. T. 2012. 'Thucydides (2)'. In *Oxford Classical Dictionary.* 4th edn. Ed. Simon Hornblower, Anthony Spawforth, and Esther Eidinow. Oxford University Press.

Wallace, Robert W. 2007. 'Plato's Sophists, Intellectual History after 450, and Sokrates'. In *The Cambridge companion to the Age of Pericles.* Ed. Loren J. Samons II. Cambridge University Press.

Waltz, Kenneth N. 1979. *Theory of International Politics.* New York: Random House.

Westlake, H. D. 1968. *Individuals in Thucydides.* Cambridge University Press.

1969. 'Hermocrates the Syracusan'. In *Essays on the Greek Historians and Greek History.* Manchester University Press.

1973. 'The Settings of Thucydidean Speeches'. In *The Speeches in Thucydides: A Collection of Original Studies.* Ed. Philip A. Stadter. Chapel Hill: University of North Carolina Press.

1982. Review of Hunter Rawlings, *The Structure of Thucydides' History. Classical Review* 32: 232–4.

2009. 'Thucydides and the uneasy peace: a study in political incompetence'. In *Thucydides.* Ed. J. Rusten. Oxford University Press.

Wheeler, Everett L., and Barry Strauss. 2007. 'Battle'. In *Cambridge History of Greek and Roman Warfare, I: Greece, the Hellenistic World and the Rise of Rome.* Ed. Philip Sabin, Hans van Wees, and Michael Whitby. Cambridge University Press.

Williams, Bernard. 1981a. 'Internal and External Reasons'. In *Moral Luck: Philosophical Essays 1973–1980.* Cambridge University Press.

1981b. 'Moral luck'. In *Moral Luck: Philosophical Papers 1973–1980.* Cambridge University Press.

1993. *Shame and Necessity.* Berkeley: University of California Press.

1995. 'Moral Luck: A Postscript'. In *Making Sense of Humanity and Other Philosophical Papers 1982–1993.* Cambridge University Press.

2002. *Truth and Truthfulness: An Essay in Genealogy.* Princeton University Press.

2005. 'Realism and Moralism'. In *In the Beginning Was the Deed.* Ed. and intro. Geoffrey Hawthorn. Princeton University Press.

Woodhead, A. G. 1960. 'Thucydides' Portrait of Cleon'. *Mnemosyne* 13: 289–317.

Yoshitake, Sumio. 2010. 'Arete and the Achievements of the War Dead: The Logic of Praise in the Athenian Funeral Oration'. In *War, Democracy and Culture in Classical Athens.* Ed. David M. Pritchard. Cambridge University Press.

Yunis, Harvey. 1996. *Taming Democracy: Models of Political Rhetoric in Classical Athens.* Ithaca: Cornell University Press.

Zumbrunnen, John. 2008. *Silence and Democracy: Athenian Politics in Thucydides' History.* University Park PA: Pennsylvania State University Press.

Index

Mynott's edition of Thucydides has full indexes of the text. This one includes the names, places and issues that signify in this book. All are arranged alphabetically except the activities of individuals and some events, alliances, arbitration, assemblies and battles, in which entities were involved; these are ordered chronologically under the relevant heads. I do not include my references to Mynott or to the commentaries by Gomme *et al.* and Hornblower.

14968668R00165

Printed in Great Britain
by Amazon.co.uk, Ltd.,
Marston Gate.